PRAISE FOR TUCKER MAX AND
GEOFFREY MILLER'S

What Women Want

"Every single page has interesting information. A great resource."
— Dr. Drew Pinsky, host of the *Loveline* radio show and
Dr. Drew On Call on HLN

"The most unexpected book of the year: world-famous evolutionary psycholo-gist meets world-famous drunken asshole. The result: a sober, solid, neces-sary, and authoritative guide not just to dating, but to becoming a better man."
— Neil Strauss, author of *The Game* and *The Truth*

"I wish I could teleport a copy of *What Women Want* back in time and give it to my thirteen-year-old self, and then instruct him to read it once a year for the next decade."
— Jake Seliger, author and founder of The Story's Story

"From the very beginning, this book plays it straight. It's about becoming a better person and creating positive, fulfilling relationships. This isn't a book with a predatory, pickup-artist mindset."
— Aubrey Marcus, founder of Onnit Fitness and
the Aubrey Marcus Podcast

"A fascinating look at mating and dating from the perspective of a guy who gained fame for doing the former."
— Adam Kovac, AskMen.com

D0830651

What Women Want

TUCKER MAX

GEOFFREY MILLER, PhD

with Nils Parker

Little, Brown and Company
New York • Boston • London

Little, Brown and Company
Hachette Book Group
1290 Avenue of the Americas, New York, NY 10104
littlebrown.com

Originally published in hardcover as *Mate* by Little, Brown and Company, September 2015
First Little, Brown trade paperback edition, September 2016

Little, Brown and Company is a division of Hachette Book Group, Inc.
The Little, Brown name and logo are trademarks of Hachette Book Group, Inc.

The publisher is not responsible for websites (or their content) that are not owned by the publisher.

The Hachette Speakers Bureau provides a wide range of authors for speaking events. To find out more, go to hachettespeakersbureau.com or call (866) 376-6591.

Photographs and images reproduced throughout the text are attributable to the following:
Model photo on page 40 by Kevin Sinclair/CC-BY-3.0; Jessica Biel photo on page 40 by Photographer's Mate 2nd Class Daniel J. McLain; Christina Hendricks photo on page 40 © Jason LaVeris / Getty Images; BMI chart drawing on page 80 by Erin Tyler; Kevin James photo on page 81 © Ray Tamarra / Getty Images; Rick James photo on page 81 © Leach Entertainment Features; Jesse James photo on page 81 by pinguino k/CC-BY-2.0; Lebron James photo on page 81 by Tim Shelby/CC-BY-2.0; Paul Newman photo on page 210 © Warner Brothers; Jon Hamm photo on page 210 © Scott Council / Getty Images.

ISBN 978-0-316-37536-8 (hc) / 978-0-316-34943-7 (international) / 978-0-316-37533-7 (pb)
Library of Congress Control Number: 2015944905

10 9 8 7 6 5 4 3 2 1

RRD-C

Printed in the United States of America

To our 17-year-old former selves, and to Bishop, Atalanta, and all the sons and daughters who deserve the great relationships we want for them.

TABLE OF CONTENTS

The Five-Step Process
to Mating Success

STEP ONE — GET YOUR HEAD STRAIGHT

STEP TWO — DEVELOP ATTRACTIVE TRAITS

STEP THREE — DISPLAY ATTRACTIVE PROOFS

STEP FOUR — GO WHERE THE WOMEN ARE

STEP FIVE — TAKE ACTION

What Women Want

INTRODUCTION — A NEW APPROACH TO MATING EDUCATION

You have no fucking idea what you're doing.

Not when it comes to sex and dating and women, anyway. That's probably why you bought this book or why someone gave it to you as a not-so-subtle hint that you need to get your shit together. Don't beat yourself up about it though, because it's not your fault.

Your culture has failed you *and* the women you're trying to meet.

For decades now, women have been wondering, *"Where are all the great guys?"* You have been wondering, *"Where are all of you going? What did I say?"* And nobody has had a decent answer for either of you.

Your primal self expected that you'd be born into a normal human tribe with wise mentors, heroic role models, and transformational rites of passage that could solve those mating problems. Your primal brain expected to find itself in a sexual culture with fun mating rituals and a decent chance of finding a girlfriend after puberty. As it should have. That kind of sexual culture had been the hunter-gatherer norm for hundreds of thousands of years. Unfortunately, you never got any of that good stuff your ancestors got.

No, you got fed a bunch of bullshit by parents, priests, professors, and politicians trying to tell you what to do, usually in service of some kind of selfish agenda that had nothing to do with your health, happiness, or mating success.

Your culture should have taught you long ago what we're going to teach you: *to be successful in mating, you simply have to become the kind of man that women have evolved to want.*

This is not a revolutionary concept; it's an evolutionary one. Human females, like all clever creatures, choose their mates according to certain criteria and preferences. If you don't fit their criteria, they won't mate with you. If you do, good news — you're in business.

It really is that basic, and there's no way around it. In biology, this process is called female choice.

Female choice is so high you can't get over it, so deep you can't get under it, so wide you can't get around it. Your only option is to accept it and embrace it. You *have* to fit their mate choice criteria. Once you do that and become that man, your future girlfriends will be attracted to you and more grateful than you can imagine—whether you're seeking one-time hookups or a lifelong marriage.

We'll show you all of this stuff. We'll explain the five principles for successful mating to give you a nice functional framework, and then we'll walk you through the five steps for getting your mating life together. That's it. That's all you need to fix your mating life, so that's all there is to this book.

It's a very simple concept, and the next 330 pages are dedicated to showing you what that is, why that is, and how to do it. If you pay attention and follow along—if you work on becoming a great guy who can offer the things women instinctively want—you will be happier, and women will be happier with you. Everyone wins.

THIS BOOK'S ORIGIN

This is not our book; it's your book. We built it from the ground up to serve your needs. It's been shaped by your emails, questions, and feedback. It even originated in the dating failures of guys like you. Here's how that happened:

This book exists because some young guys in Cincinnati were terrible with women, and they blamed Tucker Max.

At a Thanksgiving dinner, Geoff was hanging out with some of his male cousins—typical young American guys in high school or college, mostly without girlfriends. They asked about Geoff's research in evolutionary psychology and human sexuality. Geoff explained a few basics about why women love self-deprecating humor, why they value intelligence as a "good genes" trait, and how lap dancers' ovulatory cycles influence their tip earnings.

The cousins had never heard about any of that stuff. Some were fundamentalist, some were atheist; some were young Republicans; some were liberal hipsters. Their common ground was that they all adored women, sex, and dating, but they knew almost nothing about these topics.

So Geoff asked his relatives and their friends where they were learning about human mating. Then the floodgates opened. Several mentioned that they'd read Tucker's books, like *I Hope They Serve Beer in Hell, Assholes Finish First,* or *Hilarity Ensues.* They swore by these books. They weren't just entertaining stories; they were the bedrock of their sexual education—their dating bibles.

Geoff was appalled by their ignorance about mating but intrigued to hear about this Tucker person, who must be an especially wise, well-balanced, sober dating guru to merit such a devoted and diverse following. So Geoff read Tucker's books, and the mystery only deepened. The letters *W* and *T* and *F* kept running through Geoff's mind.

A few months later, Geoff was at a psychology conference in Austin, Texas, and got in touch with Tucker. They found an instant rapport, and Geoff shared the story about the Thanksgiving cousins who were Tucker Max fans.

Tucker asked, "How are they doing with women and dating?"

Geoff said, "Not very well, I think. They seem confused and frustrated. With all due respect, I'm not sure your books are the best guides to how to improve one's dating life."

Well no shit, Tucker thought. His books weren't written as education manuals. They're just funny stories about getting drunk, hooking up, and doing stupid things with his friends. Who takes dating advice from a guy who gets into a Breathalyzer contest at a sushi restaurant? Who takes sex advice from a guy who has to keep replacing his mattresses because women keep peeing on them? If anything, Tucker's stories are cautionary tales—about what *not* to do. Geoff agreed.

Tucker said, "I don't understand. You're a sex researcher and an evolutionary psychologist. You know this field; you've taught it for decades. Why didn't you just recommend a good mating guide for young men?"

Geoff said, "I tried, but it doesn't exist. Nobody's written it yet."

Tucker was flabbergasted. "How could a basic instruction manual for such a crucially important topic not exist? It has to. You must be wrong!"

No. Tucker was wrong.

Geoff proved the point. "Tucker, how did *you* learn this stuff?"

Tucker said, "Oh...right. I had to learn it by myself, through trial and error. Lots and lots of error."

Geoff and Tucker spent the whole dinner discussing the reasons for our culture's failure to educate young men about mating. Geoff explained that American schools are still surprisingly repressed about sexual education— federal grants and universities don't support sex or dating research; professors can't advise students on how to become more sexually attractive or improve their Tinder messaging skills; higher education focuses on improving students' economic prospects rather than their private lives. And most of the other advice-givers out there—religious zealots, gender feminists, or manosphere misogynists—have some twisted ideological agenda. Or the advice-givers are exploitative marketers trying to sell manipulative strategies, like most pickup artists. Or the advice is just factually wrong, without any scientific integrity, based on misunderstood third-hand accounts of the research in fields that Geoff's been publishing in for years.

Not one to shy away from big plans and bold pronouncements, Tucker started thinking out loud as Geoff described the current state of the art in sex and dating advice for men.

Tucker said, "Can you imagine how much easier and better our lives would have been if we knew at fifteen or twenty years-old everything about sex and dating that we know now? Shit, it would have even helped me at thirty. It's crazy how much better my life would have been! That advice book should exist!"

Geoff nodded in agreement, the way professors do in Socratic dialogues, when they're just waiting for you to catch up to the answer they already know.

Tucker said, "What if we did that? What if we took what we know now and made it available to every man in America, in an accessible, honest, funny way? We'd combine my street cred and your academic cred! It could be hilarious! It could have science! It could reach millions of guys who are lost and desperate! How great would that be?"

Geoff said, "And it could make millions of women a whole lot less frustrated that there aren't any good guys out there. They're looking for boyfriends, and we could help build them better boyfriends. That would be a win-win for both sexes."

So here it is—everything we wished we had understood when we were trying to learn how to cope with the thrilling, terrifying new world of women, sex, and dating.

Welcome to *What Women Want*.

THE FIVE PRINCIPLES OF MATING SUCCESS

When you first start to study a field, it seems like you have to memorize a zillion things. You don't. What you need is to identify the core principles—generally three to twelve of them—that govern the field. The million things you thought you had to memorize are simply various combinations of the core principles.

—John Reed

Mating is not a checklist of sex facts and dating tactics. There is no one-size-fits-all inventory of actions you must figure out, memorize, and complete in order. That would be nonsense. Almost nothing in life works like a scavenger hunt at a pub crawl. Don't let anyone tell you any different.

As with most things in life, mating is a complex system with a deep evolutionary logic and a few essential principles at its core. To be successful at it, you must understand these principles and then apply them to your choices and actions in the infinite number of situations you will find yourself in over the course of your life.

The goal of this book is to teach you how and where to apply those principles. The goal of this chapter is to teach you the principles themselves.

THE FIRST PRINCIPLE: MAKE DECISIONS WITH SCIENCE (NOT BIAS)

Most of the dating advice rampaging through our culture is outdated, irrelevant, or sex-negative. It got that way for one overwhelming reason: none of it is based on an empirical understanding of how humans and human mating actually work.

Instead, the conventional wisdom about dating has been defined by political and religious ideologies, family traditions, and cultural norms whose self-serving notions of how the world *should* work shaped their ideas (and most likely yours). We are going to teach you a completely different approach, one based on science and evidence.

There has never been a better time for this kind of examination than today. The science of human mating has flourished in the last thirty years, with astonishing new theories and findings in fields such as evolutionary psychology, hunter-gatherer anthropology, psychometrics, behavior genetics, and animal communication. Today, we can offer deeper insights, more evidence, and a more systematic perspective on mating than any culture ever could at any previous point in history.

We can explain not just what works with women, but *why* it works. We can explain not just what kind of traits you should develop to attract the women you're most attracted to, but *how* to develop those traits in the most efficient ways possible.

Using science and evidence to guide your mating life isn't just practical; it's also ethical. Science respects reality and helps you take responsibility for what you believe, while resisting dogma, superstition, and overconfidence in the process. Thinking critically, testing hypotheses, assessing evidence, and gauging feedback isn't just something researchers do in labs; it's also something you should do in your mating life, and we are going to show you how.

But first understand the principle: make decisions about what you believe based on the best scientific, empirical evidence you can find.

THE SECOND PRINCIPLE: ACCOUNT FOR THE WOMAN'S PERSPECTIVE

You obviously have a perspective on mating. But what so many guys fail to account for is that women have their own perspective, and it is different than yours. You have to understand it and account for it to be successful in mating.

If you don't understand women right now, that is no accident. Women evolved to be more complicated than you can understand so they could protect themselves from being seduced, manipulated, and exploited.

But trying to attract women without understanding that and them—who they are, what they want, what they're attracted to—is like heading out into the wilderness and trying to find your way through without a map or compass. It will just get you more lost—which is exactly the problem most guys face.

Sure, you could be a stubborn idiot and continue wandering around, guided by the North Star of your ridiculous sexual fantasies until finally you bump into someone willing to put up with your bullshit. But that's the fast track to becoming a forty-year-old divorced loser living alone in a man cave, surrounded by resentment, shame, and regret. There is another option: you could get out of your head and into women's heads—with curiosity, respect, and a commitment to mutual benefit. That's the fast track to mating success.

So, throughout this book, we'll focus on understanding women on several levels:

- why women evolved to have certain sexual concerns and preferences, given how prehistoric mating worked
- why women seek good genes, good partners, and good dads—not necessarily from the same guy
- why women feel anxious and vulnerable about sexual harassment, stalking, rape, sexually transmitted diseases (STDs), unwanted pregnancies, and slut-shaming
- why different women seek different sexual experiences and relationships under different conditions with different guys, from hookups to boyfriends to husbands
- why women value some key attractive traits in men, such as physical health, mental health, intelligence, willpower, kindness, and protectiveness
- why women value some key proofs of mate value in men, such as social success, material success, aesthetic style, and romantic commitment
- where women go to meet men, and how the supply-and-demand dynamics work in those mating markets

All of this boils down to a simple principle: If you always try to understand the woman's perspective—what they want, why they want it, and how to ethically give it to them—then you will find it much easier to become attractive to them, and you'll be much more successful with your mating efforts.

THE THIRD PRINCIPLE: OWN YOUR ATTRACTIVENESS

One of the main things we will teach you in this book is how to be attractive to women—specifically, how to develop the traits they find attractive. If you develop them well, we can guarantee that you will find mating success.

But this is just a guide—for it to work, you must *do the work*. You didn't choose which genes you inherited or what family you grew up in. But from this day forward, you **must take personal responsibility for your life, your choices, your habits, your traits, your mate value, and your attractiveness to women.**

Nobody else can do this work for you. Taking responsibility for your personal growth and social attractiveness has been a core principle from the ancient Stoics through Nietzsche and from existentialism to modern psychotherapy; it's acknowledging your ethical duty to yourself, your future potential, your free will, and your personal autonomy.

The reason we emphasize this is because women don't really "choose" to be attracted to you. They are attracted to some *features* (biologically, which we explain in depth later) and not attracted to others. Thus, whether or not a particular woman will be attracted to you is largely in your hands. You have to seize the opportunity to make yourself attractive to her. You can pretend you don't have a choice, that you don't have the time, brains, or resources to raise your game. But then you've simply talked yourself into perpetual mediocrity.

The downside of taking responsibility for your attractiveness is that becoming a better man will take a good amount of work. The upside is that taking charge of your attractiveness will help you have great experiences and relationships with great women that yield benefits in every other domain of life: health, money, happiness, altruism, and self-actualization.

This is because the "better boyfriend" ideal overlaps a lot with the ideals of manhood that most men aspire to. If you make yourself highly attractive to women, an amazing life tends to be a natural byproduct. For men, at least, sexual self-improvement is the road to a better overall life.

THE FOURTH PRINCIPLE: BE HONEST (WITH YOURSELF AND OTHERS)

Honesty is the bedrock of self-improvement and mating success.

If you try to fool yourself about what you really want, you'll never form the type of life you want and implement the actions necessary to get it. There are plenty of women out there who want the kind of sexual experience or relationship that you want; you just have to find them. But you can't find them if you're not honest—with them or yourself.

Honesty builds your social status, which improves mating success over the long term. Most women expect that most men are lying most of the time, and they hate it. In a world of liars, seducers, and charlatans, the man who stands up and tells the truth about the world, about himself, and about what he really wants is very rare and very attractive. There is a reason most women list honesty as one of their most-desired traits.

We are not trying to tell you that honesty is the *only thing* that works. Of course there are ways you can lie, cheat, steal, and manipulate your way into success. A lot of them, in fact. And we know most or all of those methods very well (learning what works often involves trying things that don't).

We aren't going to teach those methods, nor do we endorse them, *because they actually hurt you* in two ways:

1. **Lying reduces your long-term mating success:** Once a woman sees you as a liar, there is no coming back from that. She will almost certainly tell her friends about you, and when she does you become a pariah. Of course, you can find other women to exploit and lie to, but that is a very difficult path to long-term mating success. It is far easier to have long-term social relationships based on trust than to lie through your teeth and have to make new relationships over and over again.
2. **Lying makes you feel like shit, and it hurts your life:** The only people who can lie without emotional consequences are sociopaths. For everyone else, there are real psychological harms that come with deception. The evidence is very clear that perpetual liars have less career success, less mating success, less satisfaction in their relationships, and even shorter lives.

So if you want to learn how to lie, cheat, and manipulate women, this is the wrong book for you. We aren't moralizing or telling you to be honest for any reason other than this one:

An honest, ethical approach to mating (and life) works the best in the long term.

THE FIFTH PRINCIPLE: PLAY TO WIN-WIN

Some in society hold the cynical view that sexual relationships are a zero-sum game, meaning one person's gain is the other person's loss. This view says that in a one-night stand, the man is the seducer and the woman gets seduced, he "wins" and she "loses." In a relationship, if a man and a woman argue, one must win and the other must lose. In sexual politics, feminism's gain is patriarchy's loss. This zero-sum way of thinking assumes a perpetual "battle of the sexes," and sadly, it is common in both gender feminism and the manosphere.

This "battle of the sexes" view is totally, completely wrong. It is counterproductive, counterintuitive, and counter to thousands of generations of evolution. That is why we endorse the opposite principle:

Your mating goal is to find and create "win-win" relationships, where both you and the woman are better off because of your interaction.

Think about why you do anything that involves interacting with other people—it's because you expect to get value from it. You give a cashier money for a coffee because you value the coffee more than what you're paying for it. (This is economic trade, the foundational idea behind capitalism.) If economic trade wasn't positive-sum, then neither buyer nor seller would agree to the exchange.

The same basic principle works with friendships: you enjoy hanging out with the guys in your crew because you all benefit—or else you'd just leave. Those relationships are "win-win" as well.

This is also how human mating works when it's done honestly and ethically. Mutual benefits are the expectation, not the exception, because people avoid relationships where they don't benefit. If human mating *wasn't* mostly a positive-sum game that yielded "win-win" experiences and relationships, then *neither* sex would agree to play the game in the first place.

Don't think of mating as fighting women for victory. They are not your enemy. Think of mating as *finding* women who want the same things you want—so you can both win.

If you only want one-night stands, then we'll tell you how to find women who also want one-night stands (and there are many). You two can have sex, not talk to each other again, and you both got what you wanted, so you're both better off.

If you want to have a casual dating relationship that includes sex and companionship, then we'll tell you how to find women who want that. You two can have sex, hang out, have fun, and not commit or get into deep emotional ties, and you both get what you wanted.

If you want to find a woman to marry and build a life with, then we'll tell you how to find a woman who wants that as well. You two can explore each other, develop a relationship, commit, and have a great life together, and you both win.

The point is that when you both approach relationships from this perspective, it enables you both to win, which is the best option for everyone.

FROM THE FIVE PRINCIPLES TO THE FIVE-STEP PROCESS

As a way to guide your decisions and actions, these principles work. But principles alone are not good enough. Men also need a clear set of instructions for specific actions. That is what the rest of this book is about: a five-step process that boils everything you need to do down to the simplest possible set of facts to learn, choices to make, and actions to take.

The five steps are

1. **Get your head straight:** Fix your mental framework for thinking about women, sex, and dating; replace antique nonsense with state-of-the-art insights; develop confidence, understand women's points of view, and clarify your mating ethics and mating goals.

2. **Develop attractive traits:** Understand what women want in men and why, and then give it to them by cultivating the key traits of physical health, mental health, intelligence, willpower, tenderness, and protectiveness.

3. **Display attractive proofs:** Understand the signaling principles that underlie honest, hard-to-fake proofs of value, and construct your personal, professional, social, and romantic life around building and displaying those proofs.

4. **Go where the women are:** Understand how mating markets work, given the supply and demand of men and women; how to find women who offer the highest value and best compatibility, given your tastes and goals; and how to meet those women in specific places, from local leisure clubs to online dating apps.

5. **Take action:** Understand how to talk to women, date them, have great sex with them, and learn from your experiences to build a positive-feedback cycle of personal improvement, sexual experience, and delighted women. All of which will help you create and execute your mating plan.

These steps are simple to understand, but they're not always easy to accomplish. Anyone who tells you otherwise is selling you bullshit. We are not offering a get-laid-quick scheme. We know that a third of the dudes who bought this book haven't even read this far yet. Another third will skim the rest of this book, think some of it is cool, recommend it to their friends, and fail to change their lives or improve their mating success in any significant way.

This book is really for the last third of you—the smart, hungry guys who will get inspired to think, choose, and act. You're the guys who will bring these five principles alive. You're the guys who will delight the women in your lives—and who will be the envy of the guys who may never read this far.

THE FIVE-STEP PROCESS
TO MATING SUCCESS

STEP ONE

Get Your
Head Straight

CHAPTER 1: BUILD SELF-CONFIDENCE

Confidence doesn't come out of nowhere. It's a result of some-thing... hours and days and weeks and years of constant work and dedication.

—*Roger Staubach*

"**H**ow can I become more confident?" is by far the most common question we get asked, whether it's about approaching women, dating them, or just having sex. For the unconfident among you, it all feels like a terrifyingly uncertain nightmare, and as a result, you worry about practically everything.

What do I say? What do I do? Where do I take her? What if she doesn't like me? What if she says no? What if I'm not good at it? What if I throw up on her dog like Tucker did? What if, what if, what if...

The problem you have right now with confidence is the same one Supreme Court Justice Potter Stewart had with obscenity in 1964: you know it when you see it, but you can't for the life of you seem to define it for yourself. You are not alone. Almost nobody understands confidence at a deep level, so the advice you get about how to fix it is almost always bad. It's usually some kind of self-help platitude like "just believe in yourself" or "fake it till you make it" or "nobody can make you feel inferior without your consent." Thanks, Mom, but that shit doesn't work.

Fortunately, in the last twenty years researchers have gained a lot of new insights into the origins and nature of confidence, and they allow us, finally, to explain exactly what it is:

Confidence is the realistic expectation you have of being successful at something, given (a) your competence at it and (b) the risk involved with doing it.

Take driving, for example. When you were sixteen, your confidence behind the wheel was probably pretty low because you hadn't developed enough experience to have a realistic expectation of being good at driving, and the risk involved was disproportionately high since a car under the control of an inexperienced driver becomes a two-ton metal projectile of speeding death.

At twenty-six, however, your confidence is much higher because you've had ten or more years of experience on the road without smashing into parked cars and running over children. When you get behind the wheel now, you understand all the unseen risks and thus have a very high expectation of getting where you intend to go safe and sound.

That is confidence in a nutshell. Given competence, you anticipate success, so you're willing to take the risk—whether it's driving a car, climbing a mountain, or saying hi to a pretty woman. It applies essentially the same way across all domains of life—including mating.

CONFIDENCE REFLECTS COMPETENCE

Don't think confidence is some kind of modern phenomenon though, just because people today don't shut up about it. Confidence has been a thing for a long time. In fact, confidence is part of your genetic makeup; it evolved over thousands of generations as a mental tool to guide our decision-making around risk.

To understand why Paleolithic man evolved confidence, take this example:

You're a young early man, out on the savannah with a couple other guys from your clan, on one of your first hunts. You're camped at the mouth of a cave on the last night, guarding your kill before you make the final push back to your tribe in the morning. Somewhere out in the darkness you hear a number of menacing growls. Your instinct is to get the hell out of there (fight or flight), but one of the other men stops you. He's a little older and has been on a number of hunts just like this one. He grabs the meat and buries it, then grabs you and hunkers down to hide. This is the smart move—he knows *from experience*.

Sure, it's a risk because whatever is out there in the darkness sounds pretty hungry and keeps getting closer, but your fellow clan member doesn't seem overly worried about it. The feeling in your gut in that moment was guiding your choice because you had no experienced-based knowledge to take its place. If you had, your reaction would more likely have been calm and cool like your buddy, and you would have been the one to make the smart choice. He had confidence because he'd successfully navigated similar situations in the past. Had he not been there, you would probably have done the dumb thing and ended up losing your tribe's next meal, possibly becoming a meal yourself.

True confidence is not about *hoping* that you can take this risk (that's called courage) and overcome this challenge (that's perseverance); it's about *realistically expecting* that you can do it, based on *previously demonstrated performance*.

A confident guy *expects* the woman to engage him in conversation when he goes up to say hi and introduce himself. He *expects* her to give him her number when he asks for it. He doesn't think he deserves it or she owes it to him (unless he is *also* an entitled douchebag, which is entirely possible)—he just expects that he's going to get it, even before he says a word. Why? Because he's done this dozens if not hundreds of times, with enough success to accurately predict the likely outcome.

How can you realistically judge the likelihood of your success in a unique moment like that—or in any domain of life? Your brain does it by unconsciously integrating a bunch of data from your memory and your current state. It adds up your past training, experiences, and successes, plus your present capabilities, to guide your decisions. Your brain is like a mushy three-pound sportsbook between your ears, setting the line and shifting the odds on your immediate future.

The most annoying thing about confidence, though, is that 90 percent of the time it's dormant (or at least it should be). It should only become an issue when you're actively facing a risky challenge, not when you're eating dinner or sitting at home trying to choose between watching football or Netflix. Nobody walks around all day vacillating between confident and unconfident. That would be exhausting and pointless.

When a challenge does arise—like texting a new match on Tinder or having sex with a woman for the first time—your confidence system immediately switches on and delivers its verdict: what confidence level you should feel in this situation, given its rewards and risks in relation to your competence level.

For example, if your Tinder game is tight, and you've had good dates from it, your confidence is probably high. If you have a history of striking out with women and a reputation as a two-pump chump with new ones, your confidence is going to be low.

There is pretty much no way around this dynamic. Evolution forced us to develop confidence levels that accurately tracked our competencies. It's hard to fake true confidence now, effectively anyway, because the humans who could fake it quickly died out. They took stupid risks that they couldn't handle, and they won prehistoric "Darwin Awards" as a result—death through idiotic overconfidence. Imagine if our Paleolithic man was bigger and more blustery than his older, more experienced friend:

"Don't worry about those lions crouched in the grass out there. We'll be fine. I bet they can't even smell this meat. Besides, it's totally dark, how are they going to find us? And I could whip them anyway...Boy, they sure look fast when they sprint with their ears back like that."

There are some who would tell you that our prehistoric friend was being confident—he just guessed wrong. After all, confidence is not a guarantee of success. And those people would be right about the last part. Confidence is no guarantee of success.

But where they are wrong is in their evaluation of our friend's state of mind. If you totally believe in yourself like he did, but you haven't learned or accomplished anything yet, like he hadn't, you're not being confidently optimistic; you're being dangerously, arrogantly delusional. And natural selection—perched on the pointy ends of Mr. and Mrs. Lion's claws and teeth—will turn you into breakfast.

This is the deep evolutionary reason why you can't "fake it till you make it." To build real confidence you *must* boost real competence.

BUILD CONFIDENCE THROUGH DEMONSTRATED PERFORMANCE

So let's talk about building confidence. First thing's first: *there are no shortcuts.*

Anyone who tries to sell you their "Ten Tricks to Get Confident with Women" is selling bullshit. If they, like *The Secret*, tell you the key is just to visualize your success, then the actual secret is that they're charlatans taking your money.

Yes, you can absolutely hack your momentum-based confidence a little bit by jump-starting your mating success and launching yourself onto that upward spiral (we'll get to this in a minute), but that's just messing around at the margins of confidence. It's not addressing the core issue.

The only effective strategy for gaining real confidence is to develop skills and demonstrate performance of those skills.

Developing realistic self-confidence is truly that simple. All you have to do is get good at the things you want to feel confident about and then demonstrate those skills, to yourself and others. This means learning, practicing, and then consistently performing under real-life conditions, with real stakes, when real people are watching. Once you do that, confidence in that skill is almost automatic.

Go back to driving as an example. The first year or so, you learned how to drive in school or from your parents. You practiced on familiar roads, driving relatively short distances to and from school, running errands for your mom, going to your part-time job. You developed a little bit of confidence but nothing too crazy—like you were Dale Jr. or something, just enough to feel comfortable about getting behind the wheel. Then one weekend you took a girl to a movie theater you'd never been to before, and that night there was a driving rainstorm. That was your "oh shit" moment.

When you walked out of the theater with your date and sideways rain hit you in the face, you could have turned into a puddle of nerves who white-knuckles it all the way home at five miles per hour with your hazards flashing. But you made sure you were both buckled up and your wipers were going before you pulled out of your parking spot. You took a deep breath and then drove home at a normal-but-reduced rate of speed.

At seventeen or eighteen years old, getting your date home, having had a great time, with her being completely unaware of your lack of confidence, like you were driving Miss Daisy, will send your driving confidence through the roof. You didn't just *survive* the ordeal, you took the skills you'd developed over time and demonstrated your competence at them when it counted. Yes, this is a small thing, but confidence is a monument to consistent performance and built with thousands of small bricks of experience, not carved from one huge stone.

Situations like this are where real, true confidence is built. Confidence requires that you go through the anxiety of trying something like this long before you feel ready. In any domain, you have to go through the valley of genuinely low confidence before you can reach the peak of genuinely high confidence.

But don't misunderstand: the low confidence you feel in the moment before you decide how you are going to handle a situation is not underconfidence or neurosis or irrationality (though your ultimate decision might be). It's deep, ancient, and adaptive. It's how human learning works. The best thing you can do is accept that this is the process and develop a mature perspective.

Yes, this is totally fucking terrifying. I have no idea what I'm doing. I have zero confidence that I can get us home without killing us both. But that's OK. That's exactly what I should be feeling, since I've never done this shit before.

This perspective can give you a kind of metaconfidence: you're confident that you will be able to improve your competence at any skill if you work at it and that will lead to demonstrated performance and real confidence as a result.

The real magic happens at this metaconfidence level. The more skills you learn, the more domains you master and traits you cultivate, the more experienced you'll get at pushing through the low-confidence barrier...and the more confidence you will build.

CONFIDENCE IS USUALLY
DOMAIN-SPECIFIC

You might now be highly confident about driving, thanks to lots of practice and a lashing rainstorm, but that doesn't mean you're now automatically confident about talking to the beautiful woman in the passenger seat next to you. You might also be confident about driving automatic transmissions but not stick shifts. And all that makes complete sense, because they are totally different things.

You don't have just one overall confidence level that covers every aspect of life, because that would be stupid and maladaptive. If your odds of success in one domain don't predict your odds of success in another domain, why then should confidence in one spill over into confidence in the other?

The answer is, it *shouldn't*. As in the case of our hypothetical and now-dead prehistoric friend, the confidence he rightly had in his hunting ability should not have spilled over into his confidence in being hunted. If it hadn't, he (and his bloodline) might have survived.

You can appreciate how confidence reflects competence in particular domains when you think about mental abilities and personality traits that differ between people. More intelligent people tend to be more intellectually confident because they have more competence (developed skill and displayed performance) in learning abstract new ideas and skills. More extroverted people tend to be more socially confident because they have more competence at interacting with new people and groups. More promiscuous people tend to be more sexually confident because they have more experience hooking up with new people.

To some degree, genetic differences shape these personality differences, which in turn shape the upper and lower bounds of your confidence in these domains. But within each domain, you still have a lot of freedom to improve your confidence by building your competencies—whatever your personality. So if you're reading this right now and feel like a dumb, antisocial sex klutz, don't get too down on yourself. The only direction to go is up, and there's plenty of headroom.

MATING CONFIDENCE ADDS
UP ACROSS THE DOMAINS
THAT MATTER TO WOMEN

Women instinctively assess *everything* about you that might be important to them in a serious sexual relationship. And since women are judging your *competence* in each of these domains, your *confidence* across them automatically feeds into your overall mating confidence. The sportsbook in your mind understands this as it sets the odds on your mating future. It goes up if you have awesome strengths—such as playing sports, making money, cracking jokes, selecting wines, or going down on a woman—and it stays down if you have any embarrassing weaknesses.

Mating confidence is the sum of every specific kind of confidence you feel about every domain of competence that matters to women.

If we have been clear up to this point and you have been paying attention, right about now you should be saying, "Holy shit, this changes everything!" Because what we've just told you, if you take it to heart, can have profound implications for the rest of your mating life.

The only way to build true confidence around women is to build the competencies they desire. This means you must learn what women really want and then become a guy that has those traits. Build it and she will come (hopefully, more than once).

That's this whole book: a systematic way to boost your true mating confidence through boosting the mating-related skills that women care about and respond to.

CONFIDENCE IS ALSO ABOUT MOMENTUM

If you've had no sex with any women in the last year, you're less likely to attract women—even if you have attractive traits—because you are more likely to put off an asexual loser vibe. Women can see your late-night Google search history in your eyes.

Conversely, if you've had sex with ten women in the last month, despite having serious weaknesses as a mate, you're likely to give off some mysterious sex confidence that attracts even more women. There is a "Matthew Effect" at work in human mating:

> *Whoever gets some success will gain even more success and enjoy abundance; whoever has little success will gain even less after that and suffer misery.*
>
> —*Book of Matthew*
> *(the Apostle, not McConaughey), 13:12*

In other words, sexual success is a positive feedback loop (sex begets sex); whereas sexual failure is a downward spiral (less sex begets no sex begets Pornhub).

In human psychology, this is called "mate choice copying"—women tend to choose men who have already been chosen by other women. It's like a customer seeing that a product is the top seller on Amazon; it might not seem like the ideal product, but if all these other customers are into it, there's got to be something there.

The result is that mating confidence creates a lot of momentum—either forward momentum, like a penis-shaped express train, or static momentum, like a lonely blue-balled boulder stuck at the bottom of a hill. If only you could just push that boulder far enough up the hill that it reached the tipping point of mating success, it would turn into a rock-hard runaway train. Like Sisyphus, you've probably tried dozens of times already, without much success. It's like trying to overcome deep depression through sheer force of will. It's highly unlikely. You need some momentum.

This momentum effect in confidence is related to a cool idea in social psychology called the "sociometer theory." The idea is that humans evolved to keep track of our social popularity, status, and prestige through a kind of "social meter" in the brain that represents how well we've been getting along recently with our family, friends, and mates. The sociometer did not evolve to make us feel good or bad. It evolved to help our highly social species manage social relationships adaptively. It tells us where we stand socially so we can act accordingly.

If everybody likes and respects us, our "sociometer" goes up—which feels like increased self-confidence, self-respect, and self-esteem. If everybody hates and avoids us, the sociometer goes down like a gas gauge approaching empty—and it feels like decreased confidence.

If the sociometer reads high, we tend to approach new friends and mates and seek new opportunities for status, capitalizing on our recent success and popularity. If the sociometer reads low, we tend to avoid strangers, withdraw from public interactions, display shame and contrition, repair damaged relationships, and try to make ourselves more useful to the group.

Modern versions of sociometer theory argue that there's not just one overall sociometer analogous to overall social confidence or status. Rather, there are different sociometers to track each domain of social life—including mating life.

According to this theory, your mating sociometer reflects how well you've been doing with women over the last few weeks or months, and that mating momentum effect, along with your actual mating competencies, determines your mating confidence.

PUSH THROUGH LOW CONFIDENCE AND DEPRESSION WITH A GROWTH MINDSET

You might be thinking, *This all sounds great, but how do I even start to develop competence if I'm so depressed and unconfident that I can hardly move? How do I start to develop metaconfidence if I've never mastered any domain before? How do I push through a low-confidence barrier that's so severe I can't imagine taking action?*

In Brazilian jiu-jitsu, there is a saying: "In practice, there is no losing. There is only winning and learning. The only way to lose is to not practice."

We'll talk more about overcoming depression later, in the chapter on mental health, but for now let's just acknowledge that it is not uncommon to find oneself on a downward spiral of low confidence, passivity, failure, and shame. It's easy for us to say "build competence and the confidence will come," but in reality, once you get stuck in this spiral, it can be very hard to break out of it.

Here are some clues that you're stuck in the downward spiral:

- harsh self-judgments ("I'll suck at everything forever.")
- lack of experience ("I've never done anything like this, so why start now?")
- rehashing old failures ("I failed at that, and that, and that...")
- preoccupations with fear ("I feel terrified to even try, and that fear feels valid.")
- predictions of disaster ("If I try that, the result will be a humiliating catastrophe.")
- ruminating about obstacles ("There's no time and no money or mentors to help me.")
- adverse comparisons to others ("I'll never be as good as _____.")
- unrealistic expectations ("I should be a happily married billionaire by now.")
- perfectionism ("If I can't be the best in the world, I shouldn't even try.")
- impostor syndrome ("Even if I seem to be succeeding, I'm really just a fake.")

The first step off this downward spiral is to **acknowledge these bad feelings as natural.**

When women feel this way, our society has sympathy, and Oprah gives them cars. But when men feel this way, our society demonizes these feelings as signs of weakness, amplifying the shame and self-judgment, repeating the macho advice to "suck it up" and "get over it."

This bullshit makes the problem worse. It's impossible to pull yourself out of depression by your bootstraps when all you want to do is hang yourself with them. Bad advice can't fix bad feelings, and neither can ignoring those feelings. Don't try to push them away or pretend they're not there. These feelings evolved to protect us from harm, like our fight-or-flight responses.

Of course, it doesn't help that in Hollywood movies the hero's journey out of low competence and low confidence is always compressed into a four-minute montage of epic self-improvement, guided by a wise but stern mentor, in a picturesque setting, with an inspiring soundtrack. Thank you very much, *Rocky I, II, III, IV, V.* The real-life despair and self-doubt of the advanced beginner who finally realizes just how hard the skill is and how far he is from mastery is rarely featured. Nor is the fact that it's normal to feel fear, anxiety, self-doubt, and low confidence when faced with learning a new skill or improving a trait.

Another crucial element in moving your brain from panic to logic is to cultivate the emotional intelligence to wrap words around those feelings. Research shows that when people identify their own emotions consciously, using accurate words—"afraid," "angry," "anxious"—the amygdala, that little biological threat sensor in the brain, calms down almost instantly. At the same time, a smarter part of the prefrontal cortex goes to work inhibiting emotional overreactions so you can think coolly about what's happening.

Though the research is new, this is not a new insight. It has been taught by Buddhists in the East and philosophers in the West for 2,500 years. You can tame your negative emotions to some degree just by calling them their true names. And then, for our purposes, you can move on with learning the competencies that build confidence in all the domains that matter.

The *big* leap out of the low-self-esteem spiral, though, is to adopt a "growth mindset"—a concept developed by psychologist Carol Dweck. In a growth mindset, people only need to believe two things: (1) that their abilities can be improved through dedication and hard work rather than remain limited by their genes, backgrounds, or current situations (that is called a "fixed mindset"); and (2) that failures and setbacks can help you learn how to get better.

A growth mindset sparks a love of learning and resilience in the face of obstacles that are essential for great accomplishment. People who embrace a growth mindset actually do learn more (and more quickly) and they view challenges and failures as valuable signals to improve their skills rather than as signals that they should quit. They're like a bunch of Mr. Miyagis.

Study after study shows that almost all high-achieving people, now and in the past, had a growth mindset and consistently outperformed those with fixed mindsets. The growth mindset simply works better in life.

Whether you make the leap and do the work is up to you. We're totally confident that you can build your mating confidence if you take charge of your mating life. Eventually, you won't even have to worry about confidence anymore. You'll remember that distant, murky time in the past when you lacked confidence, and you'll be grateful that you believed in yourself enough to fix your mindset and take action.

The next step is to get out of your head—your own anxieties and insecurities—and get inside the heads of the opposite sex.

Takeaways

- Sexual confidence is a paradox because confidence reflects demonstrated performance, but it's hard to find success until you have confidence—which is what women are attracted to. The way to cut through the Gordian knot of this confidence/success paradox is to cultivate the skills and abilities that women want in a man.
- Confidence is domain-specific—being good at one thing doesn't give you confidence in something else. Domain-specific competencies do accumulate, however, and automatically raise your overall mating confidence.
- As you attract more women with your new competencies, the momentum effect kicks in, and your mating confidence will become a self-sustaining cycle of attractiveness and sex.
- The best way to get off the downward spiral of low confidence is to acknowledge the negative feelings, accept them and name them, and adopt a "growth mindset."

CHAPTER 2: UNDERSTAND WHAT IT'S LIKE TO BE A WOMAN

You never really understand a person until you consider things from his point of view...until you climb into his skin and walk around in it.

—*Atticus Finch in* To Kill a Mockingbird

We have been working with young single men in our capacities as educators, public figures, and authors for more than thirty years. In that time, the most common question we've gotten from guys centers around how to increase their confidence with women.

But there's a much deeper problem: **At least 70 percent of their questions reveal a total failure to understand the woman's point of view.**

Why does this matter? *As a man, it is impossible to be better at mating until you understand the subjective experience of a woman, because it is fundamentally different than yours in many ways.* If you can account for those differences, you will be well on your way to increased success because most men spend zero time thinking about this.

The differences start from the very beginning, at our deepest primal levels.

When a man interacts with a woman, his greatest fear is sexual rejection and humiliation. This causes him to spend as much time and energy (if not more) on defensive strategies to protect against rejection as he does on mating strategies to attract women.

Women are totally different. In these interactions, they are not much afraid of rejection. Rather, when a woman interacts with a man, **she is afraid of being physically harmed or sexually assaulted**.

Right now you're probably thinking the same thing we did when we first learned about this when we were young men: *I've never hurt a woman in my life and never would.*

And we bet you're right. You are probably perfectly safe.

But SHE doesn't know that—when she meets you, you could be Jack Ryan, Jack Sparrow, or Jack the Ripper. Any one of those is equally likely. Even more terrifying is the fact that, over the course of her life, the biggest threat to her *is men she knows*. This is not some idle, irrelevant statistic. The overwhelming majority of women that suffer physical or sexual assault suffer it at the hands of a man they know intimately.

And their fears don't stop at physical harm; they are just as vulnerable to social and emotional harm as well. Socially, you can spread lies about her or damage her reputation (with men *and* women), sometimes just by being associated with her. You can pretend you love her, get her pregnant, and then abandon her. This is only the beginning of the harms she potentially faces at your hands.

We cannot emphasize this enough: **Mating success requires cross-sex insight**. You need to understand how women evaluate your qualities and how they perceive the status, danger, opportunities, and threats that you could present. The better you learn to see these things from women's points of view, the less unattractive you will be to them and the less confused, resentful, and frustrated you will be by how they respond to you.

We're not suggesting you have to become a gender psychologist or feminize your whole worldview. You are a man, and women like men; turning into a woman would make you less attractive to (most) women.

We're telling you to simply *understand women*. And this is for the simple reason that understanding the female perspective helps you do much better with women, whatever your goal—whether it's a one-night stand, a friend with benefits, a girlfriend, or a wife. It will help you avoid and resolve arguments, saving you hours of grief. It will help you have better dates, cooler conversations, and hotter sex. It will help you to stop acting like a self-sabotaging dick. And it will also help your relationships with your mom, sisters, daughters, female friends, and coworkers.

To be clear: *the insights in this chapter are not a collection of opinions and moralizing lessons*. They are based on the best, current scientific knowledge that we have about women's psychology and sex differences. We'll also focus on women's vulnerabilities, concerns, and anxieties that you might not have considered before, because these are the aspects of the female experience that have long stood between men and a greater understanding of—and success with—women.

SHE IS TIRED OF BEING OBJECTIFIED, SO *SUBJECTIFY* HER INSTEAD

Go to a sports bar in any major city or college town on game day, and invariably you will run into a crew of gorgeous young women in skin-tight, cutoff referee outfits or school jerseys walking around, selling shot specials or beer buckets. This is how everything, not just liquor, is sold to men—hand tools, shampoo, Doritos, porn, cars. All of them shamelessly use beautiful, scantily clad women with big boobs, tight asses, and long legs as the vehicles to deliver their message. And it works.

The problem from a mating perspective (besides the obvious ethical ones) is that normal women feel this objectification acutely. On the one hand, the media have established an unrealistic expectation of beauty for them to live up to, and this makes them insecure. On the other hand, this expectation has created in women the belief that most guys care only about a woman's boob-to-ass-to-leg ratio, which is a recipe for resentment and distrust.

Here's the thing though: when women say, "Don't objectify me," they don't mean "You're never allowed to look at my boobs or notice my butt." Actually, they kind of like their boobs and butts and hope you do too, if you're a good guy and you *also* appreciate their other features, like their eyes or their opinions.

To attract women, you must be able to take their point of view and think of them not as marketing vehicles to objectify, but as living, thinking, feeling individual humans. You have to *subjectify* them: accept, understand, and acknowledge their individual, subjective consciousness.

Ironically, a great way to understand a woman's point of view is to think of her as a marketing *consumer*: a savvy customer evaluating your products (traits) and ads (proofs) to see if they'll add value to her life. If you want to guarantee mating failure, all you have to do is think of her as nothing more than an inanimate object—as an "8" or a "9," as a simplistic robot with a set of "triggers" and "hot buttons" to manipulate. At that point you've reduced your customer to nothing more than a cash dispenser, or, since we're talking about objectifying a woman, a sex dispenser.

Objectifying women isn't just a moral failure. At the purely practical level of attracting women, it's stupid. It might temporarily reduce your anxiety about approaching them (about making your pitch), because if you think of them as targets, you can try to trick yourself into thinking that they won't be judging you when you walk up to them. But they are judging you—and that's OK, as long as you understand how and why.

SHE IS PHYSICALLY VULNERABLE, AND SHE KNOWS IT

Picture this example:

You are a young, relatively inexperienced gay man. You're single, it's Friday night after a long week, and you've decided to go out and have some fun. You and some friends decide to check out a new gay bar that you've heard has a lot of hot guys.

When you walk in, you encounter an overwhelming sea of men. These guys are all as tall as NBA players, as muscular as NFL linebackers, and as sexually aggressive as a felon on his first night out of jail.

They are all bigger, stronger, faster, and hornier than you. Their heads all swivel toward you, and their eyes look you up and down like sexual Terminators.

You haven't even met them, but you can see the gears turning behind their eyes. Any one of them could grab you, carry you out of the bar, and put who knows what god knows where, and there is little you could do to stop them. You're just a piece of meat to them.

But there's strength in numbers, so you and your friends gather whatever sober courage you can muster and head to the bar. Soon enough, you've had a couple drinks, and some of these huge guys approach you and begin talking to you.

Some of them are really lame and unattractive and make crude, ham-fisted passes at you. Some are awkward and annoying. Some seem kind of angry and mean. Some are persistent and make you scared—they are much bigger than you, after all. All of these guys are very unappealing. You don't want to talk to them.

But lo and behold, some others are actually pretty intriguing. Yes, they are still big and intimidating, but they want to buy you drinks and pay you compliments. Some of them are really interesting and fun; they do amazing things with their lives and seem to really be into you. They're cocky and funny. They have that sublime masculine energy that is very appealing.

How would you feel in this situation? Nervous, worried, scared, guarded, self-conscious, and vulnerable? But also flattered, desirable, and excited (remember, you're gay in this exercise).

Some of the same male traits that frighten you the most also seem to be the most attractive to you. The guys who pose the greatest physical threat are also the same guys you can envision making you feel the safest. The guy who seems like the most egotistical player in the bar is also the one making you laugh so hard that your ribs hurt. It's all a giant, swirling, pulsating contradiction.

This is the world of sex and dating for women.

And this is what it is like for women every day, in every social situation, with straight guys just like you.

Women are surrounded by bigger, stronger, faster men who probably want to have sex with them and could take it by force. This is their experience not just at bars and clubs, but at school and work, on the street, and the subway. Men stare at them, leer at them, make crude passes at them, and interact with them all day every day, with sex clearly the subtext of every interaction— even the briefest, most innocuous nonmating exchanges.

Her: "I would also like fries with that."

Him: "Yeah, you would!"

While this is just a thought experiment, the facts that underpin it are very real. For Americans over age twenty, the average man is five inches taller than the average woman (5'9" vs. 5'4"). He's thirty pounds heavier (196 pounds vs. 166 pounds), and he carries less body fat (18 percent vs. 24 percent), so he's got about twice the upper-body strength (what he'd use to pick her up) and twice the grip strength (what he'd use to hold her down). An average woman is as physically vulnerable to an average guy as a big guy (6'0", 190 pounds) would be to the average NFL lineman (6'5", 310 pounds)—which is to say, *very vulnerable.*

Most dating advice to guys fails at this first hurdle. It's built around the assumption that men and women think alike about sex, romance, and dating without even acknowledging the basic physical differences between male and female bodies and the resulting male vs. female vulnerabilities. **This is totally wrong.** If you can understand women's sexual and physical vulnerability, dating should make a lot more sense.

For instance, if a woman seems like she's sending "mixed messages," or acting "hot and cold," or there's a mysterious push-me/pull-you erotic dance going on, it's not that she's being weird or manipulative (at least, typically). It's that she's trying to express interest from a defensive posture, and she's got a hair-trigger threat-detection system that makes her withdraw into her shell when you start pushing too hard. Maybe you really are the good guy who won't take advantage of her, but she has no way of knowing that when she first meets you. She has to evaluate you herself.

Think about how weird that whole situation is: to be sexually attracted to beings that could so easily do irreparable physical harm to you. Think about the anxiety that internal contradiction could create on a daily basis. For women who are on the more anxious and delicate side, think about the raw physical courage it must take just to go out and meet men. If she pushes when you pull, your question shouldn't be, "Why won't she have sex with me?" It should be, "Why would she *ever* put herself in a situation of sexual vulnerability with *any* guy?"

The best (and funniest) explanation of this dynamic we've ever heard comes from the famous comedian Louis C.K.:

> *The courage it takes for a woman to say yes [to a date with a man] is beyond anything I can imagine. A woman saying yes to a date with a man is literally insane, and ill advised. How do women still go out with guys, when you consider the fact that there is no greater threat to women than men? We're the number-one threat! To women! Globally and historically, we're the number-one cause of injury and mayhem to women. We're the worst thing that ever happens to them!*

And yet, here we are. Women have evolved this ambivalent arousal/fear, love/hate response to male size, strength, and power. If you want to be successful in modern mating, the more you understand this, the better you can deliver what women love while eliminating what they fear.

SHE'S BEEN DEALING WITH CREEPY DOUCHEBAGS FOR A LONG TIME

A woman can tell how well your life is going from how you look, in about two seconds. Your face and body are leaking all kinds of cues about your sexual experience, self-confidence, and personality—and she can see it all in one glance. Before you approach her, she's already decided whether she wants you to talk to her, and she's already judged your mate value and your status before you toss the first lame, derpy pickup line at her. She can smell your over-practiced PUA tricks from a mile away. It's like her superpower.

By the time you've met her, a normal American woman has spent years honing that superpower. She *had* to develop it after putting up with so much shit from lame guys hitting on her, catcalling, sexually harassing, and potentially even stalking her. Since puberty, when she started developing hips and breasts and pretty facial features, she's had to deal with creepers and sketchballs to some degree or another, and she's probably pretty sick of it.

It's hard for guys to appreciate what it would be like to grow up being stared at and sexually harassed every day of your life from age twelve onward. So instead, what you need to realize is that all this sexual attention a woman gets sows in her a fear of raw physical violence—reactive assault—that could be sparked if she ignores your come-ons, rejects you in a way you find demeaning, or dates you for six months before finding out you're a paranoid, jealous control freak.

That's the female reality of living in sexual fear. She's afraid of creeps, weirdos, crazies, losers, and stalkers. And believe us when we say that, from her perspective, they make up a high proportion of men—especially the ones likely to hit on her in inappropriate ways. Psychological and environmental factors explain much of this perspective.

The psychological research, for instance, shows that, from a woman's point of view, most guys she meets will be less kind, less agreeable, less empathic, less conscientious, less reliable, less clean—less *everything* really—than she and her friends are. Even if she accepts those sex differences, she still has to wrangle with the fact that many mental illnesses and personality disorders are more common among men (the more dangerous ones no less). These male-dominated disorders include alcoholism, drug addiction, autism, schizophrenia, narcissism, white-collar sociopathy, and criminal psychopathy. All of which make each random encounter with a man less likely to end in love and more likely to end with a fight-or-flight response.

Most guys reading this book right now are probably sitting there thinking, "WTF, I've never done any of that creepy shit. Don't lump me in with those assholes." And we agree. Most of you guys are solid dudes. You're just suffering for the actions of the highly nonrandom sample of guys who hit on every woman in sight. That's why it's so important to understand the world from a woman's perspective.

Think about women's experiences with guys like a city cop's experience with people in general. Cops spend 90 percent of their time dealing with the scummiest 5 percent of humanity. The ones who've been around a while often develop a cynical, negative, and fatalistic view of humans, based on the totality of their bitter experiences. It's not that humans are all bad. It's that cops see only the worst.

Likewise, women spend a big proportion of their time in the mating market avoiding the small percentage of guys who are the most intrusive, obnoxious, or insane. Psychopaths are sexually predatory, uninhibited, and confident, so although they're only 4 percent of the American male population, they might account for 40 percent of the men who have hit on any given woman. Guys with Asperger's are another factor; although they're often introverted (and so less likely to approach a woman), if they do approach, they're bad at reading nonverbal cues of disinterest or rejection, so they're more likely to persist beyond a woman's comfort zone. There are almost too many other types of men who do things women find repulsive to name them all.

Simply put, her experience is that the worst guys come straight at her while the best guys are nowhere to be seen.

SHE'S PROBABLY JUST NOT THAT INTO YOU, AND YOU NEED TO BE OKAY WITH THAT

The average guy finds the average woman at least somewhat sexually attractive. Think about it. The next time you're walking down the street or hanging out in a mall or student union, ask yourself seriously, *What percent of these women would I be willing to have sex with right now, if it was safe, easy, consensual, and no strings attached?*

If you're like most young guys, the answer would be well over 70 percent— even including the moms and older women. For some of you freaks, *especially* including them.

By contrast, the average woman finds the average man sexually invisible, neutral, disgusting, or repulsive. Only a tiny percentage of guys inspire immediate lust in women. And most of those guys have already moved to New York or LA to become actors or models. If you are over eighteen and haven't done that, you're not one of those guys.

This is a huge sex difference in initial choosiness, documented in both scientific research and online dating data, that plays out in every domain of sex and dating. (Of course, if a relationship develops between a man and woman, he gets a lot choosier about whether to date her exclusively, move in with her, or marry her—but we'll discuss that later in Step 4. All you need to know at this point is that women are choosier about who they have sex with; men are choosier about who they commit to.) Guys have sexual fantasies about almost all the women they know, whereas women have fantasies about virtually no men. She doesn't have as many sexual fantasies per month as you do, she doesn't masturbate nearly as much, and sex is usually more in the background of her consciousness than the foreground.

Another reason she's not attracted to most men is that she thinks their outfits are stupid and their clothes don't fit. Because they are and they don't. She's right. (Don't worry. We'll help you with this in Chapter 13, on Aesthetic Proof.) She also knows what your body would look like naked, and she probably thinks you're either a lazy loser (out of shape) or a narcissistic gym rat (in too-good shape). None of this should be particularly surprising or contentious. She likes what she likes, and, statistically, the chances are you're not it.

Where it gets problematic is when you don't get the picture and she has to tell you, because women don't like having to reject men explicitly. There is a deep evolutionary logic to this preference, and it has a lot to do with minimizing the very real risks they face from publicly humiliating their suitors. It was almost always better for an ancestral woman to keep a guy within her social orbit as a possible nonsexual friend rather than alienate or upset him. Women aren't being ambiguous and mysterious and elusive because they're "playing games" or "fucking with your head." They're just instinctively trying to reduce the risk of provoking harassment or stalking or violent retaliation.

Here's how women tell you they aren't into you: their first line of defense is simply to play it cool, professional, and neutral. They keep their physical and emotional distance, minimize contact and chatter, and eliminate any signs of affection or interest that could be misconstrued as sexual.

If that doesn't work, they might escalate the subtle rejection vibes by acting in a way that naive young men interpret as "cold" or "stuck up" or "bitchy." This vibe is not cruel—it signals that you failed to appreciate their earlier cues of disinterest, and they've reluctantly had to make their disinterest even more obvious to get it through your thick head that they do not wish to fuck you. If women wanted to be cruel when they rejected you, they would ask their brothers to cut your belly open with sharp flints and pull your guts out for the wild hyenas to eat—or whatever the equally painful equivalent on Facebook would be.

Women are trying to do the best they can to reject you without humiliating you. The more experienced and confident they are, the better they are at rejecting you obviously enough that you go away but not so obviously that you're ashamed in front of your friends and other women. But it's not their responsibility to reject you in the way that would be least costly to you; it's your responsibility to take the hint as best you can and go away.

SHE ALREADY KNOWS SHE'S PRETTY, AND SHE'S STILL SELF-CONSCIOUS

If you meet a woman who strikes you as beautiful, you're probably not the first guy to notice. In attractiveness research, men show very high agreement in their ratings of women's faces and bodies. This means that as long as she has been objectively beautiful she has been admired, hit on, masturbated to, and harassed by guys from ages sixteen to sixty, including many of her classmates, teachers, peers, coaches, coworkers, and bosses—not to mention total strangers, pickup artists, and alleged "talent scouts for modeling agencies." Many of the guys who hit on her were nasty sociopaths, because the nice guys found her too intimidating. And enough women have found her threatening that she's had trouble keeping more than a few close friends. Her beauty has already been both a blessing and a curse for years before you ever laid eyes on her.

This is one reason why it's pointless, and often counterproductive, to go up and compliment beautiful women on their beauty. Tell her something she doesn't already know and hasn't already heard from a thousand guys. Better yet, don't *tell* her anything. *Ask* her about her interests, ambitions, friends, background—anything that requires some social intelligence to appreciate behind her "hot girl" persona. Just talk to her like you already understand that (a) she's beautiful, and you both know it, (b) she's felt ambivalent about her beauty for years, and (c) she'd like to be appreciated for things she's achieved in her life through her own efforts, not through winning the genetic lottery of physical attractiveness.

Yet here is the great irony about female beauty: she's still very self-conscious about her face and her body and her clothes and her accessories. Frankly, she doesn't really understand *why* you're attracted to her. This holds true even for a very good-looking woman, because she compares herself to the world's most beautiful models and actresses, air-brushed to perfection, staring her down from the cover of every women's magazine and billboard. She doesn't typically consider what men *actually* find attractive or she misunderstands it completely.

Most women think that men are most attracted to the rail-thin models or skinny actresses that grace the covers of the magazines they buy. They're wrong. Studies show that most men are attracted to women with curves and meat on their bones; the high-fertility hourglass shapes (like Kim Kardashian, Sofia Vergara, or Halle Berry), not low-fertility apple shapes or no-fertility chopstick shapes. Also, guys prefer women who are physically healthy and capable, with strong muscles, bones, connective tissues, and immune systems, because this predicts being a sexually energetic girlfriend; a capable, protective mother; and a long-lived partner. (Think Jennifer Lawrence, Jessica Biel, Rhona Mitra, or Jennifer Garner...) Men want just the right amount of fat, in the right places, on a strong, healthy frame.

Anorexia cues (left: typical runway model) versus capability cues (middle: Jessica Biel) and fertility cues (right: Christina Hendricks)

Unfortunately, most women think the male conception of beauty is binary: "fat" (bad) or "thin" (good). So they diet using bad health advice and spotty willpower to strive for the supermodel plank shape, and they lose both their cues of fertility (boobs and butt) and their cues of capability (muscle), undermining their attractiveness.

Remember, she didn't evolve to be attracted to women or their feminine traits, so she's sort of mystified that you could find her sexually desirable in the first place. It just doesn't make sense to her. There's a part of her that was incredulous during puberty when boys were starting to notice her, and that part is still there. She's got a bit of impostor syndrome about her own erotic power.

This self-consciousness extends to nearly every aspect of her appearance, including many areas of her body and most of what she wears. Women put a lot of thought into their appearance. Everything they wear and display is probably a conscious choice. Every choice is a statement—but not every statement succeeds. Yet often, women can't tell if they've struck the right balance between formal and casual, tight and loose, sexy and slutty, classical and avant-garde, earnest and ironic. Are they projecting "sexy vamp" or "meth-head jail bait"? Are they projecting "sophisticated Brooklyn hipster" or "Jersey Real Housewife"?

The problem is that they almost never get accurate feedback about what image they're projecting. Her friends are too polite to tell her the truth one way or the other, and guys are too horny to tell the difference. Most guys are oblivious to clothes altogether, let alone the specific, conscious choices that women make. When it comes to what we wear, most of us just throw on whatever's clean.

The fact that most guys can't tell the difference between haute couture and Juicy Couture (or the respective differences in effort and taste) only amplifies her self-consciousness. And if you want to turn her self-consciousness up to 11, be the guy who can't seem to pick up on her signs of interest in you either. That one is a killer for any young woman who has put herself out there. If a woman's really interested in you, she will go out of her way to be around you and to be visible and available for you to approach. If you're oblivious enough not to get those signals, she may even have the gumption to wave at you or ask her friend to say hi. Sadly, if you're younger than twenty and/or have had sex with fewer than four women, you'll probably overlook or misinterpret all of those female choice cues. Pay more attention next time.

SHE IS WORRIED ABOUT HER SOCIAL STATUS, AND YOU'RE A BIG PART OF THAT

Just like males compete against other males for resources that matter to males, females compete against other females for resources that matter to them. Typically, female-female competition in other animals is more about food, territory, or other resources required to reproduce.

But if you're in a competitive mating market with a limited number of attractive, desirable males that all the women want, then women are going to compete against each other to get and keep those males. And they are going to use any tactics that work—seduction, manipulation, gossip, physical violence, verbal violence—anything that works to get those guys and make them stick around.

Science has started to delve into female-female competition in a serious way only in the last five years or so, and we still don't understand its intricacies very well. For example, it might seem weird to men that female-female competition would ever involve something as arbitrary as the specific brands of high-heeled shoes or handbags that women wear and carry.

But think about guys bragging about which microbrewed beer they like, which concealed-carry pistol they favor, or which car they drive. The red soles of Christian Louboutin heels and the stitching on Celine handbags don't make that much difference to their function—but the same is true for the nuances of the Congress Street IPA, the Springfield XD-S, and the Maserati Quattroporte. Both sexes are suckers for status-seeking through consumerism.

Guys know that some of our male-male competition tactics are stupid and ridiculous. Same with women. If you're smart enough to be reading this book, then the women who are smart enough to be good mates for you already understand most of the absurdities of female-female competition. They're just as disgusted by stupid women as you are by stupid men. But just as you seek social approval from guys you don't really respect, women seek social approval from women they don't really respect—and they're often appalled that they instinctively care so much about it.

This is where the similarities end, however. Women face much different social vulnerabilities. On average, they're less anxious than men about being bad at athletics, fighting, or making money. But they worry a lot more about their sexual reputations among their acquaintances, coworkers, family, and neighbors. Specifically, they fret about the existential reputational threat posed by slut-shaming in modern society.

Women are vicious to each other about slut-shaming. A woman's entire social life could be ruined by one mean sexual rumor that has been perpetuated through social media by people who barely know her. By the time a woman is out of college, she's had years of hearing women rag on other women (in their class, in their dorm, in their sorority, at their work) for being sluts and whores. Imagine the anxiety that comes with an ill-timed one-night stand or an indiscreet friend with benefits. It can be paralyzing for some women.

As a guy or even just a functional member of society, it's important to realize that female slut-shaming isn't the product of some deep self-loathing or in-group hatred. Rather, it is as prevalent as it is because a promiscuous rival is a woman's biggest threat to keeping a good boyfriend. "Sluts" aren't derogated because women are uncomfortable with their sexuality; it's because they're experts at mate poaching, which is a very real threat to most women. So when women are thinking about short-term mating with you, they're also thinking, "Who at school or work might find out about this?" and "How will I feel about this when I'm Skyping with my mom later this week?"

Female promiscuity also has a "tragedy of the commons" effect in the mating market. If one woman offers blowjobs on the second date, it's harder for other women to keep them in reserve until the fourth date as their special treat. This creates a downward spiral of young women feeling like they have to offer more and more sex to more and more guys just to stay in the mating game. Thus, slut-shaming is a way of enforcing a more restrained sexual norm on other women so that not all women have to become more promiscuous than any of them would like.

The slut-shaming then seeps down into a woman's emotional matrix, where it can fester and undermine her self-respect. That's why women typically do not feel great about themselves the morning after a one-night stand unless they have a lot of self-confidence and sexual experience. There's a reason they call the journey home the morning after a hookup the "walk of shame."

Given the risk of slut-shaming, a typical female strategy is to pursue short-term mating quietly, with a lot of plausible deniability, adaptive self-deception, and circumstantial rationalization. Any credible excuse for casual sex can reduce the slut-shaming risk—"It was my birthday," "I was drunk," "It was spring break," "It was Jamaica, after all," "I've always admired his writing."

These special-circumstance explanations help women create plausible deniability to other women that any given short-term sex was not representative of their usual longer-term mating strategy. Even the euphemisms that women use for sex ("hanging out," "hooking up," "partying," "dating," "going out together") help obscure the key issue of whether intercourse actually happened.

Understanding all this is especially important if you meet a woman who's with her friends. She knows they are watching and judging. If you talk to her for a few minutes and she's charmed, maybe she'll want to leave immediately to go have sex with you. Weirder things have happened. But she probably won't do that, because she knows she will be accountable to her friends the next time they meet. They *will* ask about what happened. She'll have to come up with a story about why fucking a guy within an hour of meeting him should not undermine her sexual reputation.

So guys in that situation should not try to steal a woman away from her friends as soon as possible. Instead, just get her number so you can text her about getting together later, in private. That way, she can make her own judgment about whether to tell her friends anything about the night, and she's much better protected against the long-term effects of slut-shaming.

Her reputational concerns don't just end with whether or not she had sex with you. If she starts dating you, that too will affect her status within her peer group, either positively or negatively. She can already anticipate how that will play out. Partly it depends on your qualities as a guy. Are you such an awesome guy that she'll get an immediate status boost from you having chosen her? Or are you such an embarrassing mess that she'll suffer a status loss— at least until she fixes you up and makes you presentable? Her friends will also judge her based on how you treat her. Are you sexually exploiting and emotionally neglecting her like that creep last year? That lowers her status. Or are you taking care of her like a potential Mr. Right would? That raises her status.

You can do everyone a huge favor before you even get to this stage by making an effort in that initial moment of contact to charm her friends—even the grumpy ones—so that they think you're a cool, funny guy and give you the benefit of the doubt from the jump.

This is as much for you and her as it is for her friends, who face a harder job in evaluating you than she does. You were an unknown quantity after all, an uncertain bet. They need time to appreciate your strengths and accept your weaknesses. But while their jury is still out, your new girlfriend will suffer a temporary loss of status. Making a good impression right away speeds up their deliberation.

SHE'S TERRIFIED OF PREGNANCY, ABANDONMENT, AND STDS

Pregnancy has been the most fundamental sex difference in mammals for more than seventy million years. Women get pregnant, men don't. Most of the sex differences in human mating strategies emerge, directly or indirectly, from that basic fact.

It's a complicated issue for young women. In the long term, pregnancy with a great husband is one of most women's greatest aspirations—it can be a true blessing. But in the short term, unwanted pregnancy is one of their biggest fears. Getting knocked up can be a career-wrecking, family-shaming, mate-value-decreasing disaster, even if the baby daddy has great genes and promises to be there when the shitty diapers hit the fan.

We know from anthropological studies of hunter-gatherer societies that if a guy abandons a woman or he has a hunting accident and gets killed, the likelihood of her baby surviving drops alarmingly. It's a potentially huge cost, and it's why women have evolved a pretty good radar for detecting unreliable flakes.

Being stuck with a little kid also seriously lowers a woman's attractiveness to future men. Whatever her mate value was before the baby, it's going to drop afterward. Very few guys want to become a step-dad, and women understand this. Their instinctive worry about unwanted pregnancy is often stronger than their conscious trust in birth control. Female mammals have been getting pregnant since before the dinosaurs went extinct. Reliable rubber condoms weren't invented until 1855. The Pill arrived only in 1960—that's just two generations of reliable female birth control. That's not enough time for evolution to have recalibrated women's mate preferences to this new reality that they could, in theory, have lots of casual short-term sex without getting pregnant.

Let's say a woman gets through high school, college, and young adulthood unscathed on the pregnancy front. She still has to worry about the armada of sexually transmitted diseases (STDs) sailing toward her aboard your dirty penis. Or at least that's what's going through her mind, unconsciously.

For STDs like gonorrhea, genital herpes, or HPV, it's much easier for the viruses or bacteria to go from your penis to her vagina than vice versa. Even if you always use condoms, there's still a risk of breakage, slippage, or incomplete coverage (if you have warts or sores near the base of your dick). When a guy gets an STD, it's usually a temporary inconvenience. When a woman gets one, it can often lead to infertility, or it can infect the baby during birth. The STD stakes are simply higher for women. This is one reason why women evolved a stronger propensity for sexual disgust toward anything that tends to promote the spread of STDs: promiscuity, group sex, anal sex, whatever. If a sexual activity has a high STD risk but doesn't bring her much pleasure, build an emotional connection with the guy, or help her pass along good genes to future babies, why would she do it?

You could be the nicest guy in the world with everything going for you, but if you roll up to a woman trying to run game, looking or smelling like you just climbed out from the bottom of a third-world public toilet, these are some of the fears that may be driving her to keep her distance. In fact, she cares more about how you smell than you can imagine. It's a mammalian thing—pheromones are real. And so is poor hygiene. Some women will decide they're interested in hooking up with a guy just from his online dating profile, and the live, in-person date is basically to see if he smells as good chemically as he looked digitally.

SHE IS JUST AS FRUSTRATED BY DATING AS YOU ARE

Even apart from women's physical vulnerabilities, sexual-reputation anxieties, and practical physical needs, women's minds evolved to be different from men's minds. They evolved to want different things at different times.

As a man, it's easy to envy women's sexual power if you're ignorant of their romantic desires. You might think, like the seduction peddlers in the PUA community often do, that if you were an attractive woman, you could sleep with any guy you wanted, get laid every weekend, and it would be awesome. And you could. But you wouldn't enjoy it. Because that's not what women evolved to want—that behavior did not serve their evolutionary interests.

In fact, this might be hard for you to believe, but it's true: **it is much harder for a highly attractive woman to get what she wants, sexually and romantically, than it is for a highly attractive man.**

Yes, every beautiful, bright woman knows she could seduce almost any man for a quick fuck. But that is rarely what she wants. She usually wants a boyfriend, at least. And her experience, if she is single, is that she has failed, over and over and over, to get the guys she really respects and admires, the great catches, the Mr. Rights, to stay with her as long as she wants.

This is due in no small part to her struggle to understand her own taste in men. There are some guys she thinks she should logically be attracted to but isn't, while there are other guys she knows she should stay away from but she can't. (We cover this in greater depth in Chapter 4: Understand What Women Want...and Why.) This internal conflict is more pronounced in younger women than older, more experienced women; but it never fully goes away, and it only makes dating that much more frustrating.

She's also frustrated by the dating scene because time is running out. Most young women want it all—education, career, money, status, love, marriage, kids, meaning, and purpose. But they can't see how all that could plausibly happen by age 40, when fertility plummets. Do the age-math. If the average American woman is about to graduate from college (typically around age 24), she might think about being a doctor—but that's another 4 years for an M.D. (until age 28), and 6 years of exhausting residency (age 34), before she can even start building her independent practice, which can take years. By the time most bright women are in their late 20s, they've realized that the clock is ticking for both their career plans and their family plans and that the two are not going to fit together very well. She's going to be looking for a guy who can help her manage these heartbreaking trade-offs.

That's why, if your early-stage relationship is going well—even just the first hour of chatting—she might want to have sex with you very soon. And if it's not going well, she probably won't have sex with you *ever*—even if you're an otherwise attractive guy. If you don't realize that even the very first hour of talking with her constitutes a type of relationship that needs some level of mutual respect and nurturance, she will especially not have sex with you.

If she does decide to have sex with you though, what she is most concerned about is not whether you will break the bed, but whether you'll break her heart. Women naturally fall for guys they've had several orgasms with. The oxytocin magic works reliably. This makes them emotionally vulnerable. The better the sex and the more they like you, the faster it happens.

So will you fuck her for one night and never call her again? That hurts for a week (or longer, if she really liked you). Will you hook up for three months until she falls in love with you, then evaporate for no obvious reason? That will hurt her for a year (or longer).

All of this makes the dating scene incredibly frustrating for women. Understand that and you'll understand why women aren't bending over backward to satisfy your unquenchable sexual thirst.

SHE HAS SEXUAL FANTASIES JUST LIKE YOU DO, EXCEPT SHE GETS A BUNCH OF SHIT FOR HERS

Men have phone sex; women talk dirty. Men are "bad boys"; women are "dirty girls." Most women have that naughty, "dirty" side that drives many of their sexual fantasies. Most of those fantasies aren't literally bad and dirty, however. Women don't fantasize about being sexually assaulted by bridge trolls on top of floating garbage skiffs. But they do fantasize about being sexually dominated and controlled by handsome, caring, and capable men who operate secretly on the fringes of acceptable society. The *Fifty Shades* series has sold more than 100 million copies for a reason.

What is a modern woman to make of this part of her sexual-emotional circuitry? She'll probably bury it deep in her private bedroom habits and worry that if she ever disclosed it to a guy, he'd be such a reductive idiot that he would think she wants to be dominated and controlled all the time, in every aspect of her life. Or worse, he might take it as license to unleash the *really* fucked up shit he's wanted to try.

It doesn't seem fair (aren't all fantasies created equal?), but the reality is that women are more prone to sexual disgust than guys are, and the average guy wants the average woman to do stuff that she'd find at least moderately gross — anal, bondage, threesomes, and more.

She's unsure how to think about this. If she holds her ground and only does what she's comfortable with, will a good boyfriend abandon her for some kinky skank? She's also vaguely aware that her dad would want to kill you for whatever you want to do to her body, and his judgment hovers over her bedroom like the Eye of Sauron. Even if she's sexually open to some of the weird shit that you want, she's not confident that she can do it right. The sexual skills they require are baffling and intimidating to her, and cultivating them would increase her risk of being slut-shamed from certain corners of her life.

And just to add insult to injury, she knows she probably won't reach orgasm the first few times she sleeps with you. When you have sex with a new woman and you're under about age sixty, you can be pretty confident that you'll enjoy the experience and be able to come. For guys, sex is reliably pleasant. But for women with a new guy, she won't feel safe and relaxed enough, or she won't be attracted enough to him yet, or he won't know her body well enough. Especially in one-night stands, most women don't climax with most men. They might still have a wonderful time — women can enjoy non-orgasmic sex a lot more than you realize, especially if you're really into them. But she usually won't reach that world-melting, mind-blowing orgasm that she might be craving.

Also, she resents your putting pressure on her to orgasm. She knows you want her to come, and she knows that to you it's some weird test of your sexual skills and gentlemanly altruism. But, honestly, if she just wanted to come, she'd have stayed home with a bottle of white wine, *Fifty Shades of Grey*, and her vibrator. If she's with you, it's because she wants *more* than just an orgasm. She wants a sexual connection. She wants to feel sexually desired. And she wants you to have a great time so you'll call her again. And often, the best way for you to give her all that is to just enjoy the hell out of her, without worrying too much about whether she comes. By all means, be great at foreplay—but do it because you love it, not like you're warming up a car engine on a cold morning.

PRACTICE PERSPECTIVE-TAKING

You should now have a much better grasp on the issues women deal with on a day-to-day, hour-to-hour, week-to-week basis. Uncertainty about and threats to their physical, emotional, and social safety surround them. You get that at a general level. But what about at the specific, individual female level? How do you grow your insights into *her* point of view? How do you *subjectify* her? You do it by practicing perspective-taking.

Next time you're in class or sitting in a Starbucks, pick out a woman in the crowd (a pretty classmate, a customer, the barista), and for a few minutes imagine yourself in her skin in the most non–*Silence of the Lambs* way possible. Then ask yourself questions like these:

- What is something unique to her life and central to her identity that is impossible for me to know just by looking at her?
- Who are the potential threats around her in this place right now?
- What does she think about all the guys in here?
- What is the likelihood she thinks I'm among the most attractive guys here?
- What parts of her body is she most embarrassed about and most proud of?
- Why did she choose to wear those specific clothes and accessories today?
- Who are her friends, and which ones would be most judgmental if she had casual sex? How does that impact her behavior and choices?

- If she got pregnant tomorrow, what would she do?
- What kind of men does she date, and do they sexually satisfy her? Are any of them here right now?

You won't necessarily guess the right answers, and you should *never* go up and ask her if your guesses are correct—unless you want to know what a restraining order looks like. This is just a thought experiment for you to practice, to put your attention on a woman's mind before you ever approach her so that you might understand her a bit better.

Women are pulling their weight in trying to understand you. They subscribe to women's magazines that devote thousands of words a month to trying to get inside your head. (Sadly, those magazines suck.) They chat with their female friends about what men might be thinking or feeling and what a man meant by this particular sentence or that particular action. They even become psych majors. If you can meet them halfway, you're going to do great. Understand this and everything we are going to tell you from this point forward will make more sense and be more effective.

Takeaways

- Mating success requires cross-sex insight—specifically, the willingness and ability to understand how women perceive the world around them and how they evaluate your qualities.
- Women are physically, emotionally, and socially vulnerable, and they know it. What makes this difficult for women is that the male traits that make women vulnerable are also some of the traits that make men more attractive.
- In most cases, women are just as worried about their social status as they are about getting pregnant, getting STDs, or getting abandoned. And you play a big role in all those areas.
- Women like sex as much as you do and are frustrated by dating as much as you are. The main difference, though, is the amount and type of pressure acting on women, especially as they get older.
- Believe it or not, it is much harder for an attractive woman to get what she wants sexually and romantically than it is for an attractive man.

CHAPTER 3: CLARIFY YOUR MATING GOALS AND ETHICS

O Lord, help me to be pure, but not yet.

—St. Augustine

At any given point in their lives, most men know what their mating goals are and what kind of relationship they want to be in. Or at least they *think* they know.

In reality, it is not uncommon to find younger and older men alike engaged in behavior and relationships that are at odds with their stated mating goals. They are, often unwittingly, lying to themselves and, as a result, lying to the women with whom they're interacting—who themselves are just as often lying about their true goals.

In modern American society, so much of the generally accepted "wisdom" about sex is based on a two-sided lie:

Lie 1 is that all women pretend to be more comfortable with short-term mating than they really are because that's supposedly the way to hook a guy into a longer-term committed relationship, which is what they all *really* want.

Lie 2 is that all men pretend to be more open to longer-term mating than they really are because that's apparently the surest way to get sex.

There are scenarios that make these lies *appear* true (e.g., where the local sex ratio is tilted and relative sexual bargaining power is wildly out of balance), but generally speaking, these lies are perniciously combined to present a picture of women using sex to get love and men using love to get sex. It is an endless charade that results, inevitably, in a heartbreaking compromise for both sexes.

The purpose of this chapter (and this entire book, really) is to short-circuit that destructive cycle and to stop the misinformation. Regardless of what you want from your mating life, there are a lot of women who want the same thing. You just need to find them and connect with them.

In order to accomplish this goal—to help men be more honest with themselves and with women so they can get what they *really* want—we need to start by helping men figure out what their mating goals actually are so they can find women with similar goals who offer real win-win relationship compatibility.

Simply put, a mating goal is nothing more than the relationship you hope results from your mating efforts. But let's be clear on the definition of *relationship* here, because many guys don't use the word correctly. A "relationship" does not automatically mean you are committed or monogamous (though it can), nor does it mean you have to hold hands at the movies and remember each other's birthdays. **A relationship is a consensual mating interaction between two parties that, ideally, is win-win for both of them.**

Every mutually agreed upon mating interaction you have with a woman—from the briefest random kissing on the dance floor to a Mormon celestial marriage that lasts beyond death into eternity—is a relationship. Your job is to figure out which of the three types of relationships you want right now: short term, medium term, or long term.

SHORT-TERM RELATIONSHIPS

(aka "hookups," "one-night stands," "casual sex," "trysts")

Short-term relationships are those where the courtship period lasts a relatively short period of time—anywhere from five minutes to five or more hours. The relationship is centered around one encounter—usually at a bar or a party or someplace like that—and typically culminates in some

REALITY CHECK TIME		
This is **NOT** a relationship	Fantasies about a woman you've never met	
	Pestering a woman to date you when she just wants to be friends	
	Thinking a woman is meant for you, despite the restraining order	

sort of sexual activity, whose end also signals the end of the relationship. You meet, you flirt, you fuck (or make out), the end.

Religion, Hollywood, and the media historically have done a great job stigmatizing casual sex. In the 1960s and 1970s, it was the domain of free-loving, freewheeling hippies. In the 1980s and 1990s, a one-night stand was a recipe for AIDS, followed quickly by death. If somehow you managed to avoid AIDS, don't worry, you almost certainly caught the worst STD of all: a baby.

Of course, if movies were to be believed, you wouldn't meet the kid until she was 16, at which point you would reevaluate your entire life, see the error of your ways for all those years, and instantly propose to your child's mother, because god forbid all either of you wanted from each other after that house party was sex.

Don't let movies, parents, teachers, or clergy fool you. There are *good things* about hooking up. There are also limiting factors that are neither good nor bad—they just *are*—that you need to consider when figuring out your mating goal.

The Good

It's fun: Even when you don't know what you're doing, the novelty of hooking up with a new person keeps the fun factor high. If you can make it enjoyable for the woman too, the fun is limitless.

Emotionally uncomplicated: When both people just want to hook up and nothing else, the emotional complications that follow from many male-female interactions tend to melt away because the only feelings that matter are the ones in your private parts. There's less fretting about what the other person is thinking. There's no "what did s/he mean by that?" afterward. There are no unrealistic expectations.

No sacrifice required: By their very nature, one-night stands and casual hookups do not require the kind of sacrifice and responsibility that comes with medium- and long-term relationships. When people talk about "no strings attached," those are the strings: sacrifice and responsibility. This makes short-term mating ideal for guys who are more focused on other things, like athletic achievement, career development, or self-improvement.

The spice of life: Variety is the spice of life, and short-term relationships let you get as spicy as you please. Variety isn't just fun in the short term. It also has long-term value, allowing you to gain a wide array of experiences (both sexual and interpersonal) and learn a lot about many different types of women, both of which will help you figure out what you like. So as your mating goals shift over time toward and between the medium term and long term, you'll have a better sense of exactly what you're looking for.

Practice makes less pathetic: Successfully hooking up with lots of different women takes time, effort, and skill. You can't just be some schmuck who points down to the boner pressing through your sweatpants and expect women to go home with you. You have to practice your courtship and dating skills.

If you're not the best-looking guy at the bar or the party, your skills will be what distinguish you from all the other decent looking guys there who want the same thing as you from the woman you are talking to. Cultivating your courtship skills also makes you a better potential mate for the medium term and long term when that time comes.

The Bad

Tastes great, but less filling: Sex with a stranger tends to be the most unsatisfying type of sex for a number of reasons: you're often drunk, you don't know her body well, you both still have your guard up, you usually can't get into the things you really like (especially if you're a kinky freak like one of the authors), and sometimes it's just awkward. Beyond the potential physical or sexual dissatisfaction, it's not uncommon for guys to feel shitty after a hookup, either about themselves for personal, moral reasons or if they feel the woman they were with regretted it or felt used.

It's hard: It takes a lot of hard work to get to the point where you can meet a woman and then a few hours later get her to agree—let alone want—to have sex with you. And to be consistently successful at it is another thing entirely. The primary reason for this is that women make their short-term mating choices with a much shorter list of criteria: looks and personality. If you are not very attractive and/or very charming, fun, or funny, you are at a distinct disadvantage to those guys who are.

Stranger danger: There is a much higher risk of negative relationship consequences from casual sex. If you have a lot of short-term sexual encounters with a lot of women, and you have made this your explicit mating goal such that all your choices were dedicated to that purpose, you will inevitably come into contact with some dangerous or crazy women (or men they interact with). To be clear, this has nothing to do with women as a gender or women who enjoy casual sex as a category. It has everything to do with playing the odds. Aggressive short-term mating is like roulette—it feels totally random, but the odds are stacked against you, and the more you spin the wheel the sooner it turns into Russian roulette. The kinds of consequences we're talking about here are things like false rape accusations, stalker ex-boyfriends, and women talking shit about you on social media.

Reputational damage: Guys who are focused on short-term relationships and are known to only care about casual sex sometimes suffer negative consequences in their social lives because women start to label them as "players." This label can affect your reputation with many different groups for an extended period of time, not just with the women you want to sleep with right now. No decent bar owner, for instance, wants a bartender who is fucking his way through the wait-staff; it's not good for his business.

Less bang for your buck: At a typical party or on an ordinary weekend night out at a bar, you might spend 4–6 hours flirting with a woman. If you're successful, those hours of effort will probably only net you 20–30 minutes of actual sexual activity. Then, when you go out the following weekend (and every weekend after) to meet a new woman, you will have to put in the exact same amount of effort for the exact same amount of sex. Thus, the "cost of acquisition" for a sexual encounter in short-term relationships stays high. On the other hand, if you were to see the first woman more often, you'd get ten times the sex for basically the same amount of courtship effort. That is the trade-off between quantity and variety/novelty: effort.

The Limits

A short-term mating strategy is not something most guys want to spend their whole lives pursuing. It's also a very hard strategy in which to find consistent success, for all the reasons we just laid out. As a result, very few guys should have mating goals centered *exclusively* around short-term relationships.

Instead, hooking up and casual sex should be the opportunistic, supplemental part of a larger mating strategy; meaning, take it when it comes, but don't go looking for it as your main mating goal.

Additionally, short-term mating can come in and out of your life as you transition between life stages, such as when you leave long-term relationships or move to new places. Most men go through more than one period in their lives when their mating goals are short-term focused. It's just that this is not the starting place on the path through dating to marriage, like some would have you believe. Be careful of falling into the trap of that type of thinking, because it has a way of reigniting that destructive cycle of self-deception and manipulation we are trying to prevent.

MEDIUM-TERM RELATIONSHIPS
(aka "dating," "friends with benefits," "seeing somebody")

In current mainstream American culture, dating can encompass everything from a few weeks of happy-hour drinks and casual sex, to several months of semi-regular sex and hanging out on the weekends, to years of nebulous quasi-commitment. Many guys will spend time in medium-term relationships, but far fewer of them than you'd think, for reasons we'll explain later. Like anything, dating has its pros and its cons, and it definitely has its limits.

The Good

More Sex, More Often: Dating someone typically creates a positive feedback loop: the more sex you have with the same woman, the quicker you gain experience, the more comfortable you get with each other, the better you get to know each other's bodies and preferences, the more she will want to have sex with you.

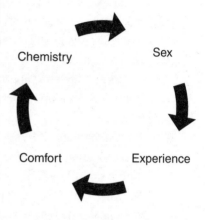

And the best part for guys who aren't ready for a long-term relationship with anyone, let alone the woman they are "seeing": you are still free to have sex with other women (at least in one author's theory).

Lower cost of acquisition: When you want to hook up with different women every weekend, you have to expend roughly the same amount of effort on every occasion. In a medium-term relationship, you have as close to a "sure thing" as you can get. After the first meeting, the first date, the first hookup, the effort for each additional sexual encounter is pretty low, especially if you don't fuck it up.

Known quantities: The threat of STDs, crazy stalkers, and reputational damage all trend down toward zero the more you get to know one woman and the longer you spend time with her.

More fulfilling: When you're dating someone, you're more likely to enjoy spending time with her vertically as well as horizontally. You'll want to take her out to eat, instead of just wanting to eat her out. You'll appreciate the person *around* the vagina as much as or more than the vagina itself, which will make you feel good about her, yourself, and whatever the two of you have decided your relationship is.

The Bad

Sleepy sex: The potential for sex to get boring and tedious in a medium-term relationship is very real. This can happen for a few reasons, especially with younger guys: (1) Your primary focus is still on novelty and variety. (2) You haven't yet learned how to choose a partner who's physically and sexually compatible with you. (3) Initially, any sex was good sex, so you went for quantity over quality, but now your priorities are shifting. If you ever find yourself in this spot, it means there is some work to do on your relationship and some choices to make. Your willingness to put in the work is a good indication of where that relationship is headed.

Tastes great, still less filling: While more emotionally satisfying than a string of short-term hookups, medium-term relationships still register fairly low on the emotional scale compared to long-term relationships. Eventually, for men and women alike, medium-term relationships, too, can become unfulfilling.

Emotional complications: The longer you are with someone, the more likely it is that feelings will develop on one side or the other, and the more likely it is that one of you will get hurt because you want more than you are getting. This is not exclusive to women; in fact, we would not even say it is *mostly* women. We have heard from, spoken with, and counseled enough brokenhearted, butt-hurt guys to know that the emotional complications of uncommitted dating with poorly defined expectations cut equally in each direction.

The Limits

As a general rule, dating is not a permanent mating goal. If they are honest with themselves, very few healthy men stay in the "playing the field" mindset for their whole lives.

Rather, it is a bridge between short- and long-term relationships. It's like a "tryout" for a more serious relationship. You've flirted and hooked up, now you're spending some time seeing how you like each other. If you like each other enough to not pursue the new and the various, then you transition out of medium-term mating into a more long-term committed relationship.

The key for men is to stay in this transitional phase long enough to know for sure if you want more but not so long that it feels like purgatory to you and a waste of time for her. We call it a "bridge" for a reason—you have to cross it in one direction or the other. If you don't—if you stay in the middle—that's when you get run over.

LONG-TERM RELATIONSHIPS

(aka "committed mating," "boyfriend-girlfriend," "partners," "marriage")

Long-term relationships are the standard boyfriend-girlfriend relationships where you have been "officially" dating long enough that you'd talk about this relationship to your friends, introduce her to people as your girlfriend, and/or commit to seeing each other exclusively. The period of time in which this relationship develops could be as short as two to four weeks, or it could take many months. It all depends on what mating goals each of you had when you met.

The defining factor in long-term relationships is the level of commitment, either in sexual exclusivity, time spent together, or both. In American culture, a long-term relationship almost always includes a pledge of monogamy and leads toward marriage. (You want to get married and still hook up with lots of women? Move to France and become president.)

The Good

Emotionally satisfying: It is far easier to achieve a high level of emotional connection and satisfaction with a committed partner. You can be emotionally vulnerable about your hopes and dreams. You can share your deepest experiences, both the greatest and the worst. Mating is ultimately about connecting and relating. The deeper the connection and the relationship go, the better it can become.

Great sex or great*est* sex?: Sex with someone you are strongly connected to emotionally is almost always the best possible sex (for lots of neurochemical reasons that are too technical to get into here). The sex can also be better because as the guardedness and insecurity decrease, the comfort and chemistry increase. You have taken the time to learn each other's preferences, how to read each other, and how to be good at doing what the other person likes, not necessarily for the express purpose of making the sex better, but to make the other person happy. Better sex — *great sex* — is just the byproduct.

Dirty deeds done dirt cheap: In a long-term relationship, assuming your sex drives are similar, the cost of acquisition for sex is at its lowest possible level. Sex is part of the deal now. You aren't competing with other men for it, like in short-term mating. And unlike in medium-term mating, there aren't (m)any preconditions or consequences attached to it. It's used less as a reward (and withheld less as a punishment), and if it isn't good once or twice, the risk of her moving on to someone else doesn't increase to DEFCON levels.

Teachable moments: You can learn far more, both about your partner and about women in general, by being in a long-term relationship. This is a product both of time with your partner and of orbiting the expanded universe of the women that are part of her life. You will learn from interacting with her friends, impressing her coworkers, and getting along with her family. These are valuable real-life skills because your relationship does not exist in a vacuum, nor does it take the place of her other relationships. It exists alongside and in concert with them. The more symbiotic you can make your long-term relationship with her family and friend relationships, the better your relationship will be and the better future potential mate you will become if this relationship ends.

The Bad

No more novelty: "Commitment" and "exclusivity" are synonyms for "you can't have sex with other people anymore." In typical long-term relationships, the sexual variety has been boiled down, by mutual agreement, to monogamy. It's you and her, baby! This can be very problematic if you're one of those guys whose itch is stronger than your self-control not to scratch it. Before you go all-in with a woman, make sure you don't actually want to go in all women instead.

Emotional risk: The big downside of long-term relationships is the risk that she could break your heart (just as you could break hers). By being emotionally open and vulnerable, you open yourself to the possibility of being deeply hurt. This is an enormous hurdle for guys with trust and abandonment issues, which also makes it the most important hurdle to overcome.

Groundhog Day: Comfort and chemistry are a great part of long-term relationships, but if you're not careful they can turn into complacency and taking things for granted. When that happens, the relationship can stagnate in many ways, including sexually, and get very stale, very quickly. You can get stuck in a rut and ultimately waste a lot of time in the relationship because the comfort and (the memory of) chemistry make it easier to stick around. This phenomenon is not exclusive to male-female relationships either; it applies to many long-term engagements: investments, careers, places that you live.

The Limits

There are seemingly no limits to a healthy, committed long-term relationship. It is an admirable mating goal and one that nearly every man is propelled toward biologically, evolutionarily, and culturally.

But do not feel the need to rush into it. You have to be ready and mature enough for a long-term relationship, or else it will fail over and over again.

Healthy is the operative word here. Having the right healthy mindset will be what makes the committed relationship successful; it doesn't work the other way around. A healthy, committed long-term relationship will be one of the greatest things you'll ever experience—right up there with your first boob grab. But it won't solve all your other problems; it will only magnify them.

RELATIONSHIP TYPE RECAP			
	Short term	*Medium term*	*Long term*
Also known as	one-night stand, hooking up, just sex	casual dating, going steady, seeing someone	committed relationship, serious dating, marriage
Typical life-stage	teens through 30s; post-divorce	college through 30s; post-divorce	late 20s onward
Typical emotion	lust	love, affection	love, attachment
Typical activity	drinking in bars, dancing in clubs, sex	going out to dinner, movies, and other activities together	watching TV, domestic activities, basic life functions
Hours of mating effort per hour of sex	very high—typically 2–10 hours of intense courtship before first hour of sex	low—be nice a few times a day for a few hours of sex a week	medium—not much mating effort required, but huge amounts of partnership effort
Key physical risks	STDs, unwanted pregnancies, fights with jealous exes	unwanted pregnancies, getting lazy	getting lazy, weak, and fat; aging
Key social risks	reputation as a "player" or "slut," social media gossip, unstable women, false rape accusations	pressure from peers, colleagues, and parents to escalate commitment;	mating skills get rusty, social network shrinks
Key emotional risks	guilt, shame, regret	romantic mania, unclear expectations, jealousy, heartbreak	boredom, drifting apart, parenting stress, infidelity, divorce

(*Continued*)

	Short term	*Medium term*	*Long term*
Learning opportunities	sample a variety of women; learn your physical & social preferences; practice basic courtship	learn about different women in more depth; learn what you like; practice sex, communication, and conflict resolution	understand one woman deeply; practice commitment, fidelity, gratitude, and forgiveness
Typical quality of sex	fun, awkward, novel, but usually conventional (kissing, oral, missionary)	passionate, consistently great, adventurous, exploratory	familiar, easy, trusting, intimate, boring
Typical expectations for future	none—just don't be an asshole in the morning	keep seeing each other unless you break up	live together, get married, have kids
Typical expectations about fidelity	none	negotiable, but usually implicit expectation that more dates implies more fidelity	usually monogamous, unless poly/open is negotiated

WHICH RELATIONSHIP IS RIGHT FOR YOU, RIGHT NOW?

Hooking up, dating, and commitment. Those are your basic options.

This book can teach you how to achieve any of those mating results, but what it cannot do is tell you which one you *should* want. No one can do that. Only you can look into yourself and determine what you desire in your own life.

This is a theme we will come back to over and over in this book: *you need to think for yourself.* We will strive to give you the information you need to do this, but *the ultimate decision about your life will always be yours.*

It's still very possible that right now you are totally lost. Maybe a recent relationship turned you upside down. Maybe you just left a repressive, sex-negative home and are experiencing the freedom of college or adult life for the first time. Maybe you've never really thought about it because you're young or, like so many guys before you, you didn't think a choice was something you could have. For any number of legitimate reasons, you may just have no idea what you want. *That's okay.*

Let's try to figure it out:

Where's Your Head at Right Now?

To figure out whether you're really more interested in shorter-term or longer-term mating at this point in your life, here's a little quiz. Answer each question as quickly and honestly as you can and from your gut and heart, not from your head.

1. **What's the longest sexual relationship you've ever had with a woman?**

   A. more than 5 years
   B. 2 to 5 years
   C. 6 months to 2 years
   D. more than a week, less than 6 months
   E. less than a week

2. **How many women have you had sex with in the last 12 months?**

   A. 0
   B. 1 or 2
   C. 3 to 5
   D. 6 to 20
   E. more than 20

3. **How many women would you want to have sex with in the next 12 months, ideally?**

   A. none or one
   B. 2 to 4
   C. 5 to 10
   D. 11 to 50
   E. more than 50

4. **For me, the most enjoyable sex is usually with a woman I've known for**

   A. more than a year
   B. between 2 weeks and a year
   C. between 2 days and 2 weeks
   D. between 1 hour and 2 days
   E. less than an hour

5. **How many years in the future would you ideally want your first child to be born (or your next child, if you already have kids)?**

   A. within the next 2 years
   B. in about 2 to 4 years
   C. in about 5 to 8 years
   D. in about 9 to 20 years
   E. I never want kids, or not until at least 20 years from now.

6. **Imagine you're 90 years old, thinking back on all the women you ever had sex with. What percentage of them have you already slept with?**

   A. At this point, I've already slept with more than 80 percent of all the women I'll ever have sex with.
   B. I've slept with about 60–80 percent of all the women I'll ever have sex with.
   C. I've slept with about half (40–60 percent) of all the women I'll ever have sex with.
   D. I've slept with about 20–40 percent of all the women I'll ever have sex with.
   E. Right now, I've slept with less than 20 percent of all the women I'll ever have sex with.

(Continued)

Scoring the quiz: Add up how many times you used each letter response. (For example, if you answered A. three times, write *3* next to A. below). Next, multiply the number next to each letter by its multiplier (0–4), and write the subtotal on each line. Then add up the five subtotals to get a grand total, and write it below.

A _____ x 0 = ___
B _____ x 1 = ___
C _____ x 2 = ___
D _____ x 3 = ___
E _____ x 4 = ___
TOTAL   = ___

This grand total represents a very rough estimate of your current mating goal: the higher your score, the shorter-term your mating orientation. The lowest possible score is 0, indicating strong interest in long-term mating, monogamy, marriage, and kids. The highest possible score is 24, indicating strong interest in short-term mating, casual sex, no commitment, and no kids. Most of you will score somewhere in-between. Generally, if your score is below 8, you're long-term oriented, 9–16 is medium-term oriented, and above 16 is short-term oriented.

Write down your current score here: ___ Does it match what you thought your mating goal was?

If this is starting to feel like a big deal and your palms are starting to sweat because it feels like you're making some kind of major life choice, calm the fuck down.

Your mating goal is not set in stone. It can change, and, in fact, it almost certainly will change many times over your life. Not just in one direction either. For instance, most guys go through multiple periods between long-term relationships where their mating goals are short-term focused. There's nothing wrong with that; it's perfectly normal.

You should revisit your mating goal as often as you'd like, and change it as you wish. If you think you want sex with lots of women but you do it and find it unrewarding, then you should reexamine your goal and change it. Or if you think you want a girlfriend but find it stifling, ask yourself why that is, and then change your goal. You can change your goal literally as much as you want, whenever you want, for almost any reason.

The point here is to understand what you want right now so you can do the things necessary to get it. This is just your specific mating goal for this exact moment in your life, nothing more.

Some more common examples of mating goals:

- I just want to have some options with women, instead of always being alone.
- I want to find a long-term girlfriend.
- I want to have as much sex as I can with as many women as possible.
- I want to casually date several different women at once.
- I want to have sex with 10 women this year.
- I want to have some relationships of any type with women, even just friendships.

Even though this decision is ultimately yours, understanding what is common among other guys can help if you're struggling to figure out what you want. The empirical evidence shows that most young men are happiest when they're in the kinds of medium-term relationships with a casual girlfriend that involve lots of sex but not much commitment.

Older guys, on the other hand, tend to be happier with a higher level of exclusivity and mutual trust (marriage-style relationships). It should be no surprise, then, that marriage is the highest predictor of happiness out there for men. (It really is.) We aren't telling you this because we think you should get married. It's what the evidence says makes most men happy, at least during most of their lives.

By no means are these the only options available to you. These are just the typical patterns, trends, and mating scripts in American dating culture and are here to give you a baseline for thinking about your own needs and goals.

Indeed, there is a whole spectacular smorgasbord of mixable and matchable mating options at your fingertips—from friends with benefits to polyamory—that you can enter into as long as you are open and honest about what you want and respect the preferences of your partner. You do that and the mating world is your oyster.

So what's your mating goal? Write it down. Seriously—literally write it down. Like, with a pen or pencil. Do it right here on this page if you're reading this in print; and if you're reading this in ebook, still write it down for real:

My Mating Goal Is _____

_____

Congratulations, you know what you want (for now)! That's great. Give yourself credit. You're already ahead of most guys, who have no idea what they're even trying to accomplish.

CLARIFYING YOUR MATING ETHICS

As you clarify your mating goals, you also need to clarify your mating ethics—the principles, rules, norms, and values that guide HOW you'll pursue your goals. These ethics need to be built into your mating goals from the ground up, based on whatever religious, political, philosophical, scientific, and personal beliefs you have.

This is NOT about becoming some paragon of virtue who seeks approval from parents, priests, philosophy professors, or feminist bloggers. Nor is it about adopting all of our—the authors'—personal values. You need to clarify your personal mating code now, *before* sexual temptations and moral dilemmas arise, because the ethical stakes in mating get higher and higher as technology advances.

If you manipulate and deceive women, you're more likely than ever to have your reputation ruined through social media and your life ruined through real-world consequences. With the rise of smartphones alone, it is infinitely easier for someone to record and publicize your sexual communications and mating behavior. Privacy is dead, but soon it will be even deader. There's nowhere left to hide unethical "seduction tactics," and they'll get you in trouble like never before with friends, police, campus conduct committees, TV news, and bloggers who trade in moral outrage.

The sooner you clarify your ethics, the better you can use ethical feedback to refine how you treat women. Inevitably, you will make ethical errors that hurt women and hurt yourself, just like you'll make practical errors in dating. The question is whether you ignore those instances or you acknowledge them, learn from them, and change your behavior accordingly.

For now, we'll just suggest a few basic moral tests you can use to guide your mating life in specific situations. These are just questions to ask yourself when a moral dilemma arises, like "Should I try to have sex with this woman even though she's drunk?"

- **The "everyone knows" heuristic:** If everyone I cared about knew what I was about to do, would I still do it?
- **The past/future heuristic:** Will I be proud of this decision a year from

now? If I had to wait a year before making this choice, would I choose to do this?

- **The hero/villain heuristic:** If I were watching a movie in which a guy was doing this with a woman, would the audience be rooting for him as the hero or booing him as the villain?
- **The YouTube heuristic:** If she recorded this whole scene with a hidden videocam and posted it to YouTube, would I be ashamed or proud?
- **The female friend heuristic:** If a guy I didn't know was doing this to my best female friend, would I want to kill him or thank him?
- **The ancestral pride heuristic:** If all of my long-dead male ancestors could see me doing this, would they say, "OMG, all the millions of man-years of blood, sweat, tears, heartbreak, and suffering we endured to produce this guy were totally worth it; we are so proud of him!"
- **The willpower heuristic:** If I had stronger willpower right now, what would I do?

This is not about us lecturing you. Clarifying your mating ethics also helps build your sexual self-confidence.

At first, worrying about ethics will feel like it cramps your style, since it removes the total douchebag option from your mating tactics. But in the longer run, having a clear sense of your sexual morality is liberating and lets you enjoy dating and sex without all the sexual guilt and shame that dogs most young men. By drawing a crisp line between good and bad in the sexual domain, you'll clear an ethical space where you are free to play, laugh, have sex, and enjoy women with a totally clear conscience. This will automatically increase your sexual self-confidence when you're interacting with women because you'll feel ethically open and honorable, like you're not hiding anything.

And guys with clear ethical values and strong moral virtues are also *highly attractive* to women, which doesn't hurt either.

Takeaways

- There are three different types of mating goals: short-term relationships, medium-term relationships, long-term relationships.
- Short-term relationships include hookups, one-night stands, and casual sex.
- Medium-term relationships are also called "uncommitted dating" or "friends with benefits."

- Long-term relationships are partnerships, boyfriend-girlfriend, or committed mating.
- Each type of relationship has its good side, its bad side, and its limits.
- All mating goals are valid.
- Clarifying your mating goals (what you seek) should include clarifying your mating ethics (how you seek it).

STEP TWO

Develop
Attractive Traits

CHAPTER 4: UNDERSTAND WHAT WOMEN WANT . . . AND WHY

The great question . . . which I have not been able to answer, despite my thirty years of research into the feminine soul, is "What does a woman want?"

—*Sigmund Freud*

Imagine a huge and powerful dragon, like Smaug from *The Hobbit*, that can survive for thousands of years, dominating its local ecosystem, eating whatever it wants, unthreatened by anything.

But the dragon never bothers to get out there and meet Mrs. Smaug, so it never reproduces. Sooner or later, it will die in some sort of dragon-related accident. When that happens, despite its thousands of years of dominance, it will qualify as a total Darwinian failure—an evolutionary dead end—because its genes for awesome survival abilities died out. They are gone forever.

If only Smaug had paid a little less attention to wrecking shops in tiny dwarf kingdoms and more attention to the mating game, maybe there'd be some baby Smaugs to continue their total domination of Middle Earth.

Well, you're no Smaug. And you are definitely not descended from ancient, celibate dragons. You are descended from sexy little fuckers that developed weird fetishes for big brains and funny stories. In fact, your lineage has an unbroken line of sexual success stretching back millions of years. (Think about that the next time you're feeling sorry for yourself, and borrow some confidence from your family tree.)

For male primates like us, it was never just about the survival of the fittest. Survival is just a means toward reproduction. And reproduction can't usually happen without getting past the challenge of female choice: the fact that female primates will not mate with just any males that happen to be alive.

Across millions of species, males have discovered only four reliable ways to break through the female choice barrier: force, trickery, bribery, and honest mating effort. In this book, we're talking about Door #4: honest mating effort. Because in a modern, moral society, if you want sex and relationships with women, honest mating effort is the only route.

You must make yourself more attractive to women, given the choice criteria they already have that are based on their evolutionary history, their cultural traditions, and their individual personalities and contexts. You can fantasize about their preferences being different—a pornotopia where beautiful women fall at your feet and do whatever you want. But in the real world, you can't argue women into changing their instinctive preferences. They either find you attractive or they don't. So your only practical and ethical point of leverage is to transform yourself into the kind of guy who completes their attraction circuits.

WOMEN EVOLVED TO WANT EFFECTIVE MEN

Women did not gather in a secret lair behind the shoe department at Neiman Marcus to watch a *Bachelor* marathon and decide on the definition of "the perfect guy" while their periods cycled together.

On the contrary, a huge amount of research done over the past thirty years has revealed that women's preferences are neither arbitrary nor confusing. They are actually very clear, and, more importantly for your mating efforts, they hold true at a deep unconscious level across all women, regardless of culture, ethnicity, social groups, or tribe. Fundamentally, they pick the same male traits over and over again and for good reasons.

This is true for all normal, healthy women, whether they know it or not. Fortunately for them, they don't need to know it (but you do) because their mate preferences and emotions do the work for them—like apps in a smartphone where you can tap on a little icon that unleashes thousands of lines of programming without you having to understand any of the underlying source code. The preferences are simple and easy to use once a woman downloads them from her parents' DNA, but there's a long evolutionary R&D process behind each one, with millions of beta testers and focus groups over thousands of generations

To understand what traits women want *in* males, you have to understand what benefits women want *from* males. Hollywood romantic comedies and Hallmark greeting cards have convinced much of our culture that the six most romantic words a man can say to a woman are "I love you" and "I am sorry." This is bullshit. In fact, if you look at actual behavior and mate choice, those six words are "Don't worry honey, I got this"—which means: we face a real problem together as a couple, but I can totally handle it as a man. I'm effective.

Females throughout nature favor effective males. To deliver effective benefits to women, you need two basic things: (1) the **ability** to be effective at life, based on having effective traits, and (2) the **willingness** to use those effective traits to do effective things and supply to females the benefits that they need for their own reproductive success.

Ability is signaled through all five of the key traits and the four key proofs that we discuss throughout the book. Willingness is signaled mostly by the tender-defender trait (Chapter 9) and romantic proof (Chapter 14). If you have amazing ability but no willingness to engage with a specific woman, you're just an unobtainable movie star to her: useful only for sexual fantasies. If you have total willingness but no ability, you're just a naive boy with a schoolyard crush: useful only in boosting her self-esteem, not for hooking up.

In biology, effectiveness is called fitness—your statistical tendency across the whole breeding pool to survive and reproduce successfully because your adaptations fit the challenges of your environment. The relationship between fitness and survival creates a deep asymmetry in nature.

It's why, for women, it's even more important to be sexually disgusted by ineffectiveness than to be sexually attracted to effectiveness. Effectiveness requires a lot—thousands of genes, hundreds of adaptations, dozens of organs, and millions of neurons working together in awesomely intricate ways to produce sustained, adaptive behavior. But there are an *infinite* number of ways to be ineffective as a male animal, from being spontaneously aborted as a blastocyst to losing competitions to rivals, and literally every point in between. Our goal is to teach you how to be as effective as possible in as many domains as possible so that more women will find you more attractive.

Consider the best comeback ever in the history of fictional male-male competition, from *The Avengers:*

> Captain America: "Big man in a suit of armor. Take that away and what are you?"
> Tony Stark/Iron Man: "Genius, billionaire, playboy, philanthropist."

Our point here is that you don't need to become Tony Stark/Iron Man to find your own personal Pepper Potts. You just need to be effective—in all the main domains of life: health, family, friends, work, play, and knowledge— because that is what women want in their men. If you can become effective at these things, you will be attractive to women.

JUMPSTART YOUR ATTRACTIVENESS: REDUCE YOUR INEFFECTIVENESS

Life effectiveness reflects biological fitness, so it's attractive to women. But for most guys, trying to increase effectiveness is less effective than reducing ineffectiveness.

Huh?

Think of it like baseball: the best way to help your team win isn't to practice hitting 400–foot home runs every day; it's to get better at not striking out all the time. It's the same way with mating. First, stop sucking. That gets you in the game. Then, work on being awesome. That wins the game.

Effectiveness is sexually attractive to most women most of the time, but ineffectiveness is sexually disgusting to *all* women *all* of the time.

No woman in any culture is erotically attracted to ineffectiveness, whether it's powerlessness or joblessness or sexual impotence or getting flustered by crises or failing to protect a baby. Thus, apart from cultivating signs of effectiveness, it can be even more important to stop showing signs of ineffectiveness. In most species, in fact, a lot of female choice is about avoiding the bad rather than approaching the good. This is why women usually have such a strong, visceral, sexual disgust toward psychopaths, narcissists, creeps, crazies, stalkers, slackers, losers, morons, etc.

A relationship with a kind, generous boyfriend could help nurture and protect a woman's body for a few months—but a relationship with a psychotic, violent boyfriend could result in permanent disability or immediate death in the blink of an eye. A one-night stand with a Mr. Olympia could result in one great baby with great genes—but a one-night stand with Mr. Syphilis could result in lifelong sterility (losing many potential babies) and premature death. For this reason, a lot of female choice is very risk-averse—the potential losses from Mr. Wrong loom larger than the potential gains from Mr. Right.

So what does this mean for you? It means you can work the asymmetry to your advantage by identifying and fixing your weak spots rather than staying stuck trying to perfect yourself in life domains that you've already handled well. Don't fixate on six-pack abs; worry about not having a keg for a stomach. Don't obsess over perfect test scores; just make sure you aren't a mouth-breathing frat douche. **Plug your gaps; don't just polish your medals.** You might have been overlooking a few of those gaps—but women always notice them.

THE THREE BASIC FORMS OF EFFECTIVENESS

When you first meet a woman, she does not care about your needs and desires. She doesn't owe you anything. You can catcall her on the street, but she does not owe you a smile. You can make her laugh in a bar, but she does not owe you a phone number. Your sexual desires are as irrelevant to her as the surface temperature of Mars.

Remember: this woman's female ancestors did not pass along their genes by giving random blowjobs to strangers. They did not reproduce by taking pity on malformed mutant-boys or forgiving abusive psycho boyfriends or getting pregnant with flakes who were likely to abandon them. **They reproduced by selecting boyfriends who offered as many of the prerequisites for effective fatherhood as possible, which ultimately shaped their mate preferences and their assessment of your mate value.** In essence, they are here because their ancestors usually picked the best guys to have sex with.

Women have three main concerns in assessing your value:

1. Does he carry good genes?

For women, the ultimate evolutionary fantasy is finding a new male lover who has awesome traits that testify to his great genetic quality, who is from a strange new tribe that offers genetic innovations unavailable domestically, and who is worth getting pregnant with tonight even if he gets killed in battle tomorrow. (There, you now understand 90 percent of women's sexual fantasies and romance novels.)

If a guy doesn't offer these kinds of good genes, there's no point in reproducing with him because natural selection will cull his inferior offspring in the next generation. Sorry to be blunt, but that's just how life works. All female animals, ever since the origins of sexual reproduction 1.2 billion years ago, want to get the best genes they can into their offspring so their offspring in turn can survive and reproduce effectively.

This might sound like a mating death sentence at first if you're not exactly setting the world on fire with your genetic profile. But all it really means in the modern mating world is that you need to accept your natural limitations, marshal the traits and proofs you do have, and step your game up in the two other ways women assess your value.

2. Will he be a good partner?

Most of the human babies born in the last million years were not conceived in short-term flings or hookups but in relationships between socially acknowledged "mates"—boyfriends and girlfriends. This means that for women, getting a good boyfriend has long been the most reliable way to ensure that your children lived past infancy and reproduced themselves.

A good boyfriend offers a fun, safe, sexy, nourishing relationship that brings the woman concrete benefits, even if she ultimately doesn't combine her eggs with his sperm, and even if they don't end up raising kids together. These benefits can be material (food, home, land, resources, money), social (reputation, popularity, status, prestige, self-esteem), protective (keep away predators, creeps, harassers, and rapists), pleasurable (his jokes make her laugh and his tongue and cock make her come), or anything else that a woman wants.

Food is a prime example. Females in thousands of species benefit from males giving them food ("nuptial gifts," "courtship feeding") before or after copulation. So any trait that predicts ability and willingness to give food can be attractive—from intelligence (learning to hunt effectively), to physical health (ability to run after game and carry back meat), to social proof (having friends who can help you hunt and butcher larger game, like giraffes or mammoths). Females across species also benefit from known males protecting them from unknown males and male gangs, so women tend to favor any bodyguard traits that make male protection more effective and reliable.

Cultivating your good boyfriend traits is important even if you don't want a girlfriend yet because the vast majority of women are more attracted to "good relationship material"—a guy who seems like a quality boyfriend or Mr. Right—than to a "player" or "boy toy."

Even a woman who is really just cruising for some hot sex will enjoy you more and feel less vulnerable to slut-shaming if she can fantasize about you being a great boyfriend. The sex will be hotter too, because most women's brains just will not let them reach orgasm if they know that you're worthless as anything other than a penis with a body attached (even if that's exactly what she's using you for). Her body will respond better if her brain's convinced that you're worth sleeping with more than just once. That's how women's sexual circuitry works.

So if you make yourself into an attractive potential boyfriend, then your sexual options become unlimited. You can downshift into a short-term hookup if you want; you can upshift into a marriage. But if you only practice being a player who pursues short-term mating, you will repel the majority of women, who want more than that.

3. Would he make a good dad?

Human males are better dads than any other males, ever, in the history of evolution. We are the masters of paternal care—helping babies and kids survive and prosper through our provisioning, protection, role-modeling, and mentorship. Think about it: male hawks might offer their kids a variety of fish, crabs, and mammals, but do they teach their kids about model rockets and Mongol battle tactics and pay for Christmas and college? No, even hawk dads suck compared to us, and they're fucking *hawks*!

We've been playing important roles in our children's lives for at least two million years. This isn't just because our male ancestors woke up one day and thought, *Wow, I really should man up and pay some attention to these kids running around.* Our paternal abilities evolved because women wanted to mate with guys who would make good dads and stepdads.

Many animals favor mates that are likely to make good parents. It's called the "good parent" process of sexual selection, and it's especially important in humans. As a result of good dads evolving, for instance, human females developed year-round sexual receptivity and the ability to pump out babies much faster than chimps or gorillas can, even though our babies need a lot more care and protection.

This paternal commitment matters immensely to women and their children. You can have great genes that produce superbabies, but if you flake out at the most critical time, it's a disaster for the woman and for the child's survival. As we said, we know from anthropological studies of hunter-gatherer societies that if a guy abandons a woman or has a fatal hunting accident, the likelihood of her baby surviving can drop a lot. Abandonment, in all its forms, exacts a huge cost, the evolutionary defense against which has resulted in exquisite creep-detection radar and attraction circuits calibrated toward dedicated, protective, caring men.

This is true even for young women who are twenty years short of this issue being immediately relevant or who don't want kids yet, if ever. Remember, an eighteen-year-old female under ancestral conditions was not twenty years away from thinking about having kids—it was more like twenty minutes. She would start having kids within about a year of starting to have sex. Every woman alive today is descended from an unbroken chain of successful mothers who raised healthy offspring, usually with a lot of help from good dads.

Ideally, a man possesses all three of these attributes—good genes, partnership, fatherhood—but women will settle for different distributions of them depending on their mating goals. That holds true even if a woman is only looking for a short-term hookup and not just if she is looking for a boyfriend or "the One."

WOMEN CONSIDER *ALL* THE TRAITS THAT MIGHT BE RELEVANT TO FUTURE REPRODUCTION

In many species, females pay attention to just one thing, one key sexual ornament—like a peacock's tail or a frog's croak—that sums up the male's whole genotype and phenotype. Some writers have claimed that female humans are the same—that they really pay attention to only one key trait, such as wealth, status, masculine energy, or emotional intelligence.

Those writers are idiots. Think about how ridiculous it would sound to you if some women's magazine blogger wrote, "Men only care about ONE THING: big boobs. That's it. Everything else is bullshit. Legs, hair, face, kindness, sense of style, professional success, sexual reputation—all bullshit."

You'd instantly realize the absurdity of that claim because you've met plenty of women with amazing boobs who you didn't find attractive because all their other traits weren't up to your standards (e.g., the big boobs were attached to a forty-five-year-old alcoholic mother of six who was ringing you up at the dollar store).

The same holds true for women. Whenever some guy writes, "Women only care about ONE THING...," women feel exasperated disgust. And they should. They can think of dozens of creeps who had that one thing and whose presence made all the blood drain from their faces and into their feet. Wealth? Women think of Donald Trump's comb-over. Status? Women think of Vladimir Putin's psychopathy. Masculine energy? Women think of Mike Tyson's rape conviction. Emotional intelligence? Women think of that annoying acroyoga guy at Burning Man—or pretty much anyone at Burning Man.

Human relationships are much more complicated. Many traits, signals, and proofs are necessary to convey all the information we need to assess in choosing mates, but none by themselves are sufficient for social and reproductive success, and some aren't even "choices" at all. Let's be very clear about this:

Attraction is an emotional, unconscious reaction to the suite of traits men present to women; it is NOT a conscious decision that they deliberate about.

This is why human courtship is long and complicated and often frustrating for both men and women. Trait assessment is, in many instances, a lightning-quick instinctive process that focuses on the deep, general, stable, heritable qualities that predict your future behavior as a genetic sire, a boyfriend, and a potential father. And that instinctive checklist of what constitutes Mr. Right or Wife Material can get pretty long.

The checklist of traits and proofs might seem daunting. But the fact that women care about many different things in men is actually great news for you. How depressing would it be if you were a peacock with a mediocre tail? You'd have no hope. Great tails evolved because they're hard-to-fake indicators of good genes and good health. If you don't have a great tail as a peacock, you're fucked—you can't just steal feathers from other dudes and glue them on your ass. This isn't Burning Man.

That's great news for the average guy: We are members of a species where females are attracted to _many_ different traits that we can cultivate and display, not just one. This means you have many options on your path to attractiveness, and all are equally valid, as they each signal effectiveness in their own way and predict a higher likelihood of social and reproductive success.

This is also why women are always digging beneath your surface. Your behavior is never just your behavior. It's always a clue to your underlying traits. Once you really understand this, a lot of blurry confusion about women will snap into sharp focus.

The more of your traits you improve, the more joy you bring to women.

Takeaways

- Women evolved to want effective men. To be an effective man, you must have the ability to be effective at life and the willingness to use that effectiveness to deliver benefits to women.
- One of the best ways to jumpstart your attractiveness is to reduce your ineffectiveness because to most women ineffectiveness is more sexually repulsive than effectiveness is sexually attractive.
- There are three primary forms of effectiveness that women consider when assessing your value:
  1. Do you carry good genes?
  2. Would you be a good partner?
  3. Would you be a good dad?
- Attraction is not a conscious decision; it is an emotional, unconscious reaction to the suite of traits and proofs you display to women.

CHAPTER 5: GET IN SHAPE

(THE PHYSICAL HEALTH TRAIT)

It is only shallow people who do not judge by appearances. The true mystery of the world is the visible, not the invisible.

—*Oscar Wilde*

If you want to get better with women, nothing will do more to increase your prospects and help achieve your mating goals than being in shape. If you are conspicuously healthy, fit, and energetic instead of the lumpy sack of hot garbage that is most guys' bodies, you're going to the head of the line.

In modern culture, we're told that choosing mates for their physical health and physical attractiveness is superficial. That is a bullshit lie. Picking people based on their looks is an evolved behavior, especially with regard to health, because health is the exact opposite of a superficial trait: it's how well your whole body works as an organic system. Visible physical health reveals how many mutations are in your DNA, what biochemical reactions are happening in every organ, what hormones are circulating in your blood. It predicts how effective you'll stay at life and how long you'll live. Physical health matters at a deep biological level, and female choice is a deeply biological activity.

So when a woman meets you for the first time, this is what she is evaluating when she sizes you up, whether her gender studies professor likes it or not. It really is that simple.

What isn't as simple is understanding precisely what we mean when we talk about physical health. We *don't* just mean the stuff your doctor was trained to worry about (like lowering your risk of suffering from heart disease in fifty years) or the ideals that men's fitness magazines are trying to sell you.

Plainly put, *good physical health is when the body of a living organism is functioning the way it was designed to function by evolution.*

There is some variance on how this *actually* looks in real life, based around things like height, body proportions, and ethnicity. But the point is, when you have the hallmarks of being in shape, you <u>look</u> healthy, and you <u>are</u> healthier.

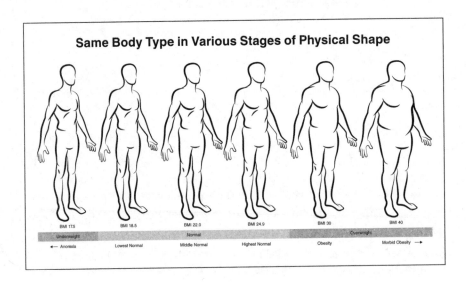

Same Body Type in Various Stages of Physical Shape

BMI 17.5	BMI 18.5	BMI 22.0	BMI 24.9	BMI 30	BMI 40
Underweight		Normal		Overweight	
← Anorexia	Lowest Normal	Middle Normal	Highest Normal	Obesity	Morbid Obesity →

There are some common misconceptions about men's health, fitness, and attractiveness that go along with this. Consider these surprising truths:

You don't need the perfect body: Women are sexually attracted to guys who are healthy, capable, and likely to live a long time. For most of them, that means a guy who is in good enough shape is good enough.

In fact, perfect can be the enemy of good, because while great shape screams "great health," it also screams "narcissistic gym rat who'll be preoccupied and unfaithful." Thus, the mating benefits of improving from bad shape to good shape are astronomical, but the benefits of going from good shape to awesome, pro athlete shape are limited.

On the James Scale of Physical Fitness, you don't want to be Kevin, but you don't want to be LeBron either. You want to be somewhere between Rick and Jesse (without all the cocaine or neo-Nazi stuff). Ultimately, it's important to realize that most women are just looking for good genes, healthy boyfriends, and long-lasting dads—not superheroes.

The Totally Anecdotal James Scale of Physical Fitness

| Kevin | Rick | Jesse | LeBron |

YOU

You don't need to be jacked like a body builder: No ancestral man would have looked like the Hulk. If a man had that much muscle mass in reality, he wouldn't have been able to effectively run, climb, stalk, hunt, scout, or dance—much less sustain his bulk with the food available. Women are looking for strong and effective men, not men who can't hug them because their pecs are in the way. Guys, we pay attention to the Hulk archetype not because women actually want to mate with the Hulk, but because the Hulk would be a formidable sexual rival for us, one who could keep us from mating with a woman. Don't confuse the guy you'd most fear with the guy that women would most want.

You don't need six-pack abs: A washboard stomach can definitely be attractive, but a preoccupation with shredding fat and signaling core muscles often strikes women as repulsively vain. Women frequently rate men with these "amazing bodies" as *less* attractive than guys who have a higher, healthier amount of fat (i.e., the energy reserves to survive infection, illness, starvation, and hardship). It takes a lot of time to reduce body fat percentage down to the "perfect abs" level (which tends to be 4–6 percent body fat), and that's time you could spend developing other more attractive traits—or on the woman herself.

With physical health what you need are the visible, nonverbal displays—the things a woman can actually *see* with her own two eyes—that signal your body's ability to do lots of things and be good at them. Your physical appearance, your body shape, your body size, your overall fitness, your energy and sexual vigor (later, we're going to show you precisely what this looks like)—these signal that you are an effective organism at a primordial level (that is, your body works and moves and survives), which is very attractive to most every woman you are going to meet.

WHY WOMEN CARE ABOUT YOUR BEING IN SHAPE

The most obvious reason you should care about your physical health, besides your own life expectancy, is that women find it very attractive. We wouldn't be talking about it if women didn't care about it because that is what this whole book is about. Like we just explained, when it comes to sex and dating, women generally (and unconsciously) look for hard-to-fake traits that display three kinds of attributes in men: (1) good genes, (2) good partner traits, and (3) good father traits.

Good physical health is one of the most reliable "honest signals" of overall genetic fitness because it is *very* hard to fake.

Most genetic mutations are harmful and hurt your health in demonstrable ways. You can wear normal-sized pants and believe with all your heart that you and some woman will make beautiful babies together one day, but if you have to whisper those sweet nothings into her ear because chronic asthma and bronchitis make it hard to breathe and talk at the same time, you can bet she is hearing something other than romance.

Furthermore, women tend to see a physically healthy guy as being healthy in all ways, which gives guys who are in shape a distinct advantage, especially in short-term mating. Attractive *and* healthy makes for an easy choice when you just want to hook up. Your physical health is the executive summary of your genetic fitness.

Healthy men also make better lovers and deliver more sexual pleasure to women. Aerobic endurance predicts how long and hard you can have sex; cardiovascular fitness (how well your blood supply works) predicts erectile function (how hard your penis can get). Women understand, viscerally, that a weak guy probably can't pick them up or flip them over and that a fat guy can't have sex very long or hold himself up on top of her.

Female sexual arousal and orgasm systems are a mate choice system designed to assess male physical health—your size, strength, stamina, sexual performance, and confidence (more on that later). So being in shape matters a lot, at both a conscious and an unconscious level.

Look at it like this: if you can't see your penis when you look down past your belly, she probably doesn't want to see it either because she knows intuitively it's packing nothing but a mushroom tip full of disappointment.

Beyond sex, physical health predicts literally how much work you can do. Work capacity was crucial to hunting, warfare, farming, and industrial labor. Though most jobs don't require as much raw physical work anymore in modern society, on a biological level women still want to know that you will be effective at getting shit done. Being in shape shows the kind of conscientious-ness and willpower necessary to set goals and restrain yourself from distrac-tions to accomplish them.

The protective capacity of a physically healthy man cannot be overlooked here. Strong men can defend themselves and their partners. Weak men can-not. Even though physical violence is much rarer than ever before in history, women are still very risk-averse and danger-aware. They've evolved to have a hair-trigger sensitivity to potential stalkers, enemy gangs, and natural disas-ters. Your potential ability to protect her and your future children—even if you never have to—is a huge part of her unconscious attraction to you.

Physical health predicts how well you can sire children—not just in terms of the genes packed into the head of every sperm, but also in terms of how many sperm you can make and how fast they can swim. (You want Navy SEALs, not Easter Seals.) Male illness leads to male infertility. Healthy dads tend to have healthy offspring. For women who are looking for long-term mates, do not think for a second that they are not acutely attuned to this rela-tionship between your physical health and your viability as a potential father.

Being able to have healthy kids is important, but being around to care for them is critical. Physical health predicts whether you'll be a long-lived, helpful, healthy, capable dad to your children (and grandchildren). Women are often thinking about the future: will you be the active kind of dad who runs around playing with the kids all day, doing fun activities until they conk out and sleep through the night from happy fatigue? Or will you be the kind of dad who sits on the couch and tells the kids to go play video games, so they get wired and cranky and stay up late and ruin your—and their mother's—sleep?

When a woman evaluates a guy who is in good shape, what she is register-ing both consciously and unconsciously is someone who is physically capa-ble and dependable; who will probably be around a long time; and who can deliver in the street and on the job, at home and in the bedroom. Without knowing much more about him, she knows that he is more likely than not to be effective at the things she cares about.

This puts him in the driver's seat when it comes to cultivating all the other traits that are important to her, because she has already given him the benefit of the doubt that he has them.

IMPROVE YOUR PHYSICAL HEALTH

If you have bad physical health genes, don't worry. Like we said, you don't have to be a quarterback to be attractive. You just have to work harder in other areas related to physical health, areas that aren't determined primarily by your genes.

That work starts now with getting in shape, and it's simpler, cheaper, and easier than you've been led to believe. There are three factors that basically determine your entire physical health: (1) sleep, (2) nutrition, and (3) exercise.

Improvement to each of these three pillars—even incremental improvement—can lead to drastic improvement in your physical health.

1. Sleep More

No one is sure yet why all mammals require sleep. What we do know is that sleep is crucial to life, and quality sleep is absolutely important for physical health. We put this first for a reason.

The CIA discovered this decades ago when they realized that sleep deprivation is one of the most effective ways to TORTURE people. Ask any new parent about the hardest part of having a baby, and their answer won't be the puking or the pooping or the crying (that was a typical Friday night in college)—it's the lack of sleep. Sleep deprivation has so many downsides that it's impossible to sustainably improve your physical health with nutrition and exercise until you fix your sleep.

And yet we deprive ourselves of sleep all the time. In fact, most Americans are chronically sleep deprived, and this makes us dumber, fatter, sicker, more dangerous, more stressed, and less attractive than we would be if we slept like normal animals. The requirement for sleep could not be simpler or clearer. To be healthy, you need **8–9 hours of sleep in a completely dark room every night.**

Right now you're probably thinking, *Yeah yeah yeah, I've gotta get sleep. Okay, next?* Do not think you can skip sleeping well. If you do, you might as well ignore everything else in this book because you won't have the energy or focus to fucking *do* any of it well.

There are six key areas to focus on for good sleep. There is an ideal situation for each area—the closer you get, the better—but don't worry about being perfect. Just be good.

Pitch-Black Room

The more ambient light you remove from your sleep area, the better. The optimal solution is to sleep in a pitch-black room. And by pitch-black, we mean as close as possible to horror-movie-monster-under-the-bed-cartoon black. If that description is not clear enough, here is a picture of Tucker's bedroom, where he gets nine hours of sleep a night:

Your eyes—even through closed eyelids—sense any light in the room, and this disrupts the release of melatonin from your pineal gland, which has been controlling sleep/wake cycles in vertebrates for more than 400 million years.

That little LED on the charger next to your pillow, the display on your alarm clock, the lights on the cable box, your phone, indicator lights on other gadgets (not to mention, if your bedroom has windows, ambient light pollution from your street)—they are all undermining hundreds of millions of years of sleep-hormone machinery inside your skull. Most people sleep in bedrooms with light leaking in from everywhere.

If you need to get more sleep, start by **eliminating those ambient light sources.** Get a different alarm clock. Turn off your phone, or flip it on its face. Tape over indicator lights. Take the TV out of your bedroom. Install blackout curtains like good hotels use in their rooms. If creating a truly pitch-black room is impossible, then at least use a sleep mask to keep the light pollution from reaching your retinas. If you can't remove the light, you might as well add the darkness.

Night-Time Screen Exposure

Electronic screens—such as those on TVs, computer monitors, tablets, and phones—produce a blue light that disrupts melatonin production much like high-intensity daylight does. This is the other way your body gets the wrong kind of light at night that makes it much harder to fall asleep and to have the right type of sleep.

Ideally, you should avoid electronic screens for two hours before going to bed. For most people, we know this seems unrealistic, but there is no shortage of nonscreen activities you could do in that time:

- Read a fucking book for once, like this one.
- Listen to podcasts (like our Mating Grounds podcast).
- Practice other skills (e.g., drawing, playing a musical instrument, speaking a foreign language, cooking, etc.) that make you a more well-rounded person and more attractive to women who can give you a whole *other* skill to practice in bed.
- Talk to people on the phone USING YOUR MOUTH instead of texting them with your fingers. (Haha, we know you won't do this.)
- Do your mindfulness meditation (discussed in chapter 6).

What's especially important *not* to do in these two hours before bed is anything involving social media. Apps like Facebook, Twitter, Snapchat, and Instagram are designed to rev up your mental excitement and provoke emotional responses (otherwise no companies would bother inserting ads in their feeds), and none of that is good for sleep. Dating apps like Tinder, Hinge, and OkCupid are even more arousing and sleep disrupting, so don't use them late in the evening, no matter how much you want to make deposits into your spank bank.

If you're all Brokeback Mountain with your screens, and you just can't quit them, don't worry—you can take baby steps into this new sleep regimen. The next-best solution is to install software on your computer (something like f.lux software) that converts your computer's blue light to soft candlelight, which doesn't inhibit sleep. Even better, it's free. Or you can buy blue-light-blocking shades. Yes, they're kind of goofy, but they really work, and they look a lot better than dark circles or giant bags under your eyes.

Consistency

Our bodies work on a consistent day-night cycle called a circadian rhythm. Basically, daytime mammals evolved to wake with the sun (when they can see and when it's worth moving around) and to go to sleep when the sun goes down (when they can't see, so they need to stay out of harm's way). If you can set your sleep schedule to follow your natural circadian rhythm, that's ideal for your hormonal health.

Almost as important as your total amount of sleep is the consistency of your sleep times. Shift work, for instance, in which companies require employees to work different hours on different days, is so catastrophic for physical and mental health that in 2007 the World Health Organization categorized shift work as a class 2A ("probable") carcinogen (i.e., a cancer-causing risk factor).

Sadly, many young guys impose a sort of shift-work schedule on themselves, thinking it's cool to have no rhyme or reason to when they sleep or wake. And they pay the price with their physical health.

So here's the thing: go to bed at a consistent time every night. If you can establish a consistent bedtime (say, 11:00 p.m.), then your body will instinctively adjust, and you'll wake up at the same time every day too (in this case, around 7:00 a.m.).

If you can increase the consistency of sleep, that amplifies the benefits of getting the right amount of sleep. Sure, you've got an inner toddler who will rebel against your wiser self. But in this case, that inner toddler is going to keep you from becoming healthier and more attractive to women. You want women keeping you up late to have great sex, not your rebellious inner toddler keeping you up late so you can watch another episode of *South Park*. You're a grown-ass man; are you really going to let a toddler boss you around?

Temperature

Humans sleep best at cooler temperatures. Most people sleep best at an ambient room temperature of 65–70 degrees Fahrenheit, and enough outside air circulation that carbon dioxide doesn't build up in their bedroom overnight. Unfortunately, most people also like to tuck into a warm and toasty bed at night, so they make the mistake of cranking up the temperature on their thermostat instead of letting their blankets and body heat do the work of warming up the bed.

Consumption

What you put into your body has a huge impact on how it sleeps, specifically stimulants, alcohol, and food. Controlling the types, the ingestion times, and the quantities of these things will better help you control your sleep patterns

   Stimulants: Minimize all stimulants after 4:00 p.m., especially ADD meds like Adderall and Ritalin, as well as caffeine sources like coffee, tea, energy drinks, and chocolate. The reason for this should be obvious—it's right in the name. *Stimulation* is the opposite of the relaxation response that helps your body fall asleep. The opposite of stimulant intake isn't alcohol or indica-heavy cannabis strains— rather, it's mindfulness, meditation, and deliberate relaxation.
   Alcohol: For most guys, alcohol works as a stimulant before it becomes a depressant. On normal nights, limit your alcohol intake to two drinks, and make sure you have the last drink at least two hours

before bed. Alcohol suppresses deep sleep and REM sleep, and it can cause dehydration, so drink lots of water before you go to bed.

Food: Avoid eating too much right before you go to bed. It's hard to sleep on a full stomach.

Anxiety

A lot of insomnia comes from unaddressed anxiety. The emotions and issues that you won't face during the day are keeping you up at night. That is why you're tossing and turning in your bed, and there is little else you can do to get better sleep besides addressing the real problems or using some sort of mindfulness exercise or meditation.

2. Eat Better

Food is the energy that your body needs to do work and meet women and have sex.

But its role goes deeper. You literally are what you eat: your body has a dynamic system with a high turnover rate. Most of the molecules in your body weren't there a year ago; they came in with your food. The food you eat now will build the body you'll have in the future. So eating better now automatically builds a better body for later.

The problem is, everything else you've been taught about food and eating by teachers, parents, and media is dangerously misinformed bullshit based on urban myths, outdated research, and food-industry propaganda.

The key thing you must understand about nutrition is this: a high-carb, low-fat diet is NOT healthy. That diet is very bad for your health, but it was the heart of the USDA food pyramid from 1992 to 2011 (it's changed now, thank god)—when most young men were learning about nutrition in school.

It's not just the USDA that is wrong; most diet and food programs don't work either. The ones that do—things like paleo, ancestral, primal, and slow-carb diets—all abide by some variation of this nutrition principle:

Eat mostly unprocessed, natural, fresh foods that humans are biologically designed to eat—like meats, vegetables, nuts, and fats—and you will be healthy. Avoid everything else as if it were poison.

Think about it like this: Tigers are animals that evolved to live in a certain biological niche. They evolved to eat certain foods: other animals smaller than themselves. When they eat those things, they are healthy. Ask any zookeeper, and she'll tell you that if you feed a vegetarian diet to a carnivorous apex predator like a tiger, it will die from malnutrition. A vegan tiger is a dead tiger.

Humans live and die by the same principle. Like all animals, we evolved in certain ecological niches, and our bodies are adapted to eat certain foods from those niches. (The difference between us and tigers is that we have a much broader range of things we can eat.) If we eat industrial, additive-laden foods that never existed in nature and that our bodies can't process (e.g., processed sugar and refined grains), we get sick. If we eat the natural foods our bodies are designed to eat, we are healthy. It's pretty simple, and the overwhelming scientific evidence now points to this strategy as the best way for humans to eat.

The Three Rules of Healthy Eating
There is so much more to say about nutrition that we can't really even begin to explain it all here, so we're going to help you understand the most important eating principles:

1. Don't eat anything with sugar in it.
[Sugar = sucrose (table sugar), glucose (grain sugar), fructose (fruit sugar), lactose (milk sugar), corn syrup]

Obviously, there is some natural sugar in otherwise very healthy foods that you should eat, like the lactose in Greek yogurt. You do not need to avoid those foods simply because they contain a small amount of natural sugar.

Rather, we're talking about the stuff where sugar is one of the first two or three ingredients on the label or where sugar has been added. That means:

	TYPE	*LIKE...*
NO	Liquid sugar	soda, fruit juices, energy drinks, Starbucks-style blended coffee drinks
	Solid sugars	candy, pudding, popsicles, cake, pie, ice cream; basically, anything Cartman would plow into his face
	Processed foods	most fast food, frozen meals, canned soups, salad dressings, condiments (e.g.,., ketchup), pasta sauce, breakfast cereals, flavored yogurts, granola & energy bars, anything with corn syrup or evaporated cane juice
	High-sugar fruits	oranges, grapes, figs, dried fruits
	"Fat-Free" foods	Foods labeled "low-fat" and "fat-free" are typically jammed with sugar; it's how manufacturers replace all the yummy flavor from fat.
	Artificial sweeteners	diet soda, Equal, Sweet & Low, Splenda—evidence shows they're an even bigger predictor of obesity than sugar

2. Don't eat anything with grains in it.

[Grains = wheat, corn, rice, barley, rye, oats, etc.—and anything made from them, e.g., corn syrup]

After sugar, grains are the second type of carbohydrates that mess with your nutritional health. Either avoid all grain carbs, or, if you must, look for "gluten-free" on your food labels and follow this chart.

	TYPE	LIKE...
NO	Liquid grains	Beer & whiskey are the worst. Drink wine (red, preferably), tequila, or most clear liquors instead.
	Bread	sandwich bread, baguettes, bread crumbs, breading, pita, tortillas, bagels—lettuce wraps are your friend.
	Flour-filled desserts	cakes, cookies, pies, pastries, muffins, donuts, brownies
	Snack chips	crackers, pretzels, tortilla chips, corn chips, bagel chips
	Pasta	rice noodles, spaghetti, linguini, lasagna, tortellini; basically, any noodle that ends in a vowel that you stuff with cheese or cover with sauce
	Cereals	breakfast cereal, granola, granola bars, oatmeal, grits
	Pizza	deep dish, flatbread, wood-fired, New York style, frozen, delivery, DiGiorno—If it has a crust and goes in a hot-ass oven, it's a no-go.

3. Eat anything else you want.

With sugars and grains off your plate, you can eat pretty much anything else. This is basically the way our ancestors ate for, oh, more than a million years before the advent of agriculture and the way our bodies are still designed to eat. It is very simple, we promise you. Here is a sample of all the things you can go buck wild on.

	TYPE	LIKE...
YES	Protein	eggs, chicken, beef, pork, lamb, fish, shrimp, shellfish—If it had eyes or a shell, you can eat the hell out of it.
	Legumes & starches	lentils, black beans, pinto beans, potatoes, sweet potatoes
	Vegetables	spinach, asparagus, peas, carrots, broccoli, green peppers, beans, etc. (no corn or vegetable oils, though). Basically, if it grows in the ground and is harvested by migrant labor, you can have it.
	Fermented or pickled foods	sauerkraut, kimchi, pickles, pickled vegetables, fish sauce, unsweetened yogurt, sour cream, cheese
	Nuts & seeds	sunflower seeds, pumpkin seeds, almonds, walnuts, cashews, hazelnuts, macadamia nuts
	Good fats & oils	butter, bone marrow, fish oil, coconut oil, olive oil, avocado, flaxseed oil

Following these three rules is intended to be a *quick and easy way* for you to see results from eating properly. But this is not at all a complete understanding of nutrition.

We highly recommend you learn more about diet and nutrition and follow one of the more comprehensive eating plans, like the paleo diet, the ancestral health diet, the perfect health diet, or the slow-carb diet.

We have extensive resources at www.TheMatingGrounds.com/diets to give you as much information on diet and nutrition as you want, and we link to the people we think know even more than we do on this subject. If you are a high-information decider, that's your next stop. If not, just stop eating sugar and grains, and you'll lose weight and be basically more healthy.

3. Exercise Smarter

As with diet, most of the information out there about getting in shape is outdated, misleading, or just plain wrong.

For example, long-duration cardio (e.g., jogging, exercise bicycling) is not very good for you, doesn't help you lose weight very effectively, and has a very poor ratio of results to time spent.

Here is the single fundamental truth about physical health that you need to understand as a guy:

Having good physical health means being physically STRONG.

There is literally nothing better a man can do for his overall health than to become physically strong. The science and evidence on this are clear.

Strength training doesn't just increase your muscle mass. It sends physiological signals throughout your body that lead to stronger joints and connective tissue, stronger bones, etc...all the way to stronger willpower in your prefrontal cortex.

Can you pick up heavy things and lift them above your head? Can you move something large from a still position? Can you carry it across distances, quickly? If you can build your overall functional strength, you'll get a lot of other health benefits for free: more muscle mass that burns more calories even at rest; more testosterone that cuts gut fat; a good cardio workout without "doing cardio." And of course, women find it extremely attractive because strength reveals good genes, good partner potential, and good dad longevity.

The Four Basic Principles of Effective Strength Workouts

1. **GO HEAVY:** Move heavy loads, not light weights. You don't get stronger without stressing your muscles, and the way to do that is with weights that are heavy (for you).

2. **GO FAST:** If you move heavy weights with very high intensity (i.e., as fast as you can, without hurting yourself, of course), that is even better. Short workouts that are very intense are much better than longer workouts at a lower intensity.

3. **DO COMPOUND MOVEMENTS:** All exercises should consist of natural, complex movements. Your body includes 206 bones and over 650 skeletal muscles. Whole-body and compound-movement exercises, like push-ups, pull-ups, and squats, use dozens of muscles to stabilize and move multiple joints. Compound movements are more efficient at training both major and minor muscles, and they build the coordination, balance, and flexibility needed to move in diverse, natural ways. Isolation movements should be avoided—no curls for the girls, no pecs for effects. They overtrain big muscles and neglect small supportive muscles and connective tissues, thus increasing injury risk.

4. **NO CHRONIC CARDIO:** Spending a lot of time doing cardio is not only a waste of time, but it can undermine your health by flooding your body with stress hormones, reducing sex hormones, and driving you to eat more grains and sugars. This is especially true for long-endurance, low-intensity cardio, like jogging or leisurely use of the elliptical machine.

On the other hand, a lot of evidence now shows that high-intensity interval training (HIIT) is amazingly effective. This means short sprints alternating with short rests. If you step on the treadmill and can effectively read a book or watch TV at the same time, *you're doing it wrong*. It's way better to do 60 seconds of maximum effort followed by 60 seconds of rest, repeated five times. Focus on how many watts of power you can generate at peak effort, not how many calories you burn overall.

There are two very simple starter programs that employ these principles to varying degrees, depending on your current level of physical fitness. These work really well and require minimal time.

Beginner Option #1 (cheap): Air Squats and Push-ups

This program is simple, easy, convenient, and free. You can do it wherever you live, in less than an hour total...*per week*. And we promise it will get you the results that matter most to women: you will lose fat everywhere and put on muscle in the areas that women find sexiest about men—the chest, arms, butt, and thighs.

The Beginner Workout	
(Cheap, At-Home, DIY)	
Air squats	20 reps
Push-ups	10 reps
Rest	30 seconds
Sets	5 (increase as you can)
Total Time	~20 minutes

You can do this program in about twenty minutes. Do it every other day to start, and then you can increase to every day if you want. You're going to alternate sets of air squats with sets of push-ups.

You'll literally just squat down as far as you can, then go all the way back up, and then go back down. You do it twenty times. Then drop and do ten push-ups. Then rest thirty seconds. Then do it again, five or ten times. If you have to start with just five sets, fine, do that.

The key to this workout is intensity. Go all-out. If your personal "all-out" is pathetic at first, who cares? It's just you alone at home and you're just getting started. It doesn't matter how bad you are. The key is to push your maximum power output so your muscles and heart get the message to raise their game—and you start to get real strength and endurance as a result.

If you have to do the push-ups from your knees rather than your toes to start, no problem, just do that. Anything that gets you through the workout. Ideally, you'll finish every workout exhausted because your power intensity has been at maximum and your work volume has been high—compared to what you're used to.

This workout is simple, but it's real, and it works. Once you start getting faster and stronger, increase the load from five sets to ten sets, and maintain the intensity. Do this for thirty days and you will see changes to your body. People you know will notice; people you don't will too.

This won't keep challenging you forever, though. If you see results and want to move up to more advanced workouts, add other body-weight exercises (like pull-ups, dips, burpees, wall sits, and ab rollouts). Then add some kettlebells, which are better than dumbbells because they require more whole-body movements and impose a heavier cardio load.

Or even better, go to The Mating Grounds site for our full list of recommended workouts, organized by convenience, time efficiency, cost efficiency, difficulty, and desired results.

Beginner Option #2 (expensive): CrossFit

The simplest and easiest thing to do (after squats and push-ups at home) is to join a gym.

But for beginners, we don't recommend that you waste time at a regular big-box gym unless what you're really looking for is athlete's foot and a hand-job in the locker room. Instead, go somewhere that is fun and effective and a place you can meet women who like working out too. Using those criteria, there's nothing better than CrossFit.

What makes CrossFit so effective compared to normal gyms is that you will be

- doing whole-body exercises that engage large numbers of muscles in safe, functional movements that require some skill
- at a place that's organized around high-intensity interval training, which is extremely time-effective
- in a fun group setting with other people who will encourage and challenge you
- overseen by a certified trainer who teaches proper form and pushes you to excellence, without compromising safety or risking injury
- in a fitness culture that's totally accepting of all body types and health levels among beginners and that encourages everyone toward success together. In fact, the more out of shape you are, the more the people of CrossFit will get behind you and encourage you.

The social aspect of CrossFit is important: having many of the same people in your class week after week builds comfort and familiarity, social accountability for showing up and doing your best, mutual support in learning the exercises, and friendly competition to push you harder.

Plus, CrossFit is an awesome way to meet women because it attracts people who are positive, hard-working, fun, smart, and hot. The women who do CrossFit tend to be in shape, socially open, and sex-positive.

If you can afford it, we highly recommend CrossFit. If you do CrossFit regularly for six months, you will see dramatic improvements in your physical health, body shape, and functional strength—but also in your sex drive, mating confidence, social network, and dating life.

DISPLAY YOUR PHYSICAL HEALTH

By now you have a good handle on what physical health is, why it's important to women, and how to improve it. Next you need to learn how to *show it off* (or signal it) to women, because having an attractive trait is useless unless the people you are trying to attract can *see it.*

This is not about becoming a self-obsessed bodybuilder who poses to show off his muscles all the time—which nauseates most women and proclaims to the world, "My ego is even bigger than my quads." Rather, it's about taking pride in your body, owning your masculinity, and displaying your good health and capabilities in ways that women naturally admire.

Your Appearance

Posture/body language: When you develop some muscle, you should feel more confident and be able to express that confidence in your posture and body language. This means simple changes, like standing tall, sitting upright, and taking up a little more space in a chair or at a party.

These things seem trivial, but they are not; women read them as honest signals of health, vitality, confidence, assertiveness, and status. They are also some of the easiest and fastest things to fix if you currently stand around shaped like a question mark, looking pathetic.

Clothes: Wearing nice clothes that fit well on a good body is one of the most potent ways to attract women. Good fit means not too loose but also not too tight: think how Hollywood actors wear their suits to the Oscars, not how a gangsta wears baggy pants. Also, clothes that reveal your *shape* don't have to reveal your *skin* (much less your junk). A great-fitting cashmere sweater will reveal your upper-body muscles and torso shape almost as well as being naked.

Your Interaction

Physical contact: If you get in better shape, you'll feel more confident about physical contact with women. If you know that your body feels strong and healthy, simple things like shaking hands, hugging, light touches, sitting close, and other random forms of contact become a way for you to signal attractiveness.

Hugging a woman to say hello or having her take your arm as you navigate a busy sidewalk are reliable signals of your physical health because she can literally *feel* it through the firmness of your embrace and the strength of your guiding arm as you walk.

The worst thing you can do as you get in shape is maintain a handshake that feels like a bag of cotton balls or hug someone like your shirt sleeves are filled with pudding.

Activity dates: When you go out with women, you should include activity dates that let you display your physical health and skills in fun, natural ways (without being an obnoxious show-off). This could include dancing, hiking, playing with dogs, playing sports she enjoys, etc. Guys who are out of shape tend to avoid these activities because they come off like sweaty, uncoordinated messes.

Sex: Being in shape makes sex much better for both of you. Strength and vigor help in foreplay; they enable you to lift her up, move her around, and be physically dominant in bed. Anaerobic fitness (strength) improves erectile function, so your penis can get harder and bigger; it also improves stamina during sex, so you don't get out of breath when fucking. Being in shape helps you recover faster after you ejaculate so you can have more sex.

Your Skills

Physical leisure activities: Once you're in decent shape, it's also great to learn useful and difficult physical skills that are also interesting and fun. These should be things you can show directly on dates, talk about credibly with the correct technical terms and funny personal stories, and possibly teach her so you can do them together; they include shooting, riding motorcycles, skiing/snowboarding, surfing, bicycling, boating, ice-skating, in-line skating, scuba diving, racquet sports, indoor climbing, outdoor technical climbing, and bar games like billiards and darts.

Dancing: This isn't just another leisure activity; it's the primordial way that humans evolved to show off their physical health, fitness, coordination, and movement skills in group settings.

There is a reason so many American women love Latin men, and we'll give you a hint: it's not their cuisine. They love the fact that an important part of Latin culture is that Latin men know how to move, especially with women as partners.

The ability to dance shows energy, coordination, stamina, flexibility, and strength, all in one fun activity. Knowing how to move your body on the dance floor also signals that you probably know how to move your body on the bedroom floor. Women will tell you: guys who can dance can fuck.

Manly stuff: Building basic competency in things that are generally regarded as masculine but that most guys can't actually do very well is a reliable signal of your physical effectiveness. These can include skills like hiking, climbing, throwing, weight lifting, swimming, hunting, horseback riding, boating, making a fire, camping, and driving a stick shift.

Women also love guys with suburban-dad skills, like using hand tools and power tools, fixing plumbing and electrical problems, assembling furniture, mowing grass, and doing car maintenance.

These things don't require Olympic-level fitness, but they give her an excuse to admire your body while you're doing something manly — *and effective* — that she can also brag about to her friends.

Team sports: There are some basic sports that women expect guys to be able to do. These vary by culture, but in America they include football, basketball, baseball, and soccer. Your ability to play these team sports with some proficiency demonstrates not just physical fitness, but also social intelligence, popularity, leadership, and aggressiveness. Women instinctively interpret your competitive ability in team sports as an index of how well you'd do in real warfare, when they and their kids would really need your protection.

If you HATE those sports, that's fine, don't do them. But be able to play at least some other sport instead. A complete lack of willingness to play any sport is a far bigger problem than not liking the popular ones.

Combat/martial arts: If ball sports are not your thing, focus on combat sports and martial arts, like mixed martial arts, jiujitsu, boxing, krav maga, and wrestling. These skills are equally reliable signals of physical fitness and also reveal your aggressiveness, emotional resilience, willpower, and ability to recover from injuries. They are really beneficial to you in many other ways as well.

Your job now is to figure out which of these things you like and care about most and then to go out and do them. Getting in shape and being physically healthy are great for your personal self-improvement, but they're even better for your mating life if you *go out and learn some new ways of using and displaying your body*.

Just start wherever you are, working on your physical fitness and your physical skills in parallel. Women appreciate what you actually do, not what you imagine.

Takeaways

- Improving your mating life starts with physical health—it is essential for living a longer, fuller life, and it is the foundation for developing all the other traits that are attractive to women.
- Physical health is not about developing washboard abs or a bodybuilder physique. It's about being able to do lots of different things effectively with your body, like any active prehistoric guy could have done, from hiking and hunting to fighting and fucking. It's about functional fitness, not body-image narcissism.
- The three keys to getting in shape are sleep, nutrition and exercise:
  1. Sleep: Get eight to nine hours of sleep in a completely dark, cool room every night at around the same time. Reduce evening exposure to electronic screens, social media, stimulants, alcohol, and anxiety.
  2. Nutrition: Stop consuming sugars and grains. Eat mostly unprocessed, natural, fresh foods that humans evolved to eat: meat, seafood, vegetables, legumes, tubers, nuts, berries, and fermented foods.
  3. Exercise: Get strong by lifting and moving heavy things at high intensity and in whole-body compound movements at a brisk pace. Avoid chronic cardio in favor of high-intensity interval training. Start with our air squats and push-ups regime. Add other body-weight exercises and kettlebells as you get stronger. Join CrossFit if you can afford it. Don't aim for the "perfect body," weightlifter muscles, or six-pack abs. Women are attracted to physical effectiveness, not physical narcissism.
- Learn effective new ways to display your health and show off your fitness: clothes that fit, confident posture, assertive body language, dynamic voice, manly skills, team sports, combat sports, leisure activities, dancing, intimate contact, and vigorous sex.

CHAPTER 6: GET HAPPY

(THE MENTAL HEALTH TRAIT)

But what is happiness except the simple harmony between a man and the life he leads?

—Albert Camus

The hardest part about happiness for most guys is that they don't actually understand what it is. Young guys especially think it means they have to be super jazzed about everything, like a cheerleader or a spazzy life coach on a manic upswing. That is totally wrong.

The last twenty years of positive psychology research has shown that happiness is really just an overall sense that life is going well. It's not mania. It's not Gary Busey running through the streets or Tom Cruise jumping up on Oprah's couch and Tebowing at her feet. When it comes to mating, it's not even acting like you're in love when you've met a woman you like.

Happiness is mainly just quiet contentment. It's appreciation for her presence in your life, the enjoyment of the food you are tasting or the beer you are drinking. Fundamentally, happiness means getting enjoyment out of your daily activities and your life.

We're not telling you that you can't be sad. It's okay to be sad sometimes. Sadness is a legitimate emotion with real functions in life. Don't be ashamed if you're sad, for whatever reason. But feel it, deal with it, and then move on.

Because if you're trying to create new relationships with women—short-, medium-, or long-term—sadness is not an attractive strategy. Women don't adopt boyfriends out of pity (they do that with puppies); they want a guy whose happiness cup overflows into theirs. Enjoying life is hugely attractive to women and a signal of good mental health.

Unfortunately, most guys take their mental health for granted. Women don't make that mistake because they are even more vulnerable to male strangers and have a lot more to lose. That's why women care just as much about the state of your mind as the state of your body.

When they see us lose our temper a little, they worry we might become dangerously aggressive. When they hear us say something oddly irrational, they worry that we're weird ("psychotic" in scientific terms). When they can tell by the smell that our bodies or clothes are unwashed, they worry we're getting too depressed to take care of ourselves.

Often they can judge our level of mental health even faster than they can judge our level of physical health (you can hide a belly, but you can't hide crazy), so you need to pay attention to this area. Everything we do or say is a potential clue to the state of our mental health, and women feel instinctive fear, anxiety, social avoidance, and sexual disgust toward guys who show signs of poor mental health.

On the positive side, some of the most sexually attractive traits that men can display to women—traits like happiness and its companions humor, resilience, playfulness, and openness—are surprisingly reliable clues of good mental health. Happiness and a good sense of humor are a guarantee of pretty good mental health because every mental disorder undermines the ability to display them. (Depressive shut-ins won't even answer the door to your knock-knock jokes.) Emotional resilience in the face of stress and setbacks is a powerful indicator of emotional stability, maturity, confidence, and optimism—and of not being anxious or psychotic. Guys with autism, severe PTSD, or catatonic schizophrenia aren't very playful with women, so playfulness means you're probably clear of those problems. Openness to new ideas and people means you probably don't have paranoid schizophrenia or social anxiety disorder.

For every mental disorder that can disrupt how your brain works to fulfill its adaptive function (which is fundamentally what mental health is), we've evolved a set of behavioral displays to show that we *don't* have that disorder. That's why women care so much about your happiness and mental health; *these traits*—happiness, sense of humor, openness, emotional resilience, playfulness—*are honest signals of sanity*.

They are the opposite of crazy cues. They're at the heart of human sexual attraction and human courtship and are some of the things women want most in men—even though we often don't realize it.

That's how evolution works. It keeps track of the links between the specific dysfunctions and the dysfunction-denying displays of excellence (through our unconscious and evolved preferences) so we don't have to. In fact, for each dimension of mental illness and mental health, there's a continuum of how well your brain works, from the very impaired, dysfunctional, and dangerous (serious mental illness) through normalcy (ordinary mental health) to the very attractive, highly functional, and beneficial (strong mental health).

Most guys who chronically struggle with women have mental health that floats between mildly harmful dysfunction and average function. Your goal as a man should be to identify where you sit along this functional spectrum and then to put in the work to improve your position (which we will show you how to do) by moving toward the attractive end.

WHY WOMEN CARE ABOUT MENTAL HEALTH

Many researchers now see evidence for a "general mental health" factor, with two major subfactors: internalizing disorders (worrying too much about what's inside your head: anxieties, depressions, phobias, delusions) and externalizing disorders (acting out too much toward other people and temptations: addictions, impulsivity, psychopathy, crime). Guys who score high on internalizing tend to end up living in their mom's basement; guys who score high on externalizing tend to end up living in their state's penitentiary. Some guys score high on both and bounce back and forth between family care, psychiatric clinics, and prisons.

From a mating perspective, the general mental health factor is one of the first things that women evaluate in men. Good mental health means a guy probably has good genes and will make a good partner and potential father. Bad mental health means he's a time suck and an energy sink and very possibly dangerous. Nobody wants to hook up with the depressed guy at the bar, let alone date him or, god forbid, marry him. Chances are those issues are going to be annoying and exhausting to deal with, which is why you have to deal with them first.

Besides poor mental health being a pain in the ass to deal with, the other reason mental health is so important to women is that it is substantially heritable—both the negative aspects and the positive aspects. If a woman chooses a guy with more issues than *National Geographic* and they have kids, even if she's able to get rid of him eventually, she won't be able to shed the antisocial, violent, destructive sons he leaves behind. On the other hand, if she chooses a guy with great mental health, she'll probably get happy, funny, emotionally stable, adaptable kids who make it much easier to be a mom—and women evolved to understand this instinctively even if they don't want kids yet.

Women have favored happy guys for thousands of generations; no doubt because they make better partners and providers. There is nothing attractive or effective, after all, about a man who responds to adversity by turtling up under the covers and listening to Coldplay on a loop. This evolutionary preference away from depression and toward happiness has resulted in much lower rates of depression in men than in women. Thus, when women see these positive mental health attributes, *they instinctively see a more effective (and thus attractive) man.*

Fortunately for women and men alike, many poor mental health traits can be managed and dealt with, and good ones are easily improved.

IMPROVE YOUR MENTAL HEALTH

Your brain does not have different rules than the rest of your body. It is a physical organ—just like all the other systems in your body—and its operation is directly tied to your overall health. And just like other parts of your body, there are things you can do right now to start getting better and seeing improvement, and there are things that take more time.

THINGS YOU CAN CHANGE
RIGHT NOW

The first three things you can work on *right now* to improve your mental health are the exact same things we outlined in the previous chapter to improve your physical health—sleep, nutrition, and exercise. These are the most important life changes that good psychiatrists and clinical psychologists recommend for their clients. They know that improving your physical health is usually *more* effective than any psychiatric medications or talk therapies that they can offer.

1. Get More Sleep

Tired brains don't work right. There are numerous studies showing that plentiful sleep improves mental health and sleep deprivation impairs it. The reason torturers around the world use sleep deprivation to drive people crazy is that it disrupts mood regulation, kills emotional resilience, induces psychosis, causes hallucinations, undermines your sense of identity, and destroys your capacity for rational thought.

And you're probably doing a lot of that to yourself already, just by staying up too late. GET EIGHT HOURS OF SLEEP EVERY NIGHT!

2. Eat Better

Malnourished brains don't work right either. Eating better will have a huge impact on your mood and stress tolerance. The standard American diet (SAD), full of processed sugars and grains, is so toxic to your mental health that it's hard to be anything other than moody and depressed on it. There's also a ton of new evidence that reducing sugars and grains in your diet changes the whole ecosystem of bacteria that live in your gut, which reduces systemic inflammation throughout your body and brain and recalibrates your hormone levels, elevating your mood.

The Microwave Bacon Mood-Booster Challenge

Most Americans eat their feelings—they try to improve their moods with carbs. This "Donuts against Depression" strategy only works as long as the sugar high lasts, and then the mood crash comes—with extra guilt and self-loathing from the weight gain. So try this for the next week instead. (Geoff loves this one.)

Every time your mood feels a little low, don't eat any carbs. Instead, eat some bacon. Get a plate, put three layers of paper towel on it, put four to six slices of good quality bacon on top, and then add another three layers of paper towel; microwave for three to five minutes until soft and warm. Eat it while watching some stand-up comedy clips on YouTube. We'll bet you feel much better throughout the week. And you'll probably lose a pound or two of fat if you're eating bacon instead of sugars and grains.

3. Exercise More

Exercise makes you feel better. The best studies show that regular exercise improves your mental health about as much as the best antidepressants and mood stabilizers—at a much lower cost and with fewer side effects. (Exercise is pro boners, not boner *pills*.) Strength conditioning may be especially useful in regulating hormones and mood—whereas chronic cardio imposes signals of stress and desperation on the brain.

It's not so much that exercise *boosts* mood; it's that a sedentary lifestyle *kills* mood. The "normal" modern American lifestyle of sitting in cars to drive, sitting at desks to work, and sitting on sofas to watch TV is outright "depressogenic": it generates some level of clinical depression in almost everyone who does it a lot. Regular daily exercise was the prehistoric norm, not the exception.

4. Get More Sunshine

Exposed to sun, your body produces more vitamin D, one of nature's most potent antidepressants and health boosters. You can take vitamin D supplements, but they don't work as well as sunshine. Your best bet is to get at least

30 minutes of sunshine per day—especially if you live at high latitude with dark winters. The same sun exposure that helps cure seasonal affective disorder can improve anyone's mood.

5. Do Lots of Small Spontaneous Things You Enjoy

Researchers have discovered that a reliable way to cultivate your own happiness is to fill your day with lots of little experiences that make you happy. Do 3–5 small, enjoyable things spaced throughout each day that distract you from grinding duties and that hit your stress reset button.

This creates a happiness feedback loop of anticipation, enjoyment, gratitude, and spontaneity. Focus on things that *increase your social engagement and support* rather than undermine your other mating and self-improvement goals—including cultivating the other traits and proofs:

- Call an old or distant friend and catch up (social proof).
- Learn a new exercise (physical proof).
- Email a favorite author or respected mentor (intelligence).
- Take your dog to the dog park and get some sun (social proof).
- Watch comedy videos (intelligence).
- Play catch with a friend (physical health, social proof).
- Practice a skill (material proof, willpower).
- Volunteer for a cause you believe in (willpower, social proof).

It's important not to sacrifice all of your small enjoyments like these in pursuit of larger, longer-term goals. Don't buy the Puritan myth that success requires shame-based self-control and brutal self-denial—or the myth of the American Dream that career success and wealth will produce sustained happiness. [We will talk more about this in Chapter 8: Get Your Life Together (The Willpower Trait).]

In fact, studies have shown that big accomplishments produce surprisingly short periods of happiness—maybe a week, maybe a month—before the mood-boosting effects fade. Goals and ambitions are important, but not because they'll increase your long-term happiness or mental health. They're important because they're worth achieving, they make your life better, the process of working toward them makes you happy, and they attract women, friends, and status.

Don't miss the enjoyment trees for the success forest. Your long-term success will depend a lot more on your long-term mental health than on accomplishing 10 percent more work today. Take the time to reboot your brain on a daily basis.

6. Do Mindfulness Meditation

Mindfulness meditation is the fastest and most powerful way to improve your mental health. We know it sounds like some convoluted New Age mumbo jumbo that only Buddhist monks and yoga-loving soccer moms would do, but it's our secret weapon for feeling happy, stable, and centered, and it can be yours too.

Exercise: How to Meditate like a Real Man

Meditation isn't a long, arduous, uncomfortable process. At its most basic, it's three steps:

1. Find a quiet place.
2. Sit there with your eyes closed.
3. Focus on your breathing.

As you focus on your breath, practice letting your thoughts and feelings come and go as they will, without judging them, reacting to them, or clinging to them. That's the mindfulness part. It sounds easy, but it's actually a real challenge to stay focused on breathing without getting caught up in your inner monologue.

The first time, try meditating for just ten minutes. Every time your mind wanders away from your breath, just make a mental note, like *Oops, silly three-pound sportsbook, there it goes again wandering off,* kindly forgive your brain, and focus back on your breath. Count how many times your mind wanders. It'll probably be at least fifty times in ten minutes if you're not used to meditating. If you can get that down to less than ten times in ten minutes, you're approaching Zen master level. If you get it down to zero times in ten minutes, you're brain-dead, and you need medical attention.

If your friends make fun of you for meditating, give them the Buddhist dare: "Don't just do something; sit there!" Give them this ten-minute mindfulness challenge, and ask for their count of mind-wandering episodes. If they *keep* making fun of you, get better friends. (We'll get to this in a minute.)

The science of meditation is very clear and provides overwhelming evidence: even twenty minutes a day doing mindfulness meditation increases happiness, vitality, emotional stability, and focus. It also decreases irritability, anxiety, depression, blood pressure, and the stress hormone cortisol. Meditation induces a physiological relaxation response in your body that counteracts daily stress.

Mindfulness helps you develop the same skills taught in cognitive behavioral therapy, one of the most effective psychotherapies: accepting your negative thoughts and anxious feelings as they come and go without taking them too seriously and then moving past them.

Not many women will list "a guy who does regular mindfulness meditation" as a mate choice criterion in their OkCupid profile, but they will all appreciate the happiness, adaptability, resilience, awareness, and playfulness that it bestows on you.

MENTAL HEALTH IMPROVEMENTS THAT TAKE MORE TIME

Some activities that improve your mental health take a little more time and a bit more emotional, physical, and financial investment. Once you've incorporated the shorter-term mental health improvements into your life, consider adding these.

1. Improve Your Circle of Friends and Your Social Relationships

People tend to turn into the average of the five people they spend the most time around. If your closest friends and colleagues are depressed, anxious, or delusional, you'll start converging toward their mental illnesses. Whereas if they're upbeat, confident, and rational, you'll raise your game just by being around them. You know why Mormons are so goddamn chipper? They're surrounded by other happy Mormons.

Spend time around the people you respect and want to be like. It can take time to find these people and develop relationships with them, especially if you've spent too long with shitty people, but it is crucial to your happiness and mental health. Just as a rising tide lifts all boats, a lowering tide makes them all run aground.

> **Who Are Your Big Five?**
>
> List the five people you spent the most time around in the last month—not just coworkers you sit near, but people you talk and hang out with. Then put a plus sign (+) next to each person who increases your happiness and a minus sign (-) next to each person who decreases your happiness.
>
> **Name:**   **+/-**
> _____   _____
> _____   _____
> _____   _____
> _____   _____
> _____   _____
>
> Now the key step: Spend less time with the minus-people and more time with plus-people. Do this exercise every month as long as you live, and you'll see a dramatic improvement in your well-being.

2. Move to a Better Place

Apart from WHO you spend time with, WHERE you spend your time also has a huge impact on your mental health. If you live in a country, city, neighborhood, or house full of miserable people, it's hard not to be miserable.

If you get depressed living in a dark, cold, rainy climate, then move somewhere else. If you feel anxious living in a fast-paced city full of strangers, move to a friendlier, more relaxed town. If you live in an apartment complex full of random loser meth-heads, just fucking move out of Indiana. If your housemates suck, move to a better house with cooler housemates.

For some of you, moving isn't realistic right now. You're either too young or too broke. Don't worry, we understand; we've been there. The important thing is to make this one of your long-term goals, because at some point you have to take responsibility for your environment as a key part of your mental health.

Later, in the chapter on mating markets, we'll give you some advice on where to move to maximize your mating opportunities with the kinds of women you favor. Just bear in mind that you will not be a positive, attractive guy if you live in a place that makes you miserable.

3. Get a Good Therapist (if needed)

If you know or think you're struggling with mental illness, you need to understand two things:

The illness isn't your fault, but it is your responsibility: Don't beat yourself up about having a medical condition that happens to affect your brain. Some people are born with physical vulnerabilities; you might have been born with an emotional or cognitive vulnerability. It's a roll of the nature/nurture dice. It probably arose from some combination of genes, random errors in brain growth before and after birth, and recent stressors or traumas. It could have happened to anyone, and in fact, most people have some sort of mental health issue.

Psychotherapy can be useful if you find the right therapist for you and your condition: A good therapist can also help build your emotional intelligence and self-control and help you construct a romantically attractive life and identity, not just solve specific mental problems. Tucker has benefited from seeing a psychoanalyst regularly. Geoff has benefited from individual and couples therapy. It's the twenty-first century. We all know that we all have issues. There's no shame in hiring a trained professional to help you with yours and to improve your mental health and your life skills. In fact, many successful women won't date a guy unless he's had some therapy. Why would they want his unresolved issues derailing their relationship?

DISPLAY YOUR MENTAL HEALTH

Women can't get inside your head and evaluate your mental health directly. So they have to rely on honest signals to evaluate it indirectly, based on your actions, mood, and behavior. We've extensively covered the five basic mental health attributes that women rate as highly attractive, but we're going to restate them here so you don't forget:

1. happiness and contentment
2. good sense of humor
3. playfulness
4. openness
5. mental resilience and adaptability

These are some of the most-desired traits that women all around the world look for in men. They are all fun for women, but they're not superficial fun.

Rather, women evolved in such a way that these traits *feel* fun to them *because* they signal your mental health—which is a deadly serious aspect of your mate value as a man. These traits show you have good genes and good partnership abilities and would make a good dad.

1. Be Happy

Some of the best ways to *display* your happiness with a woman are also the best ways to *improve* your happiness when you're by yourself.

Fill your day with lots of little things that make you happy—and then smile about them with the woman who's there. If bacon and eggs makes you happy, make two plates for breakfast after she stays overnight and enjoy them together. If you love great coffee, spend a little extra time to figure out your favorite style, and spend a little extra money to get the good stuff; then explain to her, *with enthusiasm*, why you love it. If having sex with a hot woman makes you happy, enjoy the hell out of the sex, and let her see and feel your gratitude (just don't get it in her hair).

Happiness is really a matter of taking care of yourself. It's about figuring out what actually makes you happy and doing it. If you can keep yourself happy, it demonstrates self-insight (you know yourself as a man) and self-compassion (you're kind to yourself), and predicts how kind you are capable of being to a girlfriend, to kids, and to other people.

Women often say that a great smile is the most attractive part of a man's body. This isn't because evenly spaced white teeth are so important in chewing food effectively. It's because smiles reveal happiness, happiness reveals mental health, and mental health predicts everything good in life. *If you do nothing else to improve your mental health signals, just practice feeling genuinely happy by treating yourself well.*

2. Be Funny

The human capacity for humor probably evolved at least partly through sexual selection (i.e., because women liked it) as an indicator of mental health, verbal creativity, and social intelligence.

Being funny requires you to understand other people's beliefs, assumptions, desires, fears, and values. You also have to understand social norms and how to violate them in a lighthearted, nonthreatening way. It requires a quick wit, active listening, and engagement. It's hard to do if you have any of the major mental disorders. Depressed guys don't make jokes. Schizophrenic guys don't make jokes anyone can understand.

If you can be funny and witty in one-on-one conversations with women, it's almost a guarantee that you don't have major mental health problems. Being playful on a date shows warmth and engagement. Making fun of yourself shows a resilient self-confidence that narcissists, psychopaths, and depressed people don't have. A guy who can mock his own foibles without showing low self-esteem is very attractive to women because they can be confident he's not one of those toxic, dangerous guys.

To put it another way, the psychiatrists we know often make observations like this:

> *If I'm seeing a patient and they were doing badly, but then they come in and suddenly they've got a good sense of humor, I know they're getting better. If they can make me laugh, I know the medicine's working. Their mental health is improving.*

If you are painfully unfunny, *all is not lost.* As you improve your mental health, you can also improve your sense of humor. Some people can even learn to be really funny.

Improv comedy classes are a great way to do that. They help you observe and understand people (the core of all humor). They make you better at conversation and social interaction. They break you out of your shell so you're less stiff and more playful. And they're a great way to meet women.

Practically speaking from a mating perspective, being funny only requires you to make a few jokes per date. You don't have to be Louis C. K. (even if you look like him). We know you can learn to do that.

3. Be Playful

Whereas humor is being playful with language, playfulness is being playful with everything else in life. Humans are a weirdly playful species. Other primates are playful when they're young, like human children are, but when they hit sexual maturity they become deadly serious and just stop playing. Alpha male gorillas are not frisky, jolly, or lighthearted. Try giving one of them a wet willie and see how long you can keep your face attached to your head.

Humans are unique in that we keep playing into adulthood. We have fun with each other. We play games and sports, and we tease each other. We've extended the juvenile primate playfulness into adulthood—partly because it's so attractive to mates and so useful in raising kids.

The Three Graces, Rubens (1639)

Women adore guys who can switch from serious maturity to playful immaturity and back again, as the situation demands. It's the best combination of the mature male status and young male rebelliousness—like taking your date to a museum and talking thoughtfully about the great artists of the Italian Renaissance but admitting that the works of Peter Paul Rubens are your favorite because of the subject matter, the composition, and all the big ol' titties.

There are lots of ways like that to be playful. It just requires reawakening your inner eight-year-old kid, combining it with your inner fourteen-year-old goofball self, and mixing in a dash of adult observational comedy. Here are some specific situations where you can practice playfulness with women. (We'll cover these situations and others in depth in Chapter 19: Dating Women.) Use these as inspiration to come up with your own ideas:

> **The Chuck E. Cheese's gambit:** Your culture's taught you that dating involves a certain set of fairly serious and expensive activities— dinner, movies, concerts, trips, etc. These things can be pleasant, but they don't typically result in a couple rolling around laughing

their asses off. Take a chance, and bring a woman to a place that's actually hilarious, like Chuck. E. Cheese's. It's full of games, kids, and activities that you can play with and against the woman you're with.

You might get some weird looks at first—both from your date and the kids' parents—but if you can tap into that childlike side and really have fun playing skeeball or redeeming reams of tickets for silly toys and trinkets, you can bring your date along with you into that playful mindset. Most women are tired of being so serious with men. They want a chance to feel like a kid again too.

Make stupid, self-deprecating jokes: Making fun of yourself and doing undignified things are great ways to show your playful side. If a woman balks at going to Chuck E. Cheese's, tell her not to worry "because no one can see if you're not wearing pants inside a ball pit." Or tell her you just want to recruit some child labor for your shoe factory. Tell her the only way you can get sexually aroused is by crushing the dreams of innocent children at Pop-a-Shot. You get the idea.

Obviously, you need to gauge how playful a woman is before making ridiculous jokes like this, but the point is that playfulness is disarming, it releases the dating tension, and it shows that you're open, adaptable, and happy.

Teasing: Teasing is a combination of humor and playfulness directed at the other person. If you're good at it, it can be very effective and attractive because it shows your confidence, social savvy, and awareness of social norms and how to playfully violate them.

Teasing can be tricky, however, because guys who don't understand women can overdo it and make women cry or come across as real assholes.

Imagine you're walking down the street with a woman, on your way to dinner, and you see a filthy homeless guy rooting through a garbage can. You should position yourself between him and her so she feels safe, but you can also use the opportunity to tease her by saying something like, "Wow, it really has been all downhill for your ex-boyfriend since the breakup, hasn't it?"

You're not really making fun of the homeless guy or even your date—you're teasing her about her past choice in men (which she's probably appalled by anyway) and making an awkward situation a little lighter.

Goof around when you're killing time: As you get into longer-term relationships, you'll spend a lot of time doing mundane stuff together, like going to the DMV or shopping at Target. These can either be tedious chores that make you grumpy around a woman or ripe opportunities for playfulness that make you more attractive to her—especially when she's probably equally bored.

If you're at a store like Target or Walmart, go to the dairy case and ask one of the employees where they keep the Fabergé eggs. Grab a ball from that big wire display case full of bouncy balls in the toy section and play catch with little kids who are sitting in the cart with their parents. If a kid wants a sugary cereal and his mom says no, when the mom isn't looking pass by and put eight boxes of Froot Loops in the cart. Try on ridiculous clothes in the clothing department, and then ask random people how you look in them.

All these things are fun ways to kill time. They violate some social norms and our "scripts" about how shopping is supposed to work. But nobody's harmed and people are amused.

Obviously, you want to keep in mind where the line is between playfulness and creating a public nuisance. It's one thing to grab a rubber ball and bounce it around the store. It's another to grab a baseball bat from sporting goods and play Home Run Derby with the cabbages in the produce section. From experience we can tell you that watching cabbage turn into coleslaw at 85mph is a lot of fun, but it's also a misdemeanor.

Playfulness is a mindset. It's about seeing the objects, people, and situations around you as occasions for fun rather than as serious burdens to cope with. Remember how when you're in love, the world is your playground. Women like you to have a little bit of that attitude all the time.

The key to playfulness in mating is reading the situation and the woman. The safer she feels with you, the more playful you can usually be.

4. Be Open

Openness is a general mindset that proclaims, "That looks cool. I've never done that before. I'll give that a try." You can demonstrate openness by exposing yourself to new things, foods, people, places, and cultures without getting overwhelmed, stressed, or destabilized.

Openness is attractive to women partly because it shows your ability to judge risk rationally and your emotional resilience if things go wrong. Many mental disorders undermine openness: depressed guys get stuck in ruts; socially anxious guys won't meet new people; paranoid guys won't visit new places.

Also, openness is a reliable test of your good judgment. If you're highly open-minded but you haven't yet become psychotic, that means you've exposed yourself to a lot of ideas but your brain hasn't been infected by stupid memes such as cultish religions, pseudosciences, conspiracy theories, or political extremism. So your mental health must be strong. People low on openness usually realize unconsciously that they're too mentally fragile to handle such novelty and variety.

Giving new stuff a try is the heart of displaying your openness. You can easily do it in many situations:

At the bar: Ask the bartender for the best drink she can make; if you like beer, try one you've never had before; if there are cocktail specials, order one of those. Openness isn't about *liking* any of them; it's about trying them to see if you might like them. If you don't like one, try a different one, or go back to drinking vodka sodas.

At a restaurant: Broaden your palate. Ask the waiter for the best dish on the menu; try dishes with descriptions you don't understand; order an entrée with a meat you've never had before. Experiment! Food isn't just fuel, it's an experience. And the more varied experiences you have, the more open you seem to a woman.

Movies: Watch a movie you've never heard of; see a foreign film; broaden your horizons. If you only like action movies or comedies, see a drama if that's what your date is interested in. She wants to see how you react outside your comfort zone; your willingness to try it shows openness to accepting and handling risk.

Music: You think you know which genres and bands you like, but have you ever really explored the musical landscape? Sign up for one of the streaming online music services (Pandora, Spotify, Rdio), and every day pick a random new genre and a random top station or artist within that genre. Just listen to it for at least fifteen minutes, without judgment, as if the most beautiful woman in the world really wanted to listen to it while you drove back to her place after a date. Most of the genres and stations you won't like, but you'll at least learn what "night ragas," *"canciones románticas,"* and "tropical house" mean. And you'll probably find at least a few genres and artists that you never would have discovered otherwise. That's openness.

Being highly open shows her that you can adapt to dramatic new life changes, such as living together, moving to a new city, getting married, or having kids. If you're a young guy and you're already set in your ways, that's scary to a woman. It signals that you don't have the mental health—the adaptability, resourcefulness, and resilience—to build a new relationship and a new life with a woman. And it means that you won't grow as a person—what she sees is what she'll get in you, as a boyfriend or husband, forever and ever.

5. Be Resilient and Adaptable

Mental resilience is a form of emotional intelligence. Apart from humor, play, and openness, guys can show off their mental health by displaying resilience and adaptability.

Mature, mentally healthy men deal with challenges that would make unstable boys crumble. Displaying resilience is not as simple as being funnier, more playful, or more open, however. You can't just roam the streets with a woman looking for adversity to persevere against, like some weird combination of a Spartan warrior and Mahatma Gandhi. Rather, resilience is about preparing yourself mentally for challenges of all stripes that may arise.

If you're driving down the highway with a date and a tire blows out, are you going to slam on the brakes so that your car spins into other lanes? Are you going to have a panic attack and call your mom to ask her what to do? Do you even know where your spare tire and jack are?

Here's the thing: you don't actually need to know how to change the tire yourself; you just need to know how to calmly, quickly, and *effectively* solve the problem. Displaying your resilience in a situation like that is not about the precise method of problem solving; it's about the fact that you solved it at all.

Your general adaptability and resilience are the main things that women want to see—not your specific skills in cranking a tire jack and torquing a lug wrench. If you fail to respond adaptively in a stressful situation, it's not like your date is suddenly going to hate you. She just won't be as attracted to you because your effectiveness in handling situations like these will generalize across all areas of life.

Fortunately, just as you can practice humor with your guy friends, you can practice resilience in your ordinary life. If you're out by yourself headed for lunch and the place where you wanted to eat is closed, don't berate yourself for being unprepared or cuss at the world for being unfair. Think, *How would James Bond handle this?* (or whoever your strong, effective male idol is). How would he show resilience and adaptability in that situation? He would probably think, *Not a big deal. I'll just go to the OTHER strip club in town with the free lunch buffet.* If you get into the daily habit of thinking through trouble spots and responding with some version of *Oh, it's not a big deal. How else can I solve this?* then by the time you're actually on a date with a woman and something goes wrong, your resilience and adaptability will be good to go.

If you're not quite there yet, however, there is a very simple way to practice your resilience and adaptability with women: **STOP. FUCKING. COMPLAINING.** There are few things more unattractive to a woman than a man who complains about everything instead of either grinning and bearing it or (ideally) solving his problem.

"These people are stupid." "This service is awful." "I hate romantic comedies." "Nobody in this town knows how to drive." "There's no good music anymore." Bitch, bitch, bitch, bitch, bitch, bitch, bitch.

Constant complaining and cynicism are not only signs of poor resilience, but they set a negative frame around your entire mating interaction. Instead of thinking *"Yes we can!"* you're thinking *"Just say no!"* Instead of looking for the silver lining, you're staring into the dark cloud or an abyss of bottomless misery. No woman in her right mind wants to deal with that kind of negativity — it's just not healthy, mentally or otherwise.

Takeaways

- If physical health is the bedrock of mating success, mental health is the foundation. Without it, nothing works; with it, everything in life gets easier, better, and happier. It's especially valuable in amplifying all the other traits and proofs that women like, and it reveals good genes, good partner potential, and good dad potential.

- Mental illness is instantly unattractive to women, and they can often sense it even before they notice anything about your physical health. They're not showing some arbitrary prejudice or cultural stigma; they're avoiding the very real risks and costs of interacting with guys who may be delusional, irrational, emotionally unbalanced, or otherwise dangerous — and who could pass on those problems to their kids.

- You can improve your mental health in many ways. Some are the same tactics for improving physical health: sleep, nutrition, and exercise. Others involve daily self-care: enjoying small pleasures, planning happy activities, doing gratitude exercises, and doing mindfulness meditation. Others require more dramatic life changes: making better friends, moving to a better place, learning more about your issues, and doing psychotherapy. If you have serious issues, find a good psychiatrist who knows their meds and a good clinical psychologist who does evidence-based treatments.

- The reliable signals of good mental health are some of the most attractive traits that women desire:
  1. happiness and contentment
  2. sense of humor
  3. playfulness
  4. openness
  5. mental resilience and adaptability
- You can cultivate these traits in your daily life so that when you're on dates you're already skilled at displaying your surprisingly sexy sanity.

CHAPTER 7: SMARTEN UP

(THE INTELLIGENCE TRAIT)

We should not pretend to understand the world only by the intellect. The judgment of the intellect is only part of the truth.

—*Carl Jung*

Modern society has developed into a cognitive meritocracy. If you have no idea what that means, don't worry—you're probably still smart enough to get a woman.

It means that our society values brainpower and brilliance over brawn and breeding to such a degree that intelligence is now the primary driver of your economic, social, and mating success. It doesn't pay to be stupid anymore, no matter how much you can bench press or who your dad was.

This isn't just true in school and work. It's also true in short-term mating (in ways that it took science years to understand). And it's especially true in medium- and long-term mating, when women are instinctively looking for high-IQ genes; bright, adaptable partners; and knowledgeable dads.

If you're smart and girls ignored you in high school or college, you might be skeptical that intelligence matters to women. For years you've watched from your desolate masturbation cave as hot girls fell for a parade of apparently dumb jocks and frat douches. Why did you have Sahara-like sexual dry spells while those boneheads needed an extra penis to handle all their female admirers? Aside from athletic talent, friends, social status, and a good sense of humor, what did those guys have that you didn't have?

That question answers itself: those four qualities you dismissed are actually clues to *intelligence*.

If you were a straight-A student, it's easy to think that all your male sexual rivals were stupid and undeserving. But many of those guys who seemed like idiots to you—because they didn't prioritize book smarts—actually had a lot of what's called *general intelligence,* which basically reflects how well your brain works. Those smart-enough-to-mate guys may not have understood the quantum multiverse or how to program in Python, but they knew how to read people, how to be popular and gain status in a group, and how to solve problems. They were <u>effective at the things women want.</u>

That's one reason why marines, cops, firefighters, and paramedics (professions not known for their Mensa membership) are so appealing to women. It's not just the sexy uniform on the hunky body. It's what the uniform signals— that society *officially* recognizes these guys as being effective at what they do and grants them special authority to do it. They had enough smarts to pass rigorous training and to survive real-world, high-stress challenges such as facing armed felons, enemy IEDs, toxic chemical fires, or driving ambulances at high speed through city traffic.

All of that effectiveness requires a fair amount of general intelligence. It's a real-world IQ test with the highest possible stakes. You don't need to be a genius to be a great firefighter—but being a dumb firefighter will get you killed in a hurry.

Book smarts (or academic intelligence) are important for economic success—but they're not that important for mating success because *books didn't exist in prehistory, so prehistoric women didn't evolve an instinctive attraction to bookworms.*

Instead, women evolved to value forms of intelligence that predicted who'd make a good sexual partner, life partner, and dad under natural conditions. This is what all of those jealous "smart" guys aren't smart enough to understand.

WHY WOMEN CARE ABOUT INTELLIGENCE

Several studies have shown that women can pretty accurately assess a man's intelligence from two to three minutes of face-to-face conversation. Yet there are so many amazingly brilliant dudes out there who are failures with women. Their romantic lives are as barren as their intellects are robust.

If that's you, you need to broaden your concept of intelligence so you can display it in ways that *women actually care about* because for women intelligence is no small thing. A recent BBC study of 120,000 people across fifty-three countries showed that the most attractive traits in a long-term mate were, in descending order of importance: (1) intelligence, (2) humor (which is a form of intelligence), (3) honesty, (4) kindness, (5) physical attractiveness, (6) moral values, (7) communication skills (another form of intelligence), and (8) dependability. Three of the top eight traits are related to intelligence.

In some way or another, most of these traits intersect with at least one of the facets of general intelligence: humor and communication skills depend on verbal intelligence; kindness and moral values depend on emotional intelligence; honesty and dependability depend on social intelligence. There's a lot of scientific evidence now that women feel strong romantic attraction to these facets of general intelligence:

1. **Social intelligence (SI):** "There is no 'I' in *team*" is a popular phrase about selflessness and teamwork as a foundation for success. But what it's really talking about is social intelligence—the ability to understand other people's beliefs and desires and to operate effectively in social relationships and groups for the benefit of all involved.

   Millions of years of primate social evolution have given both sexes social intelligence partly so we could manipulate, deceive, and influence others for our own interests, but also partly so we could anticipate their needs, cooperate easily, and resolve conflicts. Social intelligence is crucial for being a good partner and dad, so it is highly valued by women. Some very bright guys have a distinct weakness here, which gives people the mistaken impression that there's no connection between social intelligence and general intelligence.

2. **Emotional intelligence (EI):** For women, there is a special allure to men who can get inside their heads and know what they're thinking, sometimes before they're even consciously thinking it. This is not some crazy *Inception*-level brain-burrowing trickery. It's just emotional intelligence—the ability to understand and use your emotions to guide effective thinking and behavior and to read other people's emotions accurately in their faces, bodies, and speech.

   Over the last twenty years, advocates often claimed that EI was totally separate from IQ, but in fact, they're strongly positively correlated: bright people manage their emotions better and create better emotional connections to other people—including women. Women adore guys with high EI because they're less moody and dangerous and more empathic and cooperative—as boyfriends and dads.

3. **Verbal intelligence (VI):** Setting the whole "Leader of the Free World" thing aside, Bill Clinton is, by most accounts, a weird-haired, bulbous-nosed, hillbilly philanderer. He also has a Carnival-cruise-ship's worth of charisma, and that made him the sexiest man in America for a decade—all of it born primarily of his ability to use words effectively, to express himself articulately, to directly connect with people, and to resolve arguments and lead effectively in groups. That is verbal intelligence.

   VI is especially important in courtship because it also predicts your ability to tell good stories and jokes, to carry on an exciting conversation with active listening and good topic flow, and to have fun pillow talk after sex. Language probably evolved around a half million years ago, and women have been favoring guys with good verbal courtship skills for a very long time. (This was a central point in Geoff's book *The Mating Mind*.)

4. **Practical intelligence (PI):** It's not James Bond's Eton education that makes women's butter melt; it's his ability to drive any vehicle, use any weapon, find his way in any country, and survive any practical challenge. PI means having the "street smarts" to cope effectively with daily challenges by selecting and shaping your tactics and tools to fit your context. It means you've acquired practical, real-world skills that bookworms tend to neglect—things like understanding circuit breakers, car engines, subway maps, tax forms, barbeque recipes, and gun safety. Women's romantic fantasies often involve guys showing impressive PI in emergency situations. They instinctively value high PI as predicting effectiveness at life because a lot of challenges that potential partners and dads will face are at this level of practical problem solving, not abstract theorem proving.

   Here again, people have the mistaken impression that PI doesn't correlate with IQ because the blue-collar guys who specialize in PI-type jobs like electrician or mechanic aren't stereotyped as having much book smarts. But those guys are smart, just in a different way.

5. **Mating intelligence (MI):** If more men had even a modicum of mating intelligence this book wouldn't exist. Unfortunately, the ability to understand the other sex, anticipate their needs and desires, and display intelligence in romantically attractive ways has not been high on our list of "teachable moments" as a culture. Nor has making good choices about mating markets, dating venues, and individual women.

   MI depends a lot on all the other forms of intelligence—SI, EI, VI, and PI—and it taps deeply into general intelligence. This whole book is basically an exercise in applying your verbal intelligence (your ability to read) and general intelligence (your ability to think, learn, and act) to build up your mating intelligence.

6. **Academic intelligence (AI):** Our cognitive meritocracy puts a lot of emphasis on book smarts: doing well on the SAT, going to a good college, and getting the credentials required for most high-paying jobs. That's fair enough because book smarts are highly correlated with general intelligence, and they strongly predict your ability to succeed in school, work, and wealth building—each of which signals good partnership and fatherhood potential.

   Here's the frustrating part of academic intelligence, however: women have not evolved to feel romantic attraction to your raw IQ. They don't care that you have a Mensa card. Your intellectual *ability* is not appealing—what's appealing to women is *what you do with your intelligence,* as displayed through your social, emotional, verbal, practical, and mating intelligences.

Here's how all these different forms of intelligence overlap:

Note that general intelligence is at the top because it's the most important, it predicts all the others, and it's what women are instinctively trying to evaluate when they meet you. Mating intelligence is in the middle because it's the focus of this book; it overlaps a lot with general intelligence and draws upon all the other intelligences, which actu-

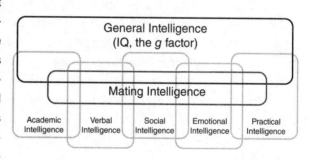

ally overlap (and correlate) with each other a lot more than the diagram shows. (For example, practical overlaps with academic; verbal overlaps with emotional, etc.)

Intelligence shows up again and again in what women want—and not just when they say they are looking for intelligence itself, but also in the attractive traits that signal good genes, good partner, and good father. Intelligence has very high heritability—almost as high as the heritability of height—and positively correlates with a wide variety of desirable, adaptive traits, like brain size, body symmetry, physical health, and longevity.

Women understand instinctively that bright dads are much more likely to have bright, healthy kids than dumb dads are—even if the sexy genius leaves after one night of pregnancy-inducing passion. The logic of female mate choice works like this: a guy's clever courtship reveals his general intelligence, which reveals his general brain function, which reveals his general genetic quality, which predicts how well his kids will survive and reproduce in turn. It's not that bright people have special genes that turbocharge their brains; they just have fewer mutations that mess up their brains than average people do. So by choosing a man who's smart, a woman gets a huge range of genetic benefits for free.

Intelligence predicts helpful cooperation and efficient division of labor in a relationship with a woman. Brighter guys are more likely to remember what's on the grocery list, when to pay the bills, and which sexual positions she likes. They are likely to achieve higher socioeconomic status, so they'll bring home more meat (if they're hunters) or money (if they're workers or entrepreneurs).

They're also more mature at any given age (remember that IQ was originally mental age divided by chronological age), with stronger ego development and moral reasoning. They also have lower rates of drug addiction, unemployment, and crime—which are huge predictors of women breaking up with and divorcing men—and they are less likely to cheat on or beat their wives, abuse their kids, or get in fights. Brighter guys also have a lower risk of death per year and so are likely to last longer as boyfriends and dads.

Intelligence also predicts teaching and mentoring ability, so brighter guys can teach their kids more effectively. Women get crushes on their teachers and professors partly because the intelligence required to teach new things to the women themselves will generalize to teaching new things to their future children.

IMPROVE YOUR INTELLIGENCE

So how can you get smarter?

Genes are not destiny, but genes do put some constraints on how smart (or dumb) you can get. You're likely to end up about as smart as the average of your two parents (who are probably smarter than you realize). But if your parents are idiots, chances are that you will be too.

Nonetheless, there are many ways you can help your brain work as attractively as possible, given the genes you have. Some involve cultivating specific intelligences, skills, and habits. Some of them just require avoiding lifestyle choices that handicap the brain health of most American men. And guess what—they are some of the same things that handicap physical and mental health.

1. Sleep and Nutrition

Chronic sleep deprivation doesn't just make you fat and weak (poor physical health) or emotionally unbalanced (poor mental health); it also makes you stupid and irrational (poor intelligence). Geoff can usually tell which of his students didn't get enough sleep the night before a seminar because they're the ones trying to make irrelevant, incoherent points. The fastest way to be smarter tomorrow is to get 8–9 hours of sleep in a completely dark room tonight.

Apart from water, your brain is made mostly of fats, so if you avoid eating animal fats and cholesterol, you're depriving your brain of the exact repair materials it needs to function. If you begin eating lots of good, brain-building fats—like grass-fed butter, coconut oil, omega 3 fatty acids, and clean animal fats—you will see a big improvement in your mental energy and clarity.

2. Learn New Things

The more you understand about the world, the more you can discuss and debate ideas with other people (including women), and the more you will turn this knowledge into actions—and the smarter and more attractive you become to women.

You don't have to become a walking Wikipedia or a Renaissance Man. Miyamoto Musashi, the greatest samurai ever (and a total Buddhist badass), said, "From one thing, know ten thousand things." If you gain real expertise in any one thing, that can be your window into understanding everything.

For example, if you really understand car engines, you've got a stockpile of mechanical metaphors for understanding more abstract processes—like "Oh, mass media combines advertising and programming to drive viewer interest? That's like a carburetor combining fuel and air to produce power!" And the more of these "mental models" you've mastered, the easier it is to find a metaphorical connection to any new concept.

What should be your first, one thing to master? Why not start with the things you already love? It could be anything—football, video games, hunting, snowboarding, whatever. Just identify something you care about, and ask yourself, *Do I really, truly, fully understand it? Could I explain its coolest details and deepest principles to someone else—like a girlfriend?*

> **What Do You Really Know About?**
>
> What topic do you think you know a lot about? _____
>
> But wait—do you really understand it as well as you think you do?
>
> Let's find out: Set a timer for sixty minutes, and write a Wikipedia entry about it. Then compare your little essay to the actual Wikipedia entry about that topic.
>
> Which is better? If yours is, then *great!* That should give you confidence. If the Wikipedia entry blows yours out of the water, maybe it's time to reevaluate, smart guy.

If you can't actually explain your favorite topic, go learn more. Even if you were bored in school because of boring teachers and boring topics, don't let that deter you from learning about what you love. You don't need a $100 textbook, and you're not accountable to standardized tests. You're free to learn in whatever way you enjoy—watching YouTube videos or Netflix documentaries, reading magazines or blogs, Skyping with your uncle who's dying to talk about his favorite hobby, etc. Overall, women care more that you are intelligent about anything and less about what that thing is.

Don't worry if you don't know a lot of different stuff yet. Just start with whatever it is you know or you like, become knowledgeable enough about it that you could teach it to someone else, and then test yourself with real people (which, of course, includes women). Can you actually explain how American football works in a way that is interesting to that cute British woman you know, who's curious about it? If not, you don't really know football—and you won't be able to use football as a metaphor to understand anything else.

3. Get Jobs That Develop Specific Intelligences

Obviously, jobs are a great way to make money so you can have a place to take women back home to, a bed to have sex on, and food to eat afterward.

But they're also a great way to cultivate specific intelligences and learn attractive new skills. Don't just choose a job for its hourly wage and convenience. That's what 90 percent of American guys do, and they stagnate. You're allowed to be more thoughtful and systematic about what work you do—even if you're a teen.

Before you take a job, you should be asking yourself a list of questions:

- *What am I going to learn, specifically and realistically?*
- *What mentors and role models will be there who can teach me?*
- *Who else will I work with?*

- *Is it a good mating market, with cool women around?* (We cover this in Chapter 15: Find the Right Mating Markets.)
- *Is it unusual and adventurous so it will give me cool stories?*

Choose the jobs that can help you overcome your personal weaknesses, amplify your strengths, and broaden your horizons. If you're shy, choose a job that requires a little more social interaction—like waiter or salesman. If you care about guns, get a job teaching in a shooting range so you get even better. If you're a small-town redneck, get a job abroad that requires travel and exposure to new cultures. Jobs can teach you more than most classes—and instead of paying for them, *you get paid for them.*

Here are just a few of our favorite job recommendations for young guys seeking to get smarter about life:

Waiter/server/bartender: Of the most socially and emotionally intelligent people we know, more than half worked as a waiter or a bartender or at some sort of service job in high school or college. If you keep your eyes and ears open in these jobs, you can learn a staggering amount about people and relationships. Your social and emotional intelligence will grow quickly—because your tips will depend on it. Your practical intelligence will flourish because you'll be struggling to master difficult skills, prioritize competing demands, and orchestrate service with coworkers. You'll also come to understand how the hospitality industry works, so you'll be much more comfortable taking a woman to any bar or restaurant anywhere in the world. And bonus: TONS of women work these jobs!

Sales: Working in retail sales is a crash course in life. It doesn't matter whether it's selling cell phones, cars, or insurance. As long as you're dealing with the full diversity of the general public, your social intelligence will grow much stronger—because your commissions will depend on it. Sales teaches you about the mutual exchange of value that defines all human relationships. You have something they want (goods or services), they have something you want (money)—the only question is whether you can make a deal. If you can sell, you can persuade. And if you can do that, you have a set of skills that applies in every relationship and every job you will ever have. And bonus: You can get sales jobs that interact with a lot of women.

Working overseas: You could take a work-study year abroad in college. You could teach English in a foreign country. You could work as a spring-break chaperone at a Mexican resort, like Tucker did in law school (instead of going to class). After school you could build the first part of your career abroad, like Geoff did for eight years in England and Germany. Travel broadens the mind and fascinates women. By exposing yourself to different people and societies, you'll strengthen your social and emotional intelligence. Exposure to new food, art, music, film, and festivals will boost your aesthetic intelligence. And by having cool adventures that make great stories, you'll become more worldly and interesting to women. The U.S. has only 7 percent of the world's land area, 6 percent of its megacities, and 4 percent of its women. To see the rest of them, go there, work there, live there, and date women there.

Start-up companies: Starting your own company—or even better, working for a small start-up—can teach you more about life, people, and money than almost anything else. If you have the brains and balls, there's nothing better to shock your brain out of the complacency that you build up in the cozy confines of your parents' home and your college. Start-ups will kick you in the teeth. They will demand more of your time, energy, and mental effort than you can imagine, in a high-risk, high-gain game. Unlike guys in well-defined jobs in big companies, those in start-ups have to master many different skills and keep lots of plates spinning in the air—building practical intelligence. Cooperating with colleagues and dealing with investors and customers build social intelligence. Learning to pitch ideas, run effective meetings, design Web content, and write good ad copy build verbal intelligence.

4. Hang Out with Intelligent People

You tend to become like the average of the five people you spend the most time with. This is a well-tested, empirically supported maxim that is *very* important for your life.

If your friends are a bunch of brainless dildos who don't read, think, discuss, or do anything, then either water has found its own level (which means you are one of them), or they are going to drag you down to the depths of their idiocy. If you want to get smarter, you need to meet, befriend, and converse and engage with people who are smart. This applies to all facets of intelligence.

Yes, if you're at school or in a smarty-pants job, you should join the clubs and professional associations where the best and brightest mingle. But if you're not going to be lighting up the Jeopardy board anytime soon, and you've started to build a life or a career in a different direction, don't spend your time with the people who have no ambition or curiosity and are just punching a clock waiting for the sweet release of death. Hang out with the people who are good at making friends. Go back into the warehouse, and check out what those guys are tinkering with on break. Sit in on the conversation in the lunchroom that seems to develop every day instead of scrolling your Twitter feed or fucking around with your fantasy lineup. Those people are cultivating and displaying forms of intelligence that you can almost certainly use more of.

5. Take Gap Years during Formal Education

This one is especially for guys in high school. If you are planning on going to college, don't go straight from high school. Sure, it's an American tradition to go straight from high school, but it's fucking stupid. There's no good reason to do it and lots of reasons not to.

Your willpower and conscientiousness are still maturing until your mid-twenties, so the longer you wait to start college, the better your self-discipline will be. Geoff has taught college for decades, and he has seen that the students who do best and benefit the most are usually the "mature students" in their early to late twenties. They are there because they've already worked, traveled, and had relationships, and now they're *seriously ready to learn.* By contrast, the eighteen-year-olds are there because their parents and teachers expected them to go. They'd rather be getting drunk and trying to hook up—the taste of freedom is still fresh on their lips.

So take a gap year—or three. If you wait, you'll grow up *before* you go to college instead of *during* it. You'll choose a better college; you'll choose a better major and courses; and you'll learn more in each course. Also, your extra maturity and mate-value will mean you'll do way better socially and sexually in college.

By the time you start, you won't be a virgin, you'll be able to drink legally, and you'll have an immense amount of experience. You will have had jobs, been places, dated diverse women, and done shit. You will understand the world in ways the eighteen-year-olds can't, and you'll basically be better at everything.

So you'll have the highest status of the guys in your freshman class, and the freshman women will fall all over you. Who are you to deny them that blessing?

Even if it's too late for you to take a gap year (because you're about to graduate from college or you're in your thirties), it's useful to think about what you would have done if you had taken a gap year—and then schedule those activities into your life. What ten things would you have loved to learn or experience on a twelve-month sabbatical from normal life that you can't learn from school or work? Of those ten, which three do you think would be most attractive to women? If you still have time to do them on an actual gap year before college, which would increase your mate value the most to college women? List them here: _____

_____

_____

Now schedule some time to do them for real!

6. Pursue the Right Kind of Education for You

There is an idea in our culture that the only "valid" education comes from formal schooling. This is BULLSHIT.

The authors of this book have six degrees between them, three of those being advanced degrees. And all of them will tell you that most of what they learned, they learned outside a classroom.

If you hate school, don't let anyone shame or stigmatize you about it. You are not alone. Many, *many* young men feel the same way, and in fact, many of the smartest, most accomplished men (and women) in America did not finish their formal schooling.

Mark Zuckerberg doesn't have a degree from Harvard, nor does Bill Gates. What they do have is a combined net worth well north of $100 billion from being founders and CEOs of two of the most important tech companies in the last thirty years. If you're not going to college, you need to think in that vein. If you start a successful company, few women will worry about where you went to school. You've already got the material proof of your practical and social intelligence.

Likewise, nobody asks where successful actors or musicians went to school. Nobody is looking at the lyrics of a Jay Z song and saying, "I like the words, but there are so many spelling mistakes. Where did that guy go to college!?"

Remember: Women can judge your intelligence quite accurately from just a few minutes of conversation. You do not need educational credentials to be a viable mate. You just need to get in the habit of learning, thinking, and exploring and then using that intelligence in ways that make your life better—which is what women want to see.

That said, formal education does have its uses in signaling intelligence. In fact, American college works better at revealing how smart you had to be to get accepted (the "credential" function) than at teaching you

---

Which Colleges Are Actually Prestigious Enough to Be Worth the Money?

Most guys wildly overestimate the prestige of the college they attend because they mistake local familiarity with global reputation. If they grew up in Phoenix, they think everybody in the world has heard of Arizona State. The truth is, most people outside the Southwest can't tell Arizona State (a decent school) from New Mexico State (a marginal school) from Blue Mountain State (a fictional, shitty school in a real-life, shitty TV show) beyond their sports programs. At the national and international levels, there just aren't that many name-brand colleges whose names most women recognize. According to the most reliable global rankings, the ten highest-prestige schools—the ones that will really grab women's interest and attention—are Harvard, Stanford, MIT, Berkeley, Cambridge, Princeton, Caltech, Columbia, U of Chicago, and Oxford. That's it.

Here are some pseudoprestigious American schools that don't even make the global top 100: Dartmouth, Emory, Tufts, UMass Amherst, Virginia, and Indiana. *Sorry, Hoos!*

---

useful things once you're there (the "human capital" function—increasing your economic value as a worker).

So if you are planning to go to college, it helps to think of your degree as an IQ credential—that will help you make better choices about where to go and why. If you are applying to colleges now, go to the most selective, most famous school you can get into. Not because it'll teach you more things, but because the name on the degree is most of the value you're going to get from it. Either go to a really good school (meaning world-famous Ivy League–level), or go to a really cheap school that has a great mating market. (We'll talk about mating markets later.)

The worst thing you can do is go to an expensive school that doesn't have great name recognition or a very high proportion of cool women, such as

Harvey Mudd, Claremont McKenna, or Oberlin. They're like buying a Hyundai Equus car: they're expensive, nobody's heard of them, and nobody's getting laid inside them.

DISPLAY YOUR INTELLIGENCE

A date is an unconscious mutual IQ test. Just as you're evaluating her brains — along with her body, personality, and background — she's evaluating yours.

She sees how you cope with mental challenges, and she unconsciously evaluates your intelligence. She asks herself things like, *Does he move gracefully and thoughtfully, or clumsily? Does he talk in interesting ways about diverse topics? Does he use good eye contact, facial expressions, and empathy? Does he know how to pronounce* ratatouille *on the prix fixe menu* (if you have taken her to a fancy restaurant)?

The answers to those subconscious questions all influence her estimate of your intelligence and, thus, your mental attractiveness. If you want to give the best answers to those questions, you need to learn the most effective ways to demonstrate your intelligence.

Here are the best indicators of intelligence, in descending order of importance to women:

1. Sense of Humor

There's a lot of research showing that a good sense of humor reveals intelligence of multiple varieties and is sexually attractive to women. In a study described in one of Geoff's papers, intelligence predicted peer-rated sense of humor, which in turn predicted success in short-term mating. On the other hand, when controlling for sense of humor, intelligence did not directly predict mating success. In other words, higher IQ seems to help in mating only insofar as it makes women find you funnier. So basically, being funny is always attractive. Unless you're trying to get laid at a funeral or the 9/11 Memorial Museum. Then you might want to save the jokes for lunch.

2. Conversation and Storytelling

According to recent research, humans evolved language at least half a million years ago. Verbal courtship and conversation developed as amazingly natural ways for us to display and judge each other's intelligence, creativity, personality, and moral value.

Nowadays, with digital technology, we display a lot of verbal intelligence when writing online dating profiles, IMs, texts, emails, and social media posts.

If anything, verbal courtship is even more important than it was a generation ago—despite most of it now happening through keyboards and text swipes rather than face to face.

What if you meet a woman at a party and she asks, "So, what's your story?" Do you have a clear, funny, engaging, short narrative about where you're from, who you are, and where you're going? If you stutter and stumble around and only manage to blurt out your name and your address, she won't be looking around desperately for your helmet and your legal guardian (which clearly you need); she'll be looking for the nearest escape.

Learn what's really interesting about your life story (it might not be the stuff you think it is), practice telling it to friends, get feedback about what's fascinating versus boring, and be ready to share the highlights with women. Know your story and make it good.

Also, be mentally engaged when you talk with women. Learn to talk articulately. Women especially value verbally intelligent guys who can talk about their feelings and emotions (this doesn't mean you have to cry). Make eye contact, look actively, have an expressive face, use gestures, and actively listen. These are the intelligence indicators that parents use to assess whether their babies' brains work right, and they're what women use on you too. If the light's on but nobody's home, they're not going to keep knocking.

Later, in the chapter on talking with women, we'll go deeper into sense of humor, conversation, and storytelling.

3. Creativity and Creative Skills

Why do you think so many men want to be musicians? Because women love musicians. That annoying guy who brings a guitar to a party and plays the one song he knows—he does it because it WORKS (at least sometimes).

Intelligence and creativity are tightly linked in the human brain, so having creative skills—like playing an instrument well or being able to draw a good portrait of a woman with paper and pencil—is a powerful, hard-to-fake signal of intelligence, and is thus deeply attractive to women.

Revive Some Skills

You probably spent hundreds of hours practicing some kind of creative skill as a kid—maybe playing piano, drawing anime, or writing short stories. Don't let all that investment go to waste. It's way easier to revive and repurpose a lapsed skill than to learn a new skill from scratch. Transform your old Mozart piano playing into some EDM keyboard skills that are actually attractive to women. Flex your short-story muscles with a blog on something you know a lot about.

But this doesn't just apply to the obvious creative arts. The romantically impressive forms of creativity can be physical (dancing, physical comedy), social (relationships, people management), verbal (conversation, storytelling), entrepreneurial (business success), or intellectual (education credentials, writing).

4. Teaching and Explaining

Remember how bored you were in school? If you looked around, you probably noticed that the girls were bored too. They craved intellectual stimulation just like you did. They wanted to learn things, but their teachers typically weren't satisfying that craving.

So, whatever you've learned, try to get comfortable with sharing it and helping women understand it better—just like you'd be thrilled if a woman explained to you how female orgasms work or why women rock the duck face in their Instagram selfies.

The topic doesn't have to be fancy (like wine) or esoteric (like French literature). If your dad was a mechanic and you learned how to tell when you need to change the oil or if your brakes are shot, the ability to explain that knowledge and teach that skill to her so she can use it for herself is very appealing. It demonstrates virtually every kind of intelligence.

Important: When teaching or explaining something to a woman, avoid mansplaining it to her like she's an innocent little kitten who is seeing the big, scary world for the first time. Being a condescending chauvinist does not make you attractive. Respect her intelligence because she is probably as smart as you are.

5. Keep It Simple, and Know When to Shut Up

A wise man once said, "Better to remain silent and be thought a fool than to speak out and remove all doubt." Often, the smartest thing you can do around other people is to shut your fucking mouth, listen, and be open to learning.

Intelligence isn't just about what you know; it's also about knowing your audience, knowing how you come across, and knowing that you don't know everything. Intellectual humility is a key sign of intelligence because the more you know, the more you realize you still have a lot to learn. When the brightest people hear an unfamiliar word or concept in conversation, they usually have the confidence to ask what it means. Their attitude is, "I don't know about that, but I'd love to learn—tell me more!"

Another sign of intelligence and humility is keeping things simple. Don't express strong views about complex topics if you don't understand them.

Don't talk about American foreign policy if you can't distinguish Iran from Iraq on a map. Don't talk about immigration if the only Mexican you know isn't even Mexican and she's on a TV show where she plays the "vaguely ethnic neighbor."

The brightest people we know are often the most plainspoken, with just the occasional technical term used precisely right. If you really want to signal intellectual insecurity to women, always use the most pretentious vocabulary: *utilize* instead of *use, empower* instead of *help*, or *take it to the next level* instead of *improve*. So simplify your vocabulary, and don't use big SAT words when small words will do.

Simple doesn't mean stupid, however. In this era of digital courtship through texting and messaging, it's especially important to avoid common errors, like confusing *you're* and *your, affect* and *effect*, or worst of all, *supposedly* and *supposably*. It won't bother some women, but bright women will assume you're iodine deficient. Before you send that next text, take a second to read it through and correct any mistakes that make it sound like you were a mistake.

Burn Your Scores

In ancient times, conquerors would burn the libraries and temples of the vanquished, not just as a show of strength, but also as a way to literally erase their history. That's what we want you to do with your test scores. Write them down:

High School GPA: ___
SAT Scores: ___, ___, ___
ACT Scores: ___, ___
IQ: ___

Now, tear this page out and burn it. Literally. Vow that you will never, ever mention any of these numbers to any woman, ever again.

Also, don't brag about your raw intelligence. Shut up about your SAT scores, your IQ, your GPA, and your class rank. Mentioning them might (or might not) reveal your high academic intelligence, but it'll certainly mark you as lacking social intelligence and mating intelligence (which are both more important for your mating prospects, as we've already discussed). Talking about them also reveals a lack of confidence and self-awareness. It's like writing an online dating profile that claims "I'm really handsome" without including any head shots or "I'm really funny!" without actually saying anything funny.

Show women, don't tell them. We will come back to that statement again and again because it is so important in almost all domains, including this one. Smart people are too busy being smart to talk much about how smart they are. Plus, there will always be someone smarter than you. Then what?

Takeaways

- Intelligence is not just book smarts (academic intelligence). General intelligence also includes social, emotional, verbal, practical, and mating intelligence—all of which are more romantically attractive to most women than book smarts.
- Women care deeply about intelligence because it reveals general genetic quality and brain function. It also predicts how effective you'll be as a partner and father.
- You can't boost your general intelligence very much because intelligence is highly heritable. But you can avoid the common lifestyle problems that make most guys dumber than they would otherwise be, like sleep deprivation, malnutrition, and micronutrient deficiencies. And you can develop specific forms of intelligence through life experiences, like hanging out with smart people, learning more about the things you love, and getting jobs that stretch your mind.
- You can also display your intelligence more effectively by cultivating a great sense of humor, improving your conversation and storytelling, learning creative skills like art or music, learning how to teach better, getting prestigious educational credentials, proving your brilliance with real-world success, and showing intellectual humility.

CHAPTER 8: GET YOUR LIFE TOGETHER

(THE WILLPOWER TRAIT)

Excellence is a habit, not an act.

—Aristotle

Willpower is the drive, resilience, and perseverance to pursue your long-term goals and honor your core values despite short-term temptations, distractions, and emotional impulses. That's it. Willpower matters because it helps you get shit done. Men with willpower do what they say they're going to do. They show up. They follow through despite setbacks and challenges. They don't give up.

Men with willpower are effective—effective at organizing their lives to realize their ambitions about what kind of men they want to become and what kind of lives they want to lead. That is the essence of willpower. And as we've told you before over and over, being effective is very, *very* attractive to women.

While intelligence is fairly fixed (at least, fixed close to the genetic set point), *you can change your willpower quite easily*, yet it's neglected by most young men. You can practice willpower in all kinds of ways, small and large, from maintaining good posture to writing term papers a week before they're due. You can preserve your limited stockpile of willpower by developing better habits that require fewer willpower-based decisions each day, like throwing out all the junk food in your home so you're never tempted.

Most importantly, you can change how you exercise self-control by changing from a self-punishing mindset to a self-compassionate mindset. In fact, one of the easiest but most effective ways to boost your willpower is to simply practice feeling more empathy toward your own future self: "What would I do today if I really cared about the self that I'll be a year from now?" Would you drink a thirty-pack of Natty Ice, eat a Taco Bell Party Pack, and play video games until 4 a.m.? Or would you do just about anything else besides that?

If you understand how willpower really works and how to develop it and deploy it effectively, it's like having a self-improvement superpower. Things gets much easier. It's the main tool you need to fix everything else in your life, and it's also immediately apparent—and attractive—to women from the first time they see you.

WHY WOMEN CARE ABOUT WILLPOWER

Anyone can cut out carbs for a week. Anyone can repress the urge to lash out in anger for a little while. Anyone can be an active listener for a night or two. From a woman's perspective, what separates the good men from the bad is the conscientious determination to do the right things for a long time, until they become part of who you are.

Women value conscientiousness (the science word for willpower) so highly—far more than men do—that in an ideal world they would want a guy who's even more conscientious than they are. Conscientiousness also has a positive genetic correlation with happiness, meaning that some of the same genes that influence one also influence the other. That's surprising if you buy into the cultural stereotype that reliable, orderly people lead boring, miserable lives while all the impulsive, immature people are out being joyful, getting drunk, skinny-dipping, and throwing pizza at cops. But then think about how much fun it is to wake up naked, in a jail cell, with a hangover, facing a misdemeanor assault charge...again. Tucker has been there, and he doesn't recommend it.

In all cultures studied so far, the women show higher average conscientiousness than the men. This means that, to most women, most men seem pretty immature, unreliable, dirty, lazy, and unambitious. That said, women also know that among men, the more conscientious ones are less likely to flirt with other attractive women and less likely to cheat in the first year of marriage. They are more reliable, thoughtful, honest, dependable, and committed in relationships. They are more comfortable with intimacy and more loving. They are also more tuned in to perceiving and caring about the emotions of other people, including their girlfriends.

In fact, across forty-six nations, higher conscientiousness predicts a stronger tendency to form long-term relationships and less interest in short-term mating. So women can use conscientiousness as a signal of your ability to make a romantic commitment. Women also correctly understand that men's conscientiousness predicts their fidelity and that the hard-working, conscientious guys who bring net benefits rather than net costs to their lives are relatively rare and precious. Thus, selecting for conscientiousness leads women to be more satisfied with their relationships and less likely to get divorced.

Women feel physically safer with more conscientious guys as well, and safe is sexy. They drive more safely, drink less when driving, and get in fewer car wrecks (a major cause of death among young women). Conscientious guys are less likely to commit violent crimes and get sent to jail and less likely to commit rash actions and take stupid risks when they're excited. Dangerous psychopaths do not just lack conscience (empathy); they also lack conscientiousness.

IMPROVE YOUR WILLPOWER— ADOPT A SELF-COMPASSION MINDSET

The most powerful way to exercise better willpower in your life is simply to change the way you talk to yourself.

Most people think of willpower issues as an inner battle between good and evil. Instead, it's about resisting the desire to do something that feels good but is actually bad for you: ordering *another* drink, supersizing the fries with that burger, texting that woman just one more time. Or it's the struggle between doing something you *want* to do (go drinking with friends) versus something you *have* to do (write a term paper). "Show some willpower!" you tell yourself. And you're half-right. The discipline to resist temptation is part of willpower, but it's only the negative facet—the part about what *not* to do.

If you're still young, the voice in your head shouting those things (the superego) sounds a lot like your parents at their bossiest and most disapproving. Immediately, the struggle turns into a generation-gap issue of mature responsibility versus the youthful rebellion of your id. The result is like a dialogue inside the head of someone with multiple personality disorder, like Gollum in *Lord of the Rings*: "Respect kind Master Frodo!" (good Smeagol) versus "Kill nasty hobbitses and steal back my Precious!" (bad Gollum).

That kind of inner argument is exactly *the wrong way* to succeed with willpower. By moralizing the issue into good versus evil, it loads way too much ethical baggage onto one little decision. *It also means that half of you always loses.*

Even if you succeed in making the "right" decision, it will feel like the wrong decision to the part of you that wants to do the "wrong" thing, and that outcome creates resentment, frustration, and a self-punishment mindset. Your

inner Gollum will end up looking for other ways to steal his Precious back when your superego/inner dad/Smeagol isn't watching as carefully. You might write the term paper tonight, but you'll be tempted to make up for this act of magnificent valor by going to Coachella and getting e-tarded on Molly all weekend so that you fail your chemistry final on Monday.

Instead of thinking of willpower as a battle between good and evil that requires suppressing and punishing part of yourself, take a self-compassionate mindset. Think of willpower as the way to cultivate more positive outcomes, habits, and traits. It is dedication to your life goals based on realistic but challenging ambitions.

It's not about turning down that fourth whiskey because you're being hard on yourself. Rather, you're turning it down *because you have more important shit to do* that your future self will be very grateful for. You're pursuing more important positive goals, like getting fit and healthy or staying safe to drive or keeping your sexual self-control so a woman wants to see you again. You are turning down that fourth whiskey because you like your future self and want to help him.

With the self-compassionate mindset, you need to think things through intelligently before you make a decision. The positive side of willpower is *the power to do* and to frame all of your *I won't*s as being in the service of those higher *I will*s. Once you do that, you're no longer using your willpower to oppress and disappoint half of yourself. You're using it to create the future self that you really care about. **Thus, willpower is really just being as kind as you can to the man you want to become.**

By doing that, you'll turn into him without feeling the inner conflict that's handicapped your willpower up to this point.

Exercise: Fix Your Nasty Self-Talk

Self-talk is how you talk to yourself about yourself in your own head. When guys with low self-compassion fuck something up, they use really nasty self-talk words and phrases, like "Total loser assclown!" "Such a stupid fucktard," or "When you absolutely, positively, gotta kill every motherfucking hope and dream in the room, there I am." Whenever you catch yourself using nasty self-talk, practice playing the devil's advocate to challenge your harsh self-judgment ("No, actually I don't *always* ruin *everything*. Maybe I'm only a *partial* assclown."), and use gentler self-talk instead ("Yep, I did mess that up, but it's not the end of the world. How can I manage things better in the future?")

Write down the five most common words, phrases, or judgments that you use to beat yourself up about your willpower failures: _____

_____

_____

_____

_____

Now write down some kinder, gentler self-talk you could substitute for these judgments, talk that frames your limited willpower in more forgiving ways but that still keep you accountable: _____

_____

_____

_____

BUILD THE RIGHT FOUNDATION

Willpower depends on the executive control parts of your brain, so the healthier your body, the better those brain parts will work.

Sleep: Again with the sleep? *Yes, because it's that important.*

Many studies show that sleep deprivation kills your willpower. Think about the last week you crammed for exams, pulling all-nighters. Did you eat healthy foods? Did you keep up your grooming regime? Or did you fall into a downward spiral of fatigue, impulsivity, bad habits, self-loathing, anxiety, and sleeplessness? Guess what—the sleep deprivation was the active ingredient in that disaster.

Nutrition: To preserve willpower, you need to eat in a way that delivers sustained, long-term energy to your body and brain. The standard American diet, with its sugar surges and crashes, does the exact opposite of that. If you eat the way we suggest in Chapter 5: Get in Shape (The Physical Health Trait), not only will your physical and mental health improve, but you'll also feel like you have more willpower.

Plus, you'll need less willpower to control what you eat. As you wean yourself off sugars and grains, your whole physiology and your gut microbiome will adapt in a few weeks, so you just won't be as interested in donuts and milkshakes. Things that used to taste bland (like roasted vegetables) will start to taste amazingly delicious, and things that used to taste sweet (like Cinnabon) will start to taste repulsive.

Exercise: Just doing regular exercise improves your willpower reserves, even before the effects are apparent in your body. Think of your exercise regime as partly training your muscles and partly training your willpower. Doing as many push-ups as you can every morning before you shower might not build your pecs as effectively as doing a serious "chest day" at the gym, but it will build your conscientiousness more effectively.

SET GOALS, AND ACCOMPLISH THEM

Willpower is like a muscle: the more you use it, the stronger it gets. One of the best ways to exercise your willpower is to set goals and work to accomplish them.

Bonus: This isn't just the best way to improve willpower; *it's also the best way to turn yourself into the person you want to be — a man who is very attractive to women.*

In fact, that's the entire point of this book. Let's be clear (and honest) here, though: *if you rely only on willpower* to improve, you will fail. Gritting your teeth and "just doing it" is a destructive fantasy that cripples many guys on their quest to better themselves. Instead, the best approach is to set goals and then build processes into your life that *are easy and automatic* and that put you on a path to accomplishing those goals. Those processes are called **habits.**

That's the irony of improving willpower by setting goals and accomplishing them using good habits: the better the habits are that you build, the more willpower you develop, and *the less you actually have to use willpower!*

There has been a ton of fantastic research over the past twenty years that has clearly explained how to create real change in your life without having to rely solely on willpower (which is impossible). We are going to teach you the general way to set and accomplish goals. You can *apply this simple process to every area* in your life that you want to improve, including every trait and proof we cover in this book.

Here are the steps:

1. Start with a single goal that is realistic and specific.
2. Make a specific plan of action, with a deadline.
3. Make your plan into an easy habit with very few decisions.
4. Make yourself accountable to others.
5. Have fun, and celebrate wins.
6. If you mess up, forgive yourself, readjust, and continue.

1. Start with a single goal that is realistic and specific.

Don't go crazy with huge goals like "Be the most attractive man on earth," or "This month, implement everything I learned in *What Women Want*." Those goals are too hard; they are either unrealistic or not specific enough to even know if you've accomplished them. The best willpower-based goals to start with have these characteristics:

- <u>They are singular</u>: Don't do everything at once. Start with the easiest thing that can help you the most. For most guys, this is one of the keystone habits—sleep, nutrition, or exercise. Your assignment is to *pick just one of these three* for now and focus on it! From there, go on to all the other things you want to improve.

- <u>They are realistic</u>: By starting small and being realistic, you're more likely to succeed and build confidence about managing your life—which helps you accomplish other goals in turn. A goal like "Get ripped" is far harder than something like "Lose some weight." It's not that you can't get ripped, but you must crawl before you can walk, and you must bust out some squats to do that.

- <u>They are specific</u>: Precisely quantify your goal so you can tell if you succeed. "Lose some weight" is not as good as "Lose five pounds."

2. Make a specific plan of action, with a deadline.

You cannot achieve any goals through sheer willpower and random effort. You must plan specific actions that you can use your willpower to execute. This is an absolutely critical step that most guys skip.

A specific plan is actionable and structured as a habitual, repeatable process that allows you to go on autopilot as you execute.

This is where you need to do your research, seek expert advice, use your intelligence, and think about alternatives. For example, bad plans look like this:

- "Lose five pounds." By when? How? No deadline and no plan of action is worthless; this is just a hope.
- "Lose five pounds within thirty days by eating less." This is too vague.
- "Lose five pounds within thirty days by fasting for thirty days." This is impossibly self-punishing.
- "Lose five pounds within thirty days by moving more and exercising." What does this mean? What exercise are you even talking about?
- "Lose five pounds within thirty days by doing two hours of cardio every day." This is inefficient and unrealistic.

Given what you've already learned in the physical health chapter, a much better plan would be this:

- "Lose five pounds within thirty days by eliminating all processed sugars and refined grains."

This plan has the benefit of being crystal clear about how you have to use your willpower, and it leaves no wiggle room for fooling yourself. You know precisely what your goal is (lose five pounds), by when you will achieve it (thirty days), how you are going to do it (cutting out sugars and grains for thirty days), and how to measure the results (after thirty days you will either have lost the weight or you won't).

3. Make your plan into an easy habit, with very few decisions.

The more you have to think about it, the harder a plan is to execute. And the more you have to use willpower, the harder the plan will be to follow. The easiest way to "just do it" is to make *it* a no-brainer to do—a habit you can follow with very few decisions and little extra effort.

For example, if your plan is to lose five pounds in thirty days by not consuming any sugar or grains and you leave all the Cap'n Crunch and mac & cheese in the cupboard, there's constant temptation that requires daily willpower to resist. That's setting yourself up for failure.

The better approach is to take ten minutes to throw out all that shit so you never have to worry about the temptation. Then replace it with foods that serve your goals. Now when you get hungry, you don't have to use willpower; there are only good foods to eat, not bad ones. By minimizing your day-to-day decision making, you're setting yourself up for success. You won't need willpower all the time; you'll only need it for half an hour once a week while grocery shopping.

Make your plan so *easy and simple you'll feel stupid if you don't do it.*

4. Make yourself accountable to others.

Friends are one of our biggest influences and can be potent allies in change. The research on this is not just clear, it is overwhelming. The best way to follow through on your plans and accomplish your goals is to pursue them with other people who will support you and to make yourself accountable to them.

Your social groups exert enormous influence on you and can help you maintain your willpower when it is lagging. In fact, research suggests this is why support groups like AA are effective. It's not the belief in a higher power; it's the social accountability from just showing up to the meetings.

Even just telling your friends you are doing something new works well. Numerous studies of people trying to lose weight have shown that those people get much better results when they tell their family and friends from the start about what they are trying to do and what their specific goals are. Social pressure is real and it works.

5. Have fun, and celebrate wins.

The number one reason people give up on good habits is that they just aren't enjoyable. It's obvious when you think about it: who wants to keep doing something they don't like? This is why most diets fail—because they suck to live on.

The research in this area is extensive and fascinating; people will do all sorts of awful, onerous tasks if they think they are fun. For example, most of us grew up hating doing math problems, but *we will pay money to do them* if someone puts them in a grid, throws them in a book, and calls it Sudoku. Yet it's incredibly hard to get people to do those same things if they don't think they are fun, even if you provide large monetary rewards.

You may be asking, "How do I make habits fun?" Well, besides picking activities you actually like doing, make them easy and simple.

If you're trying to lose five pounds but you loathe gyms and would rather die than pick up an iron bar, there are an infinite number of simpler ways to get exercise. Play ultimate Frisbee. Train for MMA. Row crew. Staple hundred-dollar bills to your clothes, and run from muggers. *We never said you had to lift weights.* The point is, anything that moves you toward your goal and that you enjoy can become a process that turns into a good habit.

The other way to make a habit fun is to celebrate your accomplishments.

Most guys handicap themselves by celebrating their progress toward some goal in a way that moves them back away from the goal—like celebrating losing five pounds by eating a Stanley Cup–sized trophy made of chocolate.

What celebration treats can you use to reward yourself *that are still consistent with your key goals*? Write down things you really enjoy doing that you'll look forward to enough that they'll inspire stronger willpower. They should be realistic (don't list "sex with Amanda Seyfried"), affordable (avoid "blow $1,000 on lapdances"), and not too addictive (stay away from "week-long meth binge!").

You should already be keeping track of your progress (this is part of being specific). Now just acknowledge the wins along the way.

Don't be an asshole to yourself here: any win, even a small one, is worth recognizing. A small win can be any concrete, implemented outcome, even if it's only of moderate importance. What matters is that you recognize it and celebrate it, even just with yourself.

If your goal is to lose five pounds, losing two pounds should be cause for a small celebration (preferably something healthy and delicious, like bacon).

Just as we talked about with the disproportionate power of small things to build happiness in the mental health chapter (Chapter 6) and the power of momentum in the self-confidence chapter (Chapter 1), a lot of small accomplishments are more motivating and rewarding than one big accomplishment, so identify and celebrate your small wins.

If you make your habits fun and exciting on their own and then reward yourself for doing them, you will *keep* doing them.

6. If you mess up, forgive yourself, readjust, and continue.

This is literally the same thing as what we said in the first part of this section: adopt a self-compassionate mindset. We put it here to make sure you pay attention and internalize that lesson because way too many guys will make mistakes, get down on themselves, and then quit.

Don't do that. We all mess up all the time. It's OK. Forgive yourself, and get back on the horse. Focus on the right habits, and work the process so you can accomplish your goals. That is willpower in a nutshell.

DISPLAY YOUR WILLPOWER

The beauty of willpower is that women can evaluate it through so many of your behaviors in so many domains of life. *Thus, if willpower is the self-*

improvement superpower, then everything you improve in your life can testify to your willpower.

Health: Your physical health is a strong indicator of willpower. Are you strong or weak, slim or fat?

Women equate being thin with having strong self-control. This is one reason high school girls can get caught up in runaway thinness competitions with their rivals that can lead to anorexia. They'll apply the same logic, with a little less cattiness, in evaluating your body.

They'll also see your muscle mass as an indicator of your willpower. It's not that women actually need you to lift a fridge that often, but they interpret physical strength achieved through regular exercise as a cue that you've got plentiful willpower to deploy in all kinds of other useful ways—like making money, taking care of kids, and staying faithful to them.

Grooming: Take showers, wash your hands, and make sure you don't smell bad. So many guys don't pay attention to this basic step because they think it doesn't affect anybody else. Guess what, Pigpen, ten minutes with you on a cramped campus shuttle on a hot day leaves a lot of victims.

Personal care products and habits are not just ways to look your best. They're also conscientiousness signals to women. A well-shaven guy has removed the most distinctive sexual ornament on the male human face—the beard. So how could he be attractive to women? Because it takes more willpower to be clean shaven every day than to grow a beard. Hairstyles that take some effort to maintain are common conscientiousness signals across human cultures as well. Armies require haircuts like the "high and tight" because they demand frequent trims and so build willpower; no basic training anywhere encourages low-maintenance dreadlocks.

If you keep your mountain man beard, make sure your haircut on top is extra precise and up to date. (This is how hipsters combine conscientiousness and manliness.) Conversely, if your haircut is called the "Bed Head," you'd better be clean shaven.

General cleanliness: Keeping your things clean is a strong signal of conscientiousness. Your car, your apartment, your furniture—if they are dirty, clean them. Even if you don't care, other people do, and they notice. **Especially women.**

Here's a good rule of thumb for cleanliness: if it is a place where she might put things in her mouth (e.g., your kitchen) or sit her naked ass down (e.g., your bathroom)—KEEP IT CLEAN. If you do that, you can earn enough willpower brownie points to compensate for other areas where you still have some work to do, like your physical fitness or your grooming.

Still, for some guys, being sufficiently clean is easier said than done because their perspective on what *dirty* actually means is so out of whack. It's not uncommon to meet guys who think that if there aren't ants and there isn't mold then it isn't dirty. These are usually the same guys who wash their towels once a month with the full moon, like a fucking werewolf.

If you're one of these guys who's not sure whether your place is clean, then before you do anything else go take ten photos of your bathroom and kitchen as they are right now—every corner and detail. Then post them to Instagram and Facebook with no filter, ask people if the rooms look clean or dirty, and wait for the comments to roll in. If that idea scares you because you're worried about what people will say, then deep down you already know your house is probably closer to outhouse than penthouse.

And those comments you're worried about are precisely what any woman visiting your home would say—or at least think—about how your cleanliness relates to your conscientiousness.

No addictions: If you are addicted to anything—junk food, porn, alcohol, drugs, work, video games, toys—it shows a fundamental lack of willpower that also reads as poor mental health. Both are woman-repellants.

Practice moderating your habits. Find that Buddhist Middle Way between overindulgence and total abstinence. If you overindulge, your willpower is weak. But if you insist on total abstinence (like AA does with drinking), you're also signaling weak willpower—as if even one beer might send you into a nine-day blackout that ends with your car planted inside a church van.

Women want men who can have all kinds of fun—and who know when to stop. This even applies to work. While being a slacker is unattractive, so is being a workaholic. From a woman's perspective, that's just another annoying addiction that steals away your time and attention from her. It might bring in more money and status than playing *Madden NFL* all day, but it leaves her equally lonely and yearning for a boyfriend who'd rather look at her face than his Excel spreadsheets.

Sexual restraint: If a woman doesn't want to sleep with you or wants to take things slow, don't get upset. Just keep calm and respect her decision—not just because it's the right thing to do, but also because it signals your willpower. If you can show sexual restraint—especially when your tipsy brain is battling your blue balls and raging hard-on—this is hugely reassuring to women. In her mind, you've positioned yourself firmly in the "good guy" rather than the "date rapist" category.

Too often, young guys act as if tonight might be the last time they'll ever have the possibility of sex, so they get desperate and pushy. That sends a huge array of attraction-killing cues to the woman: low willpower, low social and emotional intelligence, low status, immaturity, possible virginity. Showing sexual restraint also builds your willpower when you realize that you aren't going to die if you don't get to root around on top of this woman for three minutes of sweaty glory.

Takeaways

- Willpower is the drive, resilience, and perseverance to pursue your long-term goals and honor your core values despite short-term temptations, distractions, and emotional impulses.
- Your being conscientious and reliable makes women feel safe, and for women safe feels sexy.
- The most powerful way to exercise better willpower in your life is simply to change the way you talk to yourself. Most people think of willpower issues as an inner battle between good and evil; instead, think about it as self-compassion versus self-punishment.
- The best way to build willpower is to develop good habits. It's a six-step process:
  1. Start with a single goal that is realistic and specific.
  2. Make a specific plan of action, with a deadline.
  3. Make your plan into an easy habit with very few decisions.
  4. Make yourself accountable to others.
  5. Have fun, and celebrate wins.
  6. If you mess up, forgive yourself, readjust. and continue.

CHAPTER 9: THE TENDER DEFENDER

(THE AGREEABLENESS AND ASSERTIVENESS TRAITS)

Nice Guy: "Everyone told me I was supposed to be nice to women, but it gets me nowhere—they just ignore me or friend-zone me."

Asshole: "I thought assholes got more women? I get drunk, break things, and curse at people, but women just hate me."

Almost every young guy, at some point in his life, tries one of two strategies (or both) to attract women. Depending on who raised him and where he learned about dating, he thinks he has to be either a "nice guy" or an "asshole."

The problem with these strategies is that guys tend to do both completely wrong; they do the "nice guy" thing by being a cowardly doormat that no one respects, or they play the "asshole" by being a raging douche that everyone loathes.

Women don't want either of these extremes.

You know the saying that guys want "a lady in the streets and a whore in the sheets"? Well, women want something similar from men: a man who is effective and assertive to the world but sweet and kind to her. It seems weirdly contradictory, but when you break it down and understand it from the woman's perspective, it makes perfect sense.

Around the world, women list "kindness" as one of the most desired traits in a boyfriend, and it's often number one. But most guys don't get what *kind* of kindness is most attractive. Real women are attracted to displays of *real* altruism—empathy, thoughtfulness, generosity, and self-sacrifice—that deliver concrete benefits to people in need.

For example, women adore male doctors in TV shows, not just for their income, status, and intelligence but for how they save the feverish baby, bandage up the injured kid, reassure the assault victim, and ease the pain of the dying. Women want real kindness when kindness is warranted—especially toward them, their friends and family, kids, and cute animals—because it's the sign of a good lover, partner, and father.

But women also want men who can be powerful and assertive (even violent when necessary), but *only* in ways that protect them, not ways that threaten them. Women do not want volatile, mentally unstable psychopaths; they want protective, heroic leaders who won't take any shit from people and who are comfortable confronting risk and violence when needed.

Ultimately, a woman is most attracted to (and benefits most from) a kind, tender partner who can care for her and who is also a strong protector who can defend her. If she can get both benefits from one man—if he's a "tender defender"—he becomes the whole package.

If you need proof that women find the tender-defender archetype romantically compelling and sexually irresistible, just look at the media that women choose to consume: **all romance novels feature a tender defender as the hero.**

All successful romantic comedies include scenes in which the funny, nice guy finally shows his fierce, protective side. Even magazine profiles of famous leading men reflect this tender-defender duality, showing not just how strong and assertive they are but also how kind and socially aware they are.

In none of these books or movies or magazines are the heroes portrayed as cowardly pussies avoiding all conflict or as inconsiderate dicks spoiling for a fight. They care for their women, children, and friends but are tough and assertive to the world. They are stronger and more assertive than the "nice guys" and better, more caring people than the "assholes."

If you can wrap your head around the attractiveness of this tender-defender combination, you can easily become more attractive than 90 percent of guys out there.

But first we're going to break down each trait separately (agreeableness first, then assertiveness) before we show you how to bring them together.

WHY WOMEN CARE ABOUT AGREEABLENESS

Across all sexually reproducing species, lots of conflicts arise between males and females. Given that sexual conflict is common and costly, females evolved to favor males who could avoid and resolve conflicts more effectively.

Thus, women instinctively know that kinder men are less likely to inflict costs on them through deception and violence. Kinder men feel less anger and have fewer affairs. They're less likely to inflict an unwanted pregnancy on a woman. They are involved in fewer arguments, fewer fights, and fewer divorces. They are less likely to become harassers, stalkers, date rapists, wife beaters, or child abusers. Women have evolved to avoid being victimized by these exploiters, and their mate preferences for kindness are one important part of their antivictimization defenses.

Kindness makes it easier to cooperate with others to get mutual rewards in economic games and big-game hunting, so cooperative guys are better able to support a woman and kids. Kindness, empathy, and communication skills also allow couples and groups to work better as information-sharing and decision-making systems, especially in emergencies. Confronted by a cave bear (or its modern equivalent, like an income tax audit), the agreeable couple survives through communicating, cooperating, and dividing their labor; whereas the disagreeable couple succumbs to confusion and bickering and makes a nice snack for the carnivore (or the IRS).

This is the sort of partner any sane woman is looking for in both the medium and long term. If you're looking for something more than just a hookup, displaying kindness is a reliable way to signal to similarly interested women that you are one of the good ones.

For one-night stands, inexperienced women might assume that a guy who fancies himself an alpha male will be the best in bed because he'll be more energetic, adventurous, and dominant. But most women quickly learn that disagreeable guys don't bother kissing very well, don't do foreplay or cunnilingus, don't understand women's sexual arousal dynamics, and fuck for only a few minutes before they come — not a recipe for multiple orgasms.

Kind men actually make better lovers because they can hear, see, and feel what a woman wants at any given moment and respond empathically, adaptively, and creatively. Agreeable guys are also less likely to be sexually compulsive (excessively masturbating, visiting prostitutes, and having affairs) or sexually narcissistic (being sexually exploitative, entitled, and selfish).

Slow childhood development in humans, which allows mastery of more complex social and technical skills, favors much heavier paternal investment (toward kids from dads) over much longer periods of time. Kindness is crucial in becoming a good dad, and selection for kindness was central to the evolution of male paternal investment and children's survival, particularly since infanticide (baby killing) occurs in many mammal species. Kinder men are less likely to neglect, abuse, or kill a woman's existing children (the man's stepchildren) or his own children. This is not to say that women equate ordinary assholery with being a bloodthirsty baby killer, just that your kindness is reassuring to her maternal protective instincts long before she even has kids.

Even more to the point, agreeable dads tend to have agreeable kids, which makes parenting much happier and easier. If you are kind, warm, and generous, a woman can be reasonably confident that you won't fill her nursery with selfish little goblins who will make motherhood a misery. Even if women don't consciously want kids yet or understand the heritability of kindness, their mate choice systems evolved to anticipate that nice kids are easier to raise than nasty kids.

You're probably wondering, *If it's what women want, why aren't all men superkind and empathic?*

Evolution suggests two reasons. First, ancestral men who weren't kind could sometimes have kids through deceiving and coercing women or through taking from other men and groups the resources that women needed for reproduction, like land and food. The traits that predict this kind of nasty mating strategy are just as heritable as agreeableness, so they have survived through the generations.

Second, women have developed a preference for formidable guys capable of protecting them, somewhat of a trade-off against their preference for kindness. Under harsh conditions with lots of warfare and violence, it can be better for a woman to mate with a Mike Tyson than a Neil deGrasse Tyson. Thankfully, most of us don't live under such harsh conditions anymore. Otherwise, ear nibbling might have taken on a whole other dimension.

Agreeableness in all its forms is a trait that women seeking longer-term relationships cannot get enough of, as long as it's directed effectively at them or the people they care about and it doesn't devolve into spineless doormat syndrome. Like intelligence and mental health, it is not the easiest trait to cultivate, but it is certainly one of the easiest to display, which makes it an essential component of building your attractiveness.

IMPROVE YOUR AGREEABLENESS

The tendency toward selfishness, violence, and criminality in men peaks in young adulthood. To a large degree, you'll naturally grow more empathic and kind as you mature, so much of the narcissistic douchebaggery that may be holding you back with women will gradually evaporate without you even realizing it.

Prisons "reform" young felons mostly by just locking them up until their executive self-control and empathy systems mature and they literally grow out of their criminal selfishness. But we hope you can manage your own life better than a felon can. Here are some key ways to build empathy and kindness and display them better to women:

Learn to take care of animals: Women love guys with dogs because a kind dog owner will probably make a kind boyfriend and a good dad. Work or volunteer at an animal shelter, zoo, farm, or pet store. Get a pet, but a nice one: mean guys tend to get aggressive dog breeds such as Rottweilers and pit bulls; weird guys get snakes, lizards, and other creepy animals that women could turn into belts.

Learn to take care of children: If you have younger siblings, nieces, or nephews, reconnect with them and spend more time with them. Learn how to help them with homework, look after them at playgrounds, and change their diapers. Several studies have shown that women are especially attracted to guys holding other people's babies or who demonstrate child-care skills. Older women are often attracted to guys who have already raised kids with ex-wives, because if he managed to keep his kids alive so far despite years of illnesses, accidents, driving, and disasters, that's hard-to-fake proof that he's a competent tender defender, and that proof can outweigh the hassles of becoming a stepmom.

Learn to mentor young people: This can be as grueling as becoming a tenured professor or as simple as being assistant coach of a Little League team. You might be an eighteen-year-old college freshman with the lowest status on campus, but if you spend your Sundays being a Big Brother to a poor thirteen-year-old, you're an awesome role model to him, and women will see you through his eyes.

Learn to care for the sick, injured, and old: Nothing quickens a woman's pulse like seeing you help save someone with a weak pulse, and you don't need to become a pediatric neurosurgeon or an EMT to do that. In most American cities, the Red Cross offers fast, cheap certification courses in first aid/CPR, lifeguarding, emergency medical response, child care, pet first aid, and many other medical-care skills. You can also volunteer in a cancer ward, psychiatric hospital, senior citizens' home, or hospice. This is grueling, heart-breaking work, but that is precisely what makes it a reliable signal of tenderness that is both charming and inspiring to women.

Learn empathy from your entertainment: Expose yourself to media (TV, movies, documentaries, memoirs, novels) that promote empathy and understanding with a variety of people—especially women and children. Don't be afraid of sentimental, weepy, tragic, or heart-wrenching content. Sadness can promote empathy. Read good novels that expand your empathy for different kinds of characters and their internal lives.

DISPLAY YOUR AGREEABLENESS

Agreeableness is one of the harder traits to judge from someone's Facebook profile, so the in-person signals will really make the difference in successful mating.

Short-Term Signals

Project warmth: Remember *The Terminator*? Yeah, that's the exact opposite of what women want to see. Mating is not a hunt or a battle; flirting is a fun game where both sides can win. This means smiling, making eye contact, and using humor, playfulness, and nonsexual touch. Also, in your online dating profile, why not include some photos of you laughing with friends, hugging your grandma, or cuddling a puppy?

Show genuine interest in women: Don't just wait for your turn to talk so you can tell her how awesome you are. The things that *you* think make you awesome are often things women could not care less about. Be legitimately curious about the women you interact with, through active listening and information gathering (we talk about this a lot later on). Ask about her interests, and engage with her passions; that's where the awesomeness is for her.

Use self-deprecating humor: Poking fun at yourself can testify that you're a good, confident guy who doesn't take himself too seriously. But use self-deprecating humor in moderation—too much says you take your failures too seriously and have no confidence.

> **Dating Debrief**
>
> Did you really show genuine interest in the last woman you went on a date with? Here's one way to check. Think about that evening, and try to remember five facts about her: where she grew up, what she likes, where she works, anything like that.
>
> If you're like most guys, you can't think of five. If you have no fucking idea about any of them, you were paying too much attention to her lips and boobs and not enough to her memories, hopes, aspirations, and preferences.
>
> If you can rattle off five confidently for most dates you go on, you know how to show genuine interest in women, and you're on your way to becoming a tender defender (and more attractive to women).

Show empathic ability and dedication: Kindness does not begin and end with baby cuddling and puppy snuggling. When you're out on a date, tipping generously or giving money to panhandlers reveals kindness to your fellow humans. Even as a consumer, you can show kindness: your Seventh Generation dish soap says that you care about important things outside yourself—like the earth and future generations. That doesn't mean you should put a compost box in your dorm room or carry your baby cousin around in an insulated Whole Foods shopping bag as an empathy prop; it just means that awareness of these larger issues can be very attractive to women who are similarly conscious about those issues.

Be soft when you're hard: Be especially careful to stay kind, considerate, and safe when you're sexually aroused with a woman. Since sexual arousal tends to decrease agreeableness, making guys more willing to do all kinds of violent, nasty, disgusting, exploitative, creepy things, a woman can get an accurate sense of your true empathy level from how much restraint you show when your dick is hard.

Longer-Term Signals

Volunteer: Volunteering for almost any cause is an honest, hard-to-fake signal of kindness. No guy is doling out soup to poor people every Sunday morning, rain or shine, football or no football, if he doesn't *actually* care. The tricky thing here is not to brag about it too early or too obviously.

Be generous: Cultivate a social reputation for generosity by actually being generous to friends, family, strangers, the earth, society, and so on. When it comes to mating, give thoughtful, useful, and/or beautiful gifts to women (we'll cover gift ideas in the romantic proof chapter). This is a common courtship tactic across species and highly ritualized in human mating.

WHY WOMEN CARE ABOUT ASSERTIVENESS

Now that we've covered how to be tender, let's talk about the "defender" side of things. In fact, in addition to being kind and empathic, you also need to know how to be an asshole, *but in the best possible sense.*

In psychology, the term for this personality trait is "assertiveness," which is shorthand for the combination of protectiveness, decisiveness, and formidability. (It's also the positive side of low agreeableness.)

Women are definitely attracted to assertive, masculine men; no one disagrees with that. It is baked into the female biology. Women with a stronger fear of crime or violence prefer more aggressive and formidable males who can protect them. At peak fertility, just before ovulation, women are especially attracted to men who act assertive and dominant, who speak in a deep masculine voice, and who have a more masculine body shape.

This preference is so complete that often male dominance is more important than male physical attractiveness. Jason Statham and Johnny Depp walk into a party together where nobody knows them. Guess who's more likely to go home with the hottest woman in the place? It's probably going to be the Transporter, not Willy Wonka.

This impulse toward the protective is also why heroic risk taking is so attractive to women, especially for short-term mating. Risk taking implies you will put yourself out there for a woman, both literally and figuratively. Of course, since most imminent physical threats have disappeared in our modern society and most guys are complete idiots, risk taking more often takes the form of acting like a total jackass. When an attractive female is watching, for instance, male skateboarders take more risks (because of a temporary boost in testosterone), doing more impressive tricks but also suffering more crashes. Your job is to recognize the line where risk taking leaves the realm of the protective and functional and enters the land of the foolish and immature.

The genetic, partnership, and fatherhood implications of assertiveness make this line one worth understanding. Aggressive behavior, risk taking, and leadership are all heritable. Testosterone levels in males are also highly heritable, which influence aggressiveness, dominance, and not taking shit from other people (e.g., rejecting low, unfair offers in the Ultimatum Game). This is a positive attribute right up until the point when you are super agro and she has to start worrying about whether or not your kids are going to be bullies or predators.

That said, part of protectiveness and formidability is a guy's willingness to punish, ostracize, or stigmatize bad guys. This brings big benefits to the tribe and to a woman and her offspring, friends, and relatives. She has an intuitive understanding that she is safer with an assertive male—a male who understands violence.

Violence has deep evolutionary roots. To be effective hunters who can provide meat to women and children, men needed to be able to use lethal violence against animals. To be good defenders, they had to be able to protect

ancestral women and children from many prehistoric threats: natural disas-
ters, dangerous animals, predators, and out-group (rival tribes) and in-group
(psychopaths, despots) social threats. The prehistoric weapons for killing animals also overlapped with those for killing people (e.g., clubs, daggers,
spears, slings, bows and arrows), so good hunters tend to make good war-
riors who can defend women.

Feminist psychology portrays male protectiveness toward women, particularly when taken to the extreme, as a social pathology called "benevolent sexism." The protectiveness can start to look possessive and infantilizing. You
put her on a pedestal like a fragile little china doll who can't take care of herself. You swoop in like a white knight to save the day, when the day never
needed saving to begin with. A lot of women, especially older, more successful women, find this to be a huge turnoff if there's no real threat.

Yet, paradoxically, women rate "benevolently sexist" (i.e., protective) men
as most attractive, especially in romantic rather than work contexts. Also,
women who value benevolent sexism more are happier with their lives.

In other words, this is hard. Assertiveness is really a delicate balance.
What is protective and decisive to one can easily be overbearing and possessive to another. Understanding the distinction is as much about the ability to
assess threats as the ability to read the reaction of the women on the other
side of your efforts.

Yes, this means you have to learn to understand women and think for yourself. And no, there is no precise checklist of behavior that always works all the
time. Welcome to Life.

IMPROVE YOUR ASSERTIVENESS

To those for whom strength and confidence don't come naturally, assertiveness
can be an intimidating subject. It's one thing to say, "Be kind" or "Be generous."
It's another thing altogether to say, "Man up and show some fucking balls for
once, why don't you?!" But there are ways to improve your assertiveness.

Get your hands dirty: If you know how to run, climb, swim, drive, sail, fly,
use power tools, repair engines, pick locks, navigate, hunt, and use survival
skills, fire skills, tracking, and evasion—all that awesome Jason Bourne
shit—it's hard not to feel like you own the world around you. If you want to
cultivate a stronger sense of protectiveness, hardiness, and formidability, we
can't think of a better way than bending traditional sources of adversity to your
will. Just like we told you in the willpower chapter—skills matter.

Learn self-defense: Language is often your most effective form of self-defense, but it's hard to show verbal self-confidence in threatening situations if you don't have any physical self-defense skills to back it up.

This is crucial: the main point of learning how to fight in modern society is not that you'll need to win lots of actual fights. Rather, it's to cultivate the self-confidence that comes with knowing that you *could* win a fight.

It's very difficult to be an effective tender defender without this belief in your own formidability, because women can sense whether you have that capacity for defense, even if they never see you use it. How? Because *you* know it.

Remember the discussion about sociometers in chapter 1? This is another place it matters. If you don't actually know how to fight, unless you are an amazing actor, you will betray this lack of confidence, and other people *will* see it.

There are two basic ways to develop effective self-defense skills. Tucker prefers one, Geoff prefers the other, but both are valid (and you can do both):

Practical self-defense (Geoff's pick): Practical self-defense focuses on threat assessment, verbal challenges and commands, recruiting bystander witnesses, force escalation, evading multiple attackers, improvised weapons, dealing with knife and handgun threats, and legal implications of force (e.g., assault charges, civil lawsuits). It's about messy, gritty, real-life situations with no clear roles or rules and no happy outcomes.

Practical self-defense classes teach doing everything you can to avoid violence, but then escalating to no-holds-barred, very dirty street fighting if necessary. It's typically based around the Israeli discipline of krav maga (or some mixed martial arts methods), supplemented by weapons training with batons, knives, guns, and improvised weapons. These classes usually require you to attack heavily padded assailants who instill real fear and adrenaline. You focus on learning a small number of really useful moves, practiced to the point that you can use them automatically under conditions of high stress.

Mixed martial arts (MMA, Tucker's pick): Mixed martial arts is what you see on TV: UFC cage-fighting. You can learn MMA or learn the two basic component arts separately, Brazilian jiu-jitsu and Muay Thai, and you will learn how to handle yourself very well in any sort of physical altercation. This is real fighting done in a safe, controlled environment where you can learn skills, forge friendships, and explore yourself. And of course, MMA fighting methods are all real and tested.

The vast majority of "martial arts" are nothing more than stylized bullshit moves that are totally useless in a fight. For example, Taekwondo is as effective as basketball moves in a real fight. MMA is about real fighting. You get hit in the face and learn to take a punch. You get put in a choke hold and learn to apply one yourself in high-stress situations with someone trying to stop you.

What is so good about MMA (in addition to the effective skills you learn) is that it forces you to confront all of your issues with confidence, submission, and self-discipline and, in the process, teaches you who and what you are. After six months of MMA (or Brazilian jiu-jitsu or Muay Thai), it's hard not to be more confident, both with yourself and in situations.

Being a tender defender isn't simply about the willingness to defend and protect; it's about the *ability* to do it effectively and decisively. This is what proper self-defense training provides. And no amount of tenderness can substitute for it when it really counts.

DISPLAY YOUR ASSERTIVENESS

In any relationship with a woman, whether for a couple of hours or a marriage, you'll probably be in tender mode 95 percent of the time and defender mode only 5 percent of the time.

How you act in those 5 percent of defender cases will determine a larger percentage of her attraction to you than the quieter 95 percent of tender moments. That's why *how* you display assertiveness is as important as *whether* you display it at all.

Use nonverbal behavior: Project competence, vigilance, assertiveness, and formidability. "Postural openness" (taking up more space, arms out, legs apart) increases your apparent size and strength, which increases your apparent social status.

Dance, monkey, dance: Believe it or not, the energy you display while dancing is a window into your formidability. Women rate males as better dancers if they display larger, more variable, and faster arm movements. These movement patterns are correlated with objective measurements of male grip strength, upper-body strength, and cardiovascular fitness. Women can also judge male risk seeking and formidability fairly accurately from watching men dance.

Obviously, if you hate dancing, don't go out there and throw your body around like someone on crack just to impress the ladies. But if you enjoy dancing, understand that bolder is better.

Make decisions, and get shit done: Good defenders think and act fast because threats attack fast; indecisiveness can get a woman and her kids killed. Your decisiveness in ordering drinks effectively at a noisy bar gives a woman clues about your likely decisiveness in facing down a pack of wolves (or bros, which is the bigger threat to her in modern society).

Be sexually dominant: This is a powerful cue of aggressive ability and confidence and very hot to many women—especially those who are often embarrassed to ask for it. (See our list of sex resources in Chapter 20 for more on this.)

Play sports: Male athletes have higher mating success than nonathletes, and women prefer athletes who play competitive, aggressive sports, not just for their physical health but for their proven dominance in ritualized one-on-one violence (combat sports) and warfare (team sports). Women perceive male athletes as more energetic, ambitious, competitive, and promiscuous.

HOW TO COMBINE AND DISPLAY TENDER-DEFENDER TRAITS

As we've said, about 95 percent of the time in a relationship everything will be cool, and there will be no conflicts or threats. Then it's great to display your tender side. Look for opportunities to show that you're kind and considerate: acting like a gentleman, talking empathically, cooing at babies, petting dogs, and so on.

But about 5 percent of the time, your threat radar will detect some possible social conflict or physical danger, and you need to go into defender mode. Think of this as like switching from spooning in bed to jumping up to investigate a weird noise from your kitchen at night. You're no longer focused on the woman but on identifying and neutralizing the threat for the sake of the woman and yourself. This holds true even on dates, where threats are usually minor but your reactions to them are major cues to your character.

Suppose you meet a woman—maybe on Match.com or Tinder or maybe you have a class together. To keep it casual and low stress, you agree to meet up for coffee over the weekend. Coffee goes well, and it turns into brunch. You pick a place with a great vibe and a great menu. When you get there, you make sure she has the seat with the better view (demonstrating empathy in the form of literal perspective taking). She orders first—and you order decisively yourself—but then the server brings your date the wrong entrée and spills some of it on her dress.

How do you respond?

The nice-guy wimp cowers in spoon mode. He doesn't say anything to the server because he "doesn't want to make a scene," which she interprets as "doesn't have the balls to protect her" or "doesn't care about her at all." The woman might say she is happy to just eat the wrong entrée (which she isn't) and to deal with the stained dress (although she just spent two hundred dollars on it). But she'll silently seethe with resentment.

The asshole would turn way too aggressive way too early—as if it wasn't just soup spilled on his date's dress but raw sewage deliberately sprayed from a fire hose onto her wedding dress. He skips over normal knife mode (investigating possible threats and evaluating the best tactical solutions) and goes straight to katana mode, slashing wildly like a boy-samurai wielding his first two-handed sword. He'll cuss at the server, push him around, demand to see the manager, and escalate the confrontation. The woman might initially admire his decisiveness, but she will quickly realize that he's paying more attention to his own outrage than to her interests. He's not tending her or defending her; he's just picking a fight and indulging his out-of-control ego.

The tender defender politely but assertively gets the problem fixed in ways that respect the woman. He makes sure the server acknowledges the errors, without having to lose face, and suggests useful ways to correct the errors, without sounding patronizing. Does she want her original order, given how long it may take to prepare, or is she truly OK with this entrée? Does she want the restaurant to cover her dry-cleaning costs? Will the manager offer free mimosas and desserts for their trouble? He realizes the woman may feel embarrassed by the stains all over her dress and reassures her that she still looks gorgeous. He deftly resolves the situation with a combination of spoon mode and knife mode.

It's worth thinking about these sorts of issues before they come up and thinking about how to firmly, politely, and assertively deal with problems. Run some mental scenarios about how you'd deal with common date crises. For each, think about the overly agreeable spoon-mode response, the overly aggressive knife-mode response, and the perfectly balanced tender-defender response. In fact, view them not as problems but as opportunities to show off your tender-defender traits.

TENDER DEFENDER DOS AND DON'TS

DO BE	DON'T BE
Empathic	Narcissistic
Assertive	Wimpy
Protective	Psychopathic
Generous leader	Machiavellian
Altruistic	Selfish
Confident and decisive	Submissive or passive
Ready for anything	Completely oblivious or totally anxious

Takeaways

- A woman benefits from a kind, tender partner who cares for her and a strong, decisive protector who can defend her. If you can do both—if you are a "tender defender"—you become the whole package. The tender defender respects the reality of violence and death and takes the responsibility for dealing with them so women feel free to enjoy safety and life. He offers unique benefits as a good partner and good father, and his empathic heroism can also be passed along to his kids.

- Be stronger and more assertive than the "nice guys" and a better, more caring person than the "assholes," and you will be more attractive than 90 percent of guys. Learn to switch quickly and effectively from tender to tough, from spoon mode to knife mode, from caring for the vulnerable to confronting the threatening.

- The negative sides of agreeableness and assertiveness are both sexually repulsive. Cowardice, submissiveness, indecisiveness, and passivity are *hugely* unattractive to women. But so are Dark Triad traits (narcissism, Machiavellianism, and psychopathy), which signal real threats to women's well-being. To become the man that women want, you'll need to cultivate the positive sides of agreeableness and assertiveness.

- Women want to feel safe and protected from danger; if you can provide this safety and protection, you immediately become more attractive. Threats while on a date are usually minor, but women perceive your reactions to them as major cues to your character.

Step Three

Display Attractive Proofs

CHAPTER 10: SHOW THEM WHAT YOU'RE WORKING WITH

(SIGNALING THEORY)

Show, don't tell.

—The universal screenwriter's maxim

Step 2 in this book is all about understanding and improving the traits that define your mate value—such as how well your body works (physical health) and how well your self-control systems work (willpower). If you make all of those changes, or even some of them, you're going to increase your mate value. But by itself, that's not enough.

Why? Because *having* attractive traits is not the same as *displaying* attractive traits.

Signaling theory states that when you're trying to display attractive traits to women, you must follow the screenwriter's dictum: show, don't tell. You can't just claim you have a good trait; saying "I'm smart!" means nothing. You have to actually *show your intelligence and how it's already made your life better, in specific, concrete ways.*

There are countless ways to show off your traits to women. These displays, called "proofs," are the focus of Step 3—what they are, why they attract women, and how to improve them. We'll explain social proofs like dominance, status, prestige, and popularity; material proofs like resources and wealth; aesthetic proofs like taste, style, and art; and romantic proofs like gifts, love, and commitment.

In each case the signaling logic is similar: what proof of your value can you show to a woman that a man with lower value could never succeed in showing? We've already explained that women are scanning for physical, sexual, and social threats, like robbers, rapists, and embarrassing Trekkies. But women are also scanning for mating opportunities—potential lovers and boyfriends. Your signals and proofs are the main way that you get her interest from across the room. They reveal your physical, mental, and financial health. They rank you relative to other males. They testify to your good genes, your good partner ability, and good dad potential. If you don't display them, however, women can't even see you as a mate, much less feel attraction to you. You could have the highest mate value and the most amazing traits in the world, but if you don't send out any signals or proofs of your traits, you're the Invisible Man.

Make no mistake; everything you do and say is sending these signals and proofs out in all directions all the time: your clothing, your grooming, your body language, your facial expressions, your shoes, your friends, and everything else about your appearance and actions. Women are bombarded by these signals from men all around them, and they sort through them very fast and unconsciously. Have you ever tried to talk to a woman, but you felt like after one glance she'd already made up her mind about you, even before you had a chance to talk to her?

That's probably because she did. But she wasn't being a bitch. She didn't think she was better than you! She just didn't need to talk to you to figure out what kind of guy you are; she could already tell from how you looked and acted that you weren't going to be her type. *She was responding to your signals.*

If a picture speaks a thousand words, 998 of yours were "No."

GET MORE CONSCIOUS ABOUT YOUR SIGNALS

We hear a lot of bad advice from parents and teachers about life, but chances are the worst advice we get is something like this:

> *What matters is what's on the inside, not the outside. If people don't take the time to get to know you, then that's their loss.*

This is not only wrong; it is cripplingly stupid and corrosively toxic for men (or anyone) to believe.

Everything you wear, everything you do, every gesture you make tells a story about you. Women perceive these behaviors and traits and then use them to make judgments about your mate value and boyfriend potential.

Yes, what's on the inside is very important, but we can judge each other's deepest traits only by what we can observe and verify. EVERYONE judges

EVERYONE else by what's "on the outside." We do it because we're wired by evolution to show off our inner traits through our surface behavior *and to expect everyone else to do the same.*

That is the essence of signaling, and it is the heart of honest courtship, the foundation of win-win relationships, and the most powerful principle for increasing your attractiveness to women.

The entire concept of signaling goes against the incomplete advice to "just be yourself" with women. The one thing that people never mean by "just be yourself" is "make zero effort to cultivate or display any of the traits that make women feel happy, safe, impressed, and attracted."

The reality is, you can't escape signaling; you can only do it badly or do it well. Most of the guys you see out there doing well with women—especially the guys you think don't offer anything special—understand this implicitly. Many of them probably don't even have better traits than you; they just know how to signal their traits more effectively.

The problem most guys have is that they overspecialize. They figure out in high school, "Hey, I've got one or two traits where I'm a little above average, and I'm going to just run with those," and they overinvest in developing those early strengths at the expense of everything else.

Or they develop a certain narrow, stereotyped way to display their traits. They think, "Hey, I'm bright. I'm good at chess. I'm going to become a chess genius. That'll get the women." No. That doesn't work. Very rarely do women like guys who are overspecialized in some arbitrary, culture-specific proof like chess skill. It just doesn't reach deep enough into her mating instincts. No woman has ever said to herself, *You know what I want? A man who can effortlessly navigate the Luzhin Defense but can't find his ass with two hands, a map, and a flashlight.*

In nature, mating signals are almost exclusively physical traits: the peacock's tail, the lion's mane, or the elk's antlers. Displaying them is all the males can do to get females, and if they are subpar, they're shit out of luck.

But it's different for humans. For us, in addition to physical signals (which are very important), human signals are behavioral, mental, and even moral traits. Across every culture, our primal masculine mating signals—like muscularity, handsomeness, intelligence, humor, conversational skill, and musical creativity—melt women's butter and provoke sexual interest. We have a lot of ways to show women we are attractive and awesome.

HONEST COURTSHIP (OR, WHY YOU CAN'T JUST TELL A WOMAN YOU'RE GREAT)

Here's the problem with mating signals though: what keeps animals from lying about how great they are?

Of course, all males of all species would love to send signals of maximum awesomeness so they could attract all the females. They would all love to lie about having the highest possible mate value. Seriously, if all animals could send signals that they are totally formidable rivals, uncatchable prey, and hot mates, they would. Evolution rewards signals that manipulate the receiver's senses and brains into acting in the interests of the signaler: deferring to them, mating with them, or not eating them.

But evolution also rewards receivers who aren't easily duped by lies and unreliable signals. Rivals evolved to be skeptical about unmerited claims of awesome formidability. Predators evolved to be skeptical about prey pretending to be evasive or poisonous. Females evolved to be skeptical about males pretending to be amazing.

So there's a signaling arms race between signalers (e.g., males) and receivers (e.g., females). The signalers try to influence the receivers in the signalers' interests, as when males try to seduce females. And the receivers try to distinguish the genuinely useful information in the signals from the deception and manipulation, like women on dates, trying to figure out if this guy is for real or just all talk.

As is its tendency, evolution ends up at a dynamic balance point between this honesty and deception. There's always a little bit of deception around the edges, but if a signal has lasted for many generations, it probably conveys reliable information most of the time.

Humans are a tricky case when it comes to honest signaling, because language has made it so easy for us to lie. We can claim anything with words. Half the romantic comedies ever made are based on some lie a man told to impress a beautiful woman. Thus, because verbal boasts about quality are so easy to fake, women rarely rely on them, and it's always better to demonstrate a trait than to claim it verbally.

That's also why the best signals in nature, the most honest ones, tend to be the most expensive (in biological terms). Most sexual ornaments, like the peacock's tail, for instance, are quite costly. A sickly, starving, parasite-ridden, brain-damaged peacock can't strut around for hours expertly displaying a huge, symmetrical, colorful tail; therefore, any peacock that *can* must not be sickly, starving, or otherwise impaired. The cost of the signal (the tail) guarantees the quality of the signaler (the peacock), and peahens evolved to instinctively understand that conspicuous cost and precision make signals reliable.

Many signals, especially the genetic ones, combine a conspicuous waste of material with conspicuous precision of design, and both are hard to fake. Can you grow a perfectly symmetrical face and body? You can't fake that. Do all your organic parts work together with a high level of "fit and finish," like a fully loaded Lexus? Can't fake that either. Does your brain work right so it can keep a musical rhythm accurately, solve hard problems quickly, tell interesting stories, or imitate other people's behavior in accurate and funny ways? Not possible to fake any of those.

Another reliable signal is conspicuous consumption. The point of luxury goods is not actually to bring pleasure to the wealthy. It's to signal how much money they can burn. It's a reliable signal because if you're poor, you can't afford it. That applies to houses, vehicles, clothing, jewelry, education—anything you can buy that's visible to women.

Sure, you can send fake signals in some of these domains and fool some women some of the time, but experienced women are very good at detecting fake signals and sexually rejecting the guys who send them.

Here again, being honest is a useful principle, both practically and ethically. The strategy that is better than buying a twenty-thousand-dollar watch when you make forty thousand dollars in a year is to actually develop the underlying traits that the watch is a proxy for and then display them with costly signals and reliable proofs. This keeps you honest with yourself, with women, and with your signaling tactics.

THE SIGNALING CUES YOU NEED TO UNDERSTAND

The good news is that you control nearly every aspect of how you present yourself. You determine the signals you send out into the dating world. Period. And if the signals you are sending out now are bad, *you can change them* to increase your attractiveness to the women you want to meet. So enough of the signaling theory; let's make this practical. How does signaling work in your life?

It's a Friday night, it's been a long week at school or work, and you walk into a bar or a party. You get a drink and see a pretty woman across the room. If you're like most guys, your immediate reaction comes from your animal brain: "I want to rub our privates together until the white stuff comes out of the pee place." In the second that thought is ping-ponging around your brain, she sees you too. Her immediate reaction? To immediately and instinctively assess you, based on these main categories:

Size: How big are you, physically? Are you tall, average height, short? This immediate unconscious judgment is first a threat assessment. All humans assess size first because size is the best proxy for a threat in the natural world.

Shape and movement: After she takes in size and makes her threat assessment, then her brain shifts to social evaluation. Humans are the most social apes, and quite a bit of our cognitive ability is about assessing and evaluating relative social status within our group. We do this by reading the signals others send out.

Are you muscular and healthy (physical health)? How are you walking (physical health)? And what is your posture saying about your mental state (mental health)? Are you smiling and happy or angry and violent (and what does this mean about your mental state)? Her brain makes these assessments instantaneously and unconsciously and creates the appropriate emotional reactions to your signals.

Body details (sex, race, age): How old are you? What sex? What race? All the specific details of your humanness come next, after your absolute size, shape, and movements.

Clothing: Do your clothes fit? Do they look good on you? Or does it look like you robbed a schizophrenic street person's cardboard house and got dressed in the dark? Women will make very specific conclusions about you based on what you wear.

For example, if you have a suit on, that sends a very different signal than if you are wearing a nice leather jacket and comfortable jeans, and those both send very different signals than if you're wearing a ratty T-shirt with wing sauce all over it or a neon-pink tank top that has "Female Body Inspector" on it.

Jewelry and ornamentation: Everything you put on your body, like tattoos, jewelry, watches, wearable technologies—what an anthropologist would call "body ornamentation"—sends a visual signal that tells the world about who you are at an aesthetic level, and women immediately look at these things and evaluate you by them.

You may think you are "expressing yourself," and you are. But more important, you are signaling to other people who you are and what you believe. Do you wear any jewelry or have any tattoos? Are they tasteful and discreet, beautifully ornate, or gaudy and ridiculous? Do you look like a functional member of society, like a dedicated body-art enthusiast, or like a Cash Money video and a *Sons of Anarchy* gang war exploded on your body?

Again, there is nothing inherently wrong with any choice along the spectrum regarding jewelry or body art. There is only effective and ineffective—based on the women you are trying to attract.

Grooming and smell: Grooming is very important to women, and they immediately register things like your basic level of cleanliness. How clean and well groomed are you? What is your hair like (and that means from tip to tail)? What about your teeth? Nails? Skin? What condition are they in? Are you zestfully clean or a filthy pig? Do you smell like a man or a metrosexual or her uncle?

Many guys don't think about this, but smell is incredibly important to women, and it forms a large part of unconscious attraction. If you smell bad to a woman, there's pretty much nothing you can do to overcome that. She will be immediately and totally repulsed.

IMPROVE YOUR SIGNALING

Remember that *most of this happens while you're sipping your drink across the room, before you've spoken one word to her, and usually before you're even in physical proximity.* The old cliché about most communication being nonverbal is true.

You have probably figured out that very few high-quality women respond to verbal boasting because words are like the women they are determined not to be: cheap and easy.

Instead, you need to translate those words into actions. Don't *tell* women about your attractive traits and fitness indicators; *show* them. If you want to improve your signaling, this lesson alone will carry you nearly all the way. Men who have had consistent mating success understand this. They know these things about signaling:

- Funny guys don't talk about being funny. **They make you laugh.**
- Smart guys don't talk about being intelligent. **They engage your curiosity.**
- Confident guys don't talk about being confident. **They make you feel at ease.**
- Dedicated guys don't talk about being dedicated. **They act loving and faithful.**

The next four chapters in this section are all about showing. They are about signaling that you have combined those attractive traits from the inside (physical and mental health, intelligence, willpower, tender defender) and applied them effectively to your life on the outside.

They are *proof* that you are fit and effective in all the ways that women need.

CHAPTER 11: THE POWER OF POPULARITY AND PRESTIGE

(SOCIAL PROOF)

When the character of a man is not clear to you, look at his friends.
—Japanese proverb

In your mating life, it's easy to get caught in the trap of focusing only on what a specific woman thinks of you and ignoring everybody else. After all, you can't put your penis inside your social network. You can do that only with individual women.

But that approach is totally wrong. Most of the time, individual women judge your fuckability *by your social network.* So you had better have proof— *social proof*—that it exists.

Humans are a highly social species. We have flourished for hundreds of thousands of years because we operate so effectively *in* groups and *as* groups. We are referred to by primatologists as "the social ape" for a reason.

As a result, we have evolved fast, accurate abilities to evaluate each other's social standing within our groups. Over time, as we started living in larger, more diverse communities like towns, cities, and nations, we had even stronger incentives to show off our social influence—projecting strength to get resources, projecting wisdom to get followers, projecting sexual popularity to get mates.

That's why ancient chiefs erected totem poles, high priests built monumental temples, and warlords took many wives. It's also why young people today obsess over their friend counts on social media. One can tell, at a glance, who is King Deuce of Turd Island or Lord Awesome of Awesomeland.

Yes, a woman can take one look at you and get a good sense of your physical health and willpower. She can listen to you talk or check out your Facebook profile and judge how intelligent you are. But she will get a more complete sense of what kind of *man* you are, as a potential lover, partner, or father, by looking at all kinds of social proofs:

- Can she see that many people know and like you? **That's popularity.**
- Can she see people paying attention to what you do and say? **That's status.**
- Can she see people changing their minds to fit your worldview? **That's influence.**
- Can she see people respecting your skills and expertise? **That's prestige.**
- Can she see you being outgoing and socially confident? **That's extroversion.**
- Has she heard of you through media before meeting you? **That's fame.**

It is usually at this point that guys who have been chronically unsuccessful with women start hurling insults. They think that women caring about social proof just proves that women are superficial "fame whores," "jersey chasers," "gold diggers," and "groupies."

Do not become one of those bitter, misguided men. Social proof is not superficial. For hypersocial animals like us, it's about as deep a signal of personal value as anything gets.

Remember, you are a male stranger. You represent a danger to her, and the collective opinion of your social network gives a woman a huge amount of information about your traits, strengths, virtues, and social skills that she would otherwise find out only by taking the risks of getting to know you—a male stranger.

Most young guys have some toxic misconceptions that social proof really boils down to just a few simplistic cues popularized in rap videos, action movies, and PUA ebooks: *fame, money,* and *alpha-male dominance.*

Sure, fame is a compelling form of social proof. Women throw themselves at famous men. The problem is that you're as unlikely to become famous as you are to win the lottery, so any mating strategy of "first, just become a megafamous rock star/actor like Jared Leto" is stupid for most men. Some 99.999 percent of you are never going to be famous *even if you deserve to be.* That's not a judgment on your merits; that's just the reality of the global news/entertainment/media industry. Achieving fame also takes a long time—usually at least a decade of 100 percent dedication to building skills, performing them in public, and marketing your personal brand. You need *attainable, immediate* forms of social proof, not fame fantasies.

One step below fame on the "c'mon now, be serious" pyramid of social proof are money and class. We evolved in small tribal groups, where our survival and reproductive success depended crucially on other people; social reputation, goodwill, gratitude, and prestige were the main forms of wealth for our ancestors. Prehistoric men acquired and stored their wealth mostly in the form of "social capital" (real-life relationships, a form of social proof), not in the form of "monetary capital" (printed currencies, a form of material proof). Women evolved not to be "gold diggers" but "status diggers"—to favor socially skilled, popular, respected, high-status guys. Although a man's status as a *potential mate* is correlated with his wealth, political power, and socio-economic class, these are all distinct concepts, and they weren't as closely related in prehistory.

As we'll see in the next chapter, material proofs of wealth and resources are important to your attractiveness, but don't confuse them with social proofs. The guys who conflate the two are the guys who name-drop; buy expensive, exclusive things to express their "friendship"; and spend New Year's Eve and Valentine's Day with hookers in Vegas. They're douchebags, not cool, fun guys who add value to their social world, and they don't tend to do well with women.

The most toxic misunderstanding of social proof comes from the claim that you have to be a dominant "alpha male" to be attractive to women. This bullshit idea has been propagated through male culture because the pickup-artist community and the manosphere wildly misunderstood how human evolution worked.

It's true that when gorillas mate, there's a dominant alpha male who really does monopolize a local territory and the females who forage there. It's true that dominant baboons act like selfish sexual despots.

But humans are different. We evolved in much larger, multimale, multifemale groups

The Many Faces of Status

Among the Tsimane tribal people of Bolivia, there are at least four dimensions of social status. A man's physical size predicts his dominance (success in one-on-one fights), but it is the amount of social support he gets from others that predicts getting his way in a group, influencing group decisions, and being respected. Alpha-male-style dominance is sexy, but so are all the other forms of social proof.

where there is not just one dominant alpha male. Instead, human males differed in all kinds of ways—formidability, dominance, respect, status, prestige, fame, trustworthiness, and influence—in different domains of life, at different points in their life spans.

Almost all hunter-gatherer societies are pretty egalitarian, with consensus-based decision making, and any pretentious dude who tries to become a bossy alpha male quickly gets mocked and ostracized. This leads to shame, guilt, and depression. And no women.

Dominance means you use aggressiveness to take advantage of others, whereas prestige means people respect you for being useful and knowledgeable. It's prestigious men, not dominant men, who achieve higher reproductive success in tribal societies. Thus, modern social proof is more about having popularity, status, and prestige than trying to act like an alpha male.

So ignore all the bullshit advice that you have to "become an alpha" to get women, that if you just get fierce, domineering, and exploitative, everyone will love you and the world will be yours. That advice is totally ineffective and wrong.

Being known in your group (popular), attracting attention by delivering value (high-status), and provoking respect (prestigious) within your social group are the core of social proofs in our species, so that's what you should focus on.

Dominance is a highly concentrated, sexually edgy spice that you can sprinkle onto your social proof; it should never be the main ingredient. Offering a woman nothing more than dominance is like challenging her to eat a spoonful of pure cinnamon—she might give it a shot, but she'll gag and cry in the end.

WHY WOMEN CARE ABOUT SOCIAL PROOF

Social proof is at the heart of the difference between high-status and low-status males. It lets a woman see other people associating with you, being friends with you, reacting to you, and vouching for you. It's a way for you to prove your effectiveness not at one particular trait or skill but in the entire rich tapestry of human relationships writ large.

In fact, your social proof is really just the answer to one key question: **does this guy add value to people's lives?** If she can see that other people like you and appreciate the value you add to their lives, it makes it easier for her to like you too and to expect you'll add value to hers, especially at the genetic, partnership, and fatherhood levels.

In prehistory, a man's ability to get along with other men was crucial to his success in cooperative hunting of big game. Social outcasts just couldn't bring home the bacon. The same holds true today: it's very hard to make a good living as an introverted hermit, since economic success still depends heavily on social networks and getting along well with coworkers, bosses, mentors, investors, customers, clients, and fans. A guy with good social skills is much more likely to deliver useful resources to a woman and to their relationship.

In this way, social proof is a reflection of your mental health—more friends = less crazy—and there is strong heritability for mental disorders that interfere with these social relationships. There's moderate heritability for *most* social traits that have been studied, including trust, cooperation, social network structure, loneliness, quality of friendships, extroversion, entrepreneurship, and status. Choosing a guy with good popularity and prestige offers a woman some reassurance that he's not a flaming psychopath or a suicidal depressive and therefore probably won't be passing on these kinds of mental disorders to her kids.

A man's friendships also testify to his ability to protect himself and his mate from aggressive threats. Male primates form friendships based on who would make a good long-term ally in the event of in-group aggression. Similarly, male humans automatically associate mating effort with violent interindividual competition and possible intergroup warfare, so they intuitively rank their friends' importance largely on the basis of how useful they'd be as allies in a potential fight.

Not surprisingly, women instinctively prefer guys who are part of an effective protection force, like cops or soldiers. And when competing against other groups for territory, food, and other resources, any male who increases group efficiency and strength would be valuable to everyone in the group, including women. So, women naturally prefer guys who make groups work better—as manifested in good leadership, teamwork, conflict resolution, or even as a great host for a party.

If you have a broad, deep, long-standing social network, you must be fairly kind and caring, because only caring people (as opposed to narcissists and psychopaths) have the patience and empathy to build deep, close, long-lasting friendships. Women seeking boyfriends want many of the same traits that your oldest friends value: generosity, loyalty, and reliability. And since long-term sexual relationships require the same mutual responsiveness and suppression of both selfishness and wary self-protectiveness that successful friendships demand, your good friendships predict good mateships and good parental relationships.

If you have even two or three truly close friends, you're well ahead of the game compared to most guys, and women will respond. Having a solid reputation with a few great longtime friends can serve as significantly reassuring social proof to a woman about your qualities because it means you've consistently invested in other people's well-being, and you're also likely to do that for your partner and your children.

Thus, if a guy merits widespread respect (e.g., positive gossip, a reputation for altruism, or a reputation for punishing cheats), a woman can be pretty confident that he scores well on most of the traits that matter for her and your future children. Conversely, guys with poor physical health, poor mental health, low intelligence, poor willpower, low empathy, or low formidability tend to have bad reputations because they impose lots of costs and don't offer many benefits in a group.

IMPROVE YOUR SOCIAL PROOF

The importance of social proof to your mating life speaks to the importance of improving it. Popularity and prestige are not chia pets, however. They don't come in a box, and they don't grow overnight if you smear a bunch of shit on them. Instead, you have to develop them over time. There are things you can do in the next few weeks and next few months to spur them along.

In the Next Few Weeks

In the short run, improving your social proof boils down to organizing, facilitating, and improving your social interactions with people. You can do all of these things right now, starting today.

Focus on Your Interactions: When you're around people, put more effort into eye contact, warmth, active listening, conversation, and other basic social skills. Don't just do this with women; do it with everyone. Make it a habit. The same social skills work with your male friends and colleagues, and they'll respond by showing you more respect and warmth.

Project Confidence: As we saw in the confidence chapter, your sexual confidence reflects your recent mating success. Well, your social confidence reflects your recent social success. This means that social confidence is an important form of social proof. Projecting confidence—without being arrogant or overbearing—will help you seem far more socially attractive to both men and women.

One of the easiest ways to do this is to put yourself in situations where your particular strengths, virtues, skills, and expertise are highly valued by others. If you're good at distance running, join a running club, and you'll build both social proof and confidence. If you love food and know a lot about it, take a cooking class. Your passion and competence in those areas make it easier to project confidence around the other people in the club or class. And guess who likes running and cooking classes: pretty women.

Have Meals with People: Speaking of food, this is very simple, but it works very well. Sharing food helps strengthen social relationships in all primates. Having meals with people is a more instinctively compelling and relaxing way to bond with them than just meeting for drinks or activities, so whenever possible, involve food in your social gatherings. In the human mind, food sharing with a bunch of people automatically codes as "We are now in the same tribe; we are safe, familiar, and trusted."

Happy hours are awesome, but sharing a sit-down meal at a restaurant with your running club forces you to sit near people that share your interests. It helps you practice eye contact, active listening, and conversation. All these things build extroversion and display social proof.

In the Next Few Months

In the long run, improving your social proof boils down to one thing: *making good friends.* Remember though, developing a great social circle isn't just about getting women to like you; it's about improving all aspects of your life.

Join Groups and Classes That Help You Learn Social Skills: If your social skills are lacking, or even if they are just OK, you should invest in improving them. You'll benefit from the friends you make, the women you meet, and the social skills you learn in improv comedy classes, acting classes, public-speaking classes, and any other activities that teach you how to talk, listen, and command attention.

Take Social Jobs: Especially when you are young, you should pick jobs that force you to learn better social skills. Anything in sales, service, retail, tourism, or teaching can build your social intelligence and expand your social network. Almost any job in a mall builds social skills. Teaching English as a second language does too. Bartending especially does.

All of these jobs require interacting with lots of different people, over and over again, all day long. These jobs might not pay well, but look at it this way: they pay you to learn valuable social skills rather than you having to pay them for remedial social training. Also, you can meet lots of cool people and lots of single women in these sorts of jobs.

Volunteer: Volunteering is a fantastic way to boost social skills. Doing work in hospitals, mentoring (e.g., Big Brother), or working at an animal shelter allows for hundreds of interactions with people, and you get tons of practice in building all forms of social proof. Furthermore, you can meet lots of single women with hearts of gold at volunteering events.

Use Your Friends to Meet Friends: Your social network can grow quickly if you nurture it and make an effort to get to know friends of friends. This is the whole idea behind LinkedIn, the social media platform for professionals: you can make more work connections if others can see your existing connections and the people who vouch for your capabilities.

You can leverage the same network-growth effect informally. The more friends you have, the more new people you can meet. Your social network of friends, allies, mentors, and supporters grows through a combination of your existing popularity (your current social proof) and your similarity to new potential friends. Some of them might even be women who find you attractive.

Pick Your Roommates Carefully: Choose good housemates, roommates, and neighbors. If you can't afford your own place and live in a shared apartment or house, make sure you get housemates who add rather than subtract from your social proof. Having roommates that you get along with adds greatly to your life.

This isn't just a social proof issue either; from a practical perspective the last thing you want to do after a long day at school or work is come home to a house that feels like the Korean demilitarized zone. What ends up happening is you stay in your room, they stay in theirs, no one sees anybody, and you start isolating yourself.

Limit Activities That Isolate You: In modern life, a lot of young guys end up isolating themselves because they get too focused on educational credentialism (studying all the time), migratory careerism (moving all the time for work), individualistic consumerism (shopping all the time), and passive entertainment media (watching TV all the time). This turns them into lonely islands who don't know their neighbors and don't engage with local communities. Every hour you spend alone is an hour that you're failing to build your social skills, your social network, and your social proof.

If you spend all your spare time in World of Warcraft slaying monsters and messaging with your raid team, you'll feed your brain plenty of cues that you're dominant and popular, but you won't build any social skills that you can show to women—much less that they care about. Of course, gaming is fun. *It's specifically designed to provide as much addictive fun as you can possibly have through a computer!* But if you also care about getting laid, limit gaming to a few hours a week.

Use Social Media Intelligently: Having a lot of Facebook friends or Twitter followers gives social proof that you're interesting and popular, and a moderate amount of social media use can make you happier. College students attribute the highest social attractiveness and physical attractiveness to people who have about three hundred friends and attribute the highest extroversion if you have about five hundred; but above that, you look desperate, and your social status drops.

So it's worth building a Facebook profile that showcases your life story, interests, background, and enthusiasms. But once you connect with your real friends and family, don't become addicted to FB. It's a tool to facilitate your life, not what your life is about.

DISPLAY YOUR SOCIAL PROOF

OK, OK, you get it already. Status, popularity, and prestige are important. The question now is, *How do you reliably display those things?*

The answer is, you already do. *You display your social proof with everything you do in public, in any social setting.*

Eating lunch at a table full of people in the school cafeteria? Going out to the bar for happy hour with coworkers? Hanging out after class? Those are all opportunities to display your positive social traits. Where you sit, whether you're alone, who you sit with, how much you talk with them—everything testifies to your social proof, for better or worse, to every woman who's watching and to every woman they gossip with.

We won't flood you with an exhaustive list of every possible social-proof scenario; we'll focus on the most basic, reliable, effective ways to display social proof in ordinary life, in ways that boost your attractiveness to most women.

Be Outgoing

Women are attracted to extroversion because it predicts all sorts of positive traits—being friendly, talkative, assertive, funny, cooperative, and professionally successful. Extroversion is also one of the easiest traits for women to judge accurately: from face-to-face interaction, short emails, text samples from blogs, and even photos (after just .05 seconds of exposure).

But being outgoing doesn't mean you have to be the life of the party, swinging from chandeliers, dive-bombing keg stands, and floating from group to group like a social butterfly. Any one of those things can be a struggle for the introverts among you; and that's perfectly fine, because more often than not all they show is that you're a hyperactive maniac who can't hold a conversation.

At the other extreme, the loner in the corner, making love to his drink while staring furtively at women over the rim of the Solo cup, has "Stranger Danger" written all over him. Best to find a middle ground.

The good news is that even if you're not particularly extroverted, you can fake it. All that being outgoing really requires from a mating perspective is some basic human engagement: a warm smile, inviting eye contact, strong open posture, acknowledging her with words like "hello" and "how are you?" instead of the guy head nod or short bus wave. A woman wants to know that you are safe, accepted, and effective in your social environment.

Have Friends

You don't need a lot of them; in fact three great longtime friends are better than three hundred casual acquaintances. But you need to have them, and you need to spend time with them out in the world where women can see you (and you can meet the women), because having friends is worthless as social proof unless you're with them and you talk about them.

Being friends on 4chan and Xbox is great for entertainment value and even for your own version of male bonding, but it is completely ineffective in the mating game. If you want to display social fitness, prove that you're social by spending time in public with people who like you, and do cool things with them that are worth talking about later on dates: going on trips, playing sports, fixing and building things, blowing shit up (OK, maybe not that); you get the idea.

Hang Out with Women

Novelist Milan Kundera wrote, *"One of life's great secrets: women don't look for handsome men, they look for men with beautiful women."* This kind of "mate choice copying" is a big part of social proof in the mating game. It is also a good reason why you shouldn't fear being "friend-zoned" by women. Hanging out in public with an interesting female friend automatically makes you more attractive to every other woman. The easiest way to get more comfortable talking with women you *want* to sleep with is to spend a lot of time talking with female friends you *don't* want to sleep with.

Make Your Friends Part of Your Dating Life

Too many guys build a stupid firewall between their dating lives and their social lives. They worry that a woman might not like their friends and their friends might not like the woman they're seeing, so they keep them separate way too long.

That's a mistake, because to a woman, life is more social than physical. Your life isn't just your apartment; it's your social circle and your family. If you invite a woman into your bed but exclude her from your social network—your real, actual life that she knows matters to you—then she will assume you are not serious about her (i.e., you're trying to seduce and abandon her) or that you're ashamed of her (i.e., you're trying to seduce and abandon her without anyone knowing).

If you have quality friends who actually like you, they can carry a huge amount of the courtship burden on your behalf; you just have to put them in the same room as your date. She will ask them about you, and they will answer, probably in more positive terms than you realize. Although good male friends constantly bust each other's balls as a way to create camaraderie and protect against alpha-male arrogance within the group, they don't do it when you're not there (that's called shit-talking), and they definitely don't do it with women you like (that's called cock-blocking). They will paint a glowing picture of you and praise you in ways that you couldn't praise yourself without sounding like an egomaniac. And the positive traits that a woman perceives in your friends will rub off on you through a social halo effect.

We've emphasized that you tend to become the average of the five people you spend the most time with. Women intuitively understand this. So, if your five friends are smart, you'll seem smarter. If they're funny, you'll seem funnier. The sooner you introduce her to some of your friends, and the cooler your friends seem, the more she will see your virtues through their eyes.

Host Parties and Organize Events

Big social proof comes from arranging and hosting social events—parties, conferences, band practice, anything where groups of people come to your home territory and you show your generosity and leadership. These don't have to be big to-dos; even small gatherings that you organize are strong signals because they imply that you have enough popularity and prestige to incentivize a group to accept your invitation over all the other things they could do instead—like sleep, or masturbate, or masturbate and then go to sleep.

Guys with no friends don't host parties. Guys whom nobody respects don't organize events that are well attended. Pulling together a study group that is regularly attended, hosting an annual Halloween party, or acting as captain of your intramural team all display a degree of status and effectiveness that is attractive to women.

Go on Group Dates

The traditional American date—taking a woman out, one-on-one—is a great way for two people to get to know each other. You have a large, dedicated chunk of time to display your courtship ability, allowing direct verbal and non-verbal signaling and assessment. It's like a pair of chimps going off into the forest by themselves for private canoodling. And it's much easier for introverts, guys without a lot of friends, and guys who are really strong on verbal courtship.

But in the last several years, group dates (today's version of prehistoric young folks socializing around the campfire) have gotten much more popular, and rightfully so, because they are more natural and productive in many ways. They allow a woman to see how you thrive in a mixed-sex clannish group—how much your male friends respect you, how good you are at coordinating and communicating with them, and whether other females are interested in you.

Group dates with your friends get you the mating benefits of being a popular, prestigious part of a successful social group; the opportunity to split off like a couple of safari-loving chimps will arise at some point, and hopefully your "forest" isn't a bar bathroom.

Play Team Sports and Join Clubs

Team sports are just a more organized version of group dates where the game happens to be something other than mating—at least explicitly. If you're on any kind of team or in any kind of sports clubs (skiing, hiking, etc.), your participation in those groups provides women with powerful social proof of your extroversion, popularity, prestige, and leadership.

It doesn't matter if they're in the stands watching or on the field playing with you. High school women fall for the varsity quarterback because he gives the most conspicuous social proof of his leadership ability, under brutally competitive conditions, in a highly valued activity.

Adopt a Pet

The more sociable pets, such as dogs, can give unconditional love, attention, and respect to their masters. So, you can get some free social proof just by having a dog that loves you.

DO NOT get a dog just as a social proof accessory; dogs are intelligent, sensitive creatures that require care and attention. But if you're on the fence about whether to get a dog, it's worth knowing that the time and attention that you invest in caring for a dog are *exactly what make a dog's love a strong form of social proof in a woman's eyes.* A socially careless and unreliable man can't earn a dog's love and respect, so an adoring Border Collie says to any woman in the dog park, "This guy's a keeper."

Takeaways

- Social proof is not superficial. Women can get valuable intelligence about what kind of guy you are by seeing how other people interact with you. If you add value to their lives, you'll have probably accumulated some fame, popularity, dominance, status, influence, and/or prestige. Each is a reliable signal that you could probably add value to a woman's life too. Social proof also reflects many important heritable traits, good partner traits, and good dad traits.
- Don't worry about the unattainable, irrelevant, or repulsive forms of social proof like fame, wealth, or class. They are not the most efficient ways to attract women. Don't assume that only dominant alpha males are attractive to women—dominance is a sexual spice for private play, not the main ingredient in your public social proof.
- You might think you have the best individual traits in the world, but if you've never leveraged them into a good set of friends and a good social reputation, a woman can't trust that they're actually effective in real life, which means real *social* life.
- To display social proof more effectively, practice being warm and outgoing, cultivate friendships with both sexes, host social events, integrate friends into your dating life, join sports teams and clubs, and take care of a pet.
- To improve your social proofs over the next few weeks and months, put more effort into your social interactions, project confidence, share meals, join groups and classes that teach social skills, take social jobs, do volunteer work, use your friends to meet new friends, find better housemates, reduce socially isolating activities, and use social media intelligently.

CHAPTER 12: HOW RICH DO YOU NEED TO BE?

(MATERIAL PROOF)

I don't care too much for money / money can't buy me love.
— The Beatles

Now I ain't saying she's a gold digger,
But she ain't messin' with no broke niggas.

— Kanye West

One of the most pervasive assumptions in America is that women care about men only for their money. If you're being polite and condescending, you call them "superficial" or "materialistic." If you're bitter, you call them "money-hungry gold diggers." Mainly it's men from older generations who spew this stuff, but younger men can get swept up in female greed shaming too, especially when they have lost out in the competition for women against other guys who seemed to have fancier clothes, cooler cars, bigger salaries, and nicer apartments.

They tell themselves this kind of story:

> *I'm really a good guy; it's just that these gold diggers care only about fancy cars, expensive restaurants, and flashy jewelry. It's total bullshit. Money can't buy you love, man. Dating should be about who I am on the inside!*

This is wrong. But only half wrong.

Money is not *all* that women care about, but women *do* care about money for very good reasons. It would be stupid and naive to say that money isn't sexually attractive or that poverty isn't sexually repulsive. Most young women work hard and don't have enough money; why would they choose a boyfriend who makes their financial worries even worse? "Hey, honey, can you spare some change?" is not a good pickup line.

However, how much money you have is just one check mark down the list of attractive qualities. It does not have a dollar-for-dollar relationship with your mate value. In fact, when women rank the attractive male qualities, wealth rarely comes higher than seventh or eighth, because what women are really looking for in a longer-term mate is a guy who can help support a family and provide a decent life. You don't have to be rich to do that; you just can't be lazy about earning or reckless about spending.

Here's the kicker, the thing about wealth you must get: *women care less about money itself than about what it represents about the guy who made it.*

Financial success is a powerful indicator of the physical health, mental health, and willpower required for hard, sustained work; the intelligence, openness, and creativity required for a professional career or entrepreneurial success; and the right balance of agreeableness and assertiveness required to get along with coworkers and customers without being exploited.

That's why most good women don't actually care about a BMW as a car, or a managerial position as a title, or a condo on an upper floor as a living space. They care about them as *signals* of your underlying traits. Thus, your possessions are not "superficial" status symbols—they are *material proof* that you have the positive traits needed to care for a woman, raise kids, and recover from losses.

If you still don't think money is mostly about trait signaling, put yourself in a woman's shoes for a second and play a little game of "Who'd You Rather?" Imagine two guys hitting on you. One is worth $75 million because he happened to win the Powerball jackpot when he was an unemployed school bus driver. The other is worth $7.5 million because he built his own company from the ground up and now has ten employees and thousands of customers. Who would you rather go home, out, to the altar with?

Multiple studies show that women choose the entrepreneur, because his traits, like intelligence and hard work, were directly responsible for his success, whereas the lottery winner just had dumb luck.

The good news is that once you earn above a certain baseline amount (around $50,000 per year in most parts of America) and you don't squander it, you probably have enough resources that women feel assured you won't be a financial burden to them if you move in together.

Sure, being rich makes that easy, but as you'll see by the end of this chapter, being rich is not a necessary part of showing material proof. In fact, being rich on paper without translating it into an attractive, exciting life can be a turnoff—nobody's fucking Scrooge McDuck. The gold has to glitter in a way women can enjoy. This is the takeaway for you:

Almost all women would rather have an interesting, fun, kind husband with a solid middle-class income than a dull, disconnected, workaholic millionaire.

Unfortunately, a lot of guys (and some women) still think that money is central to attraction. They think they have to make a ton of it so they can wear the nicest clothes, get an expensive watch, buy a fancy sports car, and live in a huge house. Then the women will just magically appear, like monarch butterflies to milkweed, flies to honey, rappers to Scarface posters.

There is a reason people believe this, and it's not the biology of mating; it's the psychology of consumers. Modern marketing and advertising work by making both sexes feel sexually inadequate and then offering specific goods or services that promise to make them more attractive. It's called "conspicuous consumption," and men do it mostly to attract women, whereas women do it mostly to signal their status to other women. Consumerist culture has taught you that your mate value, your identity as a person, your sexual attractiveness, and your social popularity all depend on the things you buy.

This marketing myth is, of course, absolutely, empirically untrue. You've read about dozens of traits and proofs in this book that are attractive despite being free or cheap. Most of them depend a lot more on your intelligence, knowledge, willpower, and habits than on your credit limit. Don't fall into the mind trap of materialism—the deluded belief that acquiring material objects will lead directly to mating success and happiness. A Bentley Mulsanne won't fill the hole in your soul, no matter how hard you try to cram it in there.

When you finally realize the Mulsanne won't heal all your wounds and seduce all your crushes, you'll feel bitter, disappointed, and exploited. *Wait a minute, owning the Mulsanne helped Young Jeezy attract all his bitches and hos; why didn't it help me?* Maybe because you also didn't win three Grammy Awards. You ever think about that, Captain Karaoke?

This is not to say that wealth doesn't predict happiness—it does—but only indirectly, mostly through the social and sexual signaling benefits of attracting better friends and mates. In fact, materialism per se makes you less happy, nastier, and more socially isolated. Materialism isn't really about matter anyway; it's about signaling your consumer identity and traits. The materialist model of mating success just does not work.

Here's an example:

When Geoff was a grad student at Stanford, he lived in a shared house in Palo Alto. The young guy in the next bedroom was a talented integrated-chip designer. He made the equivalent of about $300,000 per year, but he paid only about $300 per month as his share of the rent. He slept on the shittiest futon you can imagine, had no clothes beyond what he bought at the Salvation Army, and drove an ancient, rusty Toyota Corolla. But he already had half a million dollars in the bank. His life goal was, "I'm going to make a million dollars, retire to Tahiti by age thirty-two, and *then* have a life."

Do you think he was happy? Nope. And you know why? Because he never had a girlfriend, and it frustrated him beyond belief. Well, no shit, Mr. Microchip! No self-respecting woman would ever want to be with a guy like that, who not only lived like a recluse but brought nothing to the table except money. What is she going to say to her family or her friends? "Hey, everyone, meet my boyfriend, the walking ATM."

No sensible woman wants that kind of life. He had *wealth,* but he didn't have *material proof of attractive traits.* Big difference.

WHY WOMEN CARE ABOUT MATERIAL PROOF

There is a very simple evolutionary explanation for why women don't care about money as much as they care about what it represents: our prehistoric ancestors didn't have money until a few thousand years ago. Women (and men) have not evolved to care about random numbers on a screen that show a bank balance or stacks of rectangular paper with numbers and pictures of old dudes with giant foreheads on them.

What they evolved to care about is *resources* (i.e., the stuff you buy with money). Resources are the prehistoric equivalent of money. So what women are really evaluating when it comes to material proof are (1) the practical resources they need to survive, reproduce, and support their kids; and (2) the mating signals and proofs of all the other traits we've talked about that make you a good potential partner and father.

While money is a relatively recent invention, inherited wealth in other forms has been important for a much longer time, and women are hardwired to select for it. Wealth could take the form of material resources (land, livestock, homes, and tools), "embodied wealth" (the biological resources like food and protection that kids require to grow strong bodies and bright minds), and "social capital" (relationships, status, prestige, and mentors) in hunter-gatherer, pastoral, and agricultural societies. Women know that richer dads give their kids an advantage, and they choose mates accordingly.

Interestingly, socioeconomic success is genetically heritable (mostly through genes for intelligence and conscientiousness), and economic behavior is a biological trait with many aspects that, recent studies have shown, are also surprisingly heritable: including risk taking, career choices, self-employment, economic policy attitudes, decision-making rationality, investment biases, and investor asset allocations.

Dumb, reckless people make dumb, reckless choices with their money. Smart, conscientious people make smart, conscientious choices, and women know this.

Money also tends to amplify the heritability of other traits. For example, wealth allows parents to provide more diverse opportunities for kids, which amplifies the heritability of intelligence. The more prosperity a couple has, the easier it is for their kids to explore the full range of their genetic potential, cultivating their strengths and minimizing their weaknesses.

Money acquired through *merit* (talent and hard work) doesn't just amplify the heritability of other traits; it objectively reveals them. If you achieve economic success through starting and building your own company (entrepreneur) or through following a professional, credential-based career (doctor, lawyer, professor), a woman can be pretty confident that you are well above average on most of the traits that matter to her: physical health (to work long hours), mental health (to endure stress), intelligence (to make good decisions), willpower (to work hard), assertiveness (to be a tough bargainer), and social skills (to work effectively with employees, peers, managers, investors, and clients).

How you spend your money matters too, since economic behavior is stable over time. This is perhaps the most important point since most men, statistically speaking, will never be rich and will have to be smart about money for most of their lives. A woman cares about your money management patterns now because they predict how you'll earn, spend, and save in the future. This is crucial to her because in long-term relationships, couples make most economic decisions jointly: their net wealth is yoked together, and they prosper together or fall into bankruptcy together.

IMPROVE YOUR MATERIAL PROOF

This book is about attracting women, not making money. There are thousands of other books on how to find jobs, build careers, earn more, balance budgets, and manage investments. We won't try to distill the world's largest genre of self-improvement advice into one all-purpose get-rich scheme. That would be stupid, and you would fail.

Instead, we'll recommend some of our favorite books and sources in the references. Here, we'll just highlight a few issues in building your wealth.

First, think about money not as an end in itself but as a means for self-improvement and mating success. In modern life, material proof *depends on* money, but the money has to be well spent in ways that bring value to women, not just ways that bring profit to marketers. "Get Rich" is NOT a good self-improvement strategy, much less a good mating strategy. *What you do with your money is the key to material proof.*

Your goal should not be to make as much as possible but to make enough to be comfortable and secure—and then to invest in mating tactics that take more skill and creativity than money so money itself becomes less relevant to your mate value. Focusing on making enough to live comfortably and date frequently frees you up to spend a lot of time on other things that you (and women) value, like becoming a more attractive and interesting guy.

DISPLAY YOUR MATERIAL PROOF

Materialism has been an enemy of good guys for a long time. It has derailed millions of potentially great relationships between young men and women who weren't able to honestly evaluate each other because of the blinding glare of bling in their eyes.

What it has prevented you from seeing is that the most attractive way to display material proof in America is NOT through the usual kind of materialism (buying expensive watches or fancy cars) but through indirect, nonobvious methods of turning your income into concrete traits, proofs, relationships, and experiences that women value.

That is the real value of money and wealth in the mating game. Money helps you improve your life and construct your own "mating niche"—your own physical, biological, and social environment that makes it easier to survive, mate, and parent. Most important, money lets you play by your own rules. Thus, money can attract a wide variety of discerning women in much deeper ways that aren't really about the *amount* of money you have or are spending.

Remember what we told you earlier? *Almost all women would rather have an interesting, fun, kind husband with a solid middle-class income than a dull, disconnected, workaholic millionaire.*

The question for you should be, How can you use the money you have to improve almost every aspect of yourself and your lifestyle and, in turn, radically improve your mating opportunities? When it comes to effectively displaying material proof, it's really about asking yourself how you are using your money.

1. **Are you in shape?** If you are rich in terms of money, but you're super skinny and wasting away, like a dumpster-diving freegan, you're giving unconscious cues to women that you are literally poor in biological terms. And that is very unattractive.

    This is one of the problems that tech millionaires—like Mr. Microchip—in Silicon Valley struggle with most. They spent their twenties sitting in the dark, staring into computer monitors, mainlining Mountain Dew and Doritos until they couldn't see straight. The result was a seven- or eight-figure bank balance and a body that looks like someone hung chicken skin and bacon over a bunch of coat hangers. And they wonder why beautiful, successful women in San Francisco aren't racing to jump into bed with them.

    Being in shape is not only attractive itself (as we discussed in the physical health chapter); it shows fitness in most of the other traits (willpower, etc.) as well. If you have or make decent money, use it to buy good food, do good exercises (like CrossFit), and buy a good mattress that helps you sleep better. That will do a lot of the heavy lifting of material proof for you.

2. **How strong is your tribe?** As we saw in the last chapter, your social proof is important to women—usually more important than your material proof. Who would be there to support you if the chips were down and you needed help? Anyone? No one? Being rich, but also being a reclusive loner or a social outcast, raises a red flag of unattraction to women.

    Fortunately, there are lots of ways to convert money into relationships. Throw some parties. Travel to visit old friends. Take new friends on fun trips. Attend charity galas.

    Why do you think rich people have such big houses? Part of it is signaling, but the other part is social. Most of the square footage isn't in the bedrooms; it's in the reception areas, kitchens, dining rooms, and pools where the parties happen, the social networks expand, and the women can see what popular and prestigious hosts they are.

3. **Do you live reasonably given your income?** If you are rich but you live and date superfrugally like Mr. Microchip, that won't be attractive to women because it won't improve their lives in any way.

However, if you make average money but you live like a sultan, that might be fun at first for a woman, but she'll worry too much about your mounting debt and/or your narcissism to get involved in any longer-term relationship.

The key is cost-effective courtship: figure out what you can realistically spend on dating, and get the most fun, humor, and novelty you can out of that dating budget. Protip: Spend your money on experiences, not possessions, and your attraction to women will go through the roof.

4. **Do you get more from your work than just money?** As we've seen again and again, your career isn't just a machine for turning your time into income. It's also a way to build traits and proofs, grow relationships and skills, achieve status and prestige, have experiences that make for funny stories, and meet women.

    Be wary of retail jobs that require you to adopt a sort of insincere, fake-nice persona to interact with customers, where managers are evaluating your "attitude" and "cheerfulness," not just your work performance. Those jobs won't help you learn to connect your real personality to real social skills.

    Avoid runaway workaholism and the cult of speed; slow down and give yourself enough leisure time to build mating skills, to manage your online dating, and to enjoy life and women. Work is a means to an end, not an end unto itself. If you let it define you instead of build you, it will swallow up your time, your identity, and your mating prospects.

5. **Do you display your creativity more than your money on dates?** Instead of spending tons of money on predictable dates, do cheaper things or make cheaper gifts that are really fun, exciting, or new. Instead of spending four hours' wages on dinner at the one expensive restaurant in town that you've heard of, spend half an hour on Yelp finding a really great little ethnic restaurant, and then spend only two hours' wages there.

    Show resourcefulness, not just resources. Instead of buying all the equipment you'd need for one sport, rent the equipment you'd need for ten dates doing different sports.

    Also, women love guys who make things. We have instincts for conspicuously wasteful consumption, but we also have instincts for conspicuously precise and creative craftsmanship. A good alternative to just buying courtship gifts (dinners, roses, cards) is to display your attractive traits by *making things yourself.* Make dinner instead of reservations; hike in the hills instead of flying to the mountains; write your own Valentine's Day poem instead of buying some trite Hallmark card.

You can also collect things that are interesting to women, that are fascinating to you, and that let you demonstrate knowledge, taste, and other traits. Collecting is a major way we display personal traits in consumer society: from art to artifacts, from books to music to cars, and everything in between.

6. **Do you have more possessions or more experiences in your life?**
    We mentioned this earlier, but it's so important it has its own section.

    The best way to be happy and attractive is to spend your money on new experiences, not new things. This is one of the most surprising results from the last two decades of happiness research.

    Most shiny new things that American guys buy just end up lost on a shelf, whereas fun new experiences, especially those shared with other people, can build permanent skills, relationships, and memories. Educational experiences can be especially good values. You can also buy shared social experiences with friends, like group snowboarding trips or Vegas road trips, that convert cash into social proof.

    The benefits of experiences aren't limited just to your own edification or your friendships. They're incredibly valuable in your romantic life as well. After all, what is a date but an experience with a person you want to see naked? The quality of shared experiences is a big predictor of happiness and cooperation in relationships. Obviously, the more money you can throw at a good experience, the higher quality it can become. But you don't have to do that if the money isn't there; just use what you do have to be selective about the experiences you share and to make them as great as you can.

    If you have to pick between being rich or being really fun and attractive to hang out with, always pick fun and attractive, because that will get the attention of 90 percent more women, and they'll be higher quality every time.

    That is, if you have to pick. You don't have to pick though. You can do both. And the way to do it is to effectively display your material proof in ways that signal not your bank balance but your underlying traits. If you can be a really smart, kind, in-shape guy with a lot of friends, who *happens* to have a lot of money, that is the best of both worlds. Then your mate value is through the roof, and you will have your pick of high-quality women who have the same mating goals as you.

Takeaways

- Women care about money, but not for the reasons you think. Your net worth isn't instinctively attractive in its own right—money was invented too recently for evolution to give women "gold-digging" instincts.
- Instead, your material proof reassures women that you won't drag them down into bankruptcy and starvation. It shows good gene, good partner, and good dad traits. It helps reveal important qualities like intelligence and willpower that contribute to your work success. Especially in longer-term mating, women value good providers, but good means good enough, not mega-rich.
- Money also empowers you to cultivate all your traits and other important proofs—social, aesthetic, and romantic. It's a shortcut for self-improvement and lifestyle improvement, and if you use it wisely, no matter how much or how little of it you have, it can open the door to all sorts of attractiveness-enhancing opportunities. It's almost always better to invest your spare dollars in improving your other core traits and proofs than in direct displays of material proof like buying prestige goods or luxury services.
- Money lets you take women on fun, creative dates and lets you make them fun, creative gifts. Spending wisely, more on experiences than things, builds a storehouse of amazing stories, diverse friends, and unusual skills. Money is worthless as an end in itself, but it can be a useful way to improve your mating life if you're smart about what it can buy (better traits and lifestyle that can attract a good woman) and what it can't buy (a good woman's love).

CHAPTER 13: STYLIN' AND PROFILIN'

(AESTHETIC PROOF)

Style is a simple way of saying complicated things.
—Jean Cocteau

A lot of men—especially in the United States—dismiss personal style and taste as the exclusive domain of the metrosexual, the feminine, and the gay. *Real men don't care about clothes, decor, or beauty,* they'll tell themselves between heated discussions about their fantasy football lineups. *That stuff is for chicks and guys who like dicks!*

There's no other way to put it: *men who think this way are penis pilots destined for failure and loneliness.*

For many of you younger guys, it's not your fault. Notions of masculinity have been tossed around like a ping-pong ball in a hurricane for the last fifty years. How can we expect you to have any idea what to do or how to do it when sexual and social mores keep changing and you get so many mixed messages from the media?

So let's not talk about the last fifty years of social development; let's talk about the last fifty thousand generations of sexual selection. Across thousands of animal species, over the millennia, females have been using the male beauty trait—otherwise known as sexual ornament—as the main signal of genetic quality in selecting their mates. Awesome male style isn't just a new gay thing; it's a *very* ancient straight thing.

In fact, Charles Darwin realized that female choice for beauty and style explains why the males of so many species evolved amazing, intricate physical traits. It's the male peacock who has all the pretty feathers, for instance. The male cardinal is the bright red one. The male lion has the giant, lush mane. In nature, it's the men who usually dress up, not the women.

These conspicuous displays evolved to signal to female eyes and brains that the male who possessed them was so fit, strong, and capable that he could easily afford to spend his energy lugging around all this risky, unnecessary bullshit just to get their attention. Sexual ornaments like iridescent feathers and sexy manes don't help the male's survival, but they do something much more important: they help him attract mates and reproduce.

This principle of attracting mates through conspicuous beauty and style extends into human courtship and mating in every culture. Self-ornamentation with hairstyles, accessories, and special clothing, for instance, is universal across both sexes in all hunter-gatherer tribal peoples and modern cultures and has deep evolutionary roots. Archaeologists found that humans have been ornamenting themselves with red ocher pigments and shell-bead necklaces for at least 90,000 years. Even Neanderthals were ornamenting themselves with cut, notched, polished talons from white-tailed eagles 130,000 years ago. There is even some evidence that our ancestors were selecting mates for their artistic skill in making stone tools since long before we were humans—over 1.5 million years ago.

Women pay a lot more attention than you realize to your stylish sexual ornaments, your artistic and musical skills, your appreciation of beauty, and the whole aesthetic dimension of your life: your grooming, scent, clothes, car, music, furnishings, apartment, Instagram feed, online dating profile, and everything else. All these things are reliable signals to women of who you are and how well you've cultivated your other traits—especially your mental health, intelligence, willpower, and empathy. If you neglect all these aesthetic signals just because you think they're metrosexual, feminine, or gay, you might as well shoot your own dick off; it's not like you're going to need it.

Because women instinctively think about your whole appearance, lifestyle, and set of possessions as a work of art, they want everything in your life (body, clothes, car, home) to be stylish, beautiful, creative, clean, and well maintained. They want evidence of *taste and thoughtfulness* in what you've chosen to surround yourself with.

Guys who are good at aesthetic proof understand this and use good taste to guide every decision in their lives: which neighborhood to live in, which restaurant to book for a dinner date, which wine to order, which bedroom candles to buy, which condom to wear. These may seem to be unrelated decisions, but they all add up to form your aesthetic proof.

If you're still young or a broke-dick college guy who lacks the experience and the means, don't worry. Developing aesthetic proof isn't just about buying the right stuff that somebody else has designed; it's also about what you can do, make, and create. Male creativity and artistic talent are major targets of sexual selection, because they demonstrate so much about how your mind works. Females in many species, for example, choose male mates for their ability to produce pleasing sounds—as in the bird song, whale song, gibbon song, and human music. Instrumental music is at least thirty-five thousand years old—based on the ages of some ancient bone and ivory flutes discovered in Germany—so women could have been selecting men partly for their musical talent for more than one thousand generations. Your creative activities and achievements in the visual arts, performing arts, literary arts, and science even predict your short-term mating success. Successful male artists have both more sexual partners *and* longer-term sexual relationships.

That should tell you all you need to know really: whether you just want to get laid or get married, having some demonstrable personal style, creative abilities, and aesthetic appreciation puts you way ahead of all those bros who think of "the arts" as mysterious, pretentious fields that only women and gay men appreciate.

Plainly put: A high level of aesthetic proof doesn't make you a pussy; it drowns you in it.

WHY WOMEN CARE ABOUT AESTHETIC PROOF

Women interpret aesthetic taste, as they do material proof, as a sign of good underlying traits, like intelligence, openness, worldliness, confidence, and social savvy.

If you wear Crocs on a first date and she excuses herself to the bathroom and never comes back, that is her aesthetic judgment ("Gross!") about one aspect of your aesthetic proof (shoes) that instantly leads her to make inferences about your deeper traits, like mental health ("What kind of crazy person wears plastic gardening shoes on a date?"), intelligence ("Who doesn't know that Crocs are awful?"), and willpower ("Does he just not give a shit about this date?").

And it turns out that women are right to select for aesthetic attractiveness. Evolutionary psychologists have found that beauty does often predict deeper traits that make for better partners. This halo effect also applies to products for similar reasons: good aesthetic design predicts consumers' ratings of product usability and practicality. This aesthetic dimension of product design isn't just hot air; it's the reason that Apple is the most valuable company in HISTORY.

The logic of aesthetic-based selection makes even more sense when you consider that physical beauty signals good genes. Across thousands of animal species, females use male sexual ornaments as indicators of genetic quality. Darwin realized that this is the reason that animals evolve so many amazing, diverse ways to flaunt their beauty. Recent studies show that Darwin was right: sexual selection has been central in the evolution of impressive visual displays among male peacocks, bowerbirds, primate faces, and primate sexual swellings and in the evolution of impressive musical displays among male songbirds. Aesthetic sexual selection has also shaped male genitalia, from those of insects to the human penis, through females favoring copulation with males that best stimulated them. Selection for beauty has roots much deeper than human culture, and it's a powerful way for females to get good genes for their offspring.

Furthermore, a dad with good aesthetic skills also makes a great mentor and playmate to kids of all ages. A man who's interested in the arts is a dad who'll have fun taking his kids to concerts, plays, museums, galleries, Hobby Lobby, and Home Depot. Women instinctively anticipate that kids will feel happier and safer in an aesthetically appealing home, so they'll favor men who seem likely to offer that. They know that kids will be more entertained by a dad who can draw, paint, sing, play instruments, and make things. Kids can also learn those skills from their fathers and increase their own popularity and mate value.

IMPROVE YOUR AESTHETIC PROOF

There are lots of ways to improve your aesthetic proof. The easier ways that you can tackle right now are in the "Display Aesthetic Proof" section, because for most of you guys, just doing them will be an improvement. Here we are going to talk about adding new skills and expertise over time to build a stronger foundation of aesthetic proof. These take longer and usually require some reading or training, but *so few guys bother doing them that you can get a big mating advantage from just a little effort.*

1. **Learn to dance:** Dance is ancient and universal across cultures, has its own distinctive aesthetic psychology, and is incredibly important to women. Yet a vast majority of men hate to dance and have never taken the time to be anything but horrible at it.

You either do the middle school Frankenstein, or you look like one of those inflatable dancing men outside car dealerships along the highway. There's really no excuse for not learning how to move your body in a way that does not look like you just climbed out of a glacial crevasse or had a seizure. If Napoleon Dynamite can do it, you can too. From how men dance, women can accurately judge their physical strength, their conscientiousness and agreeableness, and their tendencies toward sensation seeking and boredom.

These are the most useful forms of dance to learn for modern mating: basics (nightclub two-step, country two-step, hustle), East Coast Swing (ECS/Lindy hop), West Coast Swing (WCS), ballroom (waltz, foxtrot, quickstep), electronic dance (EDM/house dance), hip-hop dance, and Latin (merengue, rumba/mambo, cha-cha, tango, salsa). Don't worry about learning all of these; just pick a couple that use the music you like that's played in the kinds of places that attract the women you prefer. Dance classes almost always have a low male-to-female ratio, so they're also a great place to meet women.

2. **Learn to make music:** Musicians attract groupies for a reason: their skills make women swoon, and you don't have to be a rock god to reap the rewards. Music composition and production require good general intelligence and depend on diverse brain areas and diligent practice. Singing well is useful for serenading women, doing karaoke, building confidence, and improving your speaking voice, so take some voice lessons. Even better, learn how to play one of the most commonly available musical instruments: guitar, drums, or keyboards. And free computer programs like Audacity offer powerful ways to create your own music without needing instrumental skills at all.

Make no mistake about it: guys are into music because it works. Women like it.

3. **Learn to make stuff:** Craftsmanship—like working leather, machining metal, or making furniture—is a huge turn-on to women, not so much for what it is as for what it represents.

No woman is losing her composure over your leather punch or a miter saw. But the fact that you can harness the power of potentially lethal tools to create something beautiful and functional where before there were only hunks of wood and steel is incredibly attractive. And by learning to think like a craftsman, you'll understand better how everything is designed, put together, and works. So, your crafts skills will attract women *and* protect you from buying crappy consumer products that break easily and wear out quickly.

4. **Learn to draw:** Women love guys who can draw them accurately and observantly (as when Rose, the high-class heiress in *Titanic,* poses nude for Jack, the Irishman in steerage). Traditional artistic skills require a lot of intelligence, conscientiousness, practice, and manual dexterity, whether you're doing representational art (e.g., drawing a portrait of a woman) or ornamental art (e.g., carving a complex pattern into a wooden table).

    The key thing here is to *cultivate actual skill* rather than indulge in modernist expressionism or abstract art. The poet John Ciardi pointed out, "Modern art is what happens when painters stop looking at women and persuade themselves they have a better idea."

5. **Learn to be a better storyteller:** Storytelling is an ancient and sexy art. You don't need to write novels to tell stories that attract women. Tucker's career so far has been based on his ability to tell funny stories about his life to women and to tell funny stories about women to men.

    The best way to start getting better at storytelling is to listen to how stand-up comedians and great politicians tell stories. Read classic short stories. Pay attention to how your friends tell stories well or badly. Practice telling your best stories—especially the short version of your life story—again and again, refining the plot, pacing, and word choice based on people's reactions.

    Beyond that, there are dozens of books and an entire field of study on the mechanics of story, so we're not going to dive into all that minutiae. What you need to understand about telling a story is that often the "what" is the least important part. People who are bad at storytelling often get stuck in this mode of reporting facts one after the other: "And then…and then…and then…" without paying any attention to the context that gives those facts relevance. Your audience—especially women, who are incredibly deductive listeners—cares less about *what* happened than why it happened, when it happened, how it happened, to whom it happened and, most important of all, *how you feel about it.* Put all that detail into a story with a beginning, a middle, and an end, and you're on your way to not boring the shit out of everybody with the otherwise irrelevant details of your life!

DISPLAY AESTHETIC PROOF

We are going to get very specific in this section, because you might think you know what we're talking about, but you'll probably go out and fuck it all up. We're not going to let that happen—partly for your sake and partly so you don't blame us for failing to get a woman's number when you unironically show up at a sorority function in pleated khakis and a Bill Cosby sweater.

Of course, different women and different subcultures have different tastes. Goth women like black leather; hipster women like brown leather; kinky women like red leather. Laying down your own electronic music dance tracks in FL Studio software will impress more women in San Francisco than in San Antonio, and vice versa for playing Conway Twitty songs on the banjo.

We are not going to tell you that there is just one way to dress, or one car you must drive, or a specific shaving cream you must use. That's all bullshit.

The point is not which specific product you use but whether you are *tasteful and thoughtful* about what you've chosen and whether you display it with some flair and confidence. Instead of sweating *what* to buy or use, think instead about your mating market, your mating goals, and your mate preferences—what kind of style would the kind of girlfriend you'd like to attract want to see you display? Try things; if they don't work, try different things. Developing your own best personal style takes time, experimentation, and feedback.

That being said, there are some fundamentals you need to understand about grooming, clothing, and possessions that apply across most styles and mating markets:

1. Grooming

Grooming has deep biological roots; it's not just a cultural invention. All animals clean themselves—especially primates. The stereotype of the disheveled, dirty caveman is bullshit.

Unfortunately, a lot of guys have the wrong idea about good grooming: they think, like everything else aesthetically related, that it's superficial, feminine, or gay. This is wrong biologically—males of every species groom themselves to present their sexual ornaments in the best possible condition. And it's wrong historically—men throughout most ages and cultures took great pains to keep their hair, beards, clothes, accessories, weapons, armor, horses, livestock, and homesteads tight.

Women are attracted to guys who take care of themselves. They interpret grooming as a signal of your conscientiousness/willpower, one of your deepest personality traits. If you're well groomed, women automatically infer that you're likely to be mature, ambitious, and active. Lucky for you, all the great things that conscientiousness brings in the long term can be signaled to women by just a few more minutes of grooming each morning.

Take a good, hard look in your bathroom mirror. Inspect your head hair, beard, skin condition, teeth, fingernails, toenails, and pubic area. Are they all clean, trim, orderly, and pleasant? Would you want your sister to date a guy who takes care of himself the way that you take care of yourself? If you don't like the thought of welcoming a crusty garbage person to your Thanksgiving table every year, you need to get your grooming act together. Let's start at the top and work down.

1. Head Hair

Lots of different hairstyles can work on men, but whatever look you choose, give it at least a minimal amount of care. That means washing your hair every morning in the shower *with a good conditioner;* conditioners have plenty of cleaning power on their own, and unlike shampoo, they won't strip protective oils from your hair and scalp and promote dandruff (you need shampoo only about once a week). That also means getting regular haircuts from a good professional barber who gets to know your personal style.

Accept your hairline, whatever it is. Don't try to hide a receding hairline or baldness; work with it to find a haircut that works for you. It's OK to have a receding hairline that you accept (Bruce Willis, Vin Diesel, and Jason Statham have shaved their heads for years because they're going bald); it is extremely unsexy to do obvious things to try to hide it, such as comb-overs and two-tone dye jobs like your head is a '64 Impala with candy paint, sittin' on twenty-four-inch rims.

2. Eyebrow/Nose/Ear Hairs

Why are stray hairs poking out of your head and face in all directions? Get a good nose-hair trimmer and use it up your nostrils and in and around your ears at least once a week. Those hairs evolved to keep parasites out of your orifices; they didn't evolve to attract women. Unless you spend a lot of time rolling around with ticks and lice, you don't need those hairs.

Eyebrow maintenance is simple: your barber should trim them with every haircut so you don't look like an elderly Oxford professor, and your unibrow needs to be split in half with tweezing so you don't look like a mobster. Remember, conspicuous precision in grooming is a key signal of conscientiousness (willpower).

3. Facial Hair

Beard or no beard? Research shows that most women are most attracted to guys who haven't shaved for a few days or who've already succeeded in growing a proper, well-groomed beard. This makes sense evolutionarily: men wouldn't grow beards at all if ancestral women hadn't liked beards. In most cultures, men let their facial hair grow, and they style it carefully. In twentieth-century America for some reason, the clean-shaven look took over; it's fine as well and usually gets a neutral response from women.

In-between is bad; avoid the "trying to grow a beard but can't" look. If you grow a full beard, make sure it's well groomed in length and around the edges. If you're going for the hipster look, your beard can be mountain-man scruffy, but your head haircut must be tight, crisply parted, and conscientious so the unkempt facial hair looks purposeful. If both your beard and your head hair are messy and uncut, you come across as a homeless schizophrenic.

4. Skin Care

Many guys avoid face washing because they got soap in their eyes once during bath time when they were five years old and that was that— *never again!* If you are a chronic non-face-washer, it's time to process your toddler traumas and change your habits.

Having clear skin is important to women, because skin blemishes signal infection, disease, and poor health. The best way to have clear skin is to starve the bacteria in your pores that cause acne: avoid soda, sugar, grains, refined carbs, and caffeine. Most skin issues can be resolved by improving your diet and washing your face daily with a moisturizing soap. If you want a woman to kiss you, at least do her the courtesy of not having to worry about feeling like a napkin on a slice of pepperoni pizza.

5. Mouth and Breath

For mating purposes, your goal with oral care is to get your mouth into a condition where women will want to kiss it and keep kissing it. Kissing is how women sample your biochemistry and unconsciously assess your health. Rough, cracked, chapped lips are gross to kiss; drink more water and use lip balm.

Once women get past your lips, they're into the bacterial cesspool of your mouth, the dirtiest place in your body. Manage your mouth. You can control *which* bacteria species are dominant by changing what you eat; our nutrition recommendations will make your breath a lot better by reducing sugar-dependent bacteria.

And you can control *how many* bacteria a woman can taste in your mouth through good oral care. Brush your teeth with a good manual toothbrush when you wake up in the morning and with an electric toothbrush before you go to bed at night; dentists say this combination is better than using either alone. Also floss and use a tongue scraper after breakfast and again before you go to sleep.

Visit the dentist regularly to get cleanings, fix your problems, and motivate your daily oral hygiene (there's nothing like a cute dental hygienist praising your oral care regime to motivate regular flossing). All of this oral care will automatically protect you from bad breath, so you'll feel more confident talking and canoodling with women.

6. Body Hair

Most women want your chest, armpits, stomach, lower arms, and legs to show a bit of that manly hairiness. Women perceive hairlessness as coding for little boy, chemo patient, or porn star, so unless you have a ten-inch penis, don't shave off all your body hair.

At the same time, women don't like really hairy backs, shoulders, or butts, all of which code as terrorist, werewolf, or grandpa. If you can French-braid your back hair into your chest hair, it's time to visit the spa (or the local sheep shearer). For the most part though, as long as your body hair is not excessive in *either* direction—little sickly boy or Wolverine—then it's not a big issue for most women.

Same with pubic hair: most young American men keep some pubic hair so they look like they've gone through puberty, but they trim it so women aren't also flossing during blowjobs.

7. Hands

Women pay a surprising amount of attention to hands—the size, proportions, strength, hairiness, skin condition, nail condition, and vascularity (how prominent the veins are, a signal of strength and masculinity).

The most common complaints are that men don't keep their nails trimmed or their hands clean. Washing your hands isn't just good for their visual appeal; it's also one of the most powerful ways to protect yourself from colds and flu.

Once a week, clip your fingernails, scrape the dirt from under them, and push your cuticles up. You don't need a professional manicure, just enough nail shortness and cleanliness. A woman should be confident that if your hand gets inside her panties, it's not bringing a petri dish from the CDC with it.

Don't worry that good hand care will make your hands look feminine; what makes your hands look feminine is having no visible vascularity or grip strength from failing to lift heavy weights regularly.

8. Feet

Most guys have sexually repulsive feet, and women notice. Many women dread that moment when a guy first takes off his shoes and socks to have sex with her. They're bracing for the stinky, hairy, long-nailed horrors within that confirm they are, in fact, about to fuck a centaur. Don't have feet like a centaur, a hobbit, or any other mythical woodland creature.

Keep your toenails clipped and your feet clean, and sort out any calluses, bunions, rough patches, and fungal infections (athlete's foot). Wear clean socks every day. And for the love of god, when you're having sex, take them off! Women HATE when you keep them on.

9. Scent

A man's scent is hugely important to women. Sometimes his pheromone symphony smells so good that a woman can't resist. More often, a guy shows up for a first date, thinks he probably smells OK, but there's something just a bit "off," so there's no sex and no second date. Few women will admit he just didn't smell right, but the research on sex and scent says that's often the reason there is no "chemistry."

Your body scent has a complicated physiology influenced by what you eat, how you exercise, how much you sleep and hydrate, how much you sweat, and what your hormone levels are. This means your natural scent is a pretty informative signal of your overall health.

If you are really healthy and you stay reasonably clean, you'll probably smell really good to women. If you aren't healthy, you can't mask a bad body scent with bad cologne; you're just building a more layered tapestry of awfulness.

Beware: Cheap, nasty, unsubtle scents are added to most men's toiletries—soap, conditioner, hair gel, antiperspirant, body spray, and shaving foam. Avoid that shit. Buy unscented. Quality women don't fall for men who use Axe Body Spray.

Do not *bathe* in that stuff either, like you live inside a Long Island nightclub. Cologne is like saffron or hemlock—a little goes a long way (Geoff's favorite cologne is D.S. & Durga). Use just enough that a woman will consciously notice it only if she's well inside your personal space and sticking her nose into your neck. If someone can smell you from more than a foot away, you are using WAY too much.

The same principles apply to scent in your clothes, car, and home. Use unscented laundry detergent and fabric softeners so your clothes smell like you, not like "Pure Sport" Bounce dryer sheets. Don't hang some nasty pine scent "air freshener" in your car to mask the fast-food smell; just *clean out your car* and it will smell fine.

Don't overwhelm your bathroom with Lysol spray just before a woman comes over; just keep it clean. Don't use cheap scented candles or scent diffusers in your bedroom; women having sex want to smell you, not your Glade Plugin air freshener. If you keep your bedroom clean and open the windows a little at night, it'll smell fine.

2. Clothing

You were born with a body that you can change only to some extent. Fortunately, you can pick all the clothing you ever put on, so you have a huge amount of control over the style, quality, and fit of your clothing and the signals it sends to women.

Think about job uniforms. You want your airline pilot to be professionally dressed with a tie, jacket, epaulets, and the little winged pin rather than sporting a Dave Matthews Band T-shirt and flip-flops. You want your doctor in a white coat and stethoscope, not black leather bondage gear. And guess what—dressing the part actually makes patients respond better to doctor care.

Women assess your outfit in the same way when you are on a date. They want you to look the part of "cool potential boyfriend." They don't just judge how well dressed you are in terms of your style and wealth, however; they also judge *how much effort* you put into looking good for her. Most young men under-dress for dates, failing to understand that "looking casual and laid back" to them means "looking careless and uninterested" to women.

That said, almost anything *can* be appropriate to wear on a date (besides Crocs of course), depending on where you're going. Board shorts are fine if

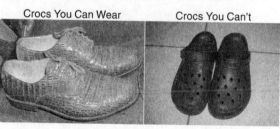

Crocs You Can Wear   Crocs You Can't

you're going to the beach. A suit is appropriate if you're going to the ballet. The reverse is not true, which we hope is obvious to you.

Fundamentally, whatever you choose to wear has to be clean, well fitted, coordinated, and socially appropriate.

Don't just throw on whatever was within reach and doesn't smell like the inside of a bus terminal. Don't look like you got dressed in the dark or you picked your outfit from a hobo's bindle. Be purposeful and considerate.

1. Own Your Clothing Signaling

Maybe you're an uppity rebel who resents women judging you by your clothing. Too bad. This is a game you can't opt out of. *Every* outfit, no matter how informal or thoughtless, sends all kinds of signals to every woman who sees it.

Dressing like a slob to show that you don't care about clothing is *still* a signal; to most women, it's a signal of immaturity, poverty, or, worst-case scenario, a big red flag about potential depression issues. So recognize what signals you want to send the world about yourself, and consciously select the clothing that best approximates those signals.

If you want the world to know you're a serious person who means business, choose darker, muted tones and more formal clothes (slacks when you could have worn jeans, an Oxford when you could have worn a polo) that button you up and appear professional.

If you want everyone to think you're sharp and irreverent and youthful, funny vintage-type T-shirts and stylish accessories (shoes, hats, bags, etc.) are going to be a staple for you. The key is to balance them with high-quality pants and jackets; otherwise, "youthful" becomes "immature," and "sharp and irreverent" can become "silly and ignorant."

2. Dress Appropriately for Your Age and Social Context

If you're a college student, dress more or less like a college student. If you are a young corporate professional, dress like one. There is some variance here of course, because different situations and subcultures call for different personal styles.

Trends change quickly though, so don't focus so much on trying to stay on trend as much as identifying the common fashion denominators for the mating market you're in. Doing that is pretty simple: pick your head up from your phone, point your eyeballs in the direction of the guys your age who are getting attention from the kinds of women you want to attract, and then wear some version of what they're wearing. Only after you learn how to play around with your personal style *within the box* of the social norms for your age and group should you try to play outside the box with more radical looks.

Many guys end up dressing inappropriately for their age, in ways that women find sexually repulsive. In grade school, the kids who dressed like old men were the ones who got destroyed. In high school, the cosplayers in superhero capes were the ones doing something else on prom night. In the adult mating game, it's the older men who dress like college kids at Coachella that get shut out.

3. Fit Trumps Fashion

Cutting-edge fashion is overrated; good fit is underappreciated. Never wear anything that a male model would wear on a runway at a fashion show, especially if it's by a designer whose clothes you've never seen in the menswear section of a decent department store (Macy's, Nordstrom, Neiman Marcus, etc.). Very few women want to date a *fashionable* guy, but many women want to date a *stylish guy who wears tasteful clothes that fit well.*

Most young men wear clothes that are too big: baggy pants, tentlike shorts, shapeless T-shirts, and saggy coats. This repulses women in several ways. It says, "I'm insecure about my size," "I don't want you to see what shape my body really is," "I can't be bothered to try on clothes in a store and see if they fit before I buy them," and "I'm so sexually insecure that I don't want to be mistaken for a gay guy who dresses well."

Look at how the leading men in romantic comedies dress; women can see their shoulder-to-waist ratio, their muscles, their amount of gut fat, their butt shape, their thigh strength, and so on. Your clothes don't have to be tight, but they should look like they FIT your body.

Your goal over the long term should be to throw out all your clothing that doesn't fit and start buying clothing that does. For now, set aside a couple of hours this weekend to go through every piece of clothing in your closet, one by one. Try every piece on, in daylight, in front of a mirror. Be brutally honest about whether it fits you. If you're lucky enough to have a high shoulder-to-waist ratio, shirts will fit you only if they are "fitted"; if they balloon out at the waist, they don't fit. Throw them out (or donate them to your younger brother or nephew if the shirts actually fit them; otherwise, donate them to a charity shop or your local landfill). If your jeans don't make your butt and legs look great, throw them out. If your coats don't fit, abandon them.

Your inner frugal granddad brain will object: "It's a perfectly good shirt; keep it; you paid for it, so it's worth something." No it isn't. It's cock-blocking you, costing you potential mating opportunities every time a woman sees it.

Dressing well in clothes that fit does not require expensive custom-made clothing. You can get 80 percent of the aesthetic benefits of a $6,000 bespoke Savile Row suit from a decent wool $299 Men's Wearhouse suit that you have tailored to fit your frame—as long as it's matched with a good pair of leather shoes.

That doesn't mean you should trot it out on a first date, or a second or a third, but it's an important piece to have in your arsenal for when you get deeper into relationships with women and are more likely to go places with her where a suit is appropriate (weddings, funerals, anniversary dinners, etc.).

The simpler you keep your tastes, the easier it is to display a personal style based on clean lines, classic looks, and good fit. The photo editors of most major magazines implicitly understand the attractiveness of simplicity. It's why you see stars of today channeling stars of yesteryear in basic looks that fit impeccably—uncomplicated jackets like a dark gray blazer, flat front wool slacks, and crisp white button-down shirts.

Paul Newman publicity photo for his first film (1954)

Jon Hamm publicity photo for the Emmy's (2015)

When buying these simple, clean, classic clothes items, it's still important to get advice. Not everything is going to look good with your skin tone, hair color, or complexion, so bring along female friends who understand men's clothes and styles. If you're still working on your social proof and have no tasteful friends to bring along, find the most experienced, intelligent salespeople and learn to read their signals. "That color looks great with your eyes" means "That doesn't fit *at all*"; "That makes you look amazingly hot!" means "That might fit OK."

4. Wash Your Damn Clothes

Your clothes should be washed regularly, look clean, and smell fresh. Any daytime clothing item exposed to sweat from your groin, feet, or underarms needs to be washed after each wearing—this includes underwear, socks, undershirts, and casual shirts. Nightwear (pajamas) and shirts worn over undershirts (e.g., dress shirts) need washing every couple of wears unless you spill shit all over them, obviously. Wash pants and jeans every three to four wears, unless you spill on them too. Suits, jackets, and outerwear need brushing after every couple of wears and dry cleaning twice a year. If you're wearing a collared, dressy shirt on a date, take the trouble to iron it—women appreciate your effort more than they notice your ironing skill.

Build a Basic Wardrobe

Every man, from fifteen to fifty-five, needs a handful of foundational items to build a wardrobe that serves him well in all his mating interactions:

- brown shoes and black shoes (leather, NO square-toed)
- brown belt and black belt (leather)
- quality dark jeans
- flat-front black dress pants
- two collared dress shirts
- two solid-color polos
- two to three quality V-neck T-shirts
- V-neck sweater
- sport coat
- peacoat/overcoat (especially if you live in a cold climate)

All these items are very versatile. They can be dressed up or down depending on the occasion. To start, stick with solid colors like white, blue, gray, black, and navy. If you insist on adding brighter colors, save them for accessories (ties, scarves, watchbands, hats, boxers) and make sure they are colors that exist in the natural world, not in a bag of tropical Skittles. (For further guidance, go to thematinggrounds.com/clothing.)

Even better, make ironing a nonissue by folding your sweaters and T-shirts properly and hanging up your shirts and pants on thick, quality-plastic or wood hangers to prevent wrinkling. The floor is not a dresser or a closet.

5. Shoes Matter

Your shoes matter more to women than you can imagine. Most American guys handicap their mating with horrible "casual" shoes that no European man would be caught dead in. Women evaluate the seriousness of your interest in them by the formality of the shoes you wear on dates. Shoes for almost all dates, except very casual or athletic activities, should be leather (or suede). Good leather shoes set you apart from the man-boys still running around in grade-school Nikes or high-school Vans. They instantly make you seem more mature, dominant, confident, and datable. Take good care of your shoes, with regular cleaning, polishing, and use of shoe trees.

3. Car and Home and Other "Stuff"

Realize that everything you take for granted about your car and home is all too apparent to a visiting woman. As a Polish proverb says, *"A guest sees more in an hour than a host sees in a year."*

1. Keep All Your Stuff Clean

Remember, women code "clean" as "safe," "mature," "reliable," and "responsible"—four very desirable qualities in a boyfriend. Keep your car washed outside and clean inside.

To most women, a tidy Toyota is more attractive than a BMW filled with fast-food wrappers, old gym bags, and used condoms. A small, clean apartment feels sexier and more romantic to most women than a luxury condo with a stinky fridge, pee stains on the bathroom floor, and filthy bed sheets.

It's especially important to keep your bathroom and kitchen clean. These are the two make-or-break areas that women pay attention to, whether they're house shopping or boyfriend shopping. If you get in the habit of doing a weekly clean for just an hour or two, it'll make your car and home much more appealing to women. You do NOT want to be the guy who brings a woman home only to have her run away in terror because she refuses to sit on any of your furniture in a skirt.

2. Clean up Clutter

Most guys have too much shit in their homes, even by their early twenties. Once a week, tidy everything that's "out," and before you put it "back" where you usually keep it, ask yourself whether it's adding any value to your life and your attractiveness. Is it truly useful, valuable, or beautiful? If not, why do you have it? Do you *really* need all eight of those enormous plastic souvenir cups from the 2010 Alamo Bowl?

Normal women hate clutter, because they're much more sensitive to the perils of dirt, dust, and vermin that could spread disease and make babies die. Being surrounded by clutter, chaos, and useless junk is also a symptom of psychosis, depression, obsessive hoarding, drug addiction, and/or unconscientious laziness. Err on the side of minimalism in your decor.

Takeaways

- The first step in improving your aesthetic proof is eliminating common errors that make men sexually repulsive to women—fixing your grooming, clothing, car, and home to eliminate things like nose hairs, zits, bad breath, dirty fingernails, nasty scents, baggy clothes, plastic shoes, car trash, and home clutter. All these problems signal poor mental health, questionable intelligence, low conscientiousness, immaturity, social isolation, and poverty to women.
- Women have been judging men based on their style, taste, aesthetic appearance, and artistic skills for more than a hundred thousand years. Modern women will judge you partly by the aesthetic proof you offer through your grooming, clothing, car, home, and artistic and musical skills. So don't worry that caring about beauty in your life will make you seem feminine or gay. Instead, take charge of your attractiveness.
- Once you've got yourself and your spaces looking tight, cultivate active performance and creative skills that are aesthetically attractive to women—things like learning to dance better, sing, play instruments, make things, draw, and tell stories. These skills all signal openness, playfulness, happiness, intelligence, willpower, and social popularity.

CHAPTER 14: SHOW HER HOW YOU FEEL

(ROMANTIC PROOF)

Romance is everything.

—*Gertrude Stein*

Women want romance. Why do you think they consume most of the romance novels, romantic comedies, romantic TV shows, and news about celebrity romances out there? They even have their own "romantic" genre of "couples" porn, where lovers actually flirt, play, and talk for a few minutes before the blowjob begins. *You mean they have names??* Exactly.

This romance stuff brings clear emotional benefits to women, but what's in it for you guys? Well, sooner or later, you're going to fall in love, and you're probably going to fuck it up. We want to help you avoid that heartbreak. This chapter teaches you how to present the "romantic proof" that women crave.

Don't worry. We're not going to preach that you must fall in love before you have sex or that all women want long-term, committed relationships. In fact, romantic proof is just as important in your dating and mating life as social, material, or aesthetic proof—*even if you're only looking for short-term mates.* Even for a one-night stand, a woman appreciates a guy who can play the romantic role and who can emotionally connect with her and eroticize whatever intimacy develops in a few hours of fun. Plus, it usually makes the sex much hotter.

BROADCASTING VS. NARROWCASTING

Broadcasting is anything you do as a guy that raises your attractiveness and apparent mate value to women in general.

Suppose you're a rock star: you're displaying your musical talent, creativity, humor, energy, and confidence onstage, and thousands of female fans respond by cheering and screaming, "Take me backstage!" or "Fill me with your tiny babies!" You might even sing a ballad or two, just to show you have a heart. But you're broadcasting these traits and proofs to every woman in the stadium; you're not focusing on any one woman.

Narrowcasting is focusing your mating effort and courtship displays on a *particular* woman. It's usually much more private, like when the rock star serenades one particular groupie in his tour bus.

Narrowcast romantic proof shows you're willing to take the time, energy, attention, and effort to prioritize a particular woman over other possible mates. Women find that very, very compelling, because you're simultaneously saying, "You're so awesome that you're worth my *best* mating effort" and "You're so much more awesome than all the other women out there that you're getting my *exclusive* mating effort—at least for this conversation, this night, or this week."

To women, a guy broadcasting his mate value often looks selfish, juvenile, sleazy, and sexually desperate, whereas a narrowcasting guy looks generous, mature, honorable, and sexually patient.

Of course, romantic proof doesn't mean you have to devote 100 percent of your time, energy, attention, and penile rigidity to just one woman. It just means you're investing enough in her, and giving up enough time that you could be spending with other women, that she's confident you really care about her over the long term. Don't automatically equate love with jealousy, romance with exclusivity, or long-term relationships with monogamy.

WHY WOMEN CARE ABOUT ROMANTIC PROOF

A lot of guys ask us, "How do I know if a woman's into me?" If you like a woman, you'd also like to know if she likes you so that you can know whether to talk to her more, to tell her that you like her, to ask her out, right?

Women are the same way. They want to know what you think about them and what your intentions are on a romantic level, because that information is very valuable to them. Women feel intense anxiety if they are not getting romantic proof from a boyfriend or husband. Feeling invisible, neglected, or taken for granted drives women nuts, and it sparks a lot of breakups and divorces.

To understand why, it helps to think about the evolutionary logic of romantic proof: *it's all about showing a guy's willingness to stay with a woman and to help take care of any kids that pop out.* Remember *March of the Penguins*, when Morgan Freeman taught us all how male emperor penguins incubated little baby penguin eggs at their feet for four months? It's no coincidence that women lost their shit over that movie.

Once a woman starts feeling safe around a man and is thinking about dating him, her self-protective instincts flare up, and she wonders, "If we have sex and I get pregnant, will he abandon me, or will he stay and help raise the kids?"

You can see this concern in pop music; most lyrics by women are basically asking, *"Hey, boy, will you really love me forever, or are you just having fun?"* Most lyrics by men are basically asking, *"Hey, girl, are you really DTF tonight, or are you just teasing me?"*

You might have very high mate value—a great body and brain, cool personality, awesome career, wonderful friends, good taste, and a romantic streak. But for a woman seeking a longer-term boyfriend or husband, that's all meaningless if you don't show romantic commitment to *her* in particular. To many women, a great guy who won't commit is just an extra-dangerous source of potential heartbreak and bitter disappointment.

So understand that women's craving for romantic proof is not some weird cultural programming, superficial whim, or capricious personality disorder. It's at the heart of protecting themselves from being seduced, impregnated, and abandoned. And apart from reducing the risk of abandonment, romantic proof gives women lots of valuable information about your good gene, good partner, and good dad potential.

Men's capacities for romantic proof couldn't have evolved to be universal across cultures if they didn't have a genetic basis. Romantic tendencies are not only stable across life but also reveal desirable, heritable personality traits and higher intelligence (higher IQ predicts lower likelihood of divorce).

For example, brighter guys will be faster to learn a woman's details and history, will be better at remembering her preferences and birthday, and will be more resourceful in organizing their romantic activities. Romance depends on conscientiousness (willpower) and agreeableness (kindness): to make a long-term relationship work, a guy has to invest in his social role as a family man, show the self-control to fulfill his commitments and resist the temptation to sleep with other women, and have the altruism to care for his own girlfriend. Romantic proof also reveals emotional stability, because depression, anxiety, and irritability distract guys from being able to take care of a woman.

IMPROVE YOUR ROMANTIC PROOF

As with any kind of hard-to-fake proof, romantic proof doesn't have to deliver any practical value to a woman; it just has to impose costs on you that would be unbearable if you tried to narrowcast them to any other woman. That's what makes it a reliable signal of intent and commitment.

So the most romantic gestures are those that cost you the most, given your abilities, preferences, and resources. If you're shy, a public declaration of love will seem especially touching. If you're cash-rich but time-poor, a woman will be much more impressed that you took the time to handcraft a unique birthday gift than if you spent a few thousand dollars on jewelry from Amazon Prime. The more the romantic gesture costs *you specifically,* the more reliable and compelling it is as a signal of your mating interest.

That said, gradual escalation is key. Too much romantic proof too early smacks of immaturity, instability, and low mate-value. If you haven't spent dozens of hours talking with a woman, you can't possibly know enough about her to actually love her for herself. You probably only love her boobs, her smile, and her last ten Facebook status updates. By narrowcasting too much romantic proof too early, you are basically saying, "For no good reason, I'm romantically fixated on you even though I've never even talked to you and know nothing about you." This reeks of desperation and is very unattractive.

What you need to understand is the typical script for how romantic signaling escalates in our culture. You already know this script at some level from watching hundreds of romances on TV and in movies; you just have to become more conscious about it so you know when you're fucking it up; then you can slow it down and take it easier.

First, you pay attention to the woman. You look at her. Don't stare like a predator, but smile and say hi. Then you talk to her and listen. This is called *having a conversation:* you learn about her, and she learns about you.

Then you invest more time in doing fun stuff together on dates, so you both learn more through shared activities and unexpected challenges. At some point you start making out and maybe having sex, so you get to know each other's bodies, passions, and kinks.

All throughout this process, your mutual interest and sexual anticipation should build slowly. Genuine, mature, choosy love grows slowly and cautiously, on the knife's edge between fear of heartbreak and hope for a shared future.

As we said, it freaks women out when you jump straight from a first date to a colossal romantic obsession without going through these stages. She knows you know nothing about her; she's just a symbol to you. Why is this guy suddenly sending me heart emoticons and links to his YouTube love-song performances when I hardly know him? That's what creeps and weirdos do. You might *feel* like you're in love after a couple of hours with a woman, but you don't have to *say* it or *act* overly romantic about it. Nurture that passion in private—that's what masturbation fantasies are for.

However, escalating romantic proof too slowly shows you're jaded, indecisive, or cynical, so women run away. Escalate just right, with your love growing in proportion to what you know about a woman, and she might just love you back and run toward a great future with you.

The best way to practice gradual escalation of romantic proof is to practice having actual medium-term and longer-term sexual relationships. You learn romantic skills by having girlfriends, learning from mistakes, resolving arguments, and understanding women better. And when you finally meet "the One" whom you want to marry and have kids with, your future wife will be thankful that you learned how to be romantic long before you met her.

DISPLAY ROMANTIC PROOF

Don't fake being in love. Why? Aside from the moral arguments—it's dishonest and it hurts women—it sets you up for catastrophic blowback. In England until 1970, a woman could have sued you for "breach of promise"; having sex was an implied promise of marriage, and if you didn't follow through, a woman could sue for serious money and ruin your reputation. The law doesn't exist anymore (thankfully), but women still feel moral outrage against guys who fake love just to get sex.

So, do not follow Ron Burgundy's lead. Instead, escalate your romantic displays only when you're *actually* falling in love and she's clearly falling for you. In the meantime, there will be a pretty big gap between how much you feel (which might be a lot) and how much you say and act upon (which might be a little for a long time), and that's exactly as it should be. What's hot to women

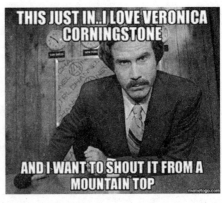

THIS JUST IN.. I LOVE VERONICA CORNINGSTONE

AND I WANT TO SHOUT IT FROM A MOUNTAIN TOP

about romance novels is the hero feeling much more than he can say, not when he says much more than he feels.

That's a high-level, strategic approach to romantic proof. Now on to the nitty-gritty, how-to, *what the fuck do I do?* parts of the equation.

Make Good Eye Contact

Have you ever been talking to someone who is looking around the room at everyone else and not paying attention to your words or your face? How does that make you feel? Like a disposable fucking loser?

It makes women feel the same way when you do it to them. And they're even more attuned to gaze direction than you are.

The simplest, most ancient forms of romantic proof are simply looking at one woman rather than at other possible mates (no wandering eye) and paying attention to her behavior and conversation rather than getting lost in your own past memories, current agendas, and future plans (no wandering mind). For all primates, including us, gaze direction and mindful attention are reliable signals of social and sexual interest.

When you're with a woman, spend most of your time looking at her in general and plenty of time looking into her eyes specifically. This doesn't mean stare like a psychotic stalker, a CIA interrogator, or a Tantric sex guru. Just look at her a little more often than you normally would.

Cultivate Good Conversation

The first duty of love is to listen.

—Philosopher Paul Tillich

Conversation is the bedrock of romantic proof. The time, attention, and humor invested in the conversation matter more than the specific subject matter.

You can talk about *anything* in a way that shows romantic proof. As you know from watching couples in public who are sickeningly in love, they can talk total nonsense for hours in a totally loving way.

However, you can talk about love itself in a way that shows zero romantic proof if your conversational style is boring, lazy, inattentive, overbearing, mansplaining, cynical, or hostile. This is one place where style can trump substance.

So what conversational style makes for good romantic proof? The main thing is mental and social effort. After she tells you her name, repeat her name to yourself until you remember it. Use active listening, pay attention to what she's saying, and give little nods and reactions as she speaks. Ask about her background, interests, values, and preferences, and weave them into your dialogue. Show energy and enthusiasm in your words, face, and gestures. Unleash your inner comedian, storyteller, reporter, and philosopher—all the creativity, knowledge, and humor that you can muster.

Above all, give her your full attention and interest. She wants mindful conversation, not mindless banter. If you're preoccupied with which cocktail to order next or analyzing that conversation with some other hot woman yesterday, you'll get that dead-eyed zombie look and she'll know your brain has gone AWOL.

Most young guys suck at paying real attention to a woman when they're talking. They worry too much about *sounding smart* and not enough about *being warm*. You can't usually talk a woman into bed by saying clever things unless you're legitimately hilarious, but you can build an emotional connection through conversation that makes her feel that spark of intimacy. And for women, there's a very short leap from emotional intimacy to physical intimacy—hot, messy, passionate sex.

Talk Respectfully about Other Women

Ex Appreciation

Think about your last three girlfriends or closest female friends. For each of them, write down the five things that you most appreciated about them *as people*—things about their minds, personalities, values, or talents (don't list physical or sexual traits like "epic tits").

When you talk about your exes on dates—if a woman asks—these are the traits to mention.

If a woman is interested in you, she'll often ask, "Hey, what were your ex-girlfriends like?" Of course, she wants to find out what you're attracted to and how she compares to them. But mostly she wants to assess your romantic capabilities (and mental health and empathy) through how you talk about them.

Do you show reliable signs of being able to feel real love for real women? Could you connect emotionally, mentally, and socially with them as people, or did you vacillate between idolizing them as goddesses and demonizing them as whores? Did your love make you committed enough to get through crises, disappointments, and arguments, or did your love evaporate at the first sign of trouble?

A woman can read all this and infer your loving-guy traits from how you talk about your exes, as well as about your sister, your mother, your female coworkers, or any other women in your life. In fact, your ability to love women as real people overlaps a lot with treating women in general as real people.

When you talk about women to a woman, make sure you are honest, caring, positive, and somewhat discreet. She is in information-gathering mode in conversations like this, but one of the things she doesn't want to learn is that if the relationship doesn't work, you'll spill all her dirty laundry to the first pretty face who asks.

Focus on Her Unique Qualities

Satirist H. L. Mencken wrote, "Love is the delusion that one woman differs from another." He was wrong. Women do differ from each other in all the same ways that men do, and different men value different qualities in women. The key to a woman's heart is not to praise her overall mate value by just calling her an "awesome 9"; any guy could do that, and he might trade up to a "10" if one comes along.

Rather, you have to gradually let her know exactly *which of her specific qualities you find uniquely irresistible* so that no other woman is likely to sweep you away.

Caution: If she has huge boobs, saying you especially love her boobs doesn't make you stand out, because most guys love boobs. She's tired of leading with her cleavage.

Focus on her qualities that most other guys would overlook—you know, like *her personality.* It might be her career, her intelligence, her extracurricular interests, her sense of humor, or refreshing honesty. It doesn't really matter, as long as it's something that is part of her identity, especially something she values or works on.

If you're especially attracted to certain qualities in a woman that most guys would find neutral, intimidating, or repulsive, that's especially valuable to her. Most guys are intimidated by very smart women, but if you're a smart guy who truly values a woman's intelligence, let her know early and often that you appreciate her brains. Don't just say, "I love you because you're smart"— that's cheap talk. Rather, *demonstrate* that you value that trait by engaging your brain with hers.

Most guys are also intimidated by very tall women, but if you adore long legs, show it by doing things that showcase her height—like playing volleyball, complimenting how great she looks in high heels at a party, or focusing a lot of sexual attention on her legs in bed. Kids have probably made fun of her for being tall since fifth grade, she's been self-conscious about it her whole life, and she's craving a guy who sees her as a leggy supermodel rather than a gangly giraffe.

Tell the Truth about Your Intentions

Love is a game that two can play and both win.
— *Actress Eva Gabor (married five times)*

When a woman asks you what you're looking for, don't fucking lie. Be honest and seek win-win relationships.

Moralizing aside, lying about your mating goals nukes your sexual confidence (if you have a conscience), risks your reputation, hurts women, undermines their trust in you, and cripples your mating strategy. Most women assume that guys are lying when they're talking about relationship intentions. Why? Because guys lie all the time: "I'm such a romantic," "I'm dying to meet the One," or "Love is so underrated these days."

Most guys — especially when they're young and horny — think they have to lure women for sex with the potential for a relationship. This is not accurate. There are MANY women who are willing to have sex without relationships, but only if you are honest.

If you are actually looking for a serious relationship, you can absolutely own it: hint on the second date that you're open to having a girlfriend if the right woman comes along, and declare on the tenth date that finding a great wife is actually your main mating goal.

But if you're *not* looking for a steady girlfriend, it's best to take the opposite tack. Tell the complete truth in a socially intelligent but clear way. Say, "Look, I may want a girlfriend and a wife and kids at some point in my life, but that's five or ten years away. Right now, I just want to have fun and meet new people and try new things."

Once you tell the truth, the woman is immediately relieved because she can give truly informed consent to whatever the evening brings. You've shown your hand, and she can either fold (run away, if she's really looking for a boyfriend) or raise you (keep flirting, if she's really looking for a hookup).

This kind of radical honesty hits an emotional reset button in most women's heads, reframing the whole interaction from "ordinary dating mind games between boy and girl" to "exciting, edgy, flirtatious conspiracy of daring truth tellers." This fundamentally changes the mating dynamic and makes short-term mating much more likely and much less shameful.

Plus, honesty is sexy to women. If you're honest about your mating goals, there's a good chance you'll be honest about everything else, and honesty is very attractive to women.

Socially intelligent honesty about your mating goals also saves your own sexual self-respect and your sense of integrity. By saying, "I'm looking to have fun and meet new people," you're NOT saying, "I just want to slay as much pussy as possible." The moral framework here is that short-term sex is fun, playful, exploratory, and a great way to make new friends rather than shameful, sinful, exploitative, or misogynist.

Get Good at Foreplay

Great foreplay is one of the most emotionally compelling forms of romantic proof to women. It shows you've got the sexual patience for a longer-term relationship rather than being desperate for immediate sexual gratification.

The key to great foreplay is to focus on both people's pleasure in each other's bodies. She wants to feel that you're doing the foreplay because you're passionately attracted to and aesthetically fascinated by every part of her body, and you're really appreciating every touch, kiss, and lick—not because you're just trying to prime the pump or, god forbid, you think it's a quid pro quo kind of situation.

For women in long-term relationships, being kissed frequently is strong romantic proof—a better signal of commitment than a boyfriend wanting sex with them. In fact, for women in longer-term relationships, foreplay really starts in the morning with the first "Hey, honey, you look great today!" or the after-lunch text that says, "My hands are going to give your hips a lot of attention tonight"; it's not limited to the few minutes before you want sex.

Embrace Sexual Passion

You might think that romantic proof means you have to care more about a woman's orgasm than about your sexual pleasure. That's not true.

Many women find it more exciting when a man gets completely carried away and really enjoys fucking them than when he's overly attentive to their own pleasure. That's the way the pirate captains fuck in romance novels, which are marketed to women, not men.

The reason women love male passion is that if you clearly find sex with them to be awesomely rewarding, you'll probably come back for more. You're starting to get hooked on her, and she likes that.

However, if you're focused only on whether a woman reaches orgasm with you, she is more likely to feel put on the spot, anxious, self-conscious, and worried that if she doesn't "perform" for you by reaching orgasm, you'll go off and find some other woman who's easily multiorgasmic.

Come Correct with Cuddling

Women instinctively understand that you'll use whatever seduction tactics you think are necessary to get them to have sex with you. The question is, how do you act after you've had sex?

Women especially value cuddling as romantic proof because it's a reliable signal that you didn't just want to fuck them once and that you actually have feelings for them that go beyond the heat of passion. Men oriented toward short-term mating view women as significantly less attractive after they come, whereas men oriented toward long-term mating experience less of this "affective shift" from preorgasmic desire to postorgasmic disgust. Thus, women can use your response after sex as a cue to your mating intentions.

Check In Regularly

> *The art of love is largely the art of persistence.*
> — *Psychotherapist Albert Ellis*

Many primates give regular "contact calls" in dense forest to let their mates know where they are. The modern equivalent is regular text messaging, liking your girlfriend's Facebook status updates, returning her phone calls, answering her emails, and chatting with her regularly. The content of the messages isn't as important as their reliability, kindness, and the time and attention required to maintain them. This is a very hard-to-fake signal of romantic commitment, because you couldn't sustain it with multiple lovers.

You might be Dr. Pussy Slayer the Sexual Superhero, but you can't keep up text chatter with more than about five women at once. At least not without seriously fucking up.

Of course, don't check in with her more often than she checks in with you—you're aiming to signal romantic reliability, not erotic obsession. And some women have a bottomless need for contact calls that no man could ever fill. You don't need to give her everything she wants; you just need to give her *enough*. That is, give her a little more than less committed guys could stand to give.

Give Gifts That Require Thought, Research, and Creativity

> *Kindness in giving creates love.*
> — *Lao Tzu*

If it's a gift you would get yourself, it's not a romantic gift; it's being selfish. If it's something you would have gotten any ex-girlfriend, it's not romantic; it's being a dickhead. If you found it in five minutes on Amazon, it's not romantic; it's lazy.

Find out her favorite kinds of flowers before you buy her flowers. It doesn't matter how pretty tiger lilies are; if she's allergic, the only ones who benefit are the makers of Benadryl and Kleenex. The best gifts tap into your own traits; making something yourself is big romantic proof and showcases your practical intelligence, willpower, and aesthetic proof.

Women care a lot about you remembering relationship-specific dates (their birthday, the date and anniversary of your first contact, first date, first kiss, first sex, marriage, etc.), romantic holidays (Valentine's Day, New Year's Eve), and minor holidays that allow romantic extended-weekend getaways (Presidents' Day, Labor Day). For each of these, you need to plan ahead—put work aside, get thoughtful gifts, make dinner and travel reservations.

Show Just Enough Jealousy

Jealousy evolved to protect a longer-term sexual relationship, so its expression reveals a mindset oriented toward longer-term commitment. Just don't be an asshole about it.

Possessive, paranoid jealousy is annoying, controlling, and oppressive to women and predicts domestic violence in the relationship. But a moderate level of mate guarding and interest in their fantasies, flirtations, and male friends signals that you're paying attention to their desires and you're serious about the relationship.

Share Interests

If she loves snowboarding, take some lessons and try it. If you know how to survive Coachella comfortably, take her and show her. Don't compartmentalize your passions. If you're *really* into motorcycles but never show her your bike or take her out on it, she'll assume that you're not serious about her. She wants to be part of your life, and if you build a wall that excludes her from your favorite hobbies, she'll feel disposable.

Show Deep Engagement Rather Than a Transactional Attitude

"Deep engagement" means you start to value the woman as an end in herself rather than a means to yours. Her happiness becomes essential to yours. You'd stick by her and care for her with a high degree of "irrational" commitment, even if she fell into a coma, got cervical cancer that required a hysterectomy, or developed schizophrenia. Economists call this "irrational" commitment because the relationship has become a net cost rather than a net benefit, so a "rational" man would leave. That's precisely why staying is the *romantic* thing to do.

A transactional attitude toward relationships means a tit-for-tat accounting that keeps track of who does what for whom and who owes more—a huge turnoff and a red flag for women.

Go Public

Contrary to the Romeo and Juliet myth that social adversity makes love stronger, relationships have lower satisfaction and worse outcomes if they aren't integrated into the lovers' social networks or if friends disapprove. Secret relationships make women less happy, even early in the courtship. Just ask the woman Tucker fucked in law school and then hustled out the door under the cover of darkness before his roommates could see.

However, married couples with strongly overlapping social networks are less likely to get divorced. Meeting a woman's friends and family, and making an effort to win their approval, is another potent signal of social accountability and reveals that you have "honorable" longer-term intentions. The more she's integrated into your social network, the more confident she can feel that you won't dump her lightly or cheat on her, because your friends would think you're a douche.

Even declaring your "relationship status" on Facebook can be strong romantic proof. A woman knows it makes you socially accountable to social media friends, so if you switched back to "single," they'd ask about why you broke up.

Takeaways

- The other traits and proofs are about broadcasting your innate qualities; romantic proof is *narrowcasting* your commitment to a specific woman about how you feel, whether it's a short-, medium-, or long-term mating scenario.

- The key to romantic proof is gradual escalation. Do not express your undying love after one date or an extra-long hug in the hallway between classes. It has to develop and grow over time, based on your interactions with the woman.
- You cannot bullshit your way through romantic proof. There is an impulse to tell a woman what you think she wants to hear, but she's heard that a thousand times. You have to be honest about your intentions and about how you feel at any given moment. That honesty tells her that your signals of interest are legitimate.
- Pay attention! There is nothing more romantic or indicative of true interest than paying attention to what a woman wants, thinks, feels, needs, or likes.

Go Where the Women Are

CHAPTER 15: FIND THE RIGHT MATING MARKETS

To know values is to know the meaning of the market.
                            —*Charles Dow (co-founder Dow Jones)*

If you are like most guys, the most important decisions you make about mating won't feel like mating decisions at all.

Where you decide to live, study, work and hang out are not just random, superficial lifestyle choices. They're crucial to your success—or failure— with women. Most mating is local, so geography matters. A lot. **The fact is, you can't meet the right women if you're in the wrong place.**

This means that your city, your college campus, your workplace, your gym, and your favorite coffee shop are not just physical locations. They're also what scientists call "mating markets."

WHAT IS A "MATING MARKET?"

Imagine a map of all the single people around you, wherever you are. The women are pink dots and the men are blue dots. Each person has a certain "dating radius"—the maximum distance they're willing to go for a date. If they have to walk, that might be two miles; if they have a car, it might be twenty miles. Each person's dating radius marks out a roughly circular territory— their pink or blue "dating zone."

Your local mating market is simply the set of all the single women and men whose dating zones overlap with yours. It's a giant Venn diagram full of lust, love, and longing.

If you're shipwrecked on a small island with just one woman, your mating market is just two people: one pink dot and one blue dot in the same tropical dating zone. Your only option is to mate with her, or spend your days making sex dolls out of coconuts and palm leaves. But her options are similarly limited: mate with you or stay celibate. Your mate value on the mainland might have been mediocre, but here, your mate value suddenly becomes relatively high.

But if you add one more guy to the island, now the woman has options, and your relative mate value might drop if the other guy's good-looking, physically healthy, or not a crazy person making sex dolls out of vegetation.

On the other hand, if you add one more woman to the island, now you have options, and the two women will probably compete harder for your attention. You'll have even higher mate value and more bargaining power to get what you want from either woman.

Most modern mating markets are much bigger than an island, but the principles are the same. About 1.6 million people live in Manhattan, and all of the single ones make up one big mating market. Whether they live in an NYU dorm, a TriBeCa loft, or an Upper East Side penthouse, they're all within fairly easy walking, subway, or taxi distance of each other. They'd all prefer not to date someone who lives up in the Bronx (a long subway ride) or down in Staten Island (a ferry ride). They're all sort of stuck with each other. Even if they never meet more than 1 percent of the opposite sex, *everybody's relative mate value is influenced by everybody else's mating options.* And since there are 30 percent more college-educated single women than college-educated single men in Manhattan, the quality guys are in short supply and can get away with acting like they're lords of an island harem.

There are lots of mating markets at intermediate scales between the tiny desert island and the vastness of Manhattan. The practicalities of meeting, dating, and travel shape how this works. Mating markets can be tiny and transient (the twenty single people at one party, for one evening) or larger and relatively fixed (a dorm floor or a law school class).

All of these mating markets, at all different scales, overlap and intersect in complicated ways. But within a given mating market, there are some simple principles that govern how men and women interact. *Understanding these mating market principles and choosing your mating markets carefully is your golden ticket to mating success.*

HOW DO MARKETS WORK?

In economics, a market is a set of sellers and buyers exchanging goods and services for money. For example, all of the customers and retailers at your nearest shopping mall form a small physical market, whereas eBay is a big online market.

If it's a free market, the exchanges are voluntary rather than forced, so sellers will sell only if they expect a net benefit from the exchange, and buyers will buy only if they also expect a net benefit. The result is mutual benefits called "gains from trade." Like romantic relationships, free markets are founded on seeking win-win interactions. You buy a shirt because you value it more than the money you exchange for it, and the store sells it because they value your money more than the shirt. This exchange maximizes everybody's well-being, and this principle largely accounts for the world's dramatic rise from medieval misery to modern prosperity.

But even free markets differ in how *efficient* they are. In an efficient market, sellers and buyers can find each other quickly and easily, can communicate what they are offering and seeking, and respond adaptively to changes in local supply and demand by raising or lowering prices. In markets that are both free and efficient, prices tend to reflect supply and demand.

But not all markets are efficient. This is a key point about markets that many people, even some economists, forget: *no central authority is in control.* Nobody has to measure supply or demand for them to affect prices. The information about supply and demand is distributed throughout the market, and buyers and sellers just act on the local cues of abundance or scarcity that they have to make the best deals they can. The prices reach an equilibrium that reflects supply and demand throughout the whole market—even though nobody knows who's in the market or anything about what they want.

Let's be very clear about one thing: most mating markets are genuine free markets that operate by the mutually beneficial exchange of value according to supply and demand, *but that doesn't mean they depend on money or are really "about" money or resources.*

It doesn't mean that dinner dates are really just economic exchanges of lobster for blowjobs. Getting surf *and* turf doesn't mean she has to play with your balls too. It also doesn't mean that your mate value depends mostly on your wealth.

A lot of people take the market metaphor too literally, to serve their own ideological agendas. Religious fundamentalists promote family values by trying to keep marriage as a socially acceptable form of prostitution in which a wife offers sex for her husband's protection and support—*but that's not how modern marriages work.* Gender feminists promote their theory that patriarchy is a zero-sum game of men economically oppressing women, which is also nonsense, as women tend to economically benefit more from marriage than men. The more cynical manosphere writers think women are just trying to con men out of their resources, while men try to con sex out of women—as if all of human mating is just one big argument between greedy hookers and horny clients. This perspective fails to recognize that men substantially benefit from marriage in emotional, social, and physical ways.

They're all wrong. They're missing the real "gains from trade" between the sexes that can happen even when no money changes hands. The mating market concept has proven useful in understanding sexual relations in all sorts of nonhuman animals that don't have money, from insect courtship to bird pair-bonding. Throughout nature, the forms of value exchanged between females and males are hardly ever monetary—and often don't even involve any material resources like food. They run much deeper.

In mating markets, males and females exchange forms of biological value, like good genes, good partner traits, and good parent abilities, that have been important for hundreds of millions of years.

As you've learned, your mate value depends mostly on the quality of your physical and mental traits, not your bank balance, and it's expressed through your social, aesthetic, and romantic proofs, not just your material proof. In fact, if you go around offering women money for sex, or implying that "romance" is just a polite smokescreen for exchanging resources, you're not just misunderstanding human mating, but you're also being an asshole and displaying very low mate value: low social and emotional intelligence, paranoid delusions that all women are gold-diggers, and zero capacity for romantic commitment. And even worse, if someone actually bites on that line, it is almost certainly someone you want nothing to do with.

The exchanges that happen in mating markets tend to be mutually beneficial (win-win), not zero-sum. This is why we harp on creating "win-win" relationships so much—that is the point of mating. The more efficient a mating market, the faster and easier it is to develop great win-win relationships, and the more of them happen.

In other words, everybody who just wants sex gets to enjoy more sex! And everybody who just wants to find a spouse is much more likely to get happily married.

Efficient mating markets make most people about as happy as they could realistically hope. Efficient markets tend to "clear" themselves, meaning that almost everybody who wants a mate finds a mate, and most romantic desires are met by an offer of some sort, from somebody. Inefficient markets, on the other hand, don't clear. They frustrate the shit out of most everyone. In inefficient mating markets, you end up with a lot of women with cats and guys with metal detectors.

Of course, mating markets differ from economic markets in lots of other ways, but the basic dynamics are similar: people get together to seek what they want and offer what they have, and their success in making deals depends on what all the other people are seeking and offering.

Here's why this matters to you: are you offering what women are looking for in your local mating market? Because if you aren't, you will fail at mating.

LEARNING YOUR MATE VALUE FROM MATING MARKETS

Mating markets also have an information-sharing function. They help you learn your local mate value, given what the local women want, and what the other local men can offer.

Given an efficient mating market, you can run little experiments to gauge your mate value: Will this gorgeous woman talk to me? No? Then how about this other, slightly less attractive one? If you can't get a "hello" from anyone but the seventy-year-old Walmart greeter—whose *job* is to say hello—you know you've got some work to do.

You can also observe how other people's apparent traits, proofs, mating goals, and mate preferences seem to be influencing their success or failure (the healthy confident guys are going home with girls, the flabby insecure wallflowers are going home with 2 a.m. pizza). And you can gossip with friends about everybody's mating successes and failures, in relation to the quality of potential mates that they pursued *(Jim finally got laid last night but made her leave under the cover of darkness before any of us woke up. Maybe she was a vampire?).*

Then you can combine all this information to guide your decisions about which women to approach and what kinds of interactions you can realistically expect. You probably do that already but don't realize it. It's based on a fundamental process called "assortative mating."

In assortative mating, similar people tend to pair up together. Brainiacs prefer brainiacs. Hipsters attract hipsters. Mormons marry Mormons (and decades of psychology research show that opposites almost never attract, so wipe that idea from your head). Similarity at the level of specific traits like these—intelligence, aesthetic style, and religion—is important.

But the most important similarity is your **overall mate value.** Generally high-quality men tend to mate with generally high-quality women, leaving mediocre people no option but to pair up with each other. And then the even lower-quality people face the hard choice between mating with another reject or staying single. **This overall "mate-value matching" ain't fair, it ain't nice, and it ain't pretty. But it's reality.** And it speaks to the power of the human desire to connect, to pair up, to mate.

Mate-value matching isn't anyone's intention. It's just the outcome of everybody wanting the highest mate-value person that they can attract, combined with the fact that human mate choice requires mutual consent. It happens naturally in every efficient mating market, from Paleolithic clans to Manhattanites on Match.com.

In modern society, the men with the highest mate values get their first pick of women. They can "afford" almost anything in their mating market. Case in point: Physically attractive guys with lots of talent, money, and fame (like Brad Pitt) are in high demand among women, so they usually get the relationships they want.

On the flip side, since beautiful, clever, and kind women (like Angelina Jolie) are in short supply and high demand, those gems can select almost any partner they want as well. When high-quality boy meets high-quality girl, they tend to pair up, and they're hard to separate for more than a fling. Brad + Angelina = "Brangelina," the super-couple.

Here's the crucial thing: once the highest-mate-value people pair off and take themselves out of the mating market, the rest of us don't just give up and stay at home masturbating to replays of *Mr. and Mrs. Smith* on TNT. We can't all be Brad Pitt, but each of us can still find a mate. We just have to settle for a woman who's not Angelina—one who has similar mate value to us, *given the other men and women left in the mating market.*

The reality is that most people end up in relationships with people who are nowhere near the top of their mating list. And that's OK, because as we saw in the romantic proof chapter, *we evolved the ability to fall deeply in love with imperfect mates.* The low-mate-value couple can enjoy making babies with each other almost as much as Brangelina can. They just might have to turn the lights off first.

So when people go "shopping" in their mating market, they quickly learn that they're not paying money for their mate; they're offering *themselves—* their own mate value—as their contribution to the deal.

What they can get in return depends on all the factors of that mating market; their own mate value, the number of men versus women, and what women in that market are demanding from men.

Why does this matter to you? Because your mate value is often determined by the mating market you are in, not an objective measure. A 7 in Milwaukee is not a 7 in Manhattan. So picking a mating market that is good for you greatly increases your ability to attract a high-quality woman.

PRINCIPLES FOR CHOOSING GOOD MATING MARKETS

You've learned already that you can't meet a woman unless you're in a mating market that includes at least one woman. You probably know that if you spend all evening playing Settlers of Catan with three male friends and no women, none of you will get laid tonight. Women aren't like State Farm insurance agents—they're not like a good neighbor, and they're not just *there* when you want them.

But that's about as far as most of you guys get. You don't think about how many or what kinds of women are within your dating zone. You don't think about the mating goals those women pursue or what traits and proofs they value in men or offer to men. You don't think about your sexual rivals—how many other men are in your mating market or what kinds of mate value they offer to women. You don't think about which mating markets are actually efficient. You don't think about any of this shit, all to your detriment.

In general, you'll achieve much more mating success and find more women who are both attractive to you and attracted to you if you know the answers to all those questions and focus your effort in mating markets that have these key features:

1. A large number of women

When it comes to mating markets, size matters. Lots of women means you have lots of choice—both in the aggregate and specific to your preferences.

If you're a very bright guy looking for a very bright woman, you're far less likely to find her outside a big city or an elite college town with lots of very smart people. If you're into freaky sex, you probably won't find your ideal partner-in-kink in your tiny Appalachian hometown. If you really like Hispanic girls, Albuquerque (population 550,000, 47 percent Hispanic) would be a much better option than Detroit (population 690,000, but only 7 percent Hispanic): you'd have a pool of 130,000 rather than 24,000 Hispanic women.

Also, in tiny mating markets, the women all know each other, which can get awkward for them. In big cities, it's easier for women to be sexually adventurous without accidentally sleeping with their best friend's ex and without their friends slut-shaming them.

2. A low sex ratio

In biology, *sex ratio is defined as the ratio of males to females in a breeding population.* If there's a high sex ratio, like three guys for every woman (e.g., a typical Comic Con or computer science class), most of the guys will fail to mate. If there's a low ratio, like two women for every man (e.g., College of Charleston or University of North Carolina), it's a mating paradise for almost every guy.

There aren't enough men to go around, so the women compete harder for men in every possible way. They'll become more emotionally generous and sexually adventurous; they'll adore you and boost your confidence rather than make you feel disposable. Also, a low sex ratio means less competition from other men—they're too busy getting laid and enjoying girlfriends to throw salt in your game or fight you. With a low sex ratio, you can relax your guard and enjoy being a lover rather than a fighter.

(We'll wait to move on for a second while you go look up flights to Raleigh-Durham.)

3. A subculture open to your mating goals

Some communities (e.g., Mormons in Utah) are more sexually conservative, and everybody expects long, chaste courtship followed by faithful marriage. If you want to find a wife and minimize your risk of marital infidelity, these communities are mating markets that will appeal to you.

But if you are into short-term mating or swinging or other sorts of very open sexual mores, there are numerous subcultures that might be more attractive mating markets. Subcultures can arise, for example, in temporary or transient situations, and those themselves become mating markets. Places with high turnover rates, like airport hotel bars, ski resorts, and tourism-based cities (Las Vegas, Orlando), tend to have a lot of short-term mating. The ultimate short-term mating destinations are, of course, Florida and Mexico beach resorts during spring break (hence Tucker's adventures in Cancun). Everybody knows that they're unlikely to see someone again after a night of passion, so expectations of romantic commitment are low.

4. A place where your mate value is competitive

Some places just attract higher-quality people who have their shit together. Major metropolises like New York, San Francisco, and London attract a lot of talent in every domain: finance, law, medicine, academia, media, and the arts. Successful people make big money and drive up rents, and people with high mate value drive up dating standards.

Those places can be very difficult for young men to compete in unless they have amazing looks, brilliant wit, early fame, or family money. If you're in a mating market like New York, understand that you'll be competing against many rich, powerful, smart, older guys who are very experienced with very attractive women. You can still compete, especially given the favorable sex ratio for men, but you need to cultivate your traits and proofs before you can expect much success.

On the other hand, it can pay to be a big fish in a small pond. If you're a medium-quality guy in a mating market where most guys are losers, your mate value will be relatively high, and lots of cute women will be interested. This often happens in smaller cities where industry's collapsed but the service sector is still functioning (so men don't have jobs but women do), or college towns where the female undergrads and grad students are sick of frat boys and listless stoners.

When you're looking for a mating market, pay as much attention to the men there, who are your rivals, as to the women there. *Women aren't measuring you against all the men on earth; they're measuring you against the other men they have access to.*

If you have your life much more together than most of the other guys in your mating market, you can do very well, even if the women seem way out of your league. You don't need to be as cool as Brad Pitt, you just have to be a little more Pitt-like than the other guys in this bar, on this night, in this town.

5. A place where your age is especially attractive

A mating market's age structure can also influence your relative mate value. Women tend to prefer slightly older men. When there aren't enough slightly older men to go around, women lower their standards and act more promiscuous. The 1960s sexual revolution was caused partly by the Baby Boom demographics: there was a huge surge of young women and young men, but the young women wanted slightly older men who were in scarce supply, so they offered more sex and expected less commitment.

The same effect still happens in most college towns: if you're a twenty-five-year-old guy in a place full of undergrads, you can do very well. Likewise if you're a decent guy in your 40s in a place full of frustrated women in their 30s (like NYC), they've already realized that most of the men at their ideal age are either married, never-married losers, or divorced-and-damaged dads. You might be the droid they've been looking for.

---

6. A place where your distinctive traits and proofs are especially attractive

Americans move around a lot, and they move to cities full of like-minded people. So different American cities develop very different social norms about particular traits and proofs.

For example, places that attract lots of good-looking people (e.g., wannabe movie stars flocking to LA) put a big premium on handsomeness, so if you have the face of an extra (like "redneck zombie #5"), don't move there.

Some places (e.g., Denver, Austin) have high expectations about physical fitness. Don't move there if you're obese, because your mate value will be appreciably low. The Gulf Coast states would be more accepting.

Some places (e.g., Cambridge, Silicon Valley) attract lots of smart people who have high expectations about book smarts. Move there if you have a Ph.D. (women will love it); don't move there if you can't spell Ph.D. (women will be repulsed).

7. Ease of meeting people

Some college campuses have buzzing student union buildings where everybody goes for lunch, and you can meet tons of women; other campuses with equal numbers of students seem like post-apocalyptic wastelands devoid of life.

Some cities have pedestrian-friendly downtowns, mixed-used developments, and great indoor malls where you can easily meet new people. Others are mostly sprawling suburbs with mini-malls where nobody gets out of the car unless absolutely necessary and the only way to meet somebody in another car is to run into them.

East Coast cities with good public transportation are much easier to get around in if you don't have a car, so your dating radius can be big even if you're poor.

Some cities (e.g., Austin) have vibrant nightlife scenes for short-term mating, others (e.g., Cincinnati) not so much. Some (e.g., Houston, Louisville) have excellent mega-churches where you can find a devout spouse, others not. Even among online dating sites, some (like OkCupid) make it much easier to find out enough about someone to send them an interesting personalized message; others (like Tinder) offer so little information in profiles that it's harder to strike up a conversation.

OkCupid Isn't Stupid: Use It to Find the City for You

To figure out which cities include lots of women who will be good matches for you, use the tools that are already out there in the online dating world. Specifically, the data-oriented dating website OkCupid.com. OkCupid has fine-tuned thousands of questions to find matches based on intelligence, personality traits, interests, and values.

To be clear, this is not about finding *specific* women; it's about figuring out which mating markets include a higher concentration of the kinds of women you like. Here's how to do it:

1. **Join OkCupid and go through the basic account setup:** Pick a username, answer the first five questions, "like" at least three women. Then enter key information in "My details," such as your ethnicity, height, and religion.

2. **Go to your profile, and click "Questions":** Answer a lot of questions, totally honestly, straight from the gut. Just remember these principles: *be honest, seek win-win relationships.* The more honest you are and the more questions you answer, the more accurate your results will be.

3. **Answer at least a couple hundred questions, across all the categories** (sex, dating, ethics, lifestyle, religion, other): For each question, you'll need to give your answer and also how you'd ideally want a woman to answer.

4. **Skip any question you don't care about, and rate every question that you do answer as "somewhat important":** the goal is to answer at least 300 questions in about an hour. You want to raise your "Highest match possible" up to at least 98%.

5. **Click on "Browse matches," and enter your basic search criteria:**
   a. women
   b. interested in men
   c. ages (e.g., 18 to 26)
   d. online in the last month (i.e., active in the mating market)
   e. and then *rank the matches by match percent* (NOT the default "Special Blend")

6. **Do this exercise once locally and a few times regionally:** Figure out which places have a lot of women who are at least an 80 percent match. That's a high enough percent that you'll have a lot in common, but a low enough percent that you're casting a reasonably wide net. Even if you're just looking for short-term mating, higher matches make it way easier to make a connection.

---

a. Locally—set your search radius to twenty miles around your current ZIP Code. Tally up the number of women above an 80 percent match. That represents your current local mating market.

b. Regionally—set your search radius to 500 miles around your current ZIP Code and do the same tally of 80+ percent matches. *Then*, do the exact same search around the seven key American cities listed below. They're not all the largest cities, but they cover more than 90 percent of American and Canadian women:

- New York (e.g., ZIP Code 11211). The radius covers most of the Eastern Seaboard, from Maine and Quebec down to Raleigh, North Carolina, and west to Cleveland.
- Chicago (ZIP Code 60601), covering most of the Midwest, from Minneapolis to Toronto, down to St. Louis and Louisville.
- Tallahassee, Florida (e.g., ZIP Code 32311), covering most of the South, from Miami to New Orleans, up to Nashville and Raleigh.
- Dallas (ZIP Code 75201), covering Texas, and up to Kansas City, Missouri, and east to Memphis, Tennessee.
- Denver (ZIP Code 80201), covering most of the Rocky Mountain cities from Montana to New Mexico and Kansas to Utah.
- Portland (ZIP Code 97209), covering all of Oregon, Washington, and British Columbia.
- Los Angeles (ZIP Code 90046), which covers almost all of California, Nevada, and Arizona.

7. **Rank the cities by number of matches:** Do these women cluster anywhere? Which city near you has the highest concentration of like-minded women? That's your nearest optimal potential mating market. Is there any good reason why you haven't moved there already? Or won't when you can? Use science, not bias, to make your decisions. Cities with more than 50 high matches are great mating markets for you.

If you do this exercise as part of choosing where to go to college or where to move after college, your dating life will be *way* easier and more fun. It doesn't hurt that it involves looking at lots of photos of beautiful women either.

Think about each potential mating market not just in terms of who's there and what they want, but how you will actually meet them and interact with them in the most basic practical ways.

TAKE ACTION AND MOVE INTO YOUR IDEAL MATING MARKETS

Think about *why* you live where you live. Was it just your arbitrary birthplace where your parents happened to settle? Did it just have the best college you could get into at the time?

Those are inertia-based reasons for living somewhere, not conscious reasons. If you're willing to move somewhere for the sake of a good education or a good job, shouldn't you be willing to move for the sake of a good potential mate?

That was a rhetorical question—of course you should be willing to. If you're not, you'll be disappointing a lot of women who'd like to meet you, and you'll be short-changing yourself.

At the very least, think about spending your time in different places than you're used to. Wherever you study, work, and hang out now might not be the ideal choice for your overall lifestyle, much less your mating success. That's OK. You didn't know how much leverage the right geography could give you.

The most important mating markets in your life, roughly from largest to smallest, are these:

1. What country you live in

Most people stay in whatever country they were born in. But that's rarely the ideal country for them to find mates. There are big differences across nations and cultures in everything related to mating, from their mating goals and sexual norms (like the Netherlands versus Saudi Arabia) to the traits and proofs that are most valued (like intelligence in England, wealth in Russia, or style in Italy).

2. What city you live in

Even within America, cities differ hugely in their populations, sex ratios, age profiles, and sexual norms (think Las Vegas vs. Salt Lake City). They differ in the ease of meeting new people and ease of traveling for dates (think walkable Boulder vs. drivable Tucson vs. undrivable LA). Some cities (like Indianapolis and Detroit) just suck for everybody who's single, and some (like Austin and Seattle) are better for most singles, but none are ideal for everybody.

The city that's ideal for you, given your goals and desires, is probably not the city you happen to be living in now. You should be willing to move to achieve the mating life you want.

---

3. What neighborhood you live in

Within each city, neighborhoods differ dramatically in all the same ways that countries and cities do. They also differ in the proportion of single people actively seeking mates: within Manhattan, think about the Upper West Side (married people with kids) vs. Tribeca (rich young banking couples with kids) vs. Greenwich Village (tons of horny NYU students). Move to neighborhoods where active singles live, study, work, and mingle. Pedestrian-friendly neighborhoods also make it much easier to bump into women than car-based suburban sprawl does.

4. Where you go to school

A low sex ratio at a college is a huge predictor of your mating success as a male student (helloooo, UNC-Chapel Hill!). Schools differ in sexual norms and mating goals, from "party schools" focused on short-term mating (Tulane, UCSB, Penn State) to Christian "ring by spring" schools where virgin students try to get engaged before their final semester (Baylor, Occidental, and any school with the word "Wesleyan" in the name). Choosing a school with a good sex ratio and sexual norms that fit your mating goals can be more important to your college experience than its academic reputation or financial aid package. It's a lot easier to study economic theory or Russian imperial history when you're not in a frozen, sexless wasteland.

5. What job you work

Work is a major mating market: a lot of people hook up with coworkers and marry work colleagues. What *kind* of job you do matters: service jobs in big restaurants, bars, coffee shops, grocery stores, malls, and bookshops let you mingle with lots of female customers and coworkers.

Where you work matters as well: an office job in a busy, pedestrian-friendly downtown offers a lot more opportunities to meet women during lunch and after work than an office job in a suburban office park. Jobs that involve conferences, trainings, and getaways are especially fun, because everybody hooks up at off-site events.

6. What social groups you join

Your social network isn't just a form of social proof; it's also a mating market in its own right. Female friends and acquaintances can become lovers, and they extend your reach into new social circles through friends of friends. Are you often hanging out with mixed-sex groups of friends who know other cool people, or are you just staying at home watching imaginary relationships between TV characters who can't introduce you to anyone?

7. What leisure activities you do

What fun things do you do on evenings and weekends? Do any women do those things? You might like guns, but shooting ranges suck for meeting women—there aren't many of them, and they're probably there learning to defend themselves against guys like you, and it's too loud to talk. If you're into live-action role-playing games (LARPing) or Civil War battle re-enactments, you'll face a sex ratio of about ten men for every woman.

On the other hand, if you take classes in salsa dancing or acroyoga or acting, you'll probably have five single women for every guy, lots of opportunities to talk, and a teacher telling them to touch you! Also try speed-dating events—local singles events specifically designed to introduce you to the largest number of women as quickly and efficiently as possible. Go where the women already are, doing the things they like.

8. What online dating sites you use

Online dating sites and mobile dating apps give you mate-search superpowers. Each site or app tends to specialize in different mating goals (e.g., Adult-FriendFinder for casual sex with "hot, horny singles…*NOW!*," Tinder and Zoosk for short-term dating, Match.com, eHarmony, and PlentyofFish for longer-term relationships, OkCupid for polyamory).

Some niche dating sites have specific clienteles (e.g., JDate for Jewish people, FarmersOnly for "good ol' country folk," 420 Singles for marijuana enthusiasts). Apps differ in how much information the profiles can contain (from tiny Tinder self-descriptions to massive OkCupid question-banks) and how much interaction the apps allow (from simple text messaging to Speed-Match's live video).

But remember, online dating is only as good as your local mating market—unless you're willing to take a plane to your first coffee date. Match.com works a *lot* better in Brooklyn than in Fresno.

We're not saying you should start packing tonight and take the next train to Brooklyn—not with all those annoying hipsters jacking up rental prices. Moving to a new country, city, or college is a serious, costly life-change that could bring massive benefits—or bitter disappointment. We're just saying you should seriously consider it.

Or you could just stay in the same city for the moment, and try to rediscover its best local mating markets. They're probably right under your nose. Think about changing jobs to somewhere surrounded by the kind of women you like. Think about what you like to do in your spare time, and go where the women are. In your social network, reach out to female friends of friends.

We've explained what mating markets are and how to find the ones that are best for you—now it's time to shop.

Takeaways

- Mating markets are geographically defined local dating zones (even if you're using online dating) that operate on the supply-and-demand dynamics of free markets in order to yield win-win outcomes for men and women whose mate-values are comparable.
- Picking the best mating markets for you, given what you want and what you offer to women, is the single most powerful way to improve your mating success. But you must understand your mating goals (what kinds of interactions or relationships you want), your mate preferences (what kinds of women you like), and your mate value (the traits and proofs that you can offer to women).
- Moving into better mating markets is a win-win for everybody. You'll have a much easier time meeting more women who value you. You'll have more dates, more sex, and better relationships. And they'll have a much easier time meeting you. *By redeploying yourself wherever more women will want you, you're bringing more joy to more women* and reducing their frustration that "there aren't any good men out there" (meaning, within easy driving distance).
- The ideal mating markets for you have these features:
  1. A large number of women of whatever age and ethnicity you prefer
  2. A low operational sex ratio (fewer men than women seeking mates)
  3. A subculture open to your mating goals (whether short term or long term)
  4. A market in which your mate-value is competitive, compared to the other guys there
  5. A market in which your age is especially attractive, given the ages of women and male rivals there
  6. A market in which your distinctive traits and proofs are especially attractive, given the women's preferences there
  7. An environment in which it's easy to meet people, given the practicalities of public life
- Don't let geographic inertia rule your mating life. Nobody else can choose your mating markets for you. Take responsibility for your attractiveness by taking responsibility for where you live and spend your time.

CHAPTER 16: BEGGARS *MUST* BE CHOOSERS

(MATE PREFERENCES)

The heart, like the stomach, wants a varied diet.

—Gustave Flaubert

If you used to be desperate to get *any* woman and you follow the advice laid out thus far in the book, soon you'll reach a point where you can attract *many* women.

That shift from any to many, from scarcity to abundance, can happen very quickly. And that's when you'll face an entirely new problem: choosing among the women who are attracted to *you*.

This is a very good problem to have. Like billionaires having to choose how they will get to work tomorrow: will it be the limo, the helicopter, the jet, or the boat? People call this an embarrassment of riches, but it's still a problem, and handling it well will be *really* important for the rest of your life.

By choosing the best women possible for you, given your preferences and mating goals, you're doing your future self a real solid. He'll be really grateful that you got so wise about women when you were still so young.

HOW MALE MATE CHOICE DIFFERS FROM FEMALE CHOICE

You've already learned how women seek men with good genes, good boy-friend potential, and good dad potential.

What you probably didn't know is that *you can use the same insights* when you're seeking good genes, good girlfriend potential, and good mom potential in women.

Women differ in all the same traits and proofs that men do, like physical fitness, emotional stability, IQ, self-control, empathy, popularity, income, and style. Almost all of these traits and proofs predict good partner and good parent potential to very similar degrees in both sexes.

Where men and women differ substantially is how they compete in the mating game. Generally speaking, it works like this:

Men compete more for short-term sex, and women compete more for long-term commitment.

For most young men, getting laid is the ultimate sexual outcome.

For most women, getting a guy to go steady as her boyfriend is a major milestone; getting him to propose marriage is the ultimate outcome.

Read that section again and again until it is seared into your brain: *men compete for sex, and women compete for commitment.*

Because of this, in most interactions with women, there's a power dynamic in mate choice that goes back and forth like a sexually-charged pendulum:

1. **Approach choice: Men choose which women to approach and talk to.** Guys usually pursue women who seem hot enough to fuck, fun enough to talk to, and sane enough not to create drama. This doesn't seem like a "mate choice" at all to most guys. It just feels like instinctive lust, intriguing chemistry, or a romantic crush. But it is still an unconscious form of choice.

2. **Sex choice: Women choose which men to have sex with.** As we've seen, women usually select guys who have the traits and proofs that offer good genes, good partner potential, and good dad potential.

3. **Relationship choice: Men choose which women to date.** After the first real hookup(s), guys start getting choosier about whether a woman is actually compelling enough to keep dating, and women tend to try to keep the guy around (assuming the woman is into him).

To recap: Boy meets girl (approach choice), girl might agree to sex (sex choice), boy might eventually commit or propose marriage (relationship choice).

This third step is where things get really interesting, because not only is post-sex choice by males rare across mammals (males in most species don't form long-term pair bonds or invest much in offspring), but in humans it is also where males have most of their mate choice power and most of their bargaining power within relationships.

If your main mating goal is short-term sex, you've probably felt the sting of thousands of rejections from women who didn't show any interest in fucking you. But among the handfuls or (if you're Tucker) hundreds of women who did fuck you, many of them probably felt the sting of your not pursuing them afterward—and you didn't even realize it.

The guys who think that women have all the power in mating are too focused on trying to get laid (sex choice by women); they're ignoring what happens the morning after: men failing to follow up after sex is often women's biggest frustration. It's what provokes women to share these kinds of confused, exasperated complaints with their female friends:

"He didn't text me after we hooked up!"

"He just never arranged a third date!"

"He's just not that into me, even after I let him try the back door!"

"He got cold feet before the wedding and left me at the altar!"

These are all examples of post-sex choice by men. They all involve men deciding not to continue a relationship and not to escalate their commitment. Women have learned to fear that post-coital shift from male lust to male indifference. It's when their power of female choice is weakest, and your power of male choice gets most brutal.

That's the step when you can get very choosy about which lover becomes your girlfriend and which girlfriend becomes your wife.

It's also a real test of your mating ethics. If you do post-sex rejections of women by going ruthlessly "scorched earth" or pulling a Houdini like an asshole, it ruins their dignity, spoils their happiness, and embitters them toward men—making the whole mating market worse for everyone.

So how should you act?

POST-SEX CHOICE IS YOUR RIGHT AS A MAN; JUST DON'T BE A DICK ABOUT IT

Women have an absolute moral right to decide who they have sex with and who they don't. Just because a woman agrees to a date or a kiss doesn't also mean she agrees to sex. She still has the right to evaluate every aspect of your mate-value, to say "No, stop!" all the way through to the end of any sexual encounter, even if she's agreed to play your little game of "just the tip." And if she rejects you *before* sex, you have no right to call her a "stuck-up cunt who needs to loosen up." That reaction alone would prove she made the right choice when she gave your penis the Heisman and ran the other way.

But this goes both ways. Men have an absolute moral right to post-sex choice, deciding which women we *continue* to have sex with and which we don't.

Assuming you're open and *honest* about your mating goals, just because you and a woman have agreed to have sex doesn't mean you've agreed to become her boyfriend. You still have the right to evaluate every aspect of her mate-value all the way through your interactions with her. And you have the right to say "No, thanks!" right up until the moment you marry her. If you reject a woman after sex, she has no right to call you a "needle-dick loser who needs to man up."

This is very important for you, because it impacts your whole mating life. **You have to get comfortable with asserting your post-sex choice rights, to have any hope of ending up in a well-chosen relationship with a high-quality woman.**

If you don't do the hard work now of practicing that open, honest post-sex assertiveness, you'll find yourself becoming a boyfriend for months, or a husband for years, maybe with the wrong woman. If you don't have the guts to say no to commitment with a woman who pushes her way into your life, because you're too concerned about being nice and not upsetting her, your weakness is doing neither of you any favors. You might regret a decade of bad marriage for the rest of your life.

Post-sex choice puts a special moral burden on men, because we have to exercise it when we've already gotten to know a woman intimately. For women, the most awkward rejections they've had to impose on guys have been things like ignoring a stranger's shitty pickup line, or telling a coworker that they just want to be friends. They don't know these guys very well, aren't empathically intertwined with them, and don't feel much guilt about spurning them. And mature, confident guys can shrug off such rejections by thinking "if only she got to know me better, she probably would have liked me more."

By contrast, if a man cuts off relations with a woman he's already had sex with, he knows her much better and they've probably had some moments of real emotional connection. It's hard for her not to take the rejection personally. She'll second-guess everything. He's already seen her boobs, so she wonders if they are too asymmetrical. He's heard her orgasm (if he's any good), so she wonders if she sounded too much like a bellowing hippo or a wounded songbird.

The pain of rejection gets exponentially worse for women if they've been dating for months, so he knows everything about her past background and future ambitions, her friends and family, her career and interests, her tastes and attitudes. Male post-sex choice at that point can be deeply wounding, because it really is a judgment about her whole worth as a woman from a man who quite possibly knows her better than her own parents do.

So remember: with the great power of male post-sex choice comes great responsibility.

Make no mistake: if you take our advice in this book, improve your attractiveness, and get more successful in dating, *you will end up disappointing a lot of women who fall for you*. The question is *how* you reject them.

Do you break their hearts like a tenth-grader—messily, stupidly, awkwardly, and insultingly? Or do you find the courage to break up like a grown-ass man—with empathic kindness but decisive clarity?

Be honest, be straight, be kind, but end it and move on. A well-managed breakup is also almost as important as a well-managed courtship, because it protects your self-image as a good guy, so you have more self-confidence about your mating ethics when you get back into the mating market.

If you know that a girlfriend wants a long-term relationship, and you know that you don't, the earlier you break up, the better for her. If you're both 25, she's only got 15 more years of decent fertility, whereas you've got at least 35 more years. A pointless 5–year relationship would burn through 1/3 of her potential motherhood years, but would only waste 1/7 of your potential fatherhood years. Respect how precious her reproductive potential is by letting her go, sooner rather than later, so she can find her real Mr. Right.

CLARIFYING YOUR MATE PREFERENCES: WHAT KIND OF WOMEN SHOULD YOU SEEK?

When your guy friends ask you what kinds of girls you like, you're probably used to rattling off a bunch of physical traits, and maybe one personality trait to show you're not a superficial douchebag. These are basically just whatever forms of cuteness would catch your eye in the first minute of gawking at a woman. You might say, "I like nice boobs, a cute butt, a pretty face, and a good sense of humor." But that kind of reply is too vague, meaningless, and misguided, on several levels.

First, you're not identifying *your* specific preferences. You're just listing features that every normal adult male human likes.

If you share your real preferences with your male friends, they will be baffled by some and try to argue passionately for the opposite, like "No way!

CrossFit girls are scary and look like dudes!" Provoking reactions like that is a sign that you've been specific and honest, not that you're weird (unless you describe your mother right down to her age, gray hair, and mom jeans).

Second, saying that you like women who are "nice," "cute," "pretty," and "good" doesn't *describe* exactly what you're seeking. Those adjectives only *evaluate* women at the vaguest possible level. Imagine trying to have phone sex with a girl who uses those kinds of words to describe how she looks and what she's wearing. *Great, so you look like my five-year-old niece at bedtime. <click!>.*

You have to get more specific: What does "pretty" mean to you? What does she do to be considered "nice" or "good"? Also, what exactly do you mean by "good sense of humor"? When she tells jokes, are they more like Sarah Silverman or your great-aunt Sarah with the Great Big Book of Puns?

Third, you're focused way too much on what guides your *approach choices* rather than your *post-sex choices*. If you're interested in any kind of interaction longer than one-night stands, you need to clarify what turn-ons would lead you to seek a second night, and what turn-offs would drive you away by the fourth night.

Different men show very strong agreement about which women are attractive enough to approach, but they differ quite a bit about what drives them nuts in relationships. It's especially important to get clarity about your post-sex choice preferences, since they're unique to you, and they'll do a lot of the heavy lifting in sorting the A+ girlfriends from the B+ girlfriends.

Exercise: Let Yourself Be Your Guide

To help you clarify what your distinctive, specific mate preferences really are, think seriously about your past crushes, lovers, and relationships.

Make a list of every memorable female from every point in your life who was sexually or romantically attractive to you, even if you never hooked up or even expressed that interest. For each one, list every single one of their pros and cons.

The key here is to be distinctive (things you liked or hated that other guys might react to differently) and specific (*exactly* what turned you on or off about the person, rather than vague evaluative terms).

You also need to be brutally honest. This is the one domain of life where you are allowed to be as choosy, narrow, sexist, racist, elitist, and judgmental as you want. It's your life and your penis.

Remember your people-centered morality: *There are no bad preferences, only bad ways to treat other people.*

Everybody has some kinky, quirky preferences that just can't be explained rationally, and you ignore them at your peril. It's not fair to get into a relationship with a woman who doesn't match your quirky ideals and then break up with her eventually, just because you couldn't admit to yourself that she wasn't what you were really looking for.

So include everything that you reacted to about lovers and crushes past, from the lowest form of raw physical lust (huge tune-in-Tokyo nipples) to the most enlightened form of spiritual connection (studied comparative religion at Berkeley).

Once you've filled your table with your whole list of women and their positive and negative traits, you've got your reference guide. Read it again and again. Study it. This is serious detective work into your own sexual circuitry. Look for patterns. Tick how many times you listed particular turn-offs and turn-ons, so you can start developing a master list of your key preferences.

This is not the list you will post on your Match.com profile; it is for your eyes only.

But it's important, because it's your personal sexual compass to what you truly like and don't like. This list will help you understand what you are looking for so that you can now go find those specific women in the mating markets where they are spending their time.

HOW TO SELECT WOMEN FOR SHORT-TERM MATING

After you've clarified your general mate preferences, you can figure out how they fit with your mating goals. Let's say you just want short-term interactions for now. That's great, but do it right. Here are some key things that guys overlook or get wrong when in hot pursuit:

1. Focus on women who send signals that they're open to short-term mating.

We get emails all the time from guys saying things like, "I met this girl and she says she wants a boyfriend and is thinking about marriage and kids soon, but I just want to hook up. What can I say to make her just want to hook up?"

Nothing, you fucking idiot! Leave her alone! She doesn't want what you want. *She even told you that specifically!*

Trying to deceive and seduce a long-term-oriented woman into a short-term interaction violates three of our five principles: it fails to understand women's perspective, it's dishonest, and it tries to impose a win-lose relationship on an unwilling victim.

Not only that, it makes things so hard on you. The way to make things easy is very clear:

If you just want to have sex, find girls who just want to have sex.

The tricky thing is that these girls into short-term mating don't go around wearing T-shirts that say "Please Fuck Me & Forget My Name." Very few women list "casual sex" as a goal in their OkCupid profile.

Why not? Because women face the risk of slut-shaming from other women, so they need plausible deniability when they send signals of openness to short-term sex.

Also, lots of clueless men confuse *selective promiscuity* (a woman's openness to one-night stands with amazing, funny, hot guys) with *indiscriminate promiscuity* (a sex worker's openness to one-hour transactions with almost any paying customer).

In fact, high-quality, sexually-open women can often be *more* selective about their short-term partners than lower-quality monogamous women can be about choosing their husbands. If you're one of the guys who mistakes selective promiscuity for being a whore, *you're one of the main reasons why women don't advertise more clearly that they're DTF if you're H-O-T.*

In our experience, here are some cues of women's openness to short-term mating. Remember, none of these clues are anywhere near 100 percent reliable. You have to cultivate your short-term mating-cue radar to detect them with even moderate accuracy.

Where She Is

Women make choices about where they go socially based on what they want sexually. Just like you select your mating markets to fit your mating goals, women do too.

Sex Parties: If you're handsome and witty and downright lucky enough to get invited to some kind of private polyamorous fuckfest, that would obviously be an ideal place for meeting a woman who's into short-term mating. They still have the power of female choice, but the women have clearly come to play, and it's quite likely that they'll fuck at least one person here. If you play your cards right, that could be you.

Bars and Clubs: The expectations aren't as clear as at a sex party, but women who are just looking to hook up with cute male strangers know that they can find plenty of such men in bars and clubs and sort through them very efficiently. However, although hookup-seekers are there in a higher proportion than almost anywhere else, *most* women in the bar or club still aren't looking to hook up—they're there to hang with friends, dance, get drunk, whatever—so don't assume.

Holiday Spots: At spring break resorts, airport hotel bars, or conferences—any place she had to take a two-or-more-hour drive or flight to get to—a woman knows that whatever man she meets is unlikely to become a long-term boyfriend, simply because he's outside her dating radius. So if a woman's showing any mating effort in her clothes, makeup, and attitude, she's probably open to short-term mating—if the right guy shows up.

Online: Few online dating sites are as blunt as the gay male app Grindr, where you can find a dude to give you a blowjob within about five minutes in any major city. But some of the heterosexual sites come close, like AdultFriendFinder or Zoosk.

Otherwise, use Tinder, Hinge, or other dating apps that don't require much verbal detail in your profile. As a rule: If the typical profile includes more than two photos but fewer than twenty words, people probably aren't looking for longer-term relationships. Even on the more respectable sites like Match.com or OkCupid, some women will tick that they're open to "short-term dating," which is as close as they can get to saying "casual sex" without being slut-shamed or attracting too many male idiots (though they will attract a lot of male idiots regardless).

How She Looks

If a woman's going out to a bar seeking a short-term mate, she's more likely to wear her sexiest outfit that accentuates all her best qualities rather than a bunch of layers that hide her shape and make her blend into the background.

When movies and TV portray women on the prowl for men, the actresses are usually dressed far sluttier than any normal women dress, so that male viewers can enjoy ogling their bodies. This is confusing to guys. Don't expect normal women seeking short-term mates in real life to dress as slutty as girls do in sex comedies or porn.

You have to learn to spot the difference between stylish (seeking boyfriend) and flirty (open to a hookup). You also have to remember that just because a woman is dressed flirty does NOT mean she wants to hook up with YOU. She's not "asking for it," and she's not "fair game"; she's simply signaling her potential willingness to be approached by the *right guys* who have their shit together.

Some women signal their mating goals in more permanent ways, like tattoos. The larger and more numerous the tattoos, the more open a woman tends to be toward short-term mating. Likewise for piercings or any kind of body modification.

Again, this does NOT mean that every girl with a "tramp stamp" or a nose stud is DTF with any random guy. It's just one partly reliable cue among many.

How She Talks

A woman who's open to a hookup might signal it through saying things like this after a few minutes of talking:

- "I just want to have fun."
- "I'm not looking for a boyfriend right now."
- "I just want to meet a lot of new people and explore my options."
- "I just got out of a long relationship and am ready to party."
- "I want more excitement in my life."

She will usually NOT say any of these things within the first hour of talking with you (unless she's really drunk):

- "If this night doesn't end with something in my butt, I will be pissed."
- "Just looking for cock right now."
- "I just want to fuck a lot of new people and explore my fetishes."
- "My ex's dick was too small, I'm looking for a huge one."
- "I want more orgasms in my life—you in?"

She might be thinking these things, but she won't say them in case anyone overhears her, or you quote her.

Of course, a woman's direct statement of interest in short-term mating with you (e.g., "Wanna get out of here?") can trump any cues based on where she is, how she looks, or how else she talks.

But even then, she might be running a kind of bait-and-switch—hooking up with you in hopes that she can convert you into a longer-term boyfriend. If you want to be confident that she'd be comfortable having sex and not expecting a second date, the other cues can be important.

The freshman virgin at the Indiana University frat party who says "Wanna get out of here?" probably has very different expectations than the twenty-eight-year-old Goth with full-sleeve tattoos in the Bronx who says the same.

2. Focus on the women who seem interested in you.

You might meet a hot woman at the bar, dressed in red leather, with "DTF" tattooed on her neck, but if she's working hard to ignore you, *leave her alone!* Focus your mating effort where it's appreciated.

That's very simple to understand, but many guys get this incredibly wrong. They try to find the hottest girl in the bar and spend all their time trying to flirt with her even when she's clearly not into them. This annoys her, wastes your time, and makes you look like a douche to every other woman there.

If you really just want a short-term hookup, it's better to take the opposite strategy: *start with the woman who's paying the most attention to you and who you'd actually want to have sex with.* If you get her back home, she'll feel almost as good in the dark as the hottest girl in the bar, and your chances with her are about twenty times higher.

3. The Dangers of Crazy Women

Some of the best women in the world are really into short-term mating with the right guys. So are some of the worst, craziest, most dangerous women. That's why short-term mating is such a high-risk game.

There's a stereotype that crazy women are easier to sleep with. Yes, some types of "craziness" make women easier to get into bed without much courtship. But the ease of courting them is negated by the horror show that they can impose on your life.

There is a big price to pay for crazy, and you won't know just

Good Slutty vs. Crazy Slutty

As a matter of basic self-protection you need to know how to distinguish between good and crazy promiscuous.

Good

- is quietly proud to be sex-positive and adventurous
- has lots of like-minded female friends
- will openly and frankly discuss exes, STD tests, and safe sex
- is comfortable with her body
- cuddles after sex but knows how to leave

Crazy

- is ashamed of her desires
- has few if any female friends
- doesn't like to talk about her past in any way
- is not comfortable with her body or what gives her pleasure
- often freaks the fuck out after sex

Avoid the crazy promiscuous ones. Their kind of craziness can ruin your life in ways you can't imagine yet. Respect these red flags.

how big it is until you find yourself still paying it off months afterwards. The blast radius from a one-night stand can reach far and wide, torching your reputation, your career, your mental health, and your self-confidence.

You might not suffer it the first three or ten times you hook up with a crazy woman. You might think "That was so easy! She was so spontaneous! The sex felt so good! I never texted her again and she didn't seem to mind!" And then you hit the one who saves your sperm or burns your fucking house down.

None of this is to say that you shouldn't hook up with lots of willing women if that's what you desire. You just need to know what the warning signs of crazy bad promiscuity are and seek out the signs of good promiscuity. If you swim in shark-infested waters without looking for the big fins poking up through the surface (and they always will) you're going to get bit sooner or later.

HOW TO PICK A WOMAN FOR LONG-TERM MATING

Good girlfriends and great wives make everything easier, happier, and more meaningful. They'll shape your whole subjective experience on a day-to-day level. If you're with a woman who's positive, stable, adaptable, and fun, that's going to rub off on you. It'll make setbacks bearable and victories sweeter. But if you're with a woman who's miserable, angry, critical, contemptuous, or snarky (*and you don't do anything about it!*), that's going to grind you into dust. Spare yourself that horrible fate.

1. What Matters the Most? Not Looks

Kim Kardashian's amazing booty? Kanye West was probably tired of it within a few months. Angelina Jolie's amazing lips? Brad Pitt probably took them for granted within a year.

After they get used to a woman's face, the shit that guys get tired of usually resides *behind* her face, in her brain. All the same traits and proofs that women are seeking in you will become things you start getting choosier and choosier about, the longer a relationship lasts and the more experience you get in longer-term relationships. This is where Kim's vocal fry, and Angelina's compulsion to turn her family into a UNICEF ad, might start to grate a little. If a long-term girlfriend proves to be less healthy, less interesting, less conscientious, or less caring than you need to live the kind of life you want, no amount of beauty will compensate.

We're not telling you to value deeper traits above their superficial attractiveness because that's morally the right thing to do. It's purely practical.

Bright guys who make some money and then chose a gorgeous but brainless trophy wife are usually miserable within six months. It's a waking nightmare to live with an intimate companion whose company you find boring. And the boredom eventually shades over into sexual disgust and emotional resentment.

You will have a better experience with her if she's smarter and more organized and has her shit together and runs her life effectively, because those qualities will help create a better life for you. That's what makes a good girlfriend.

2. Traits to Look for in a Girlfriend

The same insights we've hopefully baked into your thick skulls about how women choose men also apply when you're picking women for longer-term relationships—you just have to modify a few details, because the sexes differ a bit in how they express some of these traits, and how good versions of the traits cash out into real-life benefits. Here are some traits that will matter hugely in any long-term relationship you develop with any woman.

Her mental health: Mood is contagious, so cheerful, upbeat women will keep you happy, whereas depressed, pessimistic women will drag you down. Positive women will have more and better sex with you. Mentally healthy women avoid addictions, obsessions, and compulsions—so they spend less time, money, and energy on alcohol, nicotine, shopping, or cat-collecting. They tend to have mentally healthy relatives, so your in-laws will be more pleasant and helpful—if you have kids, there will come a time when your mother-in-law's mood and skills as a grandma can become hugely significant.

Her intelligence: Smart women make a point of feeding their brains every day with new ideas, facts, and insights, so you'll have plenty to talk about forever. Most women work, even after kids, and smarter women work better, get faster promotions, run more successful businesses, make more money, and manage it better. Smarter women give consistently better advice that can save your career from disasters (*no Jim, don't email your boss and tell him to go fuck himself*) and nudge you into brilliant opportunities.

Plus you'll have much smarter kids, so they'll require less help with homework and less guidance to keep them out of trouble, and the scholarships they'll get will save you a ton of tuition money. She'll also keep your kids safer—brighter women are safer drivers and better nurses, and they can sort through health insurance claims more effectively. The key is to recognize that she will probably not be interested in the same things you are interested in; so if she doesn't know about football strategy, engine fault codes, organic farming, or whatever else gets your rocks off, it doesn't mean she's dumb.

Her willpower: Highly conscientious women are more reliable, honest, orderly, and healthy. A high-willpower woman's less likely to cheat on you or to get fat and lazy after a baby. She'll take better care of her face, her body, her mind, her house, her career, and her kids. Whatever your income, she'll handle saving, spending, and taxes more effectively. She'll plan awesome holidays that go smoothly; she'll handle social arrangements reliably and consistently.

Her tenderness: The caring part of the tender-defender trait is especially important in seeking women for long-term relationships. A woman with good empathy, kindness, and compassion makes a much better partner, mother, and lover. Kindness helps avoid arguments, and resolve conflicts, and it sparks better make-up sex. It means that when kids arrive, a woman's first response to their distressed crying will be nurturing comfort rather than violent rejection.

Her social proof: Women on average don't care as much about climbing dominance hierarchies as about fostering tend-and-befriend connections with other women. But a woman's popularity and the quality of her social networks can still be really useful in your career and your quality of social life on evenings and weekends—because typically, the woman's friends and acquaintances account for most of a couple's socializing. Also, the more and better friends she has, the less burden is on you to be the sole entertainer and confidant in the relationship.

Her aesthetic proof: A woman with a great sense of personal style looks great and helps you look great. If you end up living together, her sense of beauty will have a big impact on the quality of your home environment and your day-to-day mood. However much money you have, a woman with good taste can create a gorgeous, functional home; a woman with bad taste will waste ungodly amounts of money on trashy clothes, ugly furniture, and badly designed houses.

Sex drive and history: Sex is obviously central to sexual relationships, and if there's a mismatch in sex drive, it's disastrous. If you end up with a wife who wants a lot less sex than you do, you will suffer for years, have resentful, frustrated affairs, and then get divorced. If you end up with a wife who wants a lot more sex than you do, you will feel nagged, unmanly, and annoyed; she will suffer for years and have the affairs, and then you'll get divorced.

Likewise, if a woman orgasms early and often when you have sex, that makes for a much happier relationship. Some women just don't come very easily, and they can usually learn to if they work on it, but it's dicey to commit to a woman who hasn't already learned how her body works.

As for her sexual history: Women go through life stages just like men do, and they tend to grow out of short-term mating, but earlier. If you're looking for a win-win longer-term relationship, you want the woman who's already sown her wild oats and already had some practice relationships. Don't be jealous of her ex-boyfriends; they helped make her the good woman you love, and now you've got her.

Takeaways

- Men have the most mate-choice power during post-sex choice.
- It is your right to exercise post-sex choice, but you have a responsibility to do it kindly and respectfully. Don't be a dick about it—no scorched earth, no Houdini vanishing acts.
- Your exes are a great guide to helping you figure out your current mate preferences. Do a full inventory of all their pros and cons; then be explicit, specific, and brutally honest. You should arrive at a much clearer understanding.
- If you're interested in short-term mating, look for women interested in the same thing and pay attention to where they are, what they wear, and what they say. But beware of the crazy ones!
- If you want a girlfriend or a wife, pay attention to the same traits and proofs she is looking for in you. If you're not sure which of those are most important to you, the qualities you admire and dislike in your mother are a good place to start.

CHAPTER 17: MEETING THE WOMEN YOU WANT

If there hadn't been women we'd still be squatting in a cave eating raw meat, because we made civilization in order to impress our girlfriends.

—Orson Welles

In this section so far we've explained how mating markets work, and how to pick good women. Those are strategic issues.

Now we're going to get tactical. We'll put the pieces together and explain precisely where, why, and how to actually meet the kind of women you want.

BARS AND CLUBS SUCK

Before we dive into the right ways to meet women, let's first get rid of a limiting belief that has probably handicapped your mating life and your sexual confidence for years: the idea that you should be able to walk into any bar, confidently approach a woman, and seduce her into a hookup...this is total bullshit and a toxic myth.

Wait, you're thinking, *how can this be?* If you've read Tucker's books, you know he did very well meeting women in dark, crowded, noisy places full of drunken rivals and tipsy women.

What you *don't* know is that Tucker is extremely outgoing, friendly, confident, loud, funny, and verbally fluent, even when drunk, in addition to being in great physical shape. Tucker in a typical bar is like a lion at a crowded savannah watering hole—he's going to drink all the water and probably take down a wildebeest. Which is to say, he happens to be very well adapted to that specific environment.

Most guys aren't like that. Which is why bars and clubs are so bad for them.

Men want to protect their physical safety, display their ability to show off attractive traits to women, and protect their sexual self-confidence. But what do most bars and clubs offer men? A set of drunk, sexually frustrated male strangers, some looking for a fight, in a noisy, crowded, chaotic environment that makes it impossible to display anything other than physical attractiveness, material proof, or extreme charisma, and a set of tipsy women, already irritable about being hit on by lots of men, ready and willing to reject you in a way that everybody can see.

You couldn't design a worse environment for men to meet women.

And it's not much better for women either. Women value their physical safety, their power of female choice, and their social safety. But what do most bars and clubs offer to them? A dark, exposed environment with few places to hide; little protection from stalking or harassment; a jostling crowd of male strangers, mostly looking for short-term hookups, who are uninhibited enough to approach any available woman; and a set of female rivals and acquaintances competing for the same men, watching who goes home with whom, who are capable of spreading malicious gossip.

The idea that bars and clubs are good places for men to meet women goes against everything in human biology.

There are virtually no cultures in history that expected their young people to find mates by throwing them randomly together into dark, noisy, threatening environments, with no structured activities or reasons for interacting, and hoping they'd sort themselves out into viable pairs. Bars and clubs present the exact opposite of a safe, easy, stress-free way to meet potential mates, to display your traits and proofs, and to work your way through a normal courtship process.

It's not your fault you're still clinging to the myth of the mating efficacy of bars and clubs; it's the fault of American bar-and-club culture, and the Hollywood system and Madison Avenue marketing machine that glamorize and celebrate it.

If you're still not convinced, look at it like this: on a deep, primal level a woman's worst fear is that a man will assault her, and a man's worst fear is that a woman will sexually humiliate him. BOTH of these elements are directly in play at bars and clubs. It literally puts men and women into the worst possible situations for mating.

Stop thinking you need to fight this natural instinct to avoid them. It's OK to not like bars and clubs as places to meet women.

MEET WOMEN THROUGH
YOUR SOCIAL LIFE

So where should you meet women?

The best way to meet a lot of women is to make your dating life an extension of your social life.

Imagine you volunteer at a community event, like a weekend park or beach cleanup, picking up trash to make the neighborhood nicer for everybody. Suppose that after you've been working alongside everyone for an hour or so, you notice that there's an attractive woman there. You hold some trash bags open for her, and she helps you load them onto a truck. You work alongside each other for another hour or so, just being cooperative and friendly. Eventually the cleanup is winding down, and you want to strike up a longer conversation with her.

Think about how much better this scenario is for meeting a woman compared to approaching a random woman in a bar:

Instead of being a potentially unsafe stranger approaching her in a dark bar, you're a guy who is part of a group she is also in, you have a legitimate reason to talk to her, and you have things to talk about related to your group or activity.

Furthermore, there are virtually no social consequences for her (or you) in talking in this situation, so you can be free to explore each other as much as you'd like.

You don't have to worry about her rejecting you, because your interactions are in the context of a volunteering event. You can interact with her in a risk-free way and get much more feedback on her attraction to you before you make a decision to actually move toward a romantic relationship.

You can show her your attractive traits in this context as well. If you've worked together for a couple of hours on a goal-directed activity like cleaning a park, she's already been judging your traits and proofs unconsciously, and she can see the attractive parts of you far easier in this setting than in a crowded bar full of other guys vying for her attention.

Even in a simple volunteering task, you have the opportunity to show her not only that you care about something she cares about, but that you're intelligent and socially conscious and that you can lead people, talk to people, etc. This gives you the chance to shine in many ways, all in a completely normal context, and in a way that is very low risk socially and psychologically.

You can use these conversations to learn all about her and find out if she is someone you'd like to pursue. She's no longer a mysterious, terrifying sex-goddess in a dark bar; she's just a sweaty, normal girl who's spent her Saturday afternoon doing the same thing you did.

Plus, the stakes remain low, since you're both there for a reason other than mate-seeking. If she's enthusiastic, your conversation easily escalates into exchanging numbers, or an immediate, informal coffee or dinner date. If she's not enthusiastic, you won't feel as hurt and upset, because the whole context isn't a high-pressure dating situation like a singles bar.

BONUS: The more social activities you do, the more people you meet. And the more people you meet, the more of their friends you meet, and the more friends you make and social activities you get invited to, where you can meet more women. Rinse and repeat.

The moral of this story is this: when you think about "meeting women," do NOT imagine trying to approach a beautiful woman you don't know in a crowded bar full of strangers. This makes you anxious for very good reasons.

Instead, think about putting yourself into social groups and activities that include women, where you do things you already enjoy with people you like. When you meet a new woman in a social context and setting based on shared interests and activities that you can talk about, you don't have to try to escalate all the way from total stranger to potential lover in just one conversation (which is very hard to do, by the way, even for the most experienced guys).

You only have to upshift from known, familiar, trusted, like-minded, socially popular guy to potential lover. And if a woman in your group thinks you're even slightly cute or interesting, *she's already anticipated that upshift in her own mind before you even say hi.* She's just waiting for you to sack up and do it.

If you're not sure which activities to do, picture the woman you are looking for right now. Imagine her lifestyle, her tastes, her activities, and her friends. Ask yourself: where are her favorite places to spend her time? What does she do for fun? And, especially, where would she go to try to meet the kind of quality men that she wants, whether as a lover, boyfriend, or husband? Make a list of all of them you think she might be into.

Let's say the list has twenty-five items. Which of those activities do you like? God forbid you take swing-dancing lessons, hate it, and find yourself dating a girl who is actually into swing dancing. *The worst!* But you will probably have overlap with at least five to ten of the activities.

Now go do those things in a social group! It really is that simple.

This is exactly what Tucker did to meet his wife—he realized she'd be an active professional who does CrossFit, so that's where he went to meet her. And he didn't meet her directly, he was introduced to her by his CrossFit coach, and now they are married.

What types of activities are there to do? There are essentially an infinite number, but we'll try to give you a list of the ones we have had success with and ones that are popular with women:

Social Activities

1. **Volunteering:** Volunteering for charities or social causes you like is one of the best ways to meet women. Tucker's met dozens of women through volunteering for his favorite causes (like no-kill animal shelters such as Austin Pets Alive, where about 80 percent of volunteers are young, single women). In fact, there is a running joke that they have no single male volunteers, because even if they start off single, they get taken fast. (This is also an example of a great mating market.)

    You get to demonstrate your tender-defender traits, meet hot girls, and help dogs. What's not to like?

2. **Group Fitness Activities:** These could be acroyoga classes, SoulCycle classes, hip-hop dance classes, or anything at your local gym (as long as the sex ratio is good, if the activity allows some conversation, and if there's a social norm of going out together sometimes after the workout).

    CrossFit is perfect for this—the intense, breathless workout of the day is usually only a small portion of the typical hour-long class, and people hang out before class and often do social activities together. Plus it selects for fit, dedicated people who tend to be successful and interesting in other parts of their lives; it has a strong subculture and group identity, so you become part of a national tribe; and it's usually around 60 percent women—most of whom are attractive and cool.

    Another option is any kind of fun amateur athletic event with a big social component. Tough Mudder and Spartan Race obstacle-course events have a lot of fun, fit women, and there are always parties and get-togethers afterward where you can talk and laugh about how dirty everybody got.

3. **Acting/improv lessons:** These are so good for building social skills and meeting women that they deserve their own entry. Drama attracts beautiful, outgoing, edgy women and not enough straight guys—these classes are typically about 70 percent female, and the whole point is to interact with them through fun role-playing, especially in the intro classes. Most classes are in the evenings and you go out for drinks afterwards. We know a ton of guys who have taken improv classes and

simultaneously improved their sense of humor, built their confidence, made great male friends, and met great women.

4. **Intramural co-ed sports leagues:** Any opportunity to play a sport with a co-ed team, especially if you're even halfway decent at it, is super fun and a great way to meet lots of women. And of course, most of these leagues are built with a social component; teams often go out to bars in large groups after games.

5. **Dance lessons:** Don't worry that you suck at dancing—*that's why you're taking lessons*. Most dance classes have a perpetual shortage of male partners and a hugely advantageous sex ratio. Focus on partner-oriented touch dance styles like salsa, tango, country, or swing, where you're switching off between women—it's like speed dating in motion. After a woman has danced with you a few times, you automatically feel familiar, safe, and manly to her.

6. **Music and singing groups:** All cities have amateur groups for instrumental music and singing where you don't have to be that good to participate. Local choirs are especially good for meeting women—the group singing puts everybody in a great mood, there are lots of women (and gay men), and there are plenty of opportunities to talk. You're also building a hugely attractive courtship skill.

School Activities

1. **Student groups:** If you're in high school or college, try a lot of extracurricular activity groups, and keep going to the ones that have lots of fun girls in them (probably not chess club or Dungeons and Dragons club— think French club, drama, yearbook, art club, the literary magazine). Focus on ones that naturally let you display your good traits and proofs, so you can have higher status in the group than you might in the school at large. Found your own group if there isn't one that appeals to you, so you get social proof as the leader.

2. **Small college seminars:** Go outside your major. Choose a juicy topic that's fun to talk about and that attracts lots of women—psychology, education, journalism, art history, English lit, and biology are all female-dominated subjects. Small seminars are great because students are encouraged to talk in class so they get to know a bit about each other, and there's time before and after class to mingle and chat about the course content. Seeing the same people every week for a semester builds familiarity and trust, both of which make you more attractive.

3. **Continuing-education classes:** Check out your local universities' continuing-education classes, which are open to any adults—including current college students. Avoid the male-dominated business, computer, and professional development classes. Focus on classes that attract young women, that involve fun interaction with other students, and that teach attractive skills—things like cooking, wine tasting, arts, crafts, music, dance, yoga, and psychology. These classes usually include a lot of middle-aged married women, but don't ignore them—they usually have younger sisters, daughters, nieces, and coworkers that they'd love to introduce you to if you seem nice.

4. **Teaching a skill in group classes:** If you have any particular skill or special knowledge about anything, you can start teaching it to people, and those people will include female students. Get whatever teaching certifications you need—it's usually easier than you think. If you know English, get your TOEFL certification and teach English to immigrants. If you know firearms, teach the women's concealed carry class at your local shooting range. If you did well on the GRE, MCAT, or LSAT, teach prep classes to college students (like Tucker did). If you're even half-decent as a teacher, female students will automatically admire and respect you.

   Important: understand the legal and social norms about dating students. In some cases (like most university-affiliated classes), you can get in big trouble for hitting on students while they're taking your class (and it's creepy).

Work Activities

1. **Conferences:** Focus on the ones that women enjoy and attend. These could be work-related or professional-development conferences (that your employer might be willing to pay for), leisure-interest conferences (Paleo *f(x)*, or TEDx events), political or religious conferences (Freedom Fest for libertarians, Evangelical revival meetings), or anything that brings a lot of like-minded people together in multi-day events that let them bump into each other repeatedly so familiarity grows. It is no coincidence that some 80% of the academics Geoff knows met their long-term mates at a conference. Plus, when they happen inside hotels, there's an extra sexual subtext—everyone's bedroom is just an elevator ride away. Add into the mix the fact that typically a large percentage of conference attendees are traveling outside their local dating zone, and it also becomes a recipe for good short-term mating opportunities.

2. **Work volunteering:** Many jobs offer charity activities. These can be just as good as volunteering on your own to meet women, so pay attention to what's available at your job and the jobs of your friends.

Local Activities

1. **Political groups:** Local activist groups focused on progressive issues are especially female-dominated, full of single women open to shorter-term mating. The Obama campaigns were incredible mating markets for young male Democrats, since most of the volunteers were college women and suburban MILFs.

   If you're conservative or libertarian, avoid the Republican or Libertarian Party groups, which skew heavily male. Instead, find local groups working for a few female-friendly progressive issues that you can genuinely support—abortion rights, animal rights, environment, education, free speech, drug legalization, anti-capitalism, LGBT rights, whatever.

2. **Religious groups:** If you're religious, make the most of it socially. Young Christians can't mingle that easily at the big, highly-structured Sunday morning services, but the Wednesday evening Bible study groups have all the perks of a college seminar. And most church groups are mostly women, so attractive young single guys are in very high demand. Pick your specific denomination carefully—no need to stay with your parents' doctrine.

   If your mating goals are longer-term, more orthodox and conservative churches (Evangelical Christian, Eastern Orthodox, Mormon, Muslim), are great places to find serious girlfriends and wives—and you'll get a huge amount of match-making help from older relatives, mentors, and do-gooders.

   If you're seeking shorter-term interactions, more liberal churches are better—progressive Christianity, Episcopalians, Presbyterians, Metropolitan Community Church, Unitarians, Reform Judaism. (Generally, churches that are gay-friendly and politically liberal tend to be more sex-positive and include women who are more open to shorter-term mating.)

3. **Meetup groups:** Meetup.com lists dozens of meetings a month in every major American city, for a vast range of interests, from digital photography to paleo eating. For each group you join, you can see the complete list of members with photos, so you can get a sense of the sex ratio and average age and attractiveness of the women. And for each planned

event, you can see exactly who plans to go. This can be a very efficient way to meet like-minded women and to learn more about cool things that fascinate you.

The beauty of **all** these activities is that even if you don't meet any attractive women at one of them, assuming you pick things you already like, then they'll still have been worth doing. They all improve your mate-value, expand your social network, and build your self-confidence, and you like doing them.

TRY ONLINE DATING

The stigma against online dating is long dead. There's absolutely no shame in that game. On the contrary, online dating is the most awesomely powerful method ever developed for meeting women.

In modern America, it is also usually the most efficient way for young men to meet desirable local women—whether for a hookup or a serious relationship. In fact, for most guys, *online dating can be your primary way to meet women*. If you're not using it, you're handicapping your sex life for no good reason.

Which Online Dating App Should You Use?

This is a fast-changing sector, and since today's hot app might become tomorrow's MySpace, we won't spend a ton of time talking about specific services. Instead, we'll give you the general principles to determine which online mating markets are good, and how to use them:

- **Your mating goals:** With more and more dating apps entering the marketplace every year, make sure to do your research and use only the online dating services that fit your needs. For example: AdultFriendFinder and Pure focus mostly on casual sex. Tinder and Zoosk focus on short-term dating. Match.com, Plenty of Fish, and OkCupid span short-term to long-term dating goals, whereas eHarmony and MatchMaker are more oriented toward long-term relationships. Ashley Madison focuses on extramarital affairs. SeekingArrangement and MissTravel match young women with sugar daddies willing to support them financially. OkCupid is especially good for alt-sex people into polyamory, BDSM, D/s, or kink. ChristianMingle is for Christians, BlackPeopleMeet is for black people, JDate is for Jewish people, OurTime is for people over 50.

- **Your mating market:** If you live in Denver, it doesn't matter how many registered users a site has in New York or Shanghai; it only matters how many Denver women are using it. You can discover how many local women there are only by trying it out in your local market.
- **Your mating preferences:** Some apps are simple to use but give you almost no information about potential mates, apart from a few photos and very brief self-descriptions. If your goal is just to meet a lot of women, Tinder is very effective, but if you're looking to meet a specific type of woman, it's not so great; it tells you a woman's age, location, appearance, and a few words about her interests but gives you no information about her background, marital status, number of kids, personality, mate preferences, or mating goals. By contrast, OkCupid allows "advanced searches" that specify your preferred height, ethnicity, education level, income, body type, drug use preferences, monogamy vs. polyamory preferences, etc.; and it allows sorting the results by match percent, amount of sexual experience, kinkiness, or even "dorkiness." This makes it much easier for everyone to find good matches — even for casual sex.

How to Set up Your Profile

Most guys fuck this up royally. Think about the whole range of traits and proofs, explained in this book, that you need to display. Most guys display only two or three of them in their profile and leave out all the others, pointlessly handicapping their attractiveness.

Photos: They're the first thing that women look at, and most guys' photos suck so badly that they're immediate deal breakers. Include several good, high-resolution photos that other people have taken of you (no selfies, unless you are under twenty-five or they are funny).

Your main profile photo should be a headshot with a warm, genuine smile. Other photos should show things like you doing something athletic (physical health), having fun with friends (social proof), traveling somewhere exotic (openness, resourcefulness), doing something productive (willpower, material proof), cuddling a pet (tender defender), and dressed up stylishly for a special event (aesthetic proof).

Show your photos to female friends and get their help selecting the best ones. You can even test-market photos by posting them on Facebook or Instagram and seeing which get the most likes.

Profile statement: Take this seriously. Before you write a first draft, look at what has worked on other people's profiles and steal their good ideas. When it's time to polish your statement, check out advice blogs like OkCupid's data blog for reference. Get feedback from friends and dates (without sounding like a desperate validation-seeking weirdo) and keep fine-tuning it.

Women don't care about what you have in common with other men. You enjoy movies, comedy, and sex? What a shock, get in line behind the other 30 million men who said the same thing.

What women want to know is what makes you *different and better* than other men. Now is the time to be honest—about your shortcomings, your awesome qualities, and your mating goals. Because if you're not, your phony attempt to sound different and better than other men will make you just like them.

Messaging women: Once your profile is done, start searching for the women who fit your mating goals and preferences. For each one who looks attractive in her photos, *read her profile carefully before you message her.* This shows respect and serious interest—it's like an early form of romantic proof. Also, the more carefully you read her words about what is important about her life, the easier it will be to engage her in conversation.

Your first message should be warm, friendly, and reassuring, showing insight into her profile and giving her a question to answer and ask in return. It should not be so long that it feels like a homework assignment or so short that it feels like 95 percent of the other messages she gets—all of which are a variation on some kind of universal douchebag haiku:

> *Yo girl, cute photo*
> *Whatchu up to right now, huh?*
> *DTF or what?*

Once a woman responds to your first message, you're off to the courtship races. The critical point to remember here, though, is that online dating is not an end in itself. The goal of exchanging messages with a woman is to bring your interaction into the real world, face to face, where you can really get to know each other and possibly touch each other's privates. All of which we will discuss shortly in Step 5.

SPEED DATING

If you're fifteen to twenty-one years old and you try to show up at a speed-dating event, people are going to think someone had to bring their kid because they couldn't find a babysitter. The target audience for speed dating tends to be older, urban, and professionally successful. But for those of you who are in your twenties or older and have some demonstrable talent or professional success, speed dating is worth a discussion.

A typical event requires advance registration, includes about twenty to forty men and women at a venue filled with small two-person tables, and involves men rotating from table to table for 3- to 8-minute dates with each woman there. The organizers give everybody a scorecard, and each person puts a check mark next to the names of anybody they're interested in meeting again. At the end of the event, everyone turns in their scorecard, and whenever there's mutual interest, the organizers forward contact information to both people a day or two after the event.

Speed dating dovetails with mating psychology in several ingenious ways:

- Everybody there is looking for some kind of mate.
- There is an equal sex ratio.
- The venue is optimized for pleasant conversation.
- The organizers are essentially professional matchmakers who can help introductions, facilitate interactions, keep people circulating, and enforce social norms.
- The structured one-on-one interactions minimize approach anxiety, interference, jostling, and cock-blocking from sexual rivals and other women.
- Face-to-face interaction means everyone can judge everyone's appearance and attributes much more accurately than in online dating.
- The 3- to 8-minute "dates" are just long enough to do "thin-slice" person perception while talking and short enough that you're not wasting much time on anyone who's not interesting to you.
- It's excellent conversation practice.
- You get clear feedback.
- It's time (~2 hours) and cost (~$40) efficient.

Takeaways

- Contrary to popular myth, bars and clubs are awful places to meet women.

- The best way to meet women is to make your mating life an extension of your social life.
- Social, school, work, and local activities are all great venues for meeting women because they do not involve many anxiety barriers.
- Online dating is the most powerful tool ever designed to meet women. The key is to use the sites and apps that are best suited to your mating goals, mating market, and mating preferences.
- While it skews older, more urban, and more professionally successful, speed dating can be a fantastically efficient way to meet many women.

STEP FIVE

Take Action

CHAPTER 18: TALKING TO WOMEN

*Language was invented for one reason, boys—to woo women—
and, in that endeavor, laziness will not do.*
    —Robin Williams in the movie Dead Poets Society *(1989)*

Language is the heart of human courtship. If you can't talk to women, they're not going to have sex with you. If you can't sustain good conversations, they won't want to be your girlfriend. If you can't resolve arguments constructively and respectfully, they won't want to marry you.

The problem is, our society's institutions don't really teach conversation skills. School teaches us our ABCs and our vocabulary, parents show us how to be polite and say "please" and "thank you" when we want something. But those vital skills that support and create huge amounts of human interaction? Forget about it—you can figure that shit out on your own.

This is doubly true for mating conversations, where women and men have very different conversational styles, layered over very different goals, depending on the stage of life they're in. And you're left to fend for yourself.

The way most guys think of it, conversation is direct verbal communication between people (talking, texting, etc.) that serves one of these purposes:

1. to communicate some news, facts, ideas, or thoughts to another person (**inform,** like a newscaster)
2. to get the other person to do something through persuasion (**influence,** like a salesman)
3. to argue a moral position or establish some objective truth (**convince,** like a philosopher)

Understanding this about conversation will make you better with parents, teachers, friends, colleagues, salespeople, and employers.

But it won't help you at all in mating situations.

Because no one ever sits down and teaches you how conversation differs in mating, you're left groping in the dark, getting drunk to dull the anxiety of uncertainty, and then resorting to pointing at your genitals like an animal, hoping she gets the picture.

THE PURPOSE OF CONVERSATION

Most guys think conversation is about the content of what they are saying, so they talk as much as possible. Or they think it's about persuading women to like them (and thus have sex with them). Or, worse, they think it's about arguing facts to arrive at some truth or consensus.

No, no, no. YOU don't understand. I went to Harvard, drive a 5-series BMW, bought all your drinks and complimented you throughout the night. Ipso facto, I have made a prima facie case for the right to habeas your corpus.

This is completely, totally wrong. Conversation in a mating context is not about persuasion or argumentation.

In mating situations, the purpose of conversation is to indirectly signal your underlying traits and begin the process of connection to the other person.

She's using your conversation to see if you are mentally stable, intelligent, kind, and empathetic. What you say and how you say it are windows into your soul. It's the best way for her to find out who you are. Conversation is her information gathering technique to check you for all the attractiveness traits that are not directly observable.

And of course, this information signaling goes both ways. You are finding out just as much about her as she is about you, as long as you're actively listening to her and not just staring at her tits while you wait for your turn to talk.

The big difference between normal conversation and mating conversation is directness. Mating conversations are primarily indirect. You know the old cliché that 93 percent of communication is nonverbal? Well that fifth-hand bullshit was based on outdated studies in a book from 1971.

But it's still true that body language is really important to communication—because most of what is being communicated is not the words themselves *but the traits and proofs that they signal.*

We already talked about this when we explained "show, don't tell." For example, you can't directly claim "I'm intelligent" and then proceed to convince a woman; you have to signal your intelligence to her indirectly by *what* you talk about and *how* you talk about it.

And if you're doing things right, conversation isn't just about indirectly signaling your underlying traits, it's also a pivotal turning point in the mating dance. As we discussed at length in Steps 2 and 3, women are already evaluating you (based on your attractiveness, your clothing, how you move, etc.) *before* you say a word. Thus, conversation, if she even lets you initiate one, is the final attraction factor for her.

Conversation is the interaction where she determines the validity of her initial attraction to you and decides whether that initial attraction is something she wants to pursue.

THE EIGHT BASIC RULES OF GOOD CONVERSATION WITH A WOMAN

If you were hoping for a checklist of things to say to a woman, you're not only out of luck, you're thinking about the subject all wrong. Every conversation with every woman will be different. That being said, there are some general principles you can apply in every situation.

We have found that the process for good conversation of any kind boils down to eight foundational rules:

1. Be a good host.

You probably feel self-conscious initiating and engaging in small talk. Well, guess what? Any woman you talk to is probably feeling that same apprehension and insecurity. She may be relieved, maybe even impressed, if you commit to taking the lead. That's why the first step in starting conversations with women is to see yourself as the host (as opposed to a follower or a guest) in any situation.

The host is in charge, and his job is to facilitate conversation. He's active, not passive, and takes the initiative in talking with people, guiding the conversation, filling in awkward pauses, introducing people, and making others feel comfortable and welcome.

Just putting yourself in the host mindset automatically changes how you approach women and boosts your confidence. Whereas the interloper worries about his own discomfort because he doesn't know everyone in the group, the host focuses on other people's social comfort and asks, "Who's here that doesn't know everyone? I'll make sure everybody's introduced to each other and feels comfortable chatting."

The next step is to transfer this warmth and openness to your nonverbal behavior.

2. SOFTEN your body language.

Long before you interact verbally, women make snap judgments about you based on your body language and facial expressions. Body language that is warm and inviting will draw others to you and make them feel comfortable conversing.

Psychologist Arthur Wassmer, Ph.D., came up with a great acronym for good body language. He called it SOFTEN:

Smile: Having a warm, sincere, friendly smile puts people at ease and is the number-one nonverbal cue for signaling your openness and warmth. After you make eye contact with someone, give her a big, genuine smile. If you're not used to smiling warmly, just practice — it's a highly learnable skill.

Open posture: Instead of standing angled away from people, with your arms crossed or in your pockets, face others directly, with your limbs taking up some space. An open posture is a clear signal of openness and confidence.

Forward lean: Leaning forward when you are listening or speaking shows someone you are paying attention. Adding a slight head tilt shows that you're comfortable with them and trust them. Another nonverbal movement to try and maintain is a slightly lower chin angle. This is especially effective if you are taller, to avoid the impression of looking down your nose at her when she speaks.

Touch: No, we're not talking about groping every woman you meet. Instead, use a good, strong handshake, where the web between your thumb and pointer finger meets theirs, to convey confidence and vitality. Obviously, shaking hands with a woman doesn't make sense in all social situations, so don't use this if it is too formal. Some women are huggers. If you find yourself in that situation, just try to match her level of closeness and firmness. Don't engulf her in a bear hug like you're about to wrestle her into a panel van and put a bag over her head.

Eye contact: Making eye contact shows you're confident, builds intimacy, and helps her feel at ease. Having shifty, leering eyes codes deeply in the mammalian brain as predatory, so do not look at women and then quickly look away as if embarrassed to be seen. It's OK to lock eyes with a woman for a beat or two, especially if you smile. Just don't track her around the party like a serial killer. You're not Dexter.

<u>Nod</u>: Whenever you listen to a woman speak, demonstrate that you're focused and interested in what she has to say by nodding occasionally and using other forms of feedback as well, like "uh-huhs" and "hmmms."

3. Establish commonality.

It's no coincidence that the "Do you know _____?" game is the dominant pattern in small talk. And almost every other pattern breaks down to finding commonalities (work, school, social groups).

Women do this because they want to use that information to make a judgment about you and your social proof. If you know a few of the same people, you're automatically in a much better position because your connection to her existing social network makes her feel safe with you. And as we've established, safety is a deep and meaningful unconscious need of hers—ignore it at your sexless peril.

There are other ways to establish commonality as well. You can ask the typical questions—where she's from, where she works, what she likes to do—and see if there's any overlap. You can also ask about features you both have, though probably at different ends of the spectrum: "How tall are you?" "Do you like having short/long hair?" Chances are you've wrestled with opinions (yours and others') on various physical features. God knows she has— probably since she was old enough to compare herself unfavorably to the Barbies she played with. The very act of having wrestled with these opinions provides common ground.

If you haven't gotten to those questions yet, however, and you are just looking for a way in, a fairly reliable way to establish a shared social connection is to make an observation on your current "mutual shared reality." Point out something obvious or noteworthy about what you are both experiencing. If you're in the same place by chance—a Whole Foods checkout line or an elevator—you can say something like, "I love Whole Foods, but I'd prefer to not have to spend my *whole paycheck* to shop here." Or "do your ears ever pop when you're going up in an elevator really fast?"

Don't worry about your opener being obvious, superficial, or even trite; in fact, *that's actually better* than if it's overly witty or incisive, because it feels more safe and familiar to her. You're not trying to stake out your ground on the topic or "run game at her," you're simply trying to extend a harmless invitation to chat, and she knows it.

This is the most polite way to do it because it gives her the choice to engage, and choice emboldens trust. Save your verbal fireworks for later, after she's reassured that you *can* do normal small talk.

And if you are in the same place by choice—CrossFit or improv class—then making an observation about your shared environment or experience is even easier (which is why we recommend doing so many activities with women, because it makes this initial conversation so simple and stress-free).

4. Gauge and respond to feedback.

Once you have begun a conversation with a woman (and even before it starts), it's absolutely crucial that you measure her responses to your words, and adjust accordingly. Specifically, you need to be attuned to her level of comfort.

If she seems comfortable, then keep talking to her and move the conversation forward.

If she seems uncomfortable, change course and try to understand what caused the discomfort so you can avoid it in the future.

Learning to accurately read female comfort and discomfort cues will help you decipher what they are thinking and how to charm them. This is something that most guys are terrible at, so even being half-decent makes you stand out in a positive way.

The important thing to remember here about gauging feedback is that it's not something you do only once. You should be taking her emotional temperature constantly and responding to it from beginning to end. That's how conversations go from bad to good and good to great, and how relationships grow from acquaintance to friend and from friend to friend with benefits.

5. Don't Act Too Excited or Too Aloof.

Studies consistently show that ratings of a conversation partner are more strongly influenced by delivery style, rather than content, and style is almost all emotional.

A lot of guys think they have to "be confident," which usually ends up reading as overexcitement. Or they feel anxious, which they compensate for by projecting aloofness. These are both unattractive.

When you are talking to a woman, especially at the beginning of the conversation, you need to project calmness and comfort to her.

This does not mean to "play it cool" like you're some kind of 1950s Mr. Slick. This isn't fucking *Grease*. The best thing you can do to project a calm attitude is be attentive, observant, and interested while staying emotionally centered.

To keep your delivery in the attractive range—when you're talking to a woman who doesn't know you well yet—make sure to *speak clearly and slowly.* Purposely slow down your delivery and take pauses.

This makes you sound more credible than fast-talkers, and helps you avoid coming across as an overeager used-car salesman. Slower speech also makes it easier to lower your voice pitch, and deeper is more attractive.

6. Ask questions and actively listen to her responses.

Charlie Rose makes millions and has a collection of friends that reads like a cross between the Forbes billionaire list and Wikipedia, and he earned it all by asking great questions and then listening to the answers. Learning those skills probably won't make you rich and famous, but it could very well get you laid, so listen up.

For women, conversation is about establishing connections and negotiating relationships. Because they have to listen in order to find common ground, most women tend to be good listeners.

Most guys, on the other hand, spend more time thinking about what to say next or wondering what the woman's nipples look like than listening to what she actually has to say.

Among men, talk is primarily a means to establish status in a hierarchical social order. They do this by exhibiting knowledge and skill and by getting attention through verbal performances like storytelling, joking, or mansplaining. In a mating context, approaching conversation like a tennis match comes off as bragging and obnoxious.

Don't look at conversation this way—at least not with women you are interested in. Instead, **think of conversation with women as a detective game, in which your goal is to learn as much about the woman as you can** by asking good questions and actually listening to the answers. If you go into the conversation knowing there is something very interesting about her, and you are determined to discover it, the questions will flow naturally.

Here are some best practices to jumpstart your new "detective game" approach:

Make the conversation about her:

This doesn't mean you don't talk, it just means you put the focus on her in order to get her to open up and tell her story. When you discover what's interesting about her and connect over it, then you can bridge into a more mutual exchange, where you talk more.

Focusing the conversation on her reveals your kindness, empathy, and social intelligence. And it provides you with the details you need to find common ground.

For instance, if you are really into cool mobile games and you find out that she is too, it will do two things: (1) it will create a connection between you that could lead to other things, and (2) it will make the conversation easy for a long period of time, as you discuss that shared interest.

Ask open-ended questions:

Most people love to talk about themselves; they just want an interested audience and a little spurring. Open-ended questions do just that.

These are the questions that don't require a simple yes or no answer—the *who, what, where, when, why, how* questions that give people the space and opportunity to really open up and tell you about themselves, all while taking the pressure off you to supply interesting conversation.

The gateway to open-ended questions is finding commonalities during the initial phase of your conversation , as we discussed earlier. Start with questions that can be answered with one or two words ("what's your favorite new game?"), and then build from there, asking clarifying questions about her answers until she gets on a roll and the conversation becomes virtually self-sustaining.

Remember: you should be gauging and responding to her feedback from your questions the entire time. If you ask about where she grew up and she rolls her eyes, stop that line of questioning and take a different tack.

Look at her, and use encouragers:

We know it's obvious, but *you need to look at women when they talk to you.*

Yes, we get that you can listen to her completely and watch the football game on the TV at the same time; so can we. But she will interpret your focus on other things as disinterest, and then she will lose interest in you.

Encouragers are simple body language indicators—like we talked about earlier—head nods or verbal cues ("uh huh," "yes," "right," "totally") that show you are listening. Don't use too many—that comes off as desperate. Just use enough so it's clear you are engaged with her and not pretending to pay attention.

Do you like being interrupted? Of course not, and neither does she.

Good listeners know never, ever to interrupt—not even if the impulse to do so comes from excitement about something she says. No matter how great your comment, cutting her off is only going to produce a reflexive negative response (at best, frustration; at worst, resentment). Let her finish, and then pause and speak slowly and calmly in response.

The one exception is if she's trailing off with a story or comment that's going nowhere, and she clearly wants to be rescued from conversational failure. In that case, by jumping in you're defending her from embarrassment, not just interrupting her.

7. Respond with validation, insight, or debate.

Conversations are a two-way street. Active listening doesn't mean you sit quietly for hours and agree with everything she says—that is passive and unattractive. It means you engage and respond accordingly. There are three basic ways to respond in conversation:

Validation

From an early age, each of us has sought the validation that comes with acceptance, and that continues right into adulthood. The degree to which an individual requires validation varies, but it remains one of the fundamental human desires and, as such, is one of the most powerful ways to connect with people, especially if it is used authentically and honestly.

One of the best ways to validate someone is through conversation. Showing interest (active listening) and then offering comforting, kind words. Respecting their thoughts and opinions. Empathizing with their point of view instead of trying to change it. All those things are conversation-based forms of validation.

Insight

The word "insight" feels profound, but it boils down to saying something that is relevant to the topic at hand and that also brings something new to the conversation. If you share an interest in something, like eating paleo, then you both will have a lot to say about it, and you should offer insight where you have it.

Generally speaking, insight is one of the most effective ways to display your traits to women in conversation; it shows you have the verbal and emotional intelligence to get what she's saying and form an appropriate response.

Debate

Active listening is great, and validation is good too, but the fastest way to get put in the friend zone is to blindly agree with everything a woman says— that's too much tender and not enough defender. No one likes a yes-man, and women find them especially unattractive.

Disagreeing with a woman is perfectly fine, and so is debate on issues you legitimately disagree about (FYI, a "woman's place is in the home" is not one of those issues).

Women will often test your intelligence, knowledge, and confidence with a bit of verbal sparring about abstract topics like politics, religion, economics, or morals. If you're just getting to know each other, chances are she is far less interested in the actual topics than she is in learning about you.

Any experienced woman knows that men won't agree with everything she says or does. The question she is asking herself is not "does he agree with my thoughts on everything," but instead "*how* does he respond when we don't agree?" Everything you say will be interpreted as an insight into your character and values.

In order to debate effectively (and attractively) with a woman, you may need to reframe your usual approach. When men disagree, they tend to use that disagreement as a way to "fight" to establish dominance. Women do not see arguments that way, especially not with men they are attracted to.

If you approach debates with women from a male-centric perspective, you will lose all of them, because more often than not, women are focused on your disagreement style rather than the merits of your argument—which is probably what you are focusing on.

Here is where you mix validation and debate. Take the time to understand her point of view (without disparaging it) before offering your own. If you debate with her in a way that validates her right to have an opinion and makes an effort to understand her point, even if you disagree with it, you'll be fine.

8. Connect with vulnerability.

We all have thoughts and feelings that we keep close to the chest, from emotionally damaging memories to unpopular views on sensitive subjects. We hide all of this from the world, until we find ourselves in a great conversation, connected enough to feel safe. Conversations move from "normal" to deep and meaningful when we start to open up and share these unpopular ideas or uncomfortable emotions.

Vulnerability isn't weakness; it's actually very powerful in conversation, when used correctly. When you "bare your neck," so to speak, and you find the courage to share even a small tidbit that lets someone know you are afraid or lonely or unsure, the other person will immediately mirror your true feelings. It's biology; she can't help it. She will feel your pain, because she has it as well (albeit about something different), and that will bring the two of you instantly closer.

Getting comfortable with deep sharing is like earning a black belt in conversation: it isn't something you use all the time, but having it gives you confidence, and your goal is to use it for good (as a means to deeper connection), not for bad (out of nervousness or because you can't think of anything else to say).

Note: Vulnerability is last in this list for a reason. It should be used sparingly, only in the right situations. Tipping your vulnerability hand within the first ten minutes of meeting someone is almost always a bad idea. Within the first hour, probably still not good. But after several hours of great conversation, then it's time to open up a bit more—not all at once, but little by little, making sure she comes with you for the ride.

HOW TO GET BETTER AT CONVERSATION

The thought of talking to a stranger makes some guys want to curl up in the fetal position. If that's you, the first thing you have to do is stop beating yourself up about it and recognize that *we all* experience some level of anxiety about social interaction at various points in our lives. Ask friends and family members you trust about their experiences with this kind of anxiety, or Google it—you'll find that it's completely normal and nothing to be ashamed of.

Once you've accepted your own feelings and gotten out of your shame spiral, it's time to fake it 'til you make it. When we talked about confidence in Chapter 1, we told you this was horrible advice. And we stand by that—for building confidence. But for getting over intense nervousness and conversation anxiety, it actually works very well.

Why?

Because most of you are fucking terrible at evaluating your own social skills, and the reality is that you're probably not doing as badly as you think.

The research pretty clearly shows that you are only marginally better than chance at understanding how others see you. And if you're laboring under the illusion that everyone can see how insanely anxious you are, think again: most of us are so focused on ourselves and our own issues that we aren't inclined to pay much attention to yours.

That might sound a little cynical, but it's actually an opportunity for improvement, because this is precisely where "fake it 'til you make it" comes in.

To fake it effectively, get an image in your head of someone who has the social skills and confidence that you want, and act the way you think *they would act* in your situation.

This generally means having a tall, confident posture, smiling more, using expansive gestures, speaking in a lower tone of voice, and all the behaviors that are consistently associated with socially confident people.

And guess what will happen if you do this? Not only will pretty much everyone accept your outward portrayal of social confidence at face value, but your body will actually respond to your "fake" behavior as if it is real confidence, as well (this is actually how your hormones work—they often follow behavior, rather than cause it). You'll actually start to *feel* more confident in short little bursts.

String enough of these bursts together over time and it will create a snowball effect of social feedback that turns your fake, short-lived confidence in social situations into real, sustained confidence. That isn't just the recipe for social confidence; that's how you build confidence, period.

What if you aren't good at conversation *at all*, so the "fake it 'til you make it" strategy doesn't work? If that sounds more like you, there are three main ways to un-suck:

1. Practice with non-mating conversations.
The best place to practice conversation is with women who are completely platonic or desexualized: family members, girlfriends of your friends, any woman who couldn't be a potential mate. This removes the pressure to perform and allows you to focus on the task at hand: learning how to have an enjoyable conversation that works.

If you don't have access to female family members, or this practice isn't working for you, there are any number of low-pressure environments you can seek out to practice conversation. One of the best places to start, believe it or not, is an old persons' home. Most assisted living facilities are full of lonely old people with nothing to do but sit there and wait for death. Those places are constantly looking for volunteers to spend time with the residents. The social pressure couldn't get much lower than that.

And, bonus, you can often find out amazing things about people—like the fact that maybe one of them has a hot granddaughter your age who has a soft spot for guys who get along with mee-maw and pee-paw.

2. Start with low-stakes mating contexts.

Once you feel confident in your basic conversational skills, (and some of you already do), you can move into conversations in a mating context.

This does not mean go to a loud bar and walk up to the hottest woman you've ever seen. Start with low-stakes mating scenarios. If you've taken our advice about mating markets and social groups, you should be in several social situations every week, meeting lots of new women just by virtue of doing new things (e.g., improv class, charity work, yoga). Those places are perfect low-stakes venues with organic opportunities to talk to women.

Another great place to practice is the mall, or any place where women are paid to talk to people. Your goal in these situations is to see if you can keep a good conversation going with someone who "has" to talk to you anyway.

The operative word there is "good." Bogarting the time of a salesgirl who works on commission at the Hollister store is not good. Naturally extending your interaction with the cute cashier for a beat or two is much better.

3. Just have fun out there.

Most men labor under a fundamental misunderstanding when it comes to sex and conversation: they see the act of talking to women *only* as a means for getting sex, which is a really shitty strategy not just for her, but for YOU.

Making the conversation transactional in this way sets you up for failure (which reduces your confidence), makes conversing harder (because you're hiding your agenda), and dredges up all sorts of shame and guilt issues that many of us have around sex.

Instead, the best way to get better at having great conversations with women is to reframe the entire purpose of talking in the first place:

When talking to women, make your only goal to have entertaining and fun conversations with them, and nothing else.

This is one of the most powerful "hacks" we know. It has helped thousands of men become very successful at mating conversations (Tucker counts this single insight as the primary source of his success with women).

We're not saying you shouldn't allow or want other things to happen. Of course you should. If you and the girl decide to go on a date, or to have sex, or anything else, that's great. But that shouldn't be *the goal* of the conversation. The goal should be to entertain yourselves, and the results will be a consequence of how well you execute that goal.

Changing your approach to "just have fun out there" has a number of immediate benefits. It builds conversational confidence instantly, it reduces awkwardness and makes conversation flow better, it enhances your attractiveness, and it makes it easier to judge whether she is interested in you.

If you're like a lot of the guys we've talked to about this, your next (and hopefully final) question about conversation is probably something like "that all sounds great, but then how do you segue to the sex part and close the deal?"

The answer (since you clearly managed to forget it in the space of a page) is, don't focus on that! You're not selling a car. *So brass tacks, honey. What's it gonna take to get you inside one of these beauties?*

You'll be surprised to find how much sexier conversation can become when you stop treating it as a means to sex or a sales close, and start treating it as an enjoyable activity in its own right, just like foreplay—because at the end of the day, **all mating conversation *is* about sex at some level.**

Sex is the subtext for every interaction you have with a woman; the sexual gap is right there between you, unspoken but palpable. Neither of you is *really* looking for a new buddy. Neither of you is *dying* to talk about the weather, or Whole Foods prices, or CrossFit (okay maybe those people are—they never shut up about it). What you're both doing is unconsciously feeling each other out, and good conversation is how that happens. The better you get at it, the more often feeling out turns to feeling *up.*

Takeaways

- Traditional conversation is about information, persuasion and argumentation. In a mating context however, conversation is about indirectly signaling your underlying traits.
- There are eight basic rules for good conversation:
  1. Be a good host.
  2. SOFTEN your body language.
  3. Establish commonality.
  4. Gauge and respond to feedback.
  5. Don't act too excited or too aloof.

6. Ask questions and actively listen to answers.
7. Respond with validation, insight, or debate.
8. Connect with vulnerability.

- To get better at conversation, you must address any negative emotions affecting your confidence and understand that everyone has suffered from some degree of social anxiety at some point in their lives.
- "Fake it 'til you make it" works wonders for overcoming nervousness and conversational anxiety.
- The key to better, more successful mating conversations is to reframe the purpose of talking to women: it can't be about getting sex; it must be about having fun and entertaining yourselves. Changing your approach to "just have fun" makes everything easier and increases your chances for mating success.

CHAPTER 19: DATING WOMEN

There are three possible parts to a date, of which at least two must be offered: entertainment, food, and affection.

— *Judith Martin, advice columnist*

Dating (or, to use the boring science-y term, "the human courtship process") has been around, in some form or another, for a long time.

Over thousands of generations, the purpose of a date (courtship) hasn't really changed much. *Dating is an opportunity for you to evaluate a woman and for her to evaluate you.* A date is just the most efficient context for the interplay of eye contact, conversation, humor, fun, and sexual chemistry that may or may not escalate into mating.

Yet you probably suck at dating. Most guys do. You don't know where to take a woman, for how long, with what expectations. You don't know how to gauge her interest or comfort level. In the back of your mind, you're hoping— half seriously—that when the check comes she'll just come out and tell you what level of sexual interaction you've earned for your effort. And it's only gotten trickier with social norms in flux, one-on-one dates giving way to group hangouts, and women ever warier of cheats, liars, and players.

And *still*, women want to go on dates. With *you idiots*, of all people! That's how ingrained courtship is in human nature, and how ingrained dating is in our culture.

A woman wants a public, romantic, memorable demonstration of your interest that makes her feel desired and that she can brag about to her girlfriends—even if she never wants to see you again, even if all you add to her life is a new item on her "deal breaker" list. A couple of drinks and some food after a hard day at school or work is just a nice bonus (if it goes well) or the cost of doing business (if it doesn't).

Here's the interesting thing about dating, though: she doesn't really care very much where you go or what you do. She doesn't care about the wine or food. She can entertain herself without you. She can drink and feed herself without you.

The whole point of the date is to provide a pleasant context for courtship, for the mutual display of fitness indicators, the sharing of life stories and the testing of sexual chemistry. It is a test you are both giving each other, and hoping the other passes, so you can move on to the fun stuff together.

If you really hit it off (if you both pass each other's mate choice tests), it doesn't matter much where you are, what you're doing, who else you're with, or how much it costs. If you're funny, charming, and engaging, you could be eating soggy fries and drinking shitty beer in a bowling alley while a gang fight erupts around you, and it won't matter to her.

In fact, if a long-term relationship develops, she's going to look back on that melee with great fondness as your romantic first-date story: *"Four people died in a hail of gunfire and screaming, but all we could see and hear was each other!"*

The relative unimportance of what you do or where you go even extends to bad dates (when either of you have failed the test). When women describe bad dates to their friends, they hardly ever mention the quality of the food, or the movie, or the miniature golf course. Their focus is on the guy and the emotions he evoked: how he made them feel uncomfortable, awkward, obligated, disgusted, or freaked out. It's rarely ever the venue or the menu that is the straw to break the date camel's back. If she does bring it up to her girlfriends, it's usually only as an exclamation point on the date's death sentence, *"And if his conceited, know-it-all blathering and awkward staring at my chest weren't bad enough, he took me to Cracker Barrel and there was a chest hair in my pancakes!"*

A woman can have an amazing date in a shitty dive bar in Cleveland if you are funny, fascinating, and thoughtful. She can have an equally horrible date at Eleven Madison Park (one of America's most incredible restaurants) if you're a boring, servile wimp or an obnoxious, loudmouth asshole.

This chapter is designed to give you ideas for things to do with women that are interesting and fun for both of you and that allow you to display all your positive attributes.

GRADING THE COURTSHIP TEST

If dating is a kind of mutual courtship test, then the traits and proofs we display toward each other through our physical and verbal behavior are the answers we give and use to grade each other. That grade is, more or less, your mating decision.

"Holy shit, I could marry this person!" (A+)

"That was great, I'm looking forward to our next date." (A-)

"Wasn't bad, probably worth a second date." (B)

"Thanks but no thanks." (C)

"Erase my number from your phone and my face from your memory." (F)

If both people give each other what amounts to a B or better, a second date's pretty likely; if it's an A+, the date's likely to last until sunrise. If either one of you is playing at a C-level or below, there's almost certainly no future for you guys—at least, if you are approaching dating with a healthy, confident mindset.

If you look at dating like this—as a way to gather information to make mating decisions—then everything else about dating that might have seemed confusing should start to make sense.

From just one date, for instance, you can evaluate each other on every trait and proof we covered in Steps 2 and 3. After a date, ask yourself about these traits and proofs:

Physical Health: Do I find her physically attractive? Is she in shape? Does she have a good body? Does she look healthy and attractive? What about her skin, hair, eyes, and posture?

Mental Health: Does she seem normal and safe, or weird and threatening? Or is she weird in ways I'm not comfortable with? Is she happy, open, playful, and fun, or depressed, paranoid, and unpredictable?

Intelligence: What is the conversation like? Is it fun for both of us? Can she read my signals? Is she listening to me? What topics does she talk about? How does she talk about me? Is she interesting?

Willpower: Does she plan things well? Was she on time or fifteen minutes late with no reasonable excuse? Does she appear to have her life together, at least to some extent? Is she generally neat and clean and organized, or sloppy and disorganized?

Tender Defender: Does she deal with people confidently and assertively, yet kindly and politely? Is she too nice or too nasty?

Social Proof: Does she have friends? Do people like her? Does she do social things? Does she comfortably find her place in new social settings, or does she melt into the background?

Material Proof: Does she dress well, live in a decent place, and have fun experiences? What kind of resources is she bringing to bear on the date? Is she self-sufficient or wholly dependent on someone else?

Aesthetic Proof: How does she dress? Does she have her own style? Does she have style at all? Are her car, apartment/dorm room, and belongings put together nicely? What kind of taste does she have in music, TV, film, art, architecture, and travel, etc.?

Romantic Proof: How much does she seem to like me? How much effort did she put into this date? Is she proud to be with me or is she trying to hide me? Is she taking extra pains to be considerate, chivalrous, attentive, and proactive about my well-being?

Mating Goals and Ethics: What kind of interaction or relationship is she looking for? Do these goals line up with mine? Is there a potential for a relationship win-win here?

Mate Preferences: What does she want in a mate? How do her mate preferences match my traits and proofs? Are her preferences thoughtful and wise, or superficial and juvenile?

Understand that the real objective of dates is not to spend a few hours feeding some cash into the service/entertainment economy; rather, it's for both people to display their best traits and proofs and to reveal their mating goals and preferences, so they can both make the best possible decisions about pursuing a mating relationship with each other.

This perspective should give you a completely different approach to dating. Now, instead of doing what other people do, or things you don't like, you can use dates to your advantage.

You can orchestrate your dates to show the best side of yourself. This has the added benefit of making the dates more fun and memorable, which also means women will almost always like them more as well.

WHERE TO GO AND WHAT TO DO

There are so many places and activities that enable you to show the best side of yourself and allow you to get to know each other, but most guys get lazy or scared and fall back on old stand-bys (dinner and a movie; drinks and more drinks) because they're trying to impress women with all the wrong things.

In reality, a good date can be any enjoyable, low-stress activity that allows both of you to learn about each other and display your best traits.

Just ask yourself the following questions as you run through your date choices. If you have more than three brain cells to rub together, you should come out the other side with some good ideas:

1. Will we be able to talk to each other and touch?
The setting of your date should allow for the right level of physical contact and conversation, particularly early in the courtship process.

Shooting guns, for example, can be a fun date, in principle—especially if you're good at it and you can teach her to be good too. However, if you're on a first date and you're at a range obeying all appropriate safety regulations, there are several barriers between you and getting to know each other—including ear protection and a metal dispenser of molten death pellets.

The last thing you want is for your date to be thinking, *"I sure hope he's not unstable because if we break up and he comes after me with a gun, he's not going to miss."*

Plainly put, you need to be able to talk to each other on a date. That means no concerts, no movies, no theater, no monster truck rallies, no shooting ranges—at least in the beginning.

Here are a few ideas to get you started:

- Café or coffee shop
- Miniature golf or batting cage
- Chuck E. Cheese's or similar place
- Museum, zoo, or aquarium
- Hiking
- Carnival or amusement park
- Medium-sized quality restaurant

2. Can you afford it comfortably?

First dates should not be expensive or elaborate; they are about information discovery and trait display. You still don't know if you like your date or if she likes you, so don't commit to a big, expensive outing until you at least know that much.

This doesn't mean you should start on the McDonald's dollar menu and make her earn her way up to super-sizing her value meal. It just means you should keep your first dates in a range you can comfortably afford, while still showing that your life is together enough that you can afford to do fun things.

As a rule of thumb, given your income, if you couldn't easily afford to go out on any given first date at least twice a week, you're spending too much—i.e., you're giving up too many other potential dates for this one woman.

Follow-up dates can swing in either direction—very cheap (a day trip to the beach) or quite expensive (a three-day weekend in the Bahamas)—depending on your goals, abilities, and resources.

The key in the beginning is to give yourself options and room to show growth. If you max out your credit card to take a girl to the nicest restaurant in town and then a concert with front-row seats for your first date, it's all downhill from there. Escalating cost on dates is a sign of escalating romantic proof and commitment, so don't shoot your wad too early.

3. Does it sound fun? Will she want to tell her friends about it?

Women like to share details about dates with their friends and relatives afterwards, like a courtship post-mortem. Your date is not just about you and her; it's a potential contribution to every conversation in her whole social life. If you add value to her other relationships, then you've added a lot of value to her life, and she'll want to see you again for more.

So when you're figuring out where to take a girl, ask yourself whether good shareable material is likely to come out of it. Does it have the potential to be distinctive and memorable and to make a good story?

Asking yourself these questions is less about finding super amazeballs places to go on dates and more about avoiding the same boring shit that isn't very fun and doesn't allow you to get to know each other. A mountain of spaghetti at Buca di Beppo and the latest superhero sequel at the local multiplex give her nothing to text home about.

Ideally, when her mom calls on Sunday afternoon and asks (*again!*) if she's met a nice guy yet, your date will be able to tell her all about you and your awesome date plan. When she goes to school or work on Monday, she'll be excited to tell her friends about what a great time you both had, instead of anxious about reporting another dud.

4. What positive traits and proofs will this activity allow me to display?

All those painfully awkward first dates you see on TV and in movies? They happen because someone gave those characters horrible fucking advice about what a person is "supposed" to do on a date. Or their screenwriters were lazy about scene-setting.

If you hate fancy food and expensive wine, *do not* take a woman to a fancy restaurant and struggle to order. There's nothing more embarrassing than asking what the "pricks ficksie" (*prix fixe*) is or why you have a spare fork next to the big fork. It will only frustrate you and make you look bad.

Instead, do things that you enjoy and are good at, ideally that overlap with her interests or desires. An ideal date is something fun that you *both* enjoy. If you both love dogs, take your dogs to the park. If you are both beer snobs, go to a nice microbrewery for a tasting.

You may not have a ton of favorite activities in common with your date, or you may not know her well enough yet to know what she likes. That should not frighten or deter you, because it can actually set you up for a great date. If you know how to do something and she doesn't, teaching her that skill can make for a fantastic date.

You can take almost any activity you like and turn it into a date if you frame it that way. If you really like archery, offer to take her to an archery range and teach her how to use a bow and arrow. She might not care about archery, but she can anticipate that this date will be new, fun, different, and memorable. It also gives you the chance to show all kinds of positive attributes: physical health, practical intelligence, patience, communication skills, and tender-defender skills.

Whereas the gun range would have been terrifying and made conversation impossible, the gentle "swoosh/thwack" of shots at the archery range allows easy conversation, and teaching her how to draw that bow requires plenty of physical contact.

IDEAS FOR DATES

There is no perfect "right date" that applies to all men in all situations. A twenty-year-old college student who likes video games and sports will have a very different ideal date than a forty-year-old computer engineer who likes math and fine wine, and they'll be dating different kinds of women. You'll have to think for yourself, but here are some ideas to get you started:

DATE LOCATIONS & ACTIVITIES		
	What/Where	*Why*
Outdoors & sporty activities	rollerblading, playground (swings, slides, etc.), climbing wall, mini-golf, Frisbee golf, kite-flying, walking in the park, bowling, go-karts, hot-air balloon ride, helicopter sightseeing, skydiving, boating, ice skating	Across the spectrum of cost, these activities are all fun, simple, and active, and they allow for conversation. They show physical skills, set you up for easy humor, enable easy physical intimacy, and expose you to a variety of dynamic, challenging environments.

Conversation & brainy activities	bookstore, coffee shop, local art galleries, art museums, science museums, history museums	If you're less athletically inclined and more cerebral, these places allow you to talk easily, showcase your intelligence and openness, and display your aesthetic proof.
Social & group activities	Farmers' market, cooking class, touring a food/drink factory (e.g., chocolate factory, winery, brewery), partnered dance lessons, karaoke with your friends, bar with bar games (e.g., billiards, darts, skeeball, shuffleboard), comedy club, improv group	That old saying that rising tides lift all ships applies very much to socially-focused date activities. If everyone is having fun, you and your date are more likely to have fun too. These dates showcase your social and aesthetic proofs, as well as your mental and physical health.

CREATE THE IDEAL (FIRST) DATE

Too many guys approach first dates as two distinct questions: (1) "Will you go out with me?" and (2) "What should we do?" This approach is a recipe for anxiety.

Add in the question, "What do you want to do?" and it becomes a recipe for failure. That shows zero conscientiousness, zero romantic investment, and zero understanding of female mating psychology.

The key to successfully setting up a first (or any) date is to take the initiative and have a specific plan ready *before* you even ask her out, so that you're essentially only asking one question. Besides, you're the one suggesting a date; shouldn't you know what the fuck you're going to do?

This does not mean you issue her an ultimatum: *"Dave & Busters, Wednesday, 6 p.m., SHARP!"* That's obnoxious.

Instead, say *"I have an idea: I want to take you to tag-team some skeeball at Dave & Buster's on Wednesday and bankrupt them of their plush toys. I was thinking 6 p.m. Does that sound like fun?"*

That shows you have been thinking about her and your time together in a concrete way. And it leaves her with three simple options for answering: (1) Yes, (2) Yes, but…, (3) No.

This is one of the reasons we advocate that you **develop a default First Date Plan**—something you can do, with only a little modification, with every woman you take on a first date. In designing your default, keep in mind that the ideal first date has three main features:

1. A weekday evening: It happens on a weekday (ideally, Wednesday or Thursday) and starts in the early evening, after work or school, when

you're both free for the rest of the night. This allows you to talk as long as you want but gives both of you an easy, respectful out if things aren't going well (i.e., you have school/work tomorrow). A weeknight date involves less pressure and expectation than a weekend date, and it leaves your weekend free for people you already know.

2. <u>An escalation option and an easy out</u>: It has an easy and mutually understood end point (like you're out of arrows at the archery range, or the bookstore is closing) but can just as easily lead to a shared meal nearby if you like each other, so you can talk more without getting hungry, and so you can buy her delicious food.

3) <u>Cheap, but not boring</u>: It's something you both like doing that you could do at least twice a week with other women.

Keeping one or even two default date plans in your back pocket means you are always ready to not just ask a girl out, but to do it with an attractive degree of specificity.

Contrary to conventional bullshit wisdom, offering a specific itinerary for a date does not make you pushy, *it makes you attractive*. She's free to turn down or modify your offer or to make a counter-offer. Remember, women can decide for themselves if your plan makes sense for them, and they can tell you if it doesn't.

That's the second part of taking the initiative: listening to and accepting her response. If she is enthusiastic about your idea (she says *yes*), great, do it.

If she's not (she says *yes, but…*), don't get offended. Don't take her negative response as a judgment of your character (unless your suggestion was something like going to Olive Garden and then paying a bunch of homeless people to fight Royal Rumble–style for the rest of your bottomless breadsticks). In which case she has probably gone from *yes, but…* to a flat-out *no*.

If you haven't offended her to the core of her being, just come up with another idea. If you want to ask her about things she's always wanted to try, that is a totally valid approach and works well with a woman who has a good head on her shoulders.

DATING ETIQUETTE

Dating etiquette tends to shift over time with sexual mores and social conventions. What was normal for your parents was probably not normal for their parents and probably isn't normal for you now, just for different reasons.

It was once right and proper, for instance, to throw your cape over a muddy puddle to ensure clean passage for a lady. That was the sixteenth century. Nowadays, the biggest problem a woman would face in that situation is wondering *why the fuck are you wearing a cape?*

Setting aside the intricacies and peculiarities of etiquette over time and across cultures, there is one overarching rule that, when applied correctly, will serve you well in all situations. We call it the Platinum Rule. It's basically the Golden Rule but for people you actually care about, whose brains aren't exact clones of your brain. It goes like this:

Treat a woman as she wants to be treated (given your new insights into what it's like to be a woman).

Think of a woman in your life whom you care about, other than your mom or your sister. How would you want some new guy to treat her on a date? Probably with courtesy and respect, right? Of course. So do that, and you'll be fine. Most everything else will come out in the wash if you and your date treat each other with mutual care and respect.

Now, there is still one lingering "dating" issue in our culture that you need to understand so you don't get blindsided—the question: **who pays, and what does it get you?**

The current American social norms hover somewhere between "the man should always pay" and "whoever initiated the date should pay," but there is no clear, consistent data or guidance on this issue that applies across the board.

That being said, the research *does* show that the majority of women want men to pay for the first few dates. Why? It's not because they're greedy gold-diggers. Well, some are, but very few of them.

It's because they are unconsciously looking for signals of your kindness, generosity, and material proof. Your picking up the check provides hard-to-fake information about your character and your resources, and that's important information for her to have.

Most men are okay with this arrangement—or at least they are used to it enough that it doesn't really register as a choice they are making.

But a surprising number of men believe that paying for dinner and dates is nothing more than a thinly veiled exchange of money for sex. This is total fucking nonsense. The "men" who perpetrate this line of garbage are angry misogynists who spend all their time trying to sleep with gold-diggers because their mothers didn't hug them enough. Fuck those guys. If you're one of them, get your shit together. If you're friends with some of them, give them this book or cut them out of your life. They're toxic and they will drag you down into a dark hateful hole with them.

Never think of paying for drinks or dinner as a down payment on sex. That sex-for-food exchange instinct is not only invalid for many reasons we don't need to get into here, but it makes women very uncomfortable (as it should, because it's *creepy*). If you are struggling with this, keeping the dates inexpensive early on is a practical way for you to pay without putting any undue pressure on the date.

READING YOUR DATE (KISSING, ESCALATION, SEX)

If there is one area of dating that makes women want to pull their hair out, it's the inability of most men to read what, to women, are blatantly obvious signals of interest (or disinterest).

They express interest and intimacy through how they dress, talk to you, look at you, sit next to you, and make physical contact with you, and they are hoping you'll read the signs correctly. That's why you need to become bilingual, so you can follow both English and "Flirtish."

Clothes

Even for a first date, a woman usually will choose what to wear very carefully, based on how likely she thinks you are to be a cute one-night stand, versus a month-long fuck-buddy, versus a potential boyfriend. Even if she's coming straight to the date from work, *she probably chose that day's outfit with your date in mind*.

There are some fairly reliable signs she's already intrigued by you (based on meeting you before, your online profile, or a friend's recommendation): new haircut and style, a manicure, high heels, little black dress or anything red, a dress or skirt rather than pants, jewelry (necklace, earrings, rings, hair ornaments), makeup, lipstick, stylish handbag. If she wears all of this, that's about as close as high-quality women ever get to "throwing themselves at you." They're saying, "You're worth bringing out my A-game, don't let me down."

More often, though, the cues from her clothing are much subtler and only reliably discernible over the course of the date or multiple dates. For instance, maybe she's wearing pants instead of a skirt because she knows they make her butt look better than anything else in her wardrobe. You won't know that until you're seen her in other things. And you will realize it only when you see her get up and walk to the bathroom and think, *Holy Christ, those pants look amazing!*

The point is, there are things to be understood from your date's choice in clothes, but only to a point. So you need to rely on conversation and contact to pick up where the perfect pants left off.

First contact

Touching on early dates is a tricky thing for both men and women because it's the first real act of physical intimacy and the first foray into personal space. You should approach touching a woman the same way you approach talking to her: be decisive and self-assured, yet gentle and protective, with the casual confidence that will provoke a positive response.

There's no reason to be hesitant. If she doesn't want you to touch her, she'll move away or let you know. The rejection will sting just the same whether you reached for her hand with a gentle, manly grip or whether you flopped your pasty paw out like a wet noodle in the general direction of her elbow.

Unlike sexual innuendo in conversation or texting, there is no plausible deniability in escalating physical intimacy. Either you reached for her hand or you didn't. Either you put your arm around her shoulder or you didn't. Any move you make that seems designed to be ambiguous or deniable shows immaturity and lack of confidence and so is much more likely to be rejected.

There are ways to engineer brief moments of contact to help you get comfortable before you initiate a bolder touch: offering your arm for her to hold onto as you walk down the street, opening the front door of the restaurant and guiding her through with your hand lightly in the small of her back, lightly touching her shoulders as you remove her coat for her before you sit down, touching fingers when you hand her something small like keys or the coat check ticket, or helping her draw the bow at the archery range while you stand behind her.

She knows damned well that most of these situations are really just excuses for you to touch each other, but they're still more romantic than the pasty-pawed elbow-slap mentioned above, and she'll appreciate that having some plausible deniability smooths the way for more physical intimacy.

Fortunately, women have their own set of signals when it comes to their openness to physical intimacy. They will place their hands or arms close to yours. They will touch your shoulder or arm to get your attention in order to tell you something interesting. They will sit closer to you or lean in to hear you even when it's clear they can hear just fine.

Your job is to recognize these signals for what they are (NOT accidents) and to initiate the next level of contact when it's appropriate. When the conversation's going well, for instance, and you've shared a few laughs, and she lightly smacks your hand in reaction to something you've just said, chances are she wants you to hold her hand.

This is a big step—at least in her mind—so your decision to either take it (and her hand) or leave it is equally important. If you take it and then intertwine fingers with her after a few minutes, that's a sign of strong mutual interest. You're moving from being "on" a date to being "in" a romantic conspiracy that will probably escalate to a kiss.

If you don't take it, she will give you another couple shots at it, but if you miss those as well, don't expect the kissing booth to be open when you walk her to the door at the end of the night.

First kiss

If you're having a great first date with a woman, and she seems like possible girlfriend material, you want to show physical interest in her early, but you want to be patient about having sex. If the conversation is clicking over drinks, you might touch her shoulder or her back if you're standing in a busy bar and creating space for yourselves like a proper tender defender. If you get some dinner, you might hold her hand for a minute after the main course if the signals are all there.

But don't try to kiss her until near the end of the date. This is a practical consideration as much as it is a comfort issue. Leaning over your entrees in the middle of a restaurant could end awkwardly or in complete disaster with spilled wine, stained shirts and her hair on fire from the votive candle in the middle of the table.

The ideal first kiss probably happens somewhere semi-private, when distractions have melted away, you've both locked eyes, at close proximity, and there's nothing more to say. If she's talking nonstop, but standing close to you, that's because she can't stand the pre-kiss tension, and that's the time to just interrupt her and kiss her.

If she's done something a little embarrassing, like spilling coffee down her coat, or slipping in her heels on the way to your car, she's feeling vulnerable and self-conscious—kiss her.

And if she's set up a situation where you clearly should kiss her, like asking you to walk her to her door after the second date and standing near you, looking alternately deep into your eyes and at your lips, then you'd better fucking kiss her, or we'll fly over there and kiss her ourselves!

Here's the thing to remember: there is no PERFECT time to kiss her. You make that time, based on the accumulation of attraction signals you have exchanged with her over the date.

Takeaways

- Dating is just the modern incarnation of the human courtship process, designed for men and women to evaluate each other for the traits and proofs we evolved to prefer and find attractive.

- A good date is any enjoyable, low-stress activity that allows you to have fun and learn about each other. It doesn't have to be expensive or complicated; in fact, it shouldn't be, in the beginning.
- The ideal first date happens on a weekday evening, allows you (or her) to easily and un-awkwardly terminate or escalate, and is inexpensive but not boring.
- Most dating etiquette is antiquated nonsense. The only rule you need to follow, given your new insights into what it's like to be a woman, is the Platinum Rule: Treat a woman as she wants to be treated.
- Reading your date's signals can be difficult and frustrating—the keys are in what she wears, how she talks, where she sits, how she looks at you, and if she touches you. Those signals can guide you through the progression of physical contact and intimacy.

CHAPTER 20: HAVING SEX

Let's talk about sex baby
Let's talk about you and me
Let's talk about all the good things
And the bad things that may be

—*Salt 'n' Pepa*

Good news: we're going to talk a lot about sex.

Bad news: we won't teach you the super-secret, double-probation, counter-clockwise McSwirley twist move guaranteed to get you all the ladies.

Because it doesn't exist. There is no "secret move."

There is no set of moves or techniques that guarantee anything. Every person's body is different, so they respond differently to different stimuli. The only move that is guaranteed to increase the *likelihood* of sexual satisfaction is mutual attraction (which is what we have told you about a hundred times at this point).

Because of that, we aren't going to get into sexual mechanics. We aren't going to hold your penis for you and push it in (the Internet is full of resources to help you with that). We're not going to tell you where the clit is, or how it works, or show you how to stimulate the g-spot (also because the best current research says that it doesn't actually exist).

Instead, we're going to talk about all the issues on the sexual landscape that are poorly understood by most men and that get in the way of mutual attraction and sexual satisfaction.

SEX IS A MEANS TO AN END, NOT AN END IN ITSELF

A lot of men, especially young men, think about sex as the entire reason to engage in mating behavior. They see sex as the destination. Reaching it is the whole point of the process—of talking to a girl or dating her or anything else.

That's why most young guys put very little thought or effort into the act of sex itself. It's just in, out, in, out. Up, down, up, down. Left, right, left, right. Like some kind of video game cheat code. Because once the penis is in the vagina, success can be declared and the rest is just a victory lap of indeterminate length.

The problem is that's not what sex is about at all.

Sex is not the finish line. It can be *a* goal, but it's not *the* goal of mating behavior, at least in the evolutionary sense. Sex works in service of your mating goals, whatever they may be—immediate physical satisfaction, building an emotional connection, reproduction, or any combination of these—not in service of itself. Sex is part of *how* you run the race, not *why* you run it.

This means that, for most people, sex isn't just about sex. And it does not end when the pumping does. Penetration, ejaculation, and relaxation—those are only mechanics. Sex includes what happens before and after the act as well. At least for women, the before and after are often the most important parts of sex, because they tell her so much about you and your connection.

Here's a great example: don't make the rookie mistake that courtship stops when foreplay begins and the clothes start coming off. You haven't "won" yet. Kissing, foreplay, petting, and sex are not just about pleasure. They're also about biological assessment. The curiosity you feel about a woman's body is genuine information-gathering. And vice versa.

A lot of what women do with a new lover is basically a quality inspection, like a mechanic looking over a used car to see if it's a lemon. If you've been on a couple of dates, she's already run the quality control on your face, your mind, and your social, material, and aesthetic proof, and she is obviously attracted enough to your traits to get naked with you. That's great.

But now she wants to assess your privates—i.e., the fitness indicators you don't wave around to the world. Your size, strength, coordination, and endurance in the sack all help her assess your physical health. Your sexual self-control and conscientious foreplay show willpower, and your understanding of her body shows intelligence, confidence, and sexual experience (social proof). Even the style of your bedroom serves as material and aesthetic proof.

There's also a hidden health-inspection function behind the apparently sweet and aimless explorations of bodies during foreplay. Example: women will feel your testicles when they're aroused. This is not because your ballsack is such a wonderful source of delight to her. It's because she evolved an interest in assessing your likely health and fertility from your junk. Bigger testicles predict higher testosterone levels, libido, sperm count, and fertility. Urologists can often predict which guys are likely to have trouble having kids just from feeling that they have small balls. On the other hand, smaller balls predict being a more involved dad who's less likely to keep pursuing short-term mating; so there's a trade-off: good sperm or good dad traits. Most women make these assessments unconsciously (but if you're dating a female urologist, *there's nowhere to hide!*).

A Urologist's Orchidometer (Testicle Measurer)

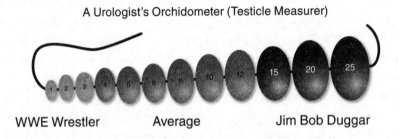

WWE Wrestler   Average   Jim Bob Duggar

Likewise, with belly shape. Women love to unbutton men's shirts and slide their hands down to feel that taut male belly. They also love that visible hip-bone curve that's only visible on guys who have a low load of abdominal fat. Why? Because a bigger belly is unattractive to women, as it has more abdominal fat and it predicts low testosterone, poor sexual performance, erectile dysfunction, and lower fertility.

The assessment process continues post-coitus as well. Women pay a lot of attention to how you act after sex, since they see your behavior as highly predictive of your future commitment level and attitude toward them. If you are aiming for a medium- or long-term mating situation and you just roll over and let her sleep in the wet spot, what she sees is low conscientiousness, low empathy, and poor tender defender-traits, which does not bode well for her.

Things are a little different in a short-term mating (e.g., one-night stand) situation. You and the woman probably don't intend on seeing each other again, and as a result, your behavior doesn't matter (within reason) because there will be no further interactions. In that case, you can both roll over and go to sleep and ignore each other (and the wet spot).

SEXUAL ESCALATION

One of the main sex questions we get from younger guys is about how to go from mutual attraction to sexual contact.

Generally speaking, there's a typical sequence of sexual behavior in our species, or at least in each culture (called an "ethogram") that looks like this:

Talking ⇒ gazing ⇒ hand-holding ⇒ hair-touching ⇒ kissing ⇒ holding ⇒ petting ⇒ genital stroking ⇒ intercourse

That's what sexual escalation looks like on the outside if you are just watching it happen between a couple.

What's happening on the *inside* of the lovers' heads, however, should feel nothing like "sexual escalation." And it certainly shouldn't feel like the man is laying siege to the woman's vagina by any means necessary, breaking down her defenses one by one.

Rather, it should feel like the natural increase of sexual tension, arousal, passion, and the giddy moment of tip-over when you both know that sex is going to happen.

We bring this up because the pick-up artist community has attempted, for years now, to teach men how to physically escalate their interactions with women through a concept they call "kino" or "kino escalation." It is similar to the famous nineteenth-century story about how to boil a live frog without its jumping out of the pot when the water gets hot. The idea is that you slowly, imperceptibly escalate the encounter (turn up the heat) in such a way as to get a woman to do things that she might not agree to (get cooked).

Plainly put: **This is terrible, creepy bullshit that psychopathic sexual predators do because they are too ashamed of themselves and their desires to honestly own them.**

This kind of behavior—whether intentional or not—is at the heart of so many awful repercussions (like date rape lawsuits) and is a strategy you should avoid like the plague (for what we hope are obvious reasons).

If you think that women have to be tricked and manipulated into having sex with you, then you either believe that women have no sexual desires and preferences of their own (which is not true) or you believe that you cannot offer the things that they want (in which case you should go back and actually read the rest of this book to acquire those traits, instead of skipping straight to the sex chapter).

The reality of modern, ethical mating is that your "sexual escalation" should begin months or years before you meet a woman, in the form of your working hard to turn yourself into the kind of man that women naturally desire. If you do that and then display these traits in a way that women can see, and then they get to know you, they will either desire you sexually—or they won't.

Of course if you do all that, and then you approach women with the express goal of having sex, they will sense it, it will repel them, and (paradoxically) you probably won't get sex. You will have shot yourself in the foot.

On the other hand, if you approach women with the goal of having fun and getting to know them, and you let your traits shine forth in a humbly confident way, then it is game on.

We know that many guys right now are saying to themselves, "But HOW do I escalate? How do I get her to have sex with me? What specifically do I say and do?"

If you're thinking that, *you've missed the point of the section AND the book.* You're still thinking about sex as something you have to trick or manipulate or persuade women into having with you—that you have to overcome their objections. Women may have objections, but your goal should not be to overcome them; your goal should be to have an interaction that is win-win for both of you.

What this means is that sexual escalation, if done right, doesn't require any convincing or persuading or defeating. She should already be into you, and she should have already decided—based on her attraction to you—whether she wants to have sex or not, so escalation is just a natural progression to what you both want.

Sex is the result of mutual attraction between a man and a woman who have the same desires, not something you get by checking off all the boxes on a To-Do-Her List.

PENIS SIZE

Yes, it's true: penis size does matter, and women like penises that are a little bit longer and thicker than average.

There's a lot of evidence for this fact. They fill the vagina just a little better, stretch the inner parts of the clitoris (the crura and bulbs), and are more exciting, especially to a woman's eyes and brains.

Even so, most guys overestimate how important penis size is to women. At one level, this book has really been one long argument that you can become highly attractive to women even if you don't have a huge penis. All the other traits and proofs add up to be much more important than penis size. If we lived in a species where females chose males just for penis size, we would have evolved tiny brains, no humor, no civilization, no love, and no courtship beyond standing up straight and naked, pointing to our huge members.

The struggle most guys face in this arena is not physical, it's mental: they underestimate their penis size relative to their perception of the population average (which is equally overestimated), and relative to what most women want. This is the porno bias effect. When it comes to penis size, porn producers select male stars who are in the top 1 percent (the Bill Gates and Warren

Buffetts of Penis), so the more porn you watch, the more warped your impression of average penis size gets.

This penis size anxiety also makes men easy prey for penis-enlargement products, which are **all** bullshit. Herbal supplements don't work. Vacuum "penis enlargers" can temporarily boost your size while your penis is in the vacuum chamber but don't result in any permanent enlargement, and they can burst blood vessels in your dick so it looks diseased. Surgery can cut a suspensory ligament so your dick hangs lower when it's flaccid, but it won't be any bigger when it's erect, and it'll be at a lower angle. Surgical injections can temporarily bulk up the girth of the penis with filler materials, but it takes a really good surgeon not to make your dick look lumpy and misshapen, plus the fillers tend to get reabsorbed, and your dick goes back to normal. Viagra makes it easier to get hard and stay hard and recover hardness after you come, but it only makes your dick harder, not bigger.

There have been many, many studies about penis size, and the data are very clear. The average American erect penis is a little above 5 inches long, measured along the top side of the penis from the tip to the pubic bone at the base. For comparison's sake, a dollar bill is about 6 inches long; only about 20 percent of guys have erect penises longer than a dollar bill; only about 3 percent have penises longer than 8 inches; only 1 in 10,000 has a ten-inch erection, and only about 5,000 men in the world have genuine twelve-inch erections.

So you can stop trying that bullshit where you measure from behind your ballsack like women who tell you how tall they are (in high heels)—there's no need to juice the numbers.

The best ways to make your dick look better are simple, cheap, safe, and healthy things we already told you to do: lose fat so your dick isn't covered by your FUPA.

Given high obesity rates even among young men now, a lot of urologists are seeing "buried penis syndrome," where gut fat and pubic fat hide the penis so it looks tiny. The pubic fat pad above and around the base of the penis is especially important to reduce, because it not only makes your penis look smaller, but it gives a woman very little firmness to grind her clit against when you're fucking her.

GO FUCK YOURSELF
(I.E., MASTURBATION)

Masturbation is a lot of fun and an important part of your sex life. You should embrace it, enjoy it, and accept it, because realistically half or more of the orgasms you have in your life will be with yourself, alone. It's no problem; it's totally normal. There should be no guilt; it happens every day, to pretty much every man on earth.

If you still have shame about masturbation, though, it should help to know that surveys indicate that basically *all* guys masturbate. Teenagers, college students, married guys with amazing wives, old guys who don't know what year it is—they all masturbate; the only difference is frequency. The exceptions are the 3 percent of religiously brainwashed freaks who say they don't (and they're probably lying).

Male human masturbation fantasies evolved sometime after our ancestors started walking upright about four million years ago (freeing the hands for "tool use") and sometime before modern humans started spreading around the world about 100,000 years ago (enabling masturbation to become universal across cultures).

Of course, many other male animals, from iguanas to chimps, also masturbate. But they can't, as far as we know, masturbate while having a complex, sustained sexual fantasy about a particular (real or imaginary) female. They can't do the "mental time travel" ("chronesthesia") that allows humans to project themselves into the past (remembering that hot senior prom date) or the future (anticipating next spring break's visit to Cancun), and they can't do the "counterfactual reasoning" that allows humans to imagine "What if this? What if that?"

Masturbation feels good. But if it only felt good—if it had no adaptive payoff—selection would have probably eliminated any tendency to masturbate. So why do men (and women) masturbate?

We're not actually sure. There are no well-established, proven theories about the evolutionary functions of male masturbation (probably because no scientist wants to be known as Dr. Jerk-Off). But there are a handful of hypotheses:

One is a learning function. Masturbation teaches you quite a bit about your penis, how to use it, and some basic sexual skills. Masturbation and various forms of mutual masturbation are used by many animals in this way.

Second is sexual release. Men, especially young men, are biologically designed to have far more mating desire than they have opportunities to fulfill it. Masturbation is a way to release some of this energy in a safe, appropriate way—to reduce sexual frustration and make it possible to show more patience and strategic self-control in mating.

The third is a reproductive function. Your sperm are constantly being made and have a relatively short lifespan (about 5–7 days, usually). Once it's been in there past that time and loses its motility (its ability to reproduce), it is basically useless. So you have to get rid of it to make way for new, living sperm that is reproductively useful. Masturbation is a way to "clear the pipes" and replace the old with the new.

The fourth theory—and this is far more speculative—has to do with sexual imprinting and fantasy. Teenage masturbation could help with learning which female traits to consider romantically attractive, by associating them with sexual pleasure.

A final possible function of masturbation becomes more relevant later, after sexual maturity, as a way to help to preserve monogamy. Even if you are in a committed, mutually fulfilling relationship, men can and do have lust that makes it tempting to cheat, or mate-switch, or abandon our mate for greener pastures. Generally, this would be a stupid idea, especially if you start having kids with your mate, because your reproductive success is probably highest if you stay with her and invest in the offspring. So along came adult male sexual fantasy and masturbation as a possible solution.

Ultimately, to masturbate is to be human. And there is no shame in being what we are.

SEXUAL SHAME AND SELF-ACCEPTANCE

One of the most important steps in having great sex with women is to accept your own sexual nature as a man.

A lot of men feel sexual shame. It can come from many places: family, society, girlfriends, other male friends. Often it takes root in puberty, when you started fantasizing and masturbating. Watching porn made you feel like your body was pudgy and your dick was small. Women who rejected you may have led you to feel like a sexually manipulative creep, so you blame your lust for your heartbreak, rather than blaming your poor understanding of women, your undeveloped fitness indicators, and your bad courtship skills. Maybe you nurture horrible memories of pissed-off authority figures saying nasty things about you or your sexual desires.

There are an almost infinite number of places and ways you could feel some level of shame about some part of your sexuality. So much of our culture treats sexuality as something shameful that it's hard to avoid sexual shame.

Most men feel, at least unconsciously, that if all of their sexual thoughts and impulses were visible to the world, other people would be horrified. For example, most men idly fantasize about having sex with over 70 percent of the women they see, but very few men would *ever* admit this fact in public (or actively pursue it).

Guess what: all guys do that, and if it's normal for all men, it's not abnormal. Stop beating yourself up for being a normal man with a normal man's desires.

Sexual shame is crippling, both emotionally (to you) and practically (to your ability to attract great women and have great sex). Your sexual desire is in many ways the core of your masculinity, the heart of your ambition, and the highest expression of nature's evolutionary quest for excellence. It

The Trojan War is one of the most important events in Greek mythology, Western civilization, and all of literature. It was a decade-long slugfest between the city of Troy and the Greeks, and it all started because

this dude	took this girl	from this dude

and his brother was like, OH HELL NO!

...and then this happened.

drove most of human evolution, exploration, invention, and creativity; and, when harnessed correctly, it has produced the most glorious expressions of human culture and genius.

This might seem weird to you, but it's true—without men lusting for beautiful, choosy women, we'd have no pyramids at Giza, no Trojan War (and thus no *Iliad* or *Odyssey*), no Roman aqueducts, no Mozart operas, no Eiffel Tower, and no *Gladiator*. Male sexual desire and mating effort has sparked a lot of great achievements, and that is a good thing. Basically, men accomplish things so women will like them and have sex with them (how many ways have we told you this already?).

The harshest truth of all you need to wrestle with is that *if you're ashamed of your lust, you're ashamed of yourself.* And you're ashamed of masculinity in general. It's not enough to respect yourself as a human being. You also have to respect yourself as a man. We talked about building confidence earlier, but part of building confidence and self-respect is respecting your lust—because it is a part of who you are as a human.

Yes, of course this also means respecting your ex-girlfriends, your future girlfriends, and your future wife. But it is entirely possible to respect all of you at the same time.

Respect for women does not need to, nor should it, compete with respect for yourself or your sexuality. When relationships work well, it is precisely because the man respects the sexual nature of his female partner and the woman respects his male sexual energy as well.

In fact, your lust is the hottest imaginable thing to women—if it's combined with all the other fitness indicators they desire, and it's in the context of a normal courtship process. For women:

Lust + loser = disgust

Lust + stranger = threat

Lust + hero (having attractive traits) + romantic context = the best thing ever

It's precisely what they love to read about in romance novels and what they love to fantasize about in bed alone at night. It's what makes them swoon. Once you've had a few dates and proved that you're charming and safe and effective, women will feel as turned on by your lust as you were turned on by their beauty.

Plainly put: *You have sexual desires, they are valid, and you have every right to pursue and satisfy them (as long as you don't hurt anyone else in the process).*

Teaching you how to do that ethically and effectively is the entire point of this book.

That being said, we recognize you probably have an avalanche of specific sex questions locked in the chamber that sits at the heart of your insecurity with women. After all, you can be attractive, effective, and good at conversation, but if you still think the clitoris is a glowing mound in the hills outside South Park, Colorado, you're kind of fucked. Or *not* fucked, as the case may be.

Accordingly, we've compiled a list of the best resources for the topics we know many of you are concerned about. These books have done a better job than we could ever do, so why try to reinvent the wheel when it already rolls?

What Women Want-Certified Sex Resources		
Subject	*Title*	*Our Thoughts*
Accepting all your freaky sexual desires	*Perv* by Jesse Bering (2014)	We're all pervs in some way or another. A great book on how to come to terms with whatever you *really* want, so you can go get it
The science behind women's sexual arousal and orgasm	*Bonk* by Mary Roach (2009)	Excellent short guide to the state of the art in sex research
Women's sexual anatomy	*Vagina* by Naomi Wolf (2009)	Explains the links between women's minds, genitals, arousal, and orgasm, and how different women are wired differently for different kinds of orgasms
Sexual fantasies	*A Billion Wicked Thoughts* by Ogi Ogas & Sai Gaddam (2012)	A goldmine of info on male versus female desires and fantasies, as revealed by huge amounts of Internet data
What women really want from sex	*Why Women Have Sex* by Cindy Meston & David Buss (2009)	A great introduction to the evolutionary logic behind women's sexual preferences, hot buttons, and kinks
How to have better sex	*Nina Hartley's Guide to Total Sex* by Nina Hartley (2006)	By a legendary porn star and sex educator, a fun, informative intro to hot sex
How to kiss better	*The Science of Kissing* by Sheril Kirshenbaum (2011)	Cool insights into the evolution, history, chemistry, and hotness of locking lips
How to go down on women	*She Comes First* by Ian Kerner (2010)	A whole book on how to give great cunnilingus. She'll be grateful.
How to help her reach orgasm	*Slow Sex* by Nicole Daedone (2011)	Explains the Orgasmic Meditation techniques for increasing women's pleasure. She'll be super grateful.
Sexual techniques	*The Guide to Getting It On* by Paul Joannides (2009)	Over 1,100 pages on all aspects of sexual mechanics
Sexual positions	*The Modern Kama Sutra* by Kamini & Kirk Thomas (2005)	An updated, illustrated version of the 2,000-year-old Indian sex manual
Domination and submission (D/s)	*Domination and Submission* by Michael Makai (2013)	Hundreds of insights into why so many women like to be "swept away" and "overwhelmed" in bed and how to bring your man-power into the bedroom
Kinky sex and power play	*The Ultimate Guide to Kink, BDSM, Role Play, and the Erotic Edge* edited by Tristan Taormino (2012)	Essays from leading kinksters about role-play, power play, rough sex, bondage, spanking, flogging, etc. Great insights into female sexual psychology even if you're just into "vanilla" sex
Polyamory	*The Ethical Slut* by Dossie Easton & Janet Hardy (2009)	The classic guide to open, honest alternatives to monogamy. Even if you just want one girlfriend, poly ideas really help you understand sexual communication and consent and how to manage jealousy.

Takeaways

- Sex is a means to an end, it is not an end in itself. Every part of sex—from foreplay through cuddling—is both an attraction-creating device and an information-gathering device.
- Cultivating the traits and proofs that are attractive to women is the only ethically legitimate way to begin sexual escalation with a woman. And the only way to continue it is through a natural, mutual progression of sexual tension. Pick-up artist "kino escalation" is predatory, psychopathic bullshit.
- The average erect penis is a touch over 5 inches. Women seem to prefer penises that are slightly larger and girthier than average but nowhere near the kind of porn-star penis that dominates the mainstream perception of penis size and female preference.
- There is an adaptive, biological function to masturbation. Studies show that pretty much everyone does it, young and old, so there should be no shame in your masturbation game.
- There are a number of reasons why men feel sexual shame, but it is critical that you accept your sexual desire and respect yourself as a man and a sexual being if you want to have more, better sex and relationships.

CHAPTER 21: CREATE YOUR MATING PLAN AND GO FORTH

A goal without a plan is just a wish.

—*Antoine de Saint-Exupéry*

This is it, the final chapter. If this were a film, this would be the *dénouement*. That little bit right before the credits and just after all the action has concluded, where the conflicts have been resolved, the story has been wrapped up, and now the main characters are telling you what's next for them while explicitly restating all the lessons you would have learned in the previous ninety minutes if you'd been paying attention.

Every man who has read this far has a similar goal: to attract more and better women to have sex with him, date him, and/or marry him. Our goal has been to teach you exactly how to do that.

Here's the thing about a goal though: *without a specific plan for how to achieve it, it's just a wish.* A fantasy. And fantasies aren't going to get you into relationships with real women.

When we were younger we *wished* we had a book like this, but it didn't exist. When we got together as grown men to create this book, we developed a detailed plan to create it, and here we are—the book you are reading is no longer a fantasy. It's in your hands.

A plan isn't just a dream with a deadline; it's a dream with every step from here to there laid out in as much detail as you'll need to execute your next steps.

So as we near the closing credits, the final question is: **what do you do now?**

If your answer isn't "put all this knowledge to work in a systematic fashion to improve my entire mating life and achieve my mating goals," then you should close this book, pick it up with both hands, and hit yourself in the head with it.

Repeatedly.

Because the time for hemming and hawing is over. No more theories or ideas, no more principles or postulations. This is the precise mating plan you are going to use to actually go out and get women. It's a straightforward 6-step process that pulls together a lot of themes from earlier chapters into a clear, actionable process that anyone can work.

YOUR MATING PLAN

1. Clarify Your Mating Goal
2. Highlight Your Attractive Traits and Work on Your Weak Ones
3. Mating Market: Find the Places and Groups That Fit You
4. Start Small, Get Wins, and Build on Them
5. Focus on Social Life and Fun
6. Try, Learn, Repeat

The process is simple, but it requires a fair amount of honest self-evaluation, a little bit of risk, and some plain-old work.

The upside is that the payoffs are immediate. If your plan is a good one, you'll quickly see improvement and find your groove. If it needs some work, you'll get instant feedback that allows you to learn from your setbacks, make changes, and see better results. If you can do that, you can end up with a plan that will turn your wish into a goal and your goal into a reality.

1. Clarify Your Mating Goal

Do you remember what your mating goal is? It's been a while since we've talked about it explicitly.

Do you just want to hook up with a lot of women? Maybe date a few and see how you feel? Possibly find the ideal long-term mate? Somewhere in between? Any of those options is a viable mating goal. If you remember, plug your mating goal into Step 1 of the Mating Plan template below.

If you don't remember, or you feel like things have changed since you started reading this book, go back to Chapter 3 and redo the Mating Goals quiz. See where your score comes out compared to the first time you took it. Then come back and we'll move forward with building out your mating plan.

Sample Mating Plan	
22 years old, recent college graduate, a good entry-level job, in a medium-sized city	
Step 1: Mating Goal	My mating goal is to meet a lot of different women and
Step 2: Highlight Attractive Traits & Work on Your Weaknesses	<u>Strength</u> I am...
Step 3: Find the Right Mating Markets	Places that reward my strengths
Step 4: **Accumulate Small Wins**	Improv <u>Small Wins</u> —Sign up —Go to 1st class —Get my first laugh —Go out after class w/people —One-on-one conversation with a female classmate
Step 5: Focus on Social Life and Fun	*Fuck it, just meet new women and have fun with them*
Step 6: Try, Learn, Repeat	Evaluate your progress and feedback, consider any changes that

2. Highlight Your Attractive Traits and Work on Your Weak Ones

The middle of this book was all about understanding the traits and proofs women find attractive, then teaching you how to display and improve them in order to build the best version of yourself and cultivate greater attraction.

In terms of your mating plan, there are two things you have to do in this area: (1) you have to highlight your attractive traits and (2) you have to work on your weak ones. The questions we asked you in the traits and proofs chapters should have given you a good sense for which traits fall into which categories.

There are a few reasons this step is important. First, highlighting your attractive traits will boost your confidence. When we struggle with women, we often think there is nothing at all attractive about us, when in reality there is a whole list of things that we have simply forgotten and thus haven't leveraged.

Secondly, figuring out what you need to work on can give you motivation and goals to work toward that aren't explicitly about success with women (which you have less control over than success with yourself). They're about self-improvement, which pays dividends in all areas of your life.

Lastly, and perhaps most importantly, clarifying what's working for you and maybe find a girlfriend.

...funny ...smart ...generous ...kind ...good at building things	Weakness I don't...	...have a lot of athletic ability ...have much money ...have a lot of experience ...have classic good looks
improv classes volunteering school groups online dating	Places that show my weakness	Sports leagues Dance clubs Hotel bars Big cities
Volunteering Small Wins —Find an organization —Go to an event —Meet the people —Lead a group	CrossFit Small Wins —Join a gym —Successful onramp —Go to first workout —Introduce self to the coach	Online Dating Small Wins —Create your profile —Find women you are attracted to —Send your first message to one of them. —Have a conversation

(this is the same for all of you)

you might need to make to your plan, given your current mating goal, strengths, and weaknesses.

what isn't helps you choose the best mating markets for you, given your goals and preferences at any particular time.

Go back to steps 2 and 3 to review your attractive traits and the weak ones that need some work. Plug the strongest and the weakest into your mating plan below. Give extra emphasis to those traits, both good and bad, that are most important to the women you want to attract.

For example, if you're horribly unathletic and you're attracted to artsy hipster girls, your athleticism isn't one of the weaknesses you need to worry about so much.

3. Mating Market: Find the Places and Groups That Fit You

Now that you have examined your strengths and weaknesses, remember what we told you: *one of the most important decisions you will ever make in your mating life is picking the right mating markets.*

You can put absolutely none of the other self-improvement knowledge in this book into practice, but if you put yourself in the right places for your current goals, preferences, and attractive traits, you will increase your mating success by a huge amount.

In the Mating Markets chapter, we broke them down by size and specificity, like a Russian nesting doll of sexual availability. We even taught you how to use OkCupid to find the neighborhoods, cities, and regions with the highest concentration of women who are 80+ percent matches. Still for many of you, the larger markets (country, state, city) are going to be fixed for some time. Moving to the Philippines to find a woman who "finally gets you" is a major life decision that few are actually prepared to make. Moving to San Francisco after college takes a chunk of change you might not have for a while.

So your focus needs to shift to the smaller, more discrete mating markets defined by simpler choices under your control (where you spend your free time, social groups you join, colleges you apply to, part-time jobs you take).

Then ask yourself two simple questions:

1. What mating markets are accessible to me and have the types of women I like, who value my attractive traits?
2. Which mating markets are disadvantageous to my prospects, given my weakest traits?

With those questions in mind, in your Mating Plan below, fill in the mating markets that would be best and worst for you in light of your goals, your preferences, and your traits. Respectively, those are the places you should concentrate most of your effort and, conversely, avoid entirely (or at least avoid spending time there with unrealistic expectations).

This might still feel somewhat abstract, so let's look at an example:

Say that an examination of your traits reveals that your strongest qualities are that you are intelligent, thoughtful, well-read, and a good listener. And your weakest qualities are that you are not classically good-looking, socially confident, or athletic.

The best mating markets for you might look like this:

- highly ranked, academically focused colleges
- most graduate schools
- intellectual social groups (book clubs, arts charities, issue activism)
- bookstores
- specific cities (Austin, TX; San Francisco, CA; Portland, OR)
- specific neighborhoods (hipster neighborhoods in larger cities)

The worst mating markets look like this:

- nightclubs and crowded bars
- athletic leagues
- big cities full of high-status men (LA, New York City, Las Vegas)
- most fraternities
- Tinder

Now, if this is you and you go to undergrad or law school at UNLV, you're looking for a girlfriend, and you tend bar at TAO nightclub to pay for tuition, you can't be too surprised if you've come up empty over and over again— despite drowning in a sea of drunk, short-term-mating focused girls ready to party every weekend. What you have to offer is not what the girls you spend the most time around are looking for. You are spending a lot of time in at least a couple suboptimal mating markets.

Once you understand what you have to offer women and where the women who value those things are, the next step is obvious: GO THERE AND INTER-ACT WITH THEM!

Seek out these mating markets, spend time in them, join their social groups and integrate yourself as fully into them as you can. That's where you will find women who will find you attractive.

This is called leverage: taking something you're already doing (using your current level of attractiveness), spending a little more time thinking about where it is valued, and using it to multiply the results dramatically. *And it is completely different than what most guys do.*

Like our hypothetical undergrad-bartender in Las Vegas, they take something that's not working (trying to find bookish, intellectual girls in clubs) and try even *harder* to make it work. Or they just do the same thing over and over, without thinking about why. If something isn't working, don't try harder or do more of it.

Avoid this strategy entirely. Do something that gives you leverage. Move someplace (eventually) with more women you match up to. Remember, you can't fit a square penis into a round vagina.

4. Start Small, Get Wins, and Build on Them

Now you're probably thinking, "That's great, but where do I start, and how *the hell* do I do all of this?" The first three parts of the Mating Plan are about iden-tification and preparation. This part is about execution.

Don't worry, we're going to start by stealing a tip from Olympic swimmers.

Researchers tracked the techniques used by USA Swimming to get its athletes ready to compete in the Olympic Games. Rather than focusing on gold medals, coaches set numerous **small, achievable goals** that the athletes focused their work toward, and then built from there. Medals were never mentioned or talked about.

They might spend a week working only on a specific aspect of their backstroke or two weeks just on starts. The result was not tedium or apathy, but rather satisfaction from numerous small and defined achievements, which in turn gave them the confidence to attempt more improvements and the energy to keep them dedicated to their training process, even though the Olympics are sometimes *years* away for some competitors.

They kept doing this for years, the progress accumulated, and before they knew it, they'd made substantial progress—*and then won gold medals* (as evidenced by the US domination in Olympic swimming medals).

Many studies have shown that painful setbacks reduce motivation much more than positive outcomes increase motivation. What this means is that when you are starting something new, it's easy for your goals to get derailed by failures at the beginning, as surely many of you have experienced. The way you overcome this pattern is to create a continual sense of forward motion by getting **small wins**—controllable opportunities that produce visible results and momentum.

For example, going to sign up for improv class is a win (that's identifying a good mating market, and working to improve your traits). Going to the first class is a win (that's entering the mating market, and taking a risk). Going out for drinks with everyone after the class is a win (that's socializing and creating relationships). Having fun and making jokes with your class out at drinks is a win (that's displaying attractive traits and creating social bonds). That's FOUR wins, before you even begin to think about any of your mating goals with any of the girls.

By themselves, none of those wins are that important. But when you string them together, this series of wins **gives you confidence,** shows that you are **on the right path,** helps you **attract other people,** and **lowers your resistance to doing other new things.** That is the positive feedback loop of creativity and productivity. And that is what we call the power of small wins.

The US Olympic Committee wasn't the only group to figure this out. Video game designers understand it as well. Video games are by their nature mostly very long and hard tasks of increasing complexity that, if you try to do all at once, produce miserable failure and the urge to throw your controller through the television.

That is why almost all games are designed with levels and numerous small goals along the way. You earn enough small rewards that you feel incentivized to keep going and going and going. They are designed precisely to capitalize on the power of small wins—which is also why they're so addictive.

If you structure your approach to new mating markets and women this way—creating momentum from small wins—you will build a meaningful track record of success and the confidence that comes with it.

5. Focus on Social Life and Fun

Almost all guys are nervous talking to really hot women. But virtually no guys are nervous talking to a sweet old grandmother.

Why?

Because of the stakes. You want the hot girl to like you so she'll mate with you (that's your goal), and that's all you're thinking about, so you focus on being perfect, not saying the wrong thing; you overanalyze everything, you overcorrect, and you choke. The science of choking is very clear—it occurs because you are worried about the outcome (the goal), which causes you to overanalyze the process.

But with Grandma, you don't have an outcome in mind. You don't have a goal. You just relax, talk like a normal person, have fun, and the conversation goes great. There is nothing at stake, so you don't choke, because you aren't worried about having a perfect process.

Well guess what—the *only difference* between the two situations (besides grandmas being huge attention sluts) is how you frame it in your mind. That's it. So how do you change the frame so you feel the same around a hot girl as you do a grandma?

You don't think about your goal at all.

Totally flush it from your mind, as if it didn't exist, and replace it with a new goal: having as much fun as you can in the moment, with the people around you. In the last chapter we talked about sex not being the goal—this is the same idea.

We call this the "love your work" model, and it works far better than any other behavioral model—especially in mating.

If you set a goal, then forget about it and instead focus on creating an enjoyable process that you love and find personally rewarding, what happens is that you end up *doing better* at achieving the goal you set in the beginning.

Tucker discovered this trick at twenty-four years old. His mating goal at the time was exclusively short term hookups, and by not thinking at all about short-term hookups when he talked to women, he immediately **tripled** the number of women he was having sex with, while putting in 50 percent less time per woman and getting higher quality women who liked him and wanted to have sex with him.

It fundamentally changed his life, and *all he did was stop thinking about sex in order to focus on meeting new women and having fun with them*. If this sounds similar to the approach to good conversation we discussed in Chapter 19, it should, because they're virtually identical. Both approaches are about removing sexual pressure and replacing it with fun.

You can do this too, right now, no matter your mating goal or your mating market. It's very simple: every time you enter your mating market (or any social situation for that matter) do this:

> *Tell yourself that your only goal is to meet new women and have as much fun with them as possible.*

We are not telling you not to care about your mating goal. Yes, your goals still exist, and yes, they are still ultimately why you are out there.

But if you leave your mating goals aside, and instead *focus on the process of meeting women and having fun*, those women you meet will be much more attracted to you, and that will allow you to come off as far more attractive to them.

We know it sounds counterintuitive. We also know it works—both science and experience point to this simple mindset shift as the key for most guys to greatly increase their success with women.

6. Try, Learn, Repeat

Over the course of his life, Tucker has gotten so drunk he quite literally shit his pants in a hotel lobby, he danced with himself in a mirror, he puked on a girl's dog, fought a minor league hockey mascot, and nuked his testosterone levels by getting a blowjob in an x-ray machine.

Despite all of this, he is rich, famous, and happily married to an amazing woman. Which is to say that at some point, as you form good habits and produce positive changes in your life:

- You will screw something up.
- You will regret a decision you made.
- You will suffer setbacks.

- You will come across new information that causes anxiety.
- You will misunderstand some of the advice we are giving you.
- You will discover something very unpleasant about yourself.

Every man on earth who is successful with women has hundreds, if not thousands, of stories about setbacks, moments of ignorance, mistakes, and bad experiences. That is how Tucker got famous—he wrote about his!

Not only should you expect mistakes, you should welcome them, because *mistakes are how you learn, and learning is how you get better.*

It's all about how you frame things: if you see setbacks as evidence that you are a failure, or as a threat to your identity in some way, then you are going to stop trying to improve so you can avoid any setbacks, and you will never get anywhere except exactly where you are.

But if you look at your actions **from a learning perspective,** it's much easier to deal with failures because you see them as opportunities. Remember the Brazilian jiu-jitsu saying we mentioned all the way back in Chapter 1? Well we love it so much, we want you to write it down and put it on your wall:

"In training, there is only winning and learning. The only way to fail is to not train."

And guess what? Your whole life is training. There is no finish line for learning (except for death). That includes learning to laugh at yourself. When it comes to rebounding from failure and growing as a man, regardless of your other goals, there may be no more important skill.

Do you know why Tucker wrote four books' worth of stories about all the stupid things he has done?

It wasn't because he knew they would form the bedrock of a new literary genre and sell millions of books (he just got lucky in that regard).

He wrote them to help alleviate all the negative emotions that arose in his life after more than a decade of doing incomprehensibly stupid things and failing with women in a breathtaking number of different ways.

It sounds counterintuitive to most young people who have spent the better part of their high school years trying to avoid detection and humiliation, but the best way to not feel awful about yourself for something stupid you did is to admit it, laugh about it, take the inevitable teasing that will come, and then move on. Don't just move on, move *forward.*

Remember, there is no exact checklist for life or love. There is no step-by-step, paint-by-numbers process that works for everyone. You have to think for yourself. You have to build your own goals, your own plan, your own life. We gave you the principles; now you have to plug them into the specifics of your life.

YOUR MATING PLAN				
Step 1 **Mating Goal**	My mating goal is _____ _____			
Step 2 **Highlight** **Attractive** **Traits &** **Work on Your** **Weaknesses**	Strength I have/am . . . _____ _____ _____	_____ _____ _____ _____	Weakness I don't/am not . . . _____ _____ _____	_____ _____ _____ _____
Step 3 **Find the** **Right** **Mating** **Markets**	Places to spend more time, that reward my strengths	_____ _____ _____ _____	Places to avoid that show my weakness	_____ _____ _____ _____
Step 4 **Accumulate** **Small Wins**	[Place #1] _____ _____ _____ _____	[Place #2] _____ _____ _____ _____	[Place #3] _____ _____ _____ _____	[Place #4] _____ _____ _____ _____
Step 5 **Forget About** **My Goal**	*Fuck it, just meet new women and have fun with them*			
Step 6 **Try, Fail,** **Learn,** **Repeat**	Evaluate your progress and feedback, consider any changes that you might need to make to your plan, given your current mating goal, strengths, and weaknesses.			

This will work exactly the same way for people who are polar opposites—only the details will be different.

WORK THE PROCESS

This book is your new starting point. It outlines a process to use in your life that you should refer to constantly, because if you do it right, the process never actually ends and you are never done getting better.

That being the case, the most crucial piece of wisdom we can leave you with is this: Keep mating a **fun** learning process, not a stressful chore.

We've dedicated our lives to understanding how mating really works. We've had thousands of conversations with women, hundreds of dates, dozens of relationships and breakups. We've woven everything we've learned from our own highly experimental lives into this book.

But we hope you won't just take our word for it. You can cultivate your own experimental attitude in your own mating life. You don't need a Ph.D. to be a scientist when it comes to dating. You just need to reconnect with your childlike curiosity about how the world works and how you can affect it. Be interested, skeptical, and inquisitive. Try things and gauge feedback; then repeat and improve the things that work, and forget the things that don't. The more playful and open-minded you get about your dating life, the more attractive to women you will become.

Mating is a lifelong journey. Success comes from learning, improving and, most importantly, having fun along the way.

POSTSCRIPT: WE'RE LEARNERS TOO, AND WE NEED YOUR FEEDBACK

A journey of a thousand miles begins with a single step.

—*Lao Tzu*

This book began as a conversation between Dr. Miller and Tucker about the lack of a fundamental guide to mating for men.

We hope this book fills that hole (pun totally intended). And we are very proud of this book. We believe it is truly different than anything else out there and will help tens of thousands of men.

That being said, we also think this is just the beginning of what this book can be.

Mating education is woefully inadequate (for men and women), and though this book has helped to lay the foundation for a solution, it is only a foundation. There is SO MUCH more that men can learn.

In fact, there is so much more we wanted to say, even in this book.

This is not an idle comment either. Our original rough draft of this book was around 400,000 words! We turned in about 230,000 words to our awesome editor at Little, Brown (John Parsley) who helped us get down to what it is now—about 120,000 words.

And those words we cut were, for the most part, additive to what you find here. In essence, we have a whole other book of material that, while similar, is not exactly the same as what you just read. There is so much more we can teach you and tell you and share with you.

We also recognize this book could be better (every author thinks that, of course). We could probably explain things more clearly, make some information more actionable, and focus on things that we may have skipped over accidentally.

Why are we telling you this? In order for this book to improve, we need your help. We see this book as the first step on a lifelong journey, the beginning of what will hopefully become a long-running series. And of course, we know we made mistakes in this version that we can improve in each subsequent edition.

So if you have the time, please head over to www.TheMatingGrounds.com/MateFeedback and give us feedback on the book.

Then, if you want to learn more, we have a popular, long-running podcast (called the Mating Grounds podcast) and an entire site dedicated to going far deeper into mating education than can be covered here.

It's the next step on the journey.

ACKNOWLEDGMENTS

This book is the brainchild of a conversation between two grown men thinking back to the struggles of their younger selves and looking forward to helping generations of young men still to come. It took an immense amount of work and it would not exist without the invaluable contributions of a number of incredibly thoughtful, supportive people, including:

Byrd Leavell is a phenomenal agent and an even better human being, an accomplishment that cannot be understated for someone who went to UVA. Byrd represented and supported us at every step of the process from conception to publication, offering insight, warnings, encouragement, and silence at all the right times.

John Parsley, our editor, to whom we are indebted. He understood everything we were trying to accomplish from Day 1, when he walked into our first meeting carrying a stack of Little Brown titles that had unique voices and great messages. Then, eighteen months later, he did it again, when he took our behemoth first draft and cut 40% out of it without losing anything important while also managing to make it *more* engaging. We think we are the only writers in history who can say their editor took a hacksaw to their book, and are glad he did it.

Sabrina Callahan, the director of publicity at Little, Brown, was open to any and every idea we had, and brought a number of her own to the table that made getting this book in front of people a pleasure instead of chore.

Jean Garnett, Miriam Parker, Mario Pulice, Malin von Euler-Hogan, Michael Noon, and the rest of the team at Little, Brown & Company were great to work with at every step. The whole team was as good as it gets in publishing. This is not bland praise. All three of us have worked with multiple publishing houses, and Little, Brown is the best.

Erin Tyler is not only a great friend, but she's a brilliant artist and graphic designer who worked seamlessly with us and the Little, Brown creative department to get us to a great cover that we all like—a result that is no easy feat, as many authors and publishers can surely attest.

Joe Antenucci, Zach Obront, Andrew Lynch, Charlie Hoehn, and all the others who read early drafts and provided valuable feedback.

Veronica Pike, Jennifer La Macchia, and Dr. Carin Perilloux were the three strongest, smartest, most engaged female influences on this book and its authors from beginning to end. This book doesn't get to where it is without them.

Individually, Geoff gives thanks for support, inspiration, ideas, and constructive criticism to: his parents, Frank and Carolyn Miller, brother Bryan, and daughter Atalanta Arden-Miller; his mentors Ken Binmore, John Brockman, Bruce Buchanan, David Buss, Leda Cosmides, Helena Cronin, Martin Daly, Robert Frank, Steve Gangestad, Gerd Gigerenzer, Linda Gottfredson, Jonathan Haidt, Nick Martin, Randy Nesse, Nigel Nicholson, Steven Pinker, Matt Ridley, Roger Shepard, Rory Sutherland, Randy Thornhill, and David Sloan Wilson; his friends and collaborators Rosalind Arden, Tim Bates, Marco del Giudice, Judith Donath, John Durant, Mia Erichson, Dylan Evans, Sara Figal, Diana Fleishman, Jennifer Freyd, Glenn Geher, Vladas Griskevicius, Martie Haselton, Scott Barry Kaufman, Matt Keller, Rob Kurzban, Barry Kuhle, Jena la Flamme, Greg Lukianoff, Eben Pagan, Brad Payne, Lars Penke, Nando Pelusi, Carin Perilloux, Kaja Perina, Arand Pierce, Nikky Prause, Catherine Randall, Chris Ryan, Andrew Shaner, Peter Todd, Rob Wiblin, Elizabeth Yeater, Ron Yeo, and Brendan Zietsch; his intellectual role models and life-of-the-mind heroes Iain M. Banks, Gary Becker, David Byrne, Leda Cosmides, Charles Darwin, Richard Dawkins, Alain de Botton, Robin Dunbar, William Eberhard, Francis Galton, Jürgen Habermas, Sam Harris, Friedrich Hayek, Christopher Hitchens, Alfred Kinsey, Herbert Marcuse, Charles Murray, John Nash, Friedrich Nietzsche, Vance Packard, Camille Paglia, Chuck Palahniuk, Karl Pearson, Michael Shermer, Dean Keith Simonton, Peter Singer, Christina Hoff Sommers, Michael Spence, Neal Stephenson, Nassim Taleb, John Tooby, Robert Trivers, Thorstein Veblen, Richard Wrangham, and Amotz Zahavi.

Individually, Tucker wants to thank: his co-authors, Nils and Geoff (pretty much everyone else is covered above).

Geoff was the intellectual engine for this book; without his expertise and deep knowledge, I would have screwed a TON of stuff up in here. All I did was add detail and narrative and examples; Geoff brought the heft and muscle.

And Nils made this happen. In a weird way, he's probably the most important author of this book. The book sounds nothing like my carefree, curse-laden writing style, and nothing like Geoff's intellectual, academic style—yet, somehow, it captures the best parts of both of our voices. Without the incredibly writing, editorial, and storytelling abilities Nils brought to the project, this book would never exist. If you're ever lucky enough to be able to work with him, leap at the chance.

FURGHER READING AND REFERENCES

Here are our suggested reading and relevant references for chapters 1 through 20. The introduction, the five principles, and final chapter on creating your mating plan don't need their own references since they anticipate or review material in other chapters. We focus on popular books that are cheap to buy and easy to read but still grounded in good evidence and sound advice, and on the most readable and fascinating of the academic books.

In case you want to dig deeper into the scientific ideas and evidence, the ebook and the Mating Grounds website also include over a thousand papers in academic journals and essays in edited books. To save space in the print edition, we've included just our "top ten" most important journal articles and book essays for each chapter. You can use Google Scholar to find most of these papers. This is very far from an exhaustive list of the relevant scientific papers—we picked recent ones, with clearly descriptive (or amusing) titles, in strong journals, by reputable researchers, with useful bibliographies. Sometimes we favored one over other similar papers just because it had a hilarious title. To avoid redundancy, we cite references only once, in the first relevant chapter, many are also relevant to later chapters.

BIBLIOGRAPHY

Chapter 1: Build Self-Confidence

Popular Books

Baumeister, R. (2012). *Willpower.* New York: Penguin Books.

Beilock (2011). *Choke.* New York: Atria Books.

Brown, B. (2010). *The gifts of imperfection.* Center City, MN: Hazelden.

Chamorro-Premuzic, T. (2013). *Confidence.* New York: Hudson Street Press.

Donovan, J. (2012). *The way of men.* Milwaukie, OR: Dissonant Hum.

Dweck, C. (2007). *Mindset: The new psychology of success.* New York: Ballantine Books.

Glover, R. A. (2003). *No more Mr. Nice Guy.* Philadelphia: Running Press.

Greene, R. (2000). *The 48 laws of power.* New York: Penguin.

Kay, K., & Shipman, C. (2014). *The Confidence Code.* New York: Harper Business.

McKay, B., & McKay, K. (2009). *The art of manliness.* HOW Books.

Northcutt, W. (2011). *The Darwin Awards: Countdown to extinction.* New York: Plume.

Sullivan, B. (2012). *Confidence beyond measure.* CreateSpace.

Academic Books

Plomin, R., et al. (2012). *Behavioral genetics* (6th Ed.). New York: Worth Publishers.

Vazire, S., & Wilson, T. D. (Eds.). (2012). *Handbook of self-knowledge.* New York: Guilford Press.

Selected Academic Papers and Essays (for the complete references list, see the ebook or the Mating Grounds website)

Bale, C., & Archer, J. (2013). Self-perceived attractiveness, romantic desirability, and self-esteem: A mating sociometer perspective. *Evolutionary Psychology, 11,* 68–84.

Denissen, J. J. A., et al. (2008). Self-esteem reactions to social interactions: Evidence for sociometer mechanisms across days, people, and nations. *Journal of Personality and Social Psychology, 95,* 181–196.

Ehrlinger, J., et al. (2008). Why the unskilled are unaware: Further explorations of (absent) self-insight among the incompetent. *Organizational Behavior and Human Decision Processes, 105,* 98–121.

Else-Quest, N. M., et al. (2012). Gender differences in self-conscious emotional experience: A meta-analysis. *Psychological Bulletin, 138,* 947–981.

Garland, E. L., et al. (2010). Upward spirals of positive emotions counter downward spirals of negativity: Insights from the broaden-and-build theory and affective neuroscience on the treatment of emotion dysfunctions and deficits in psychopathology. *Clinical Psychology Review, 30*, 849–864.

Gentile, B., et al. (2009). Gender differences in domain-specific self-esteem: A meta-analysis. *Review of General Psychology, 13*, 34–45.

Kavanagh, P. S., et al. (2010). The mating sociometer: A regulatory mechanism for mating aspirations. *Journal of Personality and Social Psychology, 99*, 120–132.

Perc, M. (2014). The Matthew Effect in empirical data. *Journal of the Royal Society Interface, 11*, 2014038.

Place, S. S., et al. (2010). Humans show mate copying after observing real mate choices. *Evolution and Human Behavior, 31*, 320–325.

Wagner, J., et al. (2013). Cherish yourself: Longitudinal patterns and conditions of self-esteem change in the transition to young adulthood. *Journal of Personality and Social Psychology, 104*, 148–163.

Chapter 2: Understand What It's Like to Be a Woman

Popular Books

Atik, C. (2013). *Modern dating: A field guide.* Ontario, Canada: Harlequin.

Behrendt, G., & Tuccillo, L. (2009). *He's just not that into you.* New York: Gallery.

Bell, L. C. (2013). *Hard to get: Twenty-something women and the paradox of sexual freedom.* Berkeley: University of California Press.

Bolick, K. (2015). *Spinster: Making a life of one's own.* New York: Crown.

Brizendine, L. (2007). *The female brain.* New York: Harmony.

Buss, D. M. (2003). *The evolution of desire* (4th Ed.). New York: Basic Books.

Buss, D. M. (2006). *The murderer next door.* New York: Penguin.

Gray, J. (2012). *Men are from Mars, women are from Venus.* New York: HarperCollins.

Hussey, M. (2013). *Get the guy.* New York: Harper Wave.

Kiehl, K. A. (2014). *The psychopath whisperer: The science of those without conscience.* New York: Crown.

Salmon, C., & Symons, D. (2003). *Warrior lovers: Erotic fiction, evolution, and female sexuality.* New Haven, CT: Yale University Press.

Sandberg, S. (2013). *Lean in: Women, work, and the will to lead.* New York: Knopf.

Academic Books

Ambady, N., & Skowronski, J. J. (Eds.). (2008). *First impressions.* New York: Guilford Press.

Arnqvist, G., & Rowe, L. (2005). *Sexual conflict.* Princeton, NJ: Princeton University Press.

Campbell, A. (2002). *A mind of her own.* New York: Oxford University Press.

Ellis, L. (2008). *Sex differences.* New York: Psychology Press.

Ellison, P. (2003). *On fertile ground: A natural history of human reproduction.* Cambridge, MA: Harvard University Press.

Geary, D. C. (2009). *Male, female: The evolution of human sex differences* (2nd Ed.). Washington, DC: American Psychological Association.

Hewlett, B. S., & Lamb, M. E. (Eds.). (2005). *Hunter-gatherer childhoods.* New Brunswick, NJ: AldineTransaction.

Hrdy, S. B. (2011). *Mothers and others.* Cambridge, MA: Belknap Press.

Lancaster, J., & Hamburg, B. (2008). *School-age pregnancy and parenthood: Biosocial perspectives* (2nd Ed.). New York: AldineTransaction.

Lancy, D. F. (2014). *The anthropology of childhood* (2nd Ed.). Cambridge: Cambridge University Press.

Mullen, P. E., et al. (2008). *Stalkers and their victims* (2nd Ed.). Cambridge: Cambridge University Press.

Muller, M. N., & Wrangham, R. W. (Eds.). (2009). *Sexual coercion in primates.* Cambridge, MA: Harvard University Press.

Royle, N. J., et al. (2012). *The evolution of parental care.* Oxford: Oxford University Press.

Shackelford, T. K., & Goetz, A. T. (Eds.). (2012). *The Oxford handbook of sexual conflict in humans.* Oxford: Oxford University Press.

Thornhill, R., & Palmer, C. T. (2001). *The natural history of rape.* Cambridge, MA: Bradford Books.

Weekes-Shackelford, V. A., & Shackelford, T. K. (Eds.). (2014). *Evolutionary perspectives on human sexual psychology and behavior.* New York: Springer.

Selected Academic Papers and Essays (see the ebook or Mating Grounds for full list)

Buss, D. M., & Duntley, J. D. (2011). The evolution of intimate partner violence. *Aggression and Violent Behavior, 16,* 411–419.

Duntley, J. D., & Shackelford, T. K. (2012). Adaptations to avoid victimization. *Aggression and Violent Behavior, 17,* 59–71.

Fleischman, D. S. (2014). Women's disgust adaptations. In V. A. Weekes-Shackelford & T. K. Shackelford (Eds.), *Evolutionary perspectives on human sexual psychology and behavior* (pp. 277–296). New York: Springer.

Galperin, A., et al. (2013). Sexual regret: Evidence for evolved sex differences. *Archives of Sexual Behavior, 42,* 1145–1161.

Haselton, M. G., et al. (2005). Sex, lies, and strategic interference: The psychology of deception between the sexes. *Personality and Social Psychology Bulletin, 31,* 3–23.

Jonason, P. K., et al. (2012). The antihero in popular culture: Life history theory and the Dark Triad personality traits. *Review of General Psychology, 16,*192–199.

Lippa, R. A. (2009). Sex differences in sex drive, sociosexuality, and height across 53 nations: Testing evolutionary and social structural theories. *Archives of Sexual Behavior, 38,* 631–651.

Marlowe, F. W. (2007). Hunting and gathering: The human sexual division of foraging labor. *Cross-Cultural Research, 41,* 170–195.

Perilloux, C., et al. (2012). The costs of rape. *Archives of Sexual Behavior, 41,* 1099–1106.

Stockley, P., & Campbell, A. (2013). Female competition and aggression: Interdisciplinary perspectives. *Philosophical Transactions of the Royal Society of London B, 368,* e20130073.

Geoff's Work

Miller, G. F. (2000). Courtship in the Pleistocene. In G. F. Miller, *The Mating Mind* (pp. 177–223). New York: Doubleday.

Miller, G. F., et al. (2007). Ovulatory cycle effects on tip earnings by lap-dancers: Economic evidence for human estrus? *Evolution and Human Behavior, 28,* 375–381.

Chapter 3: Clarify Your Mating Goals and Ethics

Popular Books

Ariely, D. (2013). *The (honest) trust about dishonesty.* New York: Harper Perennial.

Baumeister, R. F. (2010). *Is there anything good about men?* Oxford: Oxford University Press.

Blanton, B. (2005). *Radical honesty.* Stanley, VA: Sparrowhawk.

Christensen, C. M., et al. (2012). *How will you measure your life?* New York: HarperCollins.

Easton, D., & Hardy, J. W. (2009). *The ethical slut*. Berkeley, CA: Celestial Arts.

Geher, G., & Kauman, S. B. (2013). *Mating intelligence unleashed*. Oxford: Oxford University Press.

Green, R. (2004). *The art of seduction*. London: Profile Books.

Haidt, J. (2013). *The righteous mind*. New York: Vintage.

Harris, S. (2011). *The moral landscape*. New York: Free Press.

Kurzban, R. (2012). *Why everyone (else) is a hypocrite*. Princeton, NJ: Princeton University Press.

Perel, E. (2007). *Mating in captivity*. New York: Harper Perennial.

Regnerus, M. D. (2007). *Forbidden fruit: Sex and religion in the lives of American teenagers*. Oxford: Oxford University Press.

Ryan, C., & Jetha, C. (2011). *Sex at dawn*. New York: Harper Perennial.

Shermer, M. (2015). *The moral arc*. New York: Henry Holt.

Taormino, T. (2008). *Opening up*. Berkeley, CA: Cleis Press.

Tomassi, R. (2013). *The rational male*. CreateSpace.

Trivers, R. (2011). *The folly of fools*. New York: Basic Books.

Wilson, D. S. (2007). *Evolution for everyone*. McHenry, IL: Delta.

Selected Academic Papers and Essays (see the ebook or Mating Grounds for full list)

Apicella, C., & Marlowe, F. W. (2007). Men's reproductive investment decisions: Mating, parenting, and self-perceived mate value. *Human Nature, 18*, 22–34.

Ariely, D., & Loewenstein, G. (2006). The heat of the moment: The effect of sexual arousal on decision making. *Journal of Behavioral Decision Making, 19*, 87–98.

Conley, T. D., et al. (2013). A critical examination of popular assumptions about the benefits and outcomes of monogamous relationships. *Personality and Social Psychology Review, 17*, 124–141.

Finkel, E., et al. (2014). The suffocation of marriage: Climbing Mount Maslow without enough oxygen. *Psychological Inquiry, 25*, 1–41.

Jonason, P. K., & Buss, D. M. (2012). Avoiding entangling commitments: Tactics for implementing a short-term mating strategy. *Personality and Individual Differences, 52*, 606–610.

Kurzban, R., et al. (2010). Sex, drugs, and moral goals: Reproductive strategies and views about recreational drugs. *Proceedings of the Royal Society of London B, 277*, 3501–3508.

Li, N. P., & Kenrick, D. T. (2006). Sex similarities and differences in preferences for short-term mates: What, whether, and why. *Journal of Personality and Social Psychology, 90*, 468–489.

Lukaszewski, A. W., et al. (2014). Support for the condition-dependent calibration hypothesis of men's short-term mating motivation: Evidence from multiple independent samples. *Evolution & Human Behavior, 35*, 319–326.

Mitchell, M. E., et al. (2014). Need fulfillment in polyamorous relationships. *Journal of Sex Research, 51*, 329–339.

Penke, L., & Asendorpf, J. B. (2008). Beyond global sociosexual orientations: A more differentiated look at sociosexuality and its effects on courtship and romantic relationships. *Journal of Personality and Social Psychology, 95*, 1113–1135.

Geoff's Work

Geher, G., & Miller, G. F. (Eds.). (2008). *Mating intelligence*. Mahwah, NJ: Lawrence Erlbaum Associates.

Miller, G. F. (2008). Kindness, fidelity, and other sexually-selected virtues. In W. Sinnott-Armstrong (Ed.), *Moral psychology: Vol. 1. The evolution of morality: Adaptations and innateness* (pp. 209–243). Cambridge, MA: MIT Press.

Chapter 4: Understand What Women Want...and Why

Popular Books

Dixit, A. K., & Nalebuff, B. J. (2010). *The art of strategy: A game theorist's guide to success in business and life.* New York: W. W. Norton.

Kenrick, D. T. (2013). *Sex, murder, and the meaning of life.* New York: Basic Books.

Meston, C. M., & Buss, D. M. (2009). *Why women have sex.* New York: St. Martin's Griffin.

Perrett, D. (2012). *In your face: The new science of human attraction.* New York: Palgrave Macmillan.

Prioleau, B. (2013). *Swoon: Great seducers and why women love them.* New York: W. W. Norton.

Academic Books

Alcock, J. (2013). *Animal behavior* (10th Ed.). Sunderland, MA: Sinauer.

Buss, D. M. (Ed.). (2014). *Evolutionary psychology* (5th Ed.). New York: Pearson.

Buss, D. M. (Ed.). (2015). *The handbook of evolutionary psychology* (2nd Ed.). New York: Wiley.

Cronin, H. (1991). *The ant and the peacock.* Cambridge: Cambridge University Press.

Curtis, V. (2013). *Don't look, don't touch, don't eat: The science behind revulsion.* Chicago: University of Chicago Press.

Darwin, C. (1871). *The descent of man and selection in relation to sex.* London: John Murray.

Dixson, A. F. (2009). *Sexual selection and the origins of human mating systems.* Oxford: Oxford University Press.

Dixson, A. F. (2013). *Primate sexuality* (2nd Ed.). Oxford: Oxford University Press.

Gavrilets, S., & Rice, W. (Eds.). (2014). *The genetics and biology of sexual conflict.* Cold Spring Harbor, NY: Cold Spring Harbor Press.

Milam, E. L. (2011). *Looking for a few good males: Female choice in evolutionary biology.* Baltimore: Johns Hopkins University Press.

Tadelis, S. (2013). *Game theory: An introduction.* Princeton, NJ: Princeton University Press.

Thornhill, R., & Gangestad, S. W. (2008). *The evolutionary biology of human female sexuality.* Oxford: Oxford University Press.

Weekes-Shackelford, V. A., & Shackelford, T. K. (Eds.). (2014). *Evolutionary perspectives on human sexual psychology and behavior.* New York: Springer.

Selected Academic Papers and Essays (see the ebook or Mating Grounds for full list)

Buss, D. M., & Shackelford, T. K. (2008). Attractive women want it all: Good genes, economic investment, parenting proclivities, and emotional commitment. *Evolutionary Psychology, 6*(1), 134–146.

Chandler, C. H., et al. (2013). Runaway sexual selection leads to good genes. *Evolution, 67*, 110–119.

Garcia-Gonzalez, F., et al. (2015). Mating portfolios: Bet-hedging, sexual selection, and female multiple mating. *Proceedings of the Royal Society of London B, 282*, 20141525.

Gildersleeve, K., et al. (2014). Do women's mate preferences change across the ovulatory cycle? A meta-analytic review. *Psychological Bulletin, 5*, 1205–1259.

Griskevicius, V., et al. (2007). Blatant benevolence and conspicuous consumption: When romantic motives elicit costly displays. *Journal of Personality and Social Psychology, 93*, 85–102.

Jones, A. G., & Ratterman, N. L. (2009). Mate choice and sexual selection: What have we learned since Darwin? *Proceedings of the National Academy of Sciences USA, 106,* 10001–10008.

Salmon, C. (2012). The pop culture of sex: An evolutionary window on the worlds of pornography and romance. *Review of General Psychology, 16*(2), 152–160.

Stewart-Williams, S., & Thomas, A. G. (2013). The ape that thought it was a peacock: Does evolutionary psychology exaggerate human sex differences? *Psychological Inquiry, 24,* 137–168.

Todd, P. M., et al. (2012). Simple heuristics for mate choice decisions. In J. I. Krueger (Ed.), *Social judgment and decision making* (pp. 193–208). New York: Psychology Press.

Zietsch, B. P., et al. (2012). Heritability of preferences for multiple cues of mate quality in humans. *Evolution, 66,* 1762–1772.

Geoff's Work

Miller, G. F. (1997). Mate choice: From sexual cues to cognitive adaptations. In G. Cardew (Ed.), *Characterizing human psychological adaptations* (pp. 71–87). New York: John Wiley.

Miller, G. F. (2000). *The mating mind: How sexual choice shaped the evolution of human nature.* New York: Doubleday.

Miller, G. F. (2012) Sex, mutations, and marketing. *EMBO Reports, 13*(10), 880–884.

Miller, G. F., & Todd, P. M. (1998). Mate choice turns cognitive. *Trends in Cognitive Sciences, 2*(5), 190–198.

Chapter 5: Get in Shape (The Physical Health Trait)

Popular Books: General Health

Dunn, R. (2014). *The wild life of our bodies.* New York: Harper Perennial.

Durant, J. (2014). *The paleo manifesto.* New York: Harmony.

Ferriss, T. (2010). *The 4-hour body.* New York: Harmony.

Kurzweil, R., & Grossman, T. (2010). *Transcend: Nine steps to living well forever.* Emmaus, PA: Rodale.

Romaniello, J., et al. (2013). *Man 2.0: Engineering the alpha.* New York: HarperOne.

Popular Books: Sleep

Cartwright, R. D. (2012). *The twenty-four hour mind.* Oxford: Oxford University Press.

Dement, W. C. (2000). *The promise of sleep.* New York: Dell.

Duff, K. (2014). *The secret life of sleep.* New York: Atria Books.

Lockley, S. W., & Foster, R. G. (2012). *Sleep: A very short introduction.* Oxford: Oxford University Press.

Stevenson, S. (2014). *Sleep smarter.* Kolkata, India: Model House Publishing.

Popular Books: Nutrition and Diet

Asprey, D. (2014). *The bulletproof diet.* Emmaus, PA: Rodale.

Ferriss, T. (2012). *The 4-hour chef.* Boston: New Harvest.

Jaminet, P., & Jaminet, S.-C. (2012). *Perfect health diet.* New York: Scribner.

Mosley, M., & Spencer, M. (2015). *The FastDiet.* New York: Atria Books.

Perlmutter, D. (2013). *Grain brain.* New York: Little, Brown.

Pollan, M. (2009). *In defense of food: An eater's manifesto.* New York: Penguin.

Sanfilippo, D., et al. (2012). *Practical paleo.* Auberry, CA: Victory Belt Publishing.

Shanahan, C., & Shanahan, L. (2009). *Deep nutrition.* Big Box Books.

Sisson, M. (2013). *The primal blueprint.* New York: Primal Nutrition.

Walker, D. (2013). *Against all grain*. Auberry, CA: Victory Belt Publishing.

Wansink, B. (2007). *Mindless eating*. New York: Bantam.

Wolf, R. (2010). *The paleo solution*. Auberry, CA: Victory Belt Publishing.

Wrangham, R. (2010). *Catching fire: How cooking made us human*. New York: Basic Books.

Popular Books: Exercise

Bryant, J., & benShea, A. (2013). *Jailhouse strong*. CreateSpace.

Divine, M. (2014). *8 weeks to SEALFIT*. New York: St. Martin's Griffin.

Epstein, D. (2014). *The sports gene*. Rancho Santa Margarita, CA: Current Publishing.

Greenfield, B. (2014). *Beyond training: Mastering endurance, health, and life*. Auberry, CA: Victory Belt Publishing.

Herz, J. C. (2014). *Learning to breathe fire: The rise of CrossFit and the primal future of fitness*. New York: Crown Archetype.

McDougall, C. (2011). *Born to run*. New York: Random House.

Rippetoe, M. (2013). *Starting strength: Basic barbell training* (3rd Ed.). Wichita Falls, TX: Aasgard.

Starrett, K. (2013). *Becoming a supple leopard*. Auberry, CA: Victory Belt Publishing.

Starrett, K. (2014). *Ready to run*. Auberry, CA: Victory Belt Publishing.

Academic Books

Bribiescas, R. G. (2006). *Men: Evolutionary and life history*. Cambridge, MA: Harvard University Press.

De Grey, A., & Rae, M. (2008). *Ending aging*. New York: St. Martin's Griffin.

Gillette, M. U. (Ed.). (2013). *Chronobiology: Biological timing in health and disease*. Oxford, UK: Elsevier.

Gluckman, P., et al. (2009). *Principles of evolutionary medicine*. Oxford: Oxford University Press.

Kelly, R. L. (2013). *The lifeways of hunter-gatherers* (2nd Ed.). Cambridge: Cambridge University Press.

Lieberman, D. (2014). *The story of the human body: Evolution, health, and disease*. New York: Vintage.

Savalescu, J., & Bostrom, N. (Eds.). (2011). *Human enhancement*. Oxford: Oxford University Press.

Selected Academic Papers and Essays (see the ebook or Mating Grounds for full list)

Apicella, C. K. (2014). Upper-body strength predicts hunting reputation and reproductive success in Hadza hunter-gatherers. *Evolution and Human Behavior, 35*, 508–518.

Deaner, R. O., & Smith, B. A. (2013). Sex differences in sports across 50 societies. *Cross-Cultural Research, 47*(3), 268–309.

Fonken, L. K., & Nelson, R. J. (2014). The effects of light at night on circadian clocks and metabolism. *Endocrine Reviews, 35*, 648–670.

Frederick, D. A., & Haselton, M. G. (2007). Why is muscularity sexy? Tests of the fitness-indicator hypothesis. *Personality and Social Psychology Bulletin, 33*, 1167–1183.

Hugill, N., et al. (2010). The role of human body movements in mate selection. *Evolutionary Psychology, 8*(1), 66–89.

Lombardo, M. P. (2012). On the evolution of sport. *Evolutionary Psychology, 10*(1), 1–28.

McCoy, J. G., & Strecker, R. E. (2011). The cognitive cost of sleep lost. *Neurobiology and Learning and Memory, 96*, 564–582.

Puts, D. A., et al. (2012). Men's masculinity and attractiveness predict their female partners' reported orgasm frequency and timing. *Evolution and Human Behavior, 33*, 1–9.

Schulte-Hostedde, A., et al. (2008). Female mate choice is influenced by male sport participation. *Evolutionary Psychology, 6*(1), 113–124.

Straif, K., and the WHO International Agency for Research on Cancer. (2007). Carcinogenicity of shift-work, painting, and fire-fighting. *Lancet Oncology, 8*, 1065–1066.

Geoff's Work

Miller, G. F. (2000). Bodies of evidence. In G. F. Miller, *The mating mind: How sexual choice shaped the evolution of human nature* (pp. 224–257). New York: Doubleday.

Chapter 6: Get Happy (The Mental Health Trait)

Popular Books: General Mental Health and Happiness

Achor, S. (2010). *The happiness advantage.* New York: Crown Business.

Bateson, P., & Martin, P. (2013). *Play, playfulness, creativity, and innovation.* Cambridge: Cambridge University Press.

Brown, S., & Vaughan, C. (2010). *Play: How it shapes the brain, opens the imagination, and reinvigorates the soul.* New York: Penguin.

Burghardt, G. M. (2006). *The genesis of animal play.* Cambridge, MA: MIT Press.

Chodron, P. (2013). *How to meditate.* Louisville, CO: Sounds True.

Gilbert, P. (2014). *Mindful compassion.* Oakland, CA: New Harbinger.

Haidt, J. (2006). *The happiness hypothesis.* New York: Basic Books.

Harris, S. (2014). *Waking up: A guide to spirituality without religion.* New York: Simon & Schuster.

Hoehn, C. (2014). *Play it away: A workaholic's cure for anxiety.* Charliehoehn.com.

Hurley, M. H., et al. (2013). *Inside jokes: Using humor to reverse-engineer the mind.* Cambridge, MA: MIT Press.

Irvine, W. B. (2008). *A guide to the good life: The ancient art of stoic joy.* Oxford: Oxford University Press.

Kabat-Zinn, J. (2005). *Wherever you go, there you are.* New York: Hyperion.

Kaplan, S. (2013). *The hidden tools of comedy: The serious business of being funny.* Studio City, CA: Michael Wiese Productions.

Lyubomirsky, S. (2014). *The myths of happiness.* New York: Penguin.

McGraw, P., & Warner, J. (2014). *The humor code: A global search for what makes things funny.* New York: Simon & Schuster.

Perry, P. (2012). *How to stay sane.* New York: Picador.

Sacks, M. (2014). *Poking a dead frog: Conversations with today's top comedy writers.* New York: Penguin.

Salzberg, S. (2010). *Real happiness: The power of meditation.* New York: Workman Publishing.

Seligman, M. E. P. (2012). *Flourish.* New York: Atria Books.

Walsh, M., et al. (2013). *Upright Citizens Brigade comedy improvisation manual.* New York: Comedy Council of Nicea.

Williams, M., et al. (2012). *Mindfulness.* Emmaus, PA: Rodale.

Yalom, I. D. (2012). *Love's executioner, and other tales of psychotherapy* (2nd Ed.). New York: Basic Books.

Popular Books: Specific Mental Illnesses and Issues

Attwood, T. (2008). *The complete guide to Asperger's syndrome.* Philadelphia: Jessica Kingsley Publishers.

Baron-Cohen, S. (2003). *The essential difference: Men, women and the extreme male brain.* London: Allen Lane.

Frith, C., & Johnstone, E. (2003). *Schizophrenia: A very short introduction.* Oxford: Oxford University Press.

Gilbert, P. (2009). *Overcoming depression.* New York: Basic Books.

Kahn, J. P. (2012). *Angst: Origins of anxiety and depression.* Oxford: Oxford University Press.

Miklowitz, D. J. (2010). *The bipolar disorder survival guide* (2nd Ed.). New York: Guilford Press.

Robison, J. E. (2008). *Look me in the eye: My life with Asperger's.* New York: Three Rivers Press.

Rottenberg, J. (2014). *The depths: The evolutionary origins of the depression epidemic.* New York: Basic Books.

Torrey, E. F. (2013). *Surviving schizophrenia* (6th ed.). New York: Harper Perennial.

Selected Academic Papers and Essays (see the ebook or Mating Grounds for full list)

Bolier, L., et al. (2013). Positive psychology interventions: A meta-analysis of randomized controlled studies. *BMC Public Health, 13,* e119.

Del Giudice, M. (2010). Reduced fertility in patients' families is consistent with the sexual selection model of schizophrenia and schizotypy. *PLOS One, 5,* e16040.

Forgas, J. P. (2013). Don't worry, be sad! On the cognitive, motivational, and interpersonal benefits of negative mood. *Current Directions in Psychological Science, 2,* 225–232.

Hagen, E. H. (2011). Evolutionary theories of depression: A critical review. *Canadian Journal of Psychiatry, 56,* 716–726.

Howrigan, D. P., & MacDonald, K. B. (2008). Humor as a mental fitness indicator. *Evolutionary Psychology, 6*(4), 652–666.

Kim, Y. S., et al. (2012). Relationship between physical activity and general mental health. *Preventative Medicine, 55,* 458–463.

Nettle, D., & Bateson, M. (2012). The evolutionary origins of mood and its disorders. *Current Biology, 22*(17), R712–R721.

Rosen, L. D., et al. (2013). Is Facebook creating "iDisorders"? The link between clinical symptoms of psychiatric disorders and technology use, attitudes and anxiety. *Computers in Human Behavior, 29,* 1243–1254.

Treger, S., et al. (2013). Laughing and liking: Exploring the interpersonal effects of humor use in initial social interactions. *European Journal of Social Psychology, 43,* 532–543.

Wood, A. M., et al. (2010). Gratitude and well-being: A review and theoretical integration. *Clinical Psychology Review, 30,* 890–905.

Geoff's Work

Greengross, G., & Miller, G. F. (2008). Dissing oneself versus dissing rivals: Effects of status, personality, and sex on the short-term and long-term attractiveness of self-deprecating and other-deprecating humor. *Evolutionary Psychology, 6*(3), 393–408.

Greengross, G., & Miller, G. F. (2009). The Big Five personality traits of professional comedians compared to amateur comedians, comedy writers, and college students. *Personality and Individual Differences, 47,* 79–83.

Greengross, G., & Miller, G. F. (2011). Humor ability reveals intelligence, predicts mating success, and is higher in males. *Intelligence, 39,* 188–192.

Keller, M., & Miller, G. F. (2006). Resolving the paradox of common, harmful, heritable mental disorders: Which evolutionary genetic models work best? *Behavioral and Brain Sciences, 29,* 385–404.

Miller, G. F. (1997). Protean primates: The evolution of adaptive unpredictability in competition and courtship. In A. Whiten & R. W. Byrne (Eds.), *Machiavellian intelligence II* (pp. 312–340). Cambridge: Cambridge University Press.

Miller, G. F. (2009). Openness. In G. F. Miller, *Spent: Sex, evolution, and consumer behavior* (pp. 207–224). New York: Viking.

Miller, G. F. (2011). The personality/insanity continuum. In J. Brockman (Ed.), *This will make you smarter* (pp. 232–234). New York: Harper Perennial.

Miller, G. F., & Tal, I. (2007). Schizotypy versus intelligence and openness as predictors of creativity. *Schizophrenia Research, 93*(1–3), 317–324.

Shaner, A., et al. (2004). Schizophrenia as one extreme of a sexually selected fitness indicator. *Schizophrenia Research, 70*(1), 101–109.

Shaner, A., et al. (2007). Mental disorders as catastrophic failures of mating intelligence. In G. Geher & G. Miller (Eds.), *Mating intelligence* (pp. 193–223). Mahwah, NJ: Lawrence Erlbaum Associates.

Shaner, A., et al. (2008). Autism as the low-fitness extreme of a parentally selected fitness indicator. *Human Nature, 19*, 389–413.

Chapter 7: Smarten Up (The Intelligence Trait)

Popular Books

Brandon, C. (2010). *The five-year party: How colleges have given up on educating your child and what you can do about it.* Dallas: BenBella Books.

Brockman, J. (Ed.). (2012). *This will make you smarter.* New York: Harper Perennial.

De Botton, A. (2014). *The news: A user's manual.* New York: Pantheon.

Edge, D. (2003). *The gatekeepers: Inside the admissions process of a premier college.* New York: Penguin.

Ellsberg, M. (2012). *The education of millionaires.* New York: Portfolio/Penguin.

Gigerenzer, G. (2014). *Risk savvy: How to make good decisions.* New York: Viking.

Herrnstein, R. J., & Murray, C. (1996). *The bell curve.* New York: Free Press.

Hirsch, E. E. (2006). *The knowledge deficit.* New York: Houghton Mifflin.

Kahneman, D. (2013). *Thinking, fast and slow.* New York: Farrar, Straus & Giroux.

Karabel, J. (2006). *The chosen: The hidden history of admission and exclusion at Harvard, Yale, and Princeton.* New York: Mariner Books.

Kenrick, D. T., & Griskevicius, V. (2013). *The rational animal.* New York: Basic Books.

Markman, A. (2012). *Smart thinking.* New York: Perigree Books.

Murray, C. (2008). *Real education.* New York: Crown Forum.

O'Shea, J. (2013). *Gap year.* Baltimore: Johns Hopkins University Press.

Selingo, J. J. (2013). *College unbound.* Boston: New Harvest.

Watts, D. (2012). *Everything is obvious.* New York: Crown Business.

Academic Books

Bok, D. (2013). *Higher education in America.* Princeton, NJ: Princeton University Press.

Deary, I. J. (2001). *Intelligence: A very short introduction.* Oxford: Oxford University Press.

Deary, I. J., et al. (2008). *A lifetime of intelligence.* Washington, DC: American Psychological Association.

Dow, P. E. (2013). *Virtuous minds: Intellectual character development.* Downers Grove, IL: IVP Academic.

Gigerenzer, G., & Todd, P. M. (Eds.). (1999). *Simple heuristics that make us smart.* Cambridge, MA: MIT Press.

Hunt, E. (2010). *Human intelligence.* Cambridge: Cambridge University Press.

Jensen, A. R. (1998). *The g factor: The science of mental ability.* Westport, CT: Praeger.

Kaufman, A. S. (2009). *IQ testing 101.* New York: Springer.

Matthews, G., et al. (2004). *Emotional intelligence: Science and myth.* Cambridge, MA: MIT Press.

Simonton, D. K. (1999). *Origins of genius: Darwinian perspectives on creativity.* Oxford: Oxford University Press.

Simonton, D. K. (2009). *Genius 101.* New York: Springer.

Spence, A. M. (1974). *Market signaling.* Cambridge, MA: Harvard University Press.

Sterelny, K. (2012). *The evolved apprentice: How evolution made humans unique.* Cambridge, MA: MIT Press.

Sternberg, R. J., & Kaufman, S. B. (Eds.). (2011). *The Cambridge handbook of intelligence.* Cambridge: Cambridge University Press.

Suddendorf, T. (2013). *The gap: The science of what separates us from other animals.* New York: Basic Books.

Thomasello, M. (2014). *A natural history of human thinking.* Cambridge, MA: Harvard University Press.

Todd, P. M., & Gigerenzer, G. (Eds.). (2012). *Ecological rationality: Intelligence in the world.* Oxford: Oxford University Press.

Selected Academic Papers and Essays (see the ebook or Mating Grounds for full list)

Arden, R., & Plomin, R. (2006). Sex differences in variance in intelligence across childhood. *Personality and Individual Differences, 41,* 39–48.

Davies, G., et al. (2011). Genome-wide association studies establish that human intelligence is highly heritable and polygenic. *Molecular Psychiatry, 16,* 996–1005.

Gottfredson, L. S. (1997). Why *g* matters: The complexity of everyday life. *Intelligence, 24,* 79–132.

Klasios, J. (2013). Cognitive traits as sexually selected fitness indicators. *Review of General Psychology, 17*(4), 428–442.

McKeown, G. J. (2013). The analogical peacock hypothesis: The sexual selection of mind-reading and relational cognition in human communication. *Review of General Psychology, 17,* 267–287.

Muller, C., & Schumann, G. (2011). Drugs as instruments: A new framework for nonaddictive psychoactive drug use. *Behavioral and Brain Sciences, 34,* 293–310.

Murphy, N. A. (2007). Appearing smart: The impression management of intelligence, person perception accuracy, and behavior in social interaction. *Personality and Social Psychology Bulletin, 33,* 325–339.

Prokosch, M., et al. (2009). Intelligence and mate choice: Intelligent men are always appealing. *Evolution and Human Behavior, 30,* 11–20.

von Stumm, S., et al. (2011). The hungry mind: Intellectual curiosity is the third pillar of academic performance. *Perspectives on Psychological Science, 6,* 574–588.

Weisfeld, G. E., et al. (2011). Do women seek humorousness in men because it signals intelligence? A cross-cultural test. *Humor, 24,* 435–462.

Geoff's Work

Arden, R., et al. (2009). Does a fitness factor contribute to the association between intelligence and health outcomes? Evidence from medical abnormality counts among 3,654 US Veterans. *Intelligence, 37,* 581–591.

Arden, R., et al. (2009). Intelligence and semen quality are positively correlated. *Intelligence, 37,* 277–282.

Geher, G., & Miller, G. F. (Eds.). (2008). *Mating intelligence.* Mahwah, NJ: Lawrence Erlbaum Associates.

Haselton, M., & Miller, G. F. (2006). Women's fertility across the cycle increases the short-term attractiveness of creative intelligence. *Human Nature, 17*(1), 50–73.

Kaufman, S. B., et al. (2007). The role of creativity and humor in mate selection. In G. Geher & G. Miller (Eds.), *Mating intelligence* (pp. 227–262). Mahwah, NJ: Lawrence Erlbaum Associates.

Miller, G. F. (2000). Sexual selection for indicators of intelligence. In G. R. Bock et al. (Eds.), *The nature of intelligence* (pp. 260–275). New York: Wiley.

Miller, G. F. (2000). The wit to woo. In G. F. Miller, *The mating mind* (pp. 392–425). New York: Doubleday.

Miller, G. F. (2009). General intelligence. In G. F. Miller, *Spent: Sex, evolution, and consumer behavior* (pp. 187–206). New York: Viking.

Miller, G. F., & Penke, L. (2007). The evolution of human intelligence and the coefficient of additive genetic variance in human brain size. *Intelligence, 35*(2), 97–114.

Prokosch, M., et al. (2005). Intelligence tests with higher *g*-loadings show higher correlations with body symmetry: Evidence for a general fitness factor mediated by developmental stability. *Intelligence, 33*, 203–213.

Chapter 8: Get Your Life Together (The Willpower Trait)

Popular Books

Allen, D. (2002). *Getting things done*. New York: Penguin.

Baumeister, R. F., & Tierney, J. (2012). *Willpower*. New York: Penguin.

Covey, S. R. (2013). *The 7 habits of highly effective people*. New York: Simon & Schuster.

Duhigg, C. (2014). *The power of habit*. New York: Random House.

Firestone, R. W., et al. (2002). *Conquer your critical inner voice*. Oakland, CA: New Harbinger.

Gawande, A. (2010). *The checklist manifesto*. New York: Picador.

Kondo, M. (2014). *The life-changing magic of tidying up*. New York: Ten Speed Press.

Levitin, D. J. (2014). *The organized mind*. New York: Dutton.

Markman, A. (2015). *Smart change*. New York: Perigree Books.

McGonigal, K. (2013). *The willpower instinct*. New York: Avery Trade.

McKeown, G. (2014). *Essentialism: The disciplined pursuit of less*. New York: Crown Business.

Mischel, W. (2014). *The marshmallow test: Mastering self-control*. New York: Little, Brown.

Neff, K. (2011). *Self-compassion*. New York: William Morrow.

Nettle, D. (2007). *Personality*. Oxford: Oxford University Press.

Pink, D. H. (2011). *Drive*. New York: Riverhead Books.

Sax, L. (2009). *Boys adrift*. New York: Basic Books.

Academic Books

Buss, D. M., & Hawley, P. H. (Eds.). (2011). *The evolution of personality and individual differences*. Oxford: Oxford University Press.

Carere, C., & Maestripieri, D. (Eds.). (2013). *Animal personalities: Behavior, physiology, and evolution*. Chicago: University of Chicago Press.

Matthews, G., et al. (2009). *Personality traits* (3rd Ed.). Cambridge: Cambridge University Press.

Ryan, R. M. (Ed.). (2014). *The Oxford handbook of human motivation*. Oxford: Oxford University Press.

Vohs, K. D., & Baumeister, R. F. (2011). *Handbook of self-regulation: Research, theory, and applications* (2nd ed.). New York: Guilford.

Zuckerman, M. (2007). *Sensation seeking and risky behavior*. Washington, DC: American Psychological Association.

Selected Academic Papers and Essays (see the ebook or Mating Grounds for full list)

Bevilacqua, L., & Goldman, D. (2013). Genetics of impulsive behavior. *Philosophical Transactions of the Royal Society of London B, 368*, e20120380.

Del Giudice, M. (2014). Self-regulation in an evolutionary perspective. In G. H. E. Gendolla et al. (Eds.), *Handbook of biobehavioral approaches to self-regulation* (pp. 25–42). New York: Springer.

De Ridder, D. T. D., et al. (2012). Taking stock of self-control: A meta-analysis of how trait self-control relates to a wide range of behaviors. *Personality and Social Psychology Review, 16*, 76–99.

Hampton, S. E., et al. (2013). Childhood conscientiousness relates to objectively measured adult physical health four decades later. *Health Psychology, 32*, 925–928.

Inzlicht, M., et al. (2014). Exploring the mechanisms of self-control improvement. *Current Directions in Psychological Science, 23*, 302–307.

Kross, E., et al. (2014). Self-talk as a regulatory mechanism: How you do it matters. *Journal of Personality and Social Psychology, 106*, 304–324.

Lally, P., & Gardner, B. (2013). Promoting habit formation. *Health Psychology Review, 7*, S137–S153.

Schmitt, D. P., et al. (2008). Big Five traits related to short-term mating: From personality to promiscuity across 46 nations. *Evolutionary Psychology, 6*(2), 246–282.

Tidwell, N. S., & Eastwick, P. W. (2013). Sex differences in succumbing to sexual temptations: A function of impulse or control? *Personality and Social Psychology Bulletin, 39*, 1620–1633.

Zietsch, B. P., et al. (2010). Genetic and environmental influences on risky sexual behavior and its relationship with personality. *Behavior Genetics, 40*(1), 12–21.

Geoff's Work

Miller, G. F. (2007). Sexual selection for moral virtues. *Quarterly Review of Biology, 82*(2), 97–125.

Miller, G. F. (2009). Conscientiousness. In G. F. Miller, *Spent: Sex, evolution, and consumer behavior* (pp. 225–239). New York: Viking.

Penke, L., et al. (2007). The evolutionary genetics of personality. *European Journal of Personality, 21*(5), 549–587.

Chapter 9: The Tender Defender (The Agreeableness and Assertiveness Traits)

Popular Books

De Becker, G. (1999). *The gift of fear.* New York: Dell.

De Waal, F. (2010). *The age of empathy.* New York: Broadway Books.

Gonzales, L. (2004). *Deep survival: Who lives, who dies, and why.* New York: W. W. Norton.

Gottschall, J. (2015). *The professor in the cage: Why men fight and why we like to watch.* New York: Penguin.

Grossman, D., & Christensen, L. W. (2008). *On combat: The psychology and physiology of deadly conflict in war and peace* (3rd Ed.). Warrior Science Publications.

Houston, P., et al. (2013). *Spy the lie: Former CIA officers teach you how to detect deception.* New York: St. Martin's Press.

Kane, L. A., et al. (2009). *The little black book of violence: What every young man needs to know about fighting.* Wolfeboro, NH: YMAA Publication Center.

LaFrance, M. (2011). *Lip service: Smiles in life, death, trust, lies, work, memory, sex, and politics.* New York: W. W. Norton.

McConnell, P. B. (2003). *The other end of the leash: Why we do what we do around dogs.* New York: Ballantine Books.

Miller, R. (2008). *Meditations on violence: A comparison of martial arts training and real world violence.* Wolfeboro, NH: YMAA Publication Center.

Pinker, S. (2012). *The better angels of our nature: Why violence has declined.* New York: Penguin.

Plantinga, A. (2014). *400 things cops know: Street-smart lessons from a veteran patrolman.* Fresno, CA: Quill Driver Books.

Schaffer, B. (2013). *Way of the warrior: The philosophy of law enforcement.* CreateSpace.

Sherwood, B. (2010). *The survivors club: The secrets and science that could save your life.* New York: Grand Central Publishing.

Sommers, C. H. (2013). *The way against boys: How misguided policies are harming our young men.* New York: Simon & Schuster.

Stout, M. (2005). *The sociopath next door.* New York: Harmony.

Academic Books

Flesch, W. (2009). *Comeuppance: Costly signaling, altruistic punishment, and other biological components of fiction.* Cambridge, MA: Harvard University Press.

Gat, A. (2008). *War in human civilization.* Oxford: Oxford University Press.

Gottschall, J. (2008). *The rape of Troy: Evolution, violence, and the world of Homer.* Cambridge: Cambridge University Press.

Hardy, I. C. W., & Briffa, M. (Eds.). (2013). *Animal contests.* Cambridge: Cambridge University Press.

Hausfater, G., & Hrdy, S. B. (2008). *Infanticide: Comparative and evolutionary perspectives.* Chicago: AldineTransaction.

Shackelford, T. K. (2012). *The Oxford handbook of evolutionary perspectives on violence, homicide, and war.* Oxford: Oxford University Press.

Shackelford, T. K., & Hansen, R. D. (Eds.). (2013). *The evolution of violence.* New York: Springer.

Selected Academic Papers and Essays (see the ebook or Mating Grounds for full list)

Ainsworth, S. E., & Maner, J. K. (2012). Sex begets violence: Mating motives, social dominance, and physical aggression in men. *Journal of Personality and Social Psychology, 103*(5), 819–829.

Archer, J. (2009). Does sexual selection explain human sex differences in aggression? *Behavioral and Brain Sciences, 32,* 249–266.

Gambacorta, D., & Ketelaar, T. (2013). Dominance and deference: Men inhibit creative displays during mate competition when their competitor is strong. *Evolution and Human Behavior, 34,* 330–333.

Goetz, J. L., et al. (2010). Compassion: An evolutionary analysis and empirical review. *Psychological Bulletin, 136,* 351–374.

Griskevicius, V., et al. (2009). Aggress to impress: Hostility as an evolved context-dependent strategy. *Journal of Personality and Social Psychology, 96*(5), 980–994.

Kruger, D. J., & Fitzgerald, C. J. (2011). Reproductive strategies and relationships preferences associated with prestigious and dominant men. *Personality and Individual Differences, 50,* 365–369.

McDonald, M. M., et al. (2012). Evolution and the psychology of intergroup conflict: The male warrior hypothesis. *Philosophical Transactions of the Royal Society of London B, 367,* 670–679.

Preston, S. D. (2013). The origins of altruism in offspring care. *Psychological Bulletin, 139*, 1305–1341.

Ronay, R., & von Hippel, W. (2010). The presence of an attractive woman elevates testosterone and physical risk taking in young men. *Social Psychological and Personality Science, 1*(1), 57–64.

Sell, A., et al. (2012). The importance of physical strength to human males. *Human Nature, 23*, 30–44.

Geoff's Work

Miller, G. F. (2007). Sexual selection for moral virtues. *Quarterly Review of Biology, 82*, 97–125.

Miller, G. F. (2009). Agreeableness. In G. F. Miller, *Spent: Sex, evolution, and consumer behavior* (pp. 240–254). New York: Viking.

Chapter 10: Show Them What You're Working With (Signaling Theory)

Popular Books

Bradbury, J. W., & Vehrencamp, S. L. (2011). Principles of animal communication (2nd Ed.). Sunderland, MA: Sinauer Associates.

Maynard Smith, J., & Harper, D. (2003). *Animal signals.* Oxford: Oxford University Press.

Neiva, E. (2007). *Communication games.* Berlin: Mouton de Gruyter.

Pentland, A. (2008). *Honest signals and how they shape our world.* Cambridge, MA: MIT Press.

Searcy, W. A., & Nowicki, S. (2005). *The evolution of animal communication.* Princeton, NJ: Princeton University Press.

Stegmann, U. E. (Ed.). (2013). *Animal communication theory.* Cambridge: Cambridge University Press.

Stevens, M. (2013). *Sensory ecology, behavior, and evolution.* Oxford: Oxford University Press.

Veblen, T. (1899). *The theory of the leisure class.* New York: Macmillan.

Zahavi, A., & Zahavi, A. (1997). *The handicap principle: A missing piece of Darwin's puzzle.* Oxford: Oxford University Press.

Selected Academic Papers and Essays (see the ebook or Mating Grounds for full list)

Bird, R. B., & Smith, E. A. (2005). Signaling theory, strategic interaction, and symbolic capital. *Current Anthropology, 46*, 221–248.

Castellano, S., & Cermelli, P. (2010). Attractive amplifiers in sexual selection: Where efficacy meets honesty. *Evolutionary Ecology, 24*, 1187–1197.

Dessalles, J.-L. (2014). Optimal investment in social signals. *Evolution, 68*, 1640–1650.

Higham, J. P. (2014). How does honest costly signaling work? *Behavioral Ecology, 25*, 8–11.

Hill, G. E. (2011). Condition-dependent traits as signals of the functionality of vital cellular processes. *Biology Letters, 14*, 625–634.

Kraaijeveld, K., et al. (2007). The evolution of mutual ornamentation. *Animal Behaviour, 74*, 657–677.

Schaedelin, F. C., & Taborsky, M. (2009). Extended phenotypes as signals. *Biological Reviews, 84*, 293–313.

Spence, M. (2002). Signaling in retrospect and the informational structure of markets. *American Economic Review, 92*, 424–459.

Tazzyman, S. J., et al. (2014). Signaling efficacy drives the evolution of larger sexual ornaments by sexual selection. *Evolution, 68*(1), 216–229.

Tibbetts, E. A. (2014). The evolution of honest communication: Integrating social and physiological costs of ornamentation. *Integrative and Comparative Biology, 54*, 578–590.

Geoff's Work

Miller, G. F. (1998). Review of the book *The handicap principle*. *Evolution and Human Behavior, 19*(5), 343–347.

Miller, G. F. (1999). Sexual selection for cultural displays. In R. Dunbar et al. (Eds.), *The evolution of culture* (pp. 71–91). Edinburgh: Edinburgh University Press.

Miller, G. F. (2000). Marketing. In J. Brockman (Ed.), *The greatest inventions of the last 2,000 years* (pp. 121–126). New York: Simon & Schuster.

Miller, G. F. (2000). Mental traits as fitness indicators: Expanding evolutionary psychology's adaptationism. In D. LeCroy & P. Moller (Eds.), *Evolutionary perspectives on human reproductive behavior* (pp. 62–74). New York: New York Academy of Sciences.

Miller, G. F. (2000). A mind fit for mating. In G. F. Miller, *The mating mind* (pp. 99–137). New York: Doubleday.

Miller, G. F. (2009). The Central Six. In G. F. Miller, *Spent: Sex, evolution, and consumer behavior* (pp. 144–170). New York: Viking.

Miller, G. F. (2009). Conspicuous Waste, Precision, and Reputation. In G. F. Miller, *Spent: Sex, evolution, and consumer behavior* (pp. 112–127). New York: Viking.

Miller, G. F. (2009). Flaunting Fitness. In G. F. Miller, *Spent: Sex, evolution, and consumer behavior* (pp. 90–111). New York: Viking.

Miller, G. F. (2009). Self-Branding Bodies, Self-Marketing Minds. In G. F. Miller, *Spent: Sex, evolution, and consumer behavior* (pp. 128–143). New York: Viking.

Miller, G. F. (2009). Traits That Consumers Flaunt and Marketers Ignore. In G. F. Miller, *Spent: Sex, evolution, and consumer behavior* (pp. 171–186). New York: Viking.

Chapter 11: The Power of Popularity and Prestige (Social Proof)

Popular Books

Cabane, O. F. (2013). *The charisma myth.* New York: Portfolio.

Cain, S. (2013). *Quiet.* New York: Broadway Books.

Carnegie, D. (1936). *How to win friends and influence people.* New York: Simon and Schuster.

Cialdini, R. (2008). *Influence* (5th Ed.). Boston: Allyn & Bacon.

Ellsberg, M. (2010). *The power of eye contact.* New York: William Morrow.

Grandin, T., & Barron, S. (2005). *The unwritten rules of social relationships.* Arlington, TX: Future Horizons.

Hoffman, R. (2012). *The start-up of you.* New York: Crown Business.

Lieberman, M. D. (2015). *Social: Why our brains are wired to connect.* New York: Broadway Books.

Putnam, R. D. (2001). *Bowling alone.* New York: Simon & Schuster.

Ronson, J. (2015). *So you've been publicly shamed.* New York: Riverhead Books.

Academic Books

Baumeister, R. (2005). *The cultural animal.* Oxford: Oxford University Press.

Boesch, C. (2009). *The real chimpanzee: Sex strategies in the forest.* Cambridge: Cambridge University Press.

Boyd, D. (2014). *It's complicated: The social lives of networked teens.* New Haven, CT: Yale University Press.

Caldarelli, G., & Catanzaro, M. (2012). *Networks: A very short introduction.* Oxford: Oxford University Press.

Donath, J. (2014). *The social machine: Designs for living online.* Cambridge, MA: MIT Press.

Emery, N., et al. (Eds.). (2008). *Social intelligence: From brain to culture.* Oxford: Oxford University Press.

Forgas, J. P., et al. (Eds.). (2007). *Evolution and the social mind.* New York: Psychology Press.

Gamble, C., et al. (2014). *Thinking big: How the evolution of social life shaped the human mind.* London: Thames & Hudson.

Graziano, M. S. A. (2013). *Consciousness and the social brain.* Oxford: Oxford University Press.

Harcourt, A. H., & Stewart, K. J. (2007). *Gorilla society: Conflict, compromise, and cooperation between the sexes.* Chicago: University of Chicago Press.

Hertwig, R., et al. (Eds.). (2012). *Simple heuristics in a social world.* Oxford: Oxford University Press.

Hruschka, D. J. (2010). *Friendship: Development, ecology, and evolution of a relationship.* Berkeley: University of California Press.

Jacquet, J. (2015). *Is shame necessary? New uses for an old tool.* New York: Pantheon Books.

Just, P. (2000). *Social and cultural anthropology: A very short introduction.* Oxford: Oxford University Press.

Mitani, J. C., et al. (Eds.). (2012). *The evolution of primate societies.* Chicago: University of Chicago Press.

Schaller, M., et al. (Eds.). (2006). *Evolution and social psychology.* New York: Psychology Press.

Wilson, E. O. (2013). *The social conquest of earth.* New York: Liveright.

Selected Academic Papers and Essays (see the ebook or Mating Grounds for full list)

Apicella, C., et al. (2012). Social networks and cooperation in hunter-gatherers. *Nature, 481*(7382), 497–501.

Cheng, J. T., et al. (2013). Two ways to the top: Evidence that dominance and prestige are distinct yet viable avenues to social rank and influence. *Journal of Personality and Social Psychology, 104*(1), 103–125.

Dezecache, G., & Dunbar, R. I. M. (2012). Sharing the joke: The size of natural laughter groups. *Evolution and Human Behavior, 33*, 775–779.

Fiske, S. T., et al. (2007). Universal dimensions of social cognition: Warmth and competence. *Trends in Cognitive Sciences, 11*, 77–83.

Lewis, D. M. G., et al. (2011). Friends with benefits: The evolved psychology of same- and opposite-sex friendship. *Evolutionary Psychology, 9*, 543–563.

Lukaszewski, A. W., & von Rueden, C. R. (2015). The extraversion continuum in evolutionary perspective: A review of recent theory and evidence. *Personality and Individual Differences, 77*, 186–192.

Price, M. E., & Van Vugt, M. (2014). The evolution of leader-follower reciprocity: The theory of service-for-prestige. *Frontiers in Human Neuroscience, 8*, e363.

Seyfarth, R. M., & Cheney, D. L. (2012). The evolutionary origins of friendship. *Annual Review of Psychology, 63*, 153–177.

Sundie, J. M., et al. (2012). The world's (truly) oldest profession: Social influence in evolutionary perspective. *Social Influence, 7*, 134–153.

Winegard, B. M., et al. (2013). If you've got it, flaunt it: Humans flaunt attractive partners to enhance their status and desirability. *PLOS ONE, 8*(8), e72000.

Geoff's Work

Miller, G. F. (2000). Memetic evolution and human culture. *Quarterly Review of Biology, 75*(4), 434–436.

Chapter 12: How Rich Do You Need to Be? (Material Proof)

Popular Books

Allen, R. C. (2011). *Global economic history: A very short introduction.* Oxford: Oxford University Press.

Altucher, J., & Costolo, D. (2013). *Choose yourself.* CreateSpace.

Armstrong, J. (2012). *How to worry less about money.* New York: Picador.

Clarey, A. (2013). *Bachelor pad economics.* CreateSpace.

Conniff, R. (2002). *The natural history of the rich.* New York: W. W. Norton.

Conniff, R. (2005). *The beast in the corner office.* New York: Crown Business.

De Botton, A. (2004). *Status anxiety.* New York: Penguin.

De Botton, A. (2010). *The pleasures and sorrows of work.* New York: Vintage.

Diamandis, P. H., & Kotler, S. (2014). *Abundance.* New York: Free Press.

Ferriss, T. (2009). *The 4-hour work week.* New York: Harmony.

Frank, R. H. (2000). *Luxury fever.* Princeton, NJ: Princeton University Press.

Frank, R. H. (2010). *What price the moral high ground? How to succeed without selling your soul.* Princeton, NJ: Princeton University Press.

Frank, R. H., & Cook, P. J. (1995). *The winner-take-all society.* New York: Free Press.

Gini, A. (2000). *My job, my self.* New York: Routledge.

Guillebeau, C. (2012). *The $100 startup.* New York: Crown Business.

Hoehn, C. (2014). *Recession-proof graduate.* Charliehoehn.com.

Hyatt, M. (2012). *Platform.* Nashville, TN: Thomas Nelson.

Kaufman, J. (2012). *The personal MBA.* New York: Portfolio.

Krznaric, R. (2013). *How to find fulfilling work.* New York: Picador.

Leavitt, S. D., & Dubner, S. J. (2009). *Freakonomics.* New York: Harper Perennial.

Pink, D. (2013). *To sell is human.* New York: Riverhead Books.

Ridley, M. (2011). *The rational optimist.* New York: Harper Perennial.

Ries, E. (2011). *The lean startup.* New York: Crown Business.

Seabright, P. (2010). *The company of strangers.* Princeton, NJ: Princeton University Press.

Shermer, M. (2007). *The mind of the market.* New York: Times Books.

Stanley, T. J., & Danko, W. D. (2010). *The millionaire next door.* Lanham, MD: Taylor Trade.

Thiel, P. (2014). *Zero to one.* New York: Crown Business.

Wheelan, C. (2010). *Naked economics.* New York: W. W. Norton.

Academic Books

Arrow, K., et al. (2000). *Meritocracy and economic inequality.* Princeton, NJ: Princeton University Press.

Clark, G., (2007). *A farewell to alms.* Princeton, NJ: Princeton University Press.

Earle, T. (2002). *Bronze age economics.* Boulder, CO: Westview Press.

English, J. F. (2005). *The economy of prestige.* Cambridge, MA: Harvard University Press.

Flannery, K., & Marcus, J. (2012). *The creation of inequality.* Cambridge, MA: Harvard University Press.

Furnham, A. (2006). *Just for the money? What really motivates us at work.* London: Cyan Communications.

Furnham, A. (2008). *Personality and intelligence at work.* New York: Psychology Press.

Hochschild, A. (2003). *The managed heart.* Berkeley: University of California Press.

McCloskey, D. N. (2007). *The bourgeois virtues.* Chicago: University of Chicago Press.

Preston, S. D., et al. (2014). *The interdisciplinary science of consumption.* Cambridge, MA: MIT Press.

Saad, G. (2007). *The evolutionary bases of consumption.* Mahwah, NJ: Lawrence Erlbaum Associates.

Saad, G. (Ed.). (2011). *Evolutionary psychology in the business sciences.* New York: Springer.

Taleb, N. N. (2012). *Antifragile.* New York: Penguin.

Zelizer, V. A. (2013). *Economic lives.* Princeton, NJ: Princeton University Press.

Selected Academic Papers and Essays (see the ebook or Mating Grounds for full list)

Baumeister, R. F., & Vohs, K. D. (2004). Sexual economics: Sex as female resource for social exchange in heterosexual interactions. *Personality and Social Psychology Review, 8,* 339–363.

Dunn, E. W., et al. (2011). If money doesn't make you happy, then you probably aren't spending it right. *Journal of Consumer Psychology, 21,* 115–125.

Durante, K. M., et al. (2014). Money, status, and the ovulatory cycle. *Journal of Marketing Research, 51,* 27–39.

Gilovich, T., et al. (2015). A wonderful life: Experiential consumption and the pursuit of happiness. *Journal of Consumer Psychology, 25,* 152–165.

Griskevicius, V., & Kenrick, D. T. (2013). Fundamental motives: How evolutionary needs influence consumer behavior. *Journal of Consumer Psychology, 23*(3), 372–386.

Iredale, W., et al. (2008). Showing off in humans: Male generosity as a mating signal. *Evolutionary Psychology, 6,* 386–392.

Nettle, D., & Pollet, T. V. (2008). Natural selection on male wealth in humans. *American Naturalist, 172,* 658–666.

Sozou, P. D., & Seymour, R. M. (2005). Costly but worthless gifts facilitate courtship. *Proceedings of the Royal Society of London B, 272,* 1877–1884.

Strenze, R. (2007). Intelligence and socioeconomic success: A meta-analytic review of longitudinal research. *Intelligence, 35,* 401–426.

Sundie, J. M., et al. (2011). Peacocks, Porsches, and Thorstein Veblen: Conspicuous consumption as a sexual signaling system. *Journal of Personality and Social Psychology, 100,* 664–680.

Geoff's Work

Miller, G. (1998, February 20). Waste is good. *Prospect,* 18–23.

Miller, G. (2000). Marketing. In J. Brockman (Ed.), *The greatest inventions of the last 2,000 years* (pp. 121–126). New York: Simon & Schuster.

Miller, G. (2007). Runaway consumerism explains the Fermi paradox. In J. Brockman (Ed.), *What is your dangerous idea?* (pp. 240–243). New York: Harper Perennial.

Miller, G. F. (2009). *Spent: Sex, evolution, and consumer behavior.* New York: Viking.

Miller, G. F. (2012). Sex, evolution, and marketing. *EMBO Reports, 13*(10), 880–884.

Miller, G. F. (2013). Twenty-seven thoughts about multiple selves, sustainable consumption, and human evolution. In H. C. M. van Trijp (Ed.), *Encouraging sustainable behavior* (pp. 27–35). Oxford, UK: Psychology Press.

Chapter 13: Stylin' and Profilin' (Aesthetic Proof)

Popular Books

Byrne, D. (2013). *How music works.* San Francisco: McSweeney's.

Dutton, D. (2008). *The art instinct.* London: Bloomsbury Press.

Eco, U. (2012). *History of beauty.* New York: Rizzoli.

Edwards, B. (2012). *Drawing on the right side of the brain* (4th Ed.). New York: Tarcher.

Gosling, S. D. (2008). *Snoop: What your stuff says about you.* New York: Basic Books.

Hovey, H. H. (2013). *Heirloom modern.* New York: Rizzoli.

Kandel, E. (2012). *The age of insight.* New York: Random House.

Levitin, D. (2007). *This is your brain on music.* New York: Plume/Penguin.

Marcus, G. (2012). *Guitar zero: The science of becoming musical at any age.* New York: Penguin.

Peres, D. (2007). *Details men's style manual.* New York: Gotham.

Postrel, V. (2004). *The substance of style.* New York: Harper Perennial.

Postrel, V. (2013). *The power of glamour.* New York: Simon & Schuster.

Roetzel, B. (2012). *Gentleman: A timeless guide to fashion.* Potsdam, Germany: H. F. Ullmann.

Scruton, R. (2011). *Beauty: A very short introduction.* Oxford: Oxford University Press.

Thornton, S. (2009). *Seven days in the art world.* New York: W. W. Norton.

Academic Books

Carroll, J. (2011). *Reading human nature.* New York: State University of New York Press.

Catchpole, C. K., & Slater, P. J. B. (2008). *Bird song* (2nd Ed.). Cambridge: Cambridge University Press.

Chatterjee, A. (2013). *The aesthetic brain.* Oxford: Oxford University Press.

Davies, S. (2015). *The artful species.* Oxford: Oxford University Press.

Dawkins, R. (1999). *The extended phenotype.* Oxford: Oxford University Press.

Gombrich, E. H. (1994). *A sense of order.* London: Phaidon Press.

Gombrich, E. H. (2000). *Art and illusion.* London: Phaidon Press.

Hersey, G. L. (1996). *The evolution of allure.* Cambridge, MA: MIT Press.

Hersey, G. L. (1999). *The monumental impulse.* Cambridge, MA: MIT Press.

Huron, D. (2006). *Sweet anticipation: Music and the psychology of expectation.* Cambridge, MA: MIT Press.

Jablonski, N. G. (2006). *Skin: A natural history.* Berkeley: University of California Press.

Malagouris, L. (2013). *How things shape the mind.* Cambridge, MA: MIT Press.

Mithen, S. (2007). *The singing Neanderthals.* Cambridge, MA: Harvard University Press.

Steiner, W. (2001). *Venus in exile.* New York: Free Press.

Veblen, T. (1914). *The instinct of workmanship and the state of the industrial arts.* New York: Macmillan.

Voland, E., & Grammer, K. (Eds.). (2003). *Evolutionary aesthetics.* New York: Springer.

Selected Academic Papers and Essays (see the ebook or Mating Grounds for full list)

Arden, R., et al. (2014). Genes influence young children's human figure drawings and their association with intelligence a decade later. *Psychological Science, 25*, 1843–1850.

Charlton, B. D. (2014). Menstrual cycle phase alters women's sexual preferences for composers of more complex music. *Proceedings of the Royal Society of London B, 281*, e20140403.

Clegg, H., et al. (2011). Status and mating success amongst visual artists. *Frontiers in Psychology, 2*, e310.

Fink, B., et al. (2015). Integrating body movement into attractiveness research. *Frontiers in Psychology, 6*, e220.

Gillath, O., et al. (2012). Shoes as a source of first impressions. *Journal of Research in Personality, 46*, 423–430.

Griskevicius, V., et al. (2006). Peacocks, Picasso, and parental investment: The effects of romantic motives on creativity. *Journal of Personality and Social Psychology, 91*, 63–76.

Gueguen, N., et al. (2014). Men's music ability and attractiveness to women in a real-life courtship context. *Psychology of Music, 42*, 545–549.

Kelley, L. A., & Endler, J. A. (2012). Male great bowerbirds create forced perspective illusions with consistently different individual quality. *Proceedings of the National Academy of Sciences USA, 109*(51), 20980–20985.

Plourde, A. M. (2009). The origins of prestige goods as honest signals of skill and knowledge. *Human Nature, 19*, 374–388.

Weege, B., et al. (2012). Women's visual attention to variation in men's dance quality. *Personality and Individual Differences, 53*, 236–240.

Geoff's Work

Blythe, P. W., et al. (1999). How motion reveals intention: Categorizing social interactions. In G. Gigerenzer & P. Todd. (Eds.), *Simple heuristics that make us smart* (pp. 257–285). Oxford: Oxford University Press.

Miller, G. F. (1999). Sexual selection for cultural displays. In R. Dunbar et al. (Eds.), *The evolution of culture* (pp. 71–91). Edinburgh: Edinburgh University Press.

Miller, G. F. (2000). Arts of seduction. In G. F. Miller, *The mating mind* (pp. 258–291). New York: Doubleday.

Miller, G. F. (2000). Evolution of human music through sexual selection. In N. L. Wallin et al. (Eds.), *The origins of music* (pp. 329–360). Cambridge, MA: MIT Press.

Miller, G. F. (2000). Ornamental genius. In G. F. Miller, *The mating mind* (pp. 138–175). New York: Doubleday.

Miller, G. F. (2001). Aesthetic fitness: How sexual selection shaped artistic virtuosity as a fitness indicator and aesthetic preferences as mate choice criteria. *Bulletin of Psychology and the Arts, 2*(1), 20–25.

Miller, G. F. (2014, March 29). Stuff: The bare necessities, then and now. *New Scientist, 2962*, 41–42.

Chapter 14: Show Her How You Feel (Romantic Proof)

Popular Books

Brown, B. (2012). *Daring greatly.* New York: Gotham.

Buss, D. M. (2000). *The dangerous passion.* New York: Free Press.

Conley, D. (2015). *Parentology.* New York: Simon & Schuster.

Coontz, S. (2006). *Marriage, a history: How love conquered marriage.* New York: Penguin.

Fisher, H. (2010). *Why him? Why her?* New York: Holt.

Frank, R. H. (1988). *Passions within reason.* New York: W. W. Norton.

Gottman, J. (2011). *The science of trust.* New York: W. W. Norton.

Gottman, J., & Silver, N. (2013). *What makes love last?* New York: Simon & Schuster.

Hawley, K. (2012). *Trust: A very short introduction.* Oxford: Oxford University Press.

Johnson, S. (2013). *Love sense.* New York: Little, Brown.

Levine, A., & Heller, R. (2012). *Attached.* New York: Tarcher.

Mead, R. (2008). *One perfect day: The selling of the American wedding.* New York: Penguin.

Young, L., & Alexander, B. (2014). *The chemistry between us.* Rancho Santa Margarita, CA: Current Publishing.

Zak, P. (2013). *The moral molecule: How trust works.* New York: Plume.

Academic Books

Becker, G. S. (2005). *A treatise on the family.* Cambridge, MA: Harvard University Press.

Boesch, C., & Reichart, U. (Eds.) (2003). *The evolution of monogamy.* Cambridge: Cambridge University Press.

Lettmaier, S. (2010). *Broken engagements: The action for breach of promise of marriage and the feminine ideal, 1800–1940.* Oxford: Oxford University Press.

Nesse, R. M. (Ed.). (2001). *Evolution and the capacity for commitment.* New York: Russell Sage.

Salmon, C., & Shackelford, T. K. (Eds.). (2011). *The Oxford handbook of evolutionary family psychology.* Oxford: Oxford University Press.

Simpson, J. A., & Campbell, L. (Eds.). (2013). *Handbook of close relationships.* Oxford: Oxford University Press.

Selected Academic Papers and Essays (see the ebook or Mating Grounds for full list)

Ackerman, J. M., et al. (2011). Let's get serious: Communicating commitment in romantic relationships. *Journal of Personality and Social Psychology, 100,* 1079–1094.

Cronk, L., & Dunham, B. (2007). Amounts spent on engagement rings reflect aspects of male and female mate quality. *Human Nature, 18,* 329–333.

Drouin, M., & Landgraff, C. (2012). Texting, sexting, and attachment in college students' romantic relationships. *Computers in Human Behavior, 28,* 444–449.

Galperin, A., & Haselton, M. (2010). Predictors of how often and when people fall in love. *Evolutionary Psychology, 8*(1), 5–28.

Gavrilets, S. (2012). Human origins and the transition from promiscuity to pair-bonding. *Proceedings of the National Academy of Sciences USA, 109*(25), 9923–9928.

Henrich, J., et al. (2012). The puzzle of monogamous marriage. *Philosophical Transactions of the Royal Society of London B, 367*(1589), 657–669.

Malouff, J. M., et al. (2014). Trait emotional intelligence and romantic relationship satisfaction: A meta-analysis. *American Journal of Family Therapy, 42*(1), 53–66.

Muise, A., et al. (2014). Post-sex affectionate exchanges promote sexual and relationship satisfaction. *Archives of Sexual Behavior, 43*(7), 1391–1402.

Paik, A., & Woodley, V. (2012). Symbols and investments as signals: Courtship behaviors in adolescent sexual relationships. *Rationality and Society, 24,* 3–36.

Seymour, R. M., & Sozou, P. D. (2009). Duration of courtship effort as a costly signal. *Journal of Theoretical Biology, 256,* 1–13.

Geoff's Work

Miller, G. F. (2007). Sexual selection for moral virtues. *Quarterly Review of Biology, 82*(2), 97–125.

Chapter 15: Find the Right Mating Markets

Popular Books

Bishop, B. (2009). *The big sort.* New York: Mariner Books.

Florida, R. (2009). *Who's your city?* New York: Basic Books.

Frank, R. H. (2008). *The economic naturalist.* New York: Basic Books.

Frank, R. H. (2011). *The Darwin economy: Liberty, competition, and the common good.* Princeton, NJ: Princeton University Press.

Frank, R. H. (2014). *Microeconomics and behavior* (9th Ed.). New York: McGraw-Hill.

Moretti, E. (2013). *The new geography of jobs.* New York: Mariner Books.

Speck, J. (2013). *Walkable city.* New York: North Point Press.

Weiner, E. (2009). *The geography of bliss.* New York: Twelve.

Woodard, C. (2012). *American nations: A history of the eleven rival regional cultures of North America.* New York: Penguin.

Selected Academic Papers and Essays (see the ebook or Mating Grounds for full list)

Durante, K. D., et al. (2012). Sex ratio and women's career choice: Does a scarcity of men lead women to choose briefcase over baby? *Journal of Personality and Social Psychology, 103*, 121–134.

Griskevicius, V., et al. (2012). The financial consequences of too many men: Sex ratio effects on saving, borrowing, and spending. *Journal of Personality and Social Psychology, 102*, 69–80.

Kandrik, M., et al. (2015). Scarcity of female mates predicts regional variation in men's and women's sociosexual orientation across US states. *Evolution and Human Behavior, 36*, 206-210.

Kokko, H., & Rankin, D. J. (2006). Lonely hearts of sex in the city? Density-dependent effects in mating systems. *Philosophical Transactions of the Royal Society of London B, 361*, 319–334.

Kruger, D. J. (2009). When men are scarce, good men are even harder to find: Life history, the sex ratio, and the proportion of men married. *Journal of Social, Evolutionary, and Cultural Psychology, 3*, 93–104.

Lenton, A. P., et al. (2009). The relationship between number of potential mates and mating skew in humans. *Animal Behavior, 77*, 55–60.

Noe, R., & Hammerstein, P. (1994). Biological markets: Supply-and-demand determine the effect of partner choice in cooperation, mutualism, and mating. *Behavioral Ecology and Sociobiology, 35*, 1–11.

Pollet, T. V., & Nettle, D. (2008). Driving a hard bargain: Sex ratio and male marriage success in a historical US population. *Biology Letters, 4*, 31–33.

Regnerus, M. (2012). Mating market dynamics, sex-ratio imbalances, and their consequences. *Society, 49*, 500–505.

Siow, A. (2008). How does the marriage market clear? An empirical framework. *Canadian Journal of Economics, 41*, 1121–1155.

Chapter 16: Beggars *Must* Be Choosers (Mate Preferences)

Popular Books

Kreisman, J. J., & Straus, H. (2010). *I hate you—don't leave me: Understanding the borderline personality.* New York: Perigree.

Navarro, J. (2014). *Dangerous personalities.* Emmaus, PA: Rodale.

Tashiro, T. (2014). *The science of happily ever after.* Ontario, Canada: Harlequin.

Smith, H. (2014). *Men on strike: Why men are boycotting marriage, fatherhood, and the American Dream.* New York: Encounter Books.

Selected Academic Papers and Essays (see the ebook or Mating Grounds for full list)

Cloud, J. M., & Perilloux, C. (2014). Bodily attractiveness as a window to women's fertility and reproductive value. In V. A. Weekes-Shackelford & T. K. Shackelford (Eds.), *Evolutionary perspectives on human sexual psychology and behavior* (pp. 135–152). Oxford: Oxford University Press.

Donnellan, M. B., et al. (2004). The Big Five and enduring marriages. *Journal of Research in Personality, 38*(5), 481–504.

Edward, D. A., & Chapman, T. (2011). The evolution and significance of male mate choice. *Trends in Ecology & Evolution, 26*, 647–654.

Haselton, M. G., & Gildersleeve, K. (2011). Can men detect ovulation? *Current Directions in Psychological Science, 20*, 87–91

Jaeger, M. M. (2011). "A thing of beauty is a joy forever"? Returns to physical attractiveness over the life course. *Social Forces, 89*, 983–1003.

Leichsenring, F., et al. (2011). Borderline personality disorder. *Lancet, 377*, 74–84.

Simpson, V. J., et al. (2014). Evidence to suggest that women's sexual behavior is influenced by hip width rather than waist-to-hip ratio. *Archives of Sexual Behavior, 43*, 1367–1371.

Smith, A., et al. (2011). Sexual and relationship satisfaction among heterosexual men and women: The importance of desired frequency of sex. *Journal of Sex & Marital Therapy, 37*, 104–115.

Swami, V. (2012). Written on the body? Individual differences between British adults who do and do not obtain a first tattoo. *Scandinavian Journal of Psychology, 53*, 407–412.

Willoughby, B. J., & Vitas, J. (2012). Sexual desire discrepancy: The effect of individual differences in desired and actual sexual frequency on dating couples. *Archives of Sexual Behavior, 41*, 477–486.

Geoff's Work

Hooper, P., & Miller, G. F. (2008). Mutual mate choice can drive ornament evolution even under perfect monogamy. *Adaptive Behavior, 16*(1), 53–70.

Miller, G. F. (2011, April 27). Genes fit for a queen: How Kate won her mate. *New Scientist, 210*, 38–39.

Miller, G. F. (2013). Mutual mate choice models as the red pill in evolutionary psychology: Long delayed, much needed, ideologically challenging, and hard to swallow. *Psychological Inquiry, 24*, 207–210.

Chapter 17: Meeting the Women You Want

Popular Books

Adshade, M. (2013). *Dollars and sex.* San Francisco: Chronicle Books.

Bogle, K. A. (2008). *Hooking up: Sex, dating, and relationships on campus.* New York: New York University Press.

Boyd, D. (2015). *It's complicated: The social lives of networked teens.* New Haven, CT: Yale University Press.

Chambers, D. (2013). *Social media and personal relationships.* New York: Palgrave Macmillan.

Pinker, S. (2014). *The sense of style: The thinking person's guide to writing in the 21st century.* New York: Viking.

Regnerus, M., & Uecker, J. (2011). *Premarital sex in America.* Oxford: Oxford University Press.

Rudder, C. (2014). *Dataclysm: Who we are when we think no one's looking.* New York: Crown.

Slater, D. (2014). *A million first dates: Solving the puzzle on online dating.* Rancho Santa Margarita, CA: Current Publishing.

Turkle, S. (2012). *Alone together: Why we expect more from technology and less from each other.* New York: Basic Books.

Webb, A. (2014). *Data, a love story: How I cracked the online dating code to meet my match.* New York: Plume.

Selected Academic Papers and Essays (see the ebook or Mating Grounds for full list)

Aditi, P. (2014). Is online better than offline for meeting partners? Depends: Are you looking to marry or to date? *Cyberpsychology, Behavior, and Social Networking, 17*, 664–667.

Brand, R. J., et al. (2012). What is beautiful is good, even online: Correlations between photo attractiveness and text attractiveness in men's online dating profiles. *Computers in Human Behavior, 28*, 166–170.

Doering, N. M. (2009). The Internet's impact on sexuality: A critical review of 15 years of research. *Computers in Human Behavior, 25*, 1089–1101.

Finkel, E. J., et al. (2012). Online dating: A critical analysis from the perspective of psychological science. *Psychological Science in the Public Interest, 13*, 3–66.

Garcia, J. R., et al. (2012). Sexual hookup culture: A review. *Review of General Psychology, 16*, 161–176.

Goetz, C. D. (2013). What do women's advertised mate preferences reveal? An analysis of video dating profiles. *Evolutionary Psychology, 11*, 383–391.

Hall, J. A., et al. (2010). Strategic misrepresentation in online dating: The effects of gender, self-monitoring, and personality traits. *Journal of Social and Personal Relationships, 27*, 117–135.

Lenton, A., & Francesconi, M. (2010). How humans cognitively manage an abundance of mate options. *Psychological Science, 21*, 528–533.

Place, S. S., et al. (2012). Judging romantic interest of others from thin slices is a cross-cultural ability. *Evolution and Human Behavior, 33*, 547–550.

Tifferet, S., & Vilnai-Yavetz, I. (2014). *Gender differences in Facebook self-presentation: An international randomized study. Computers in Human Behavior, 35, 388–399.*

Geoff's Work

Todd, P.M., & Miller, G. F. (1999). From pride and prejudice to persuasion: Satisficing in mate search. In G. Gigerenzer & P. Todd (Eds.), *Simple heuristics that make us smart* (pp. 286–308). Oxford: Oxford University Press.

Chapter 18: Talking to Women

Popular Books

Cabane, O. (2013). *The charisma myth.* New York: Crown Business.

Carnegie, D. (1936). *How to win friends and influence people.* New York: Simon and Schuster.

Cialdini, R. (2007). *Influence.* New York: Crown Business.

Dreeke, R. (2011). *It's not all about me.* CreateSpace.

Ekman, P. (2007). *Emotions revealed.* New York: Holt.

Epley, N. (2014). *Mindwise.* New York: Basic Books.

Gottschall, J. (2013). *The storytelling animal.* New York: Mariner Books.

Goulston, M. (2009). *Just listen.* New York: Random House.

Lieberman, M. (2012). *Social.* New York: Little, Brown.

Navarro, J. (2008). *What every body is saying.* New York: Harper Perennial.

Tannen, D. (2007). *You just don't understand: Women and men in conversation.* New York: William Morrow.

Tannen, D. (2011). *That's not what I meant!* New York: Basic Books.

Thompson, G. J., & Jenkins, J. B. (2013). *Verbal judo: The gentle art of persuasion.* New York: William Morrow.

Wassmer, A. C. (1978). *Making contact.* New York: Dial Press.

Academic Books

Boyd, B. (2009). *On the origin of stories.* Cambridge, MA: Harvard University Press.

Burling, R. (2005). *The talking ape.* Oxford: Oxford University Press.

Dessalles, J.-L. (2007). *Why we talk: The evolutionary origins of language.* Oxford: Oxford University Press.

Fitch, W. T. (2010). *The evolution of language.* Cambridge: Cambridge University Press.

Gottschall, J., & Wilson, D. S. (Eds.). (2005). *The literary animal.* Evanston, IL: Northwestern University Press.

Pinker, S. (2008). *The stuff of thought: Language as a window into human nature.* New York: Penguin.

Toye, R. (2013). *Rhetoric: A very short introduction.* Oxford: Oxford University Press.

Selected Academic Papers and Essays (see the ebook or Mating Grounds for full list)

Bale, C., et al. (2006). Chat-up lines as male sexual displays. *Personality and Individual Differences, 40*(4), 655–664.

Frisby, B. N., et al. (2011). Flirtatious communication: An experimental examination of perceptions of social-sexual communication motivated by evolutionary forces. *Sex Roles, 64,* 682–694.

Gersick, A., & Kurzban, R. (2014). Covert sexual signaling: Human flirtation and implications for other social species. *Evolutionary Psychology, 12,* 549–569.

Lange, B. P., & Euler, H. A. (2014). Writers have groupies, too: High-quality literature production and mating success. *Evolutionary Behavioral Sciences, 8,* 20–30.

Locke, J. L., & Bogin, B. (2006). Language and life history: A new perspective on the development and evolution of human language. *Behavioral and Brain Sciences, 29*(3), 259–280.

Newman, M. L., et al. (2008). Gender differences in language use: An analysis of 14,000 text samples. *Discourse Processes, 45,* 211–236.

Rosen, M., & López, H. (2009). Menstrual cycle shifts in attentional bias for courtship language. *Evolution and Human Behavior, 30,* 131–140.

Rosenberg, J., & Tunney, R. J. (2008). Human vocabulary use as display. *Evolutionary Psychology, 6,* 538–549.

Senko, C., & Fyffe, V. (2010). An evolutionary perspective on effective vs. ineffective pick-up lines. *Journal of Social Psychology, 150,* 648–667.

Toma, C. L., & Hancock, J. T. (2012). What lies beneath: The linguistic traces of deception in online dating profiles. *Journal of Communication, 62,* 78–92.

Geoff's Work

Miller, G. F. (2000). Cyrano and Scheherazade. In G. F. Miller, *The mating mind* (pp. 341–391). New York: Doubleday.

Miller, G. F. (2002). How did language evolve? In H. Swain (Ed.), *Big questions in science* (pp. 79–90). London: Jonathan Cape.

Miller, G. F., et al. (2012). The heritability and genetic correlates of mobile phone use: A twin study of consumer behaviour. *Twin Research and Human Genetics, 15*(1), 97–106.

Chapter 19: Dating Women

Popular Books

Behrendt, G., & Ruotola, A. (2013). *It's just a f***ing date.* New York: Diversion Books.

Burton, N. (2011). *The little black book of big red flags.* Avon, MA: Adams Media.

Gray, C. (2011). *From shy to social: The shy man's guide to personal & dating success.* Sunbow Press.

Gray, J. (2005). *Mars and Venus on a date.* New York: Harper Perennial.

Kinrys, M. (2013). *Get inside her: Dirty dating tips & secrets from a woman.* Grayslake, IL: Velocity House.

Pease, B., & Pease, N. (2006). *The definitive book of body language.* New York: Bantam.

Selected Academic Papers and Essays (see the ebook or Mating Grounds for full list)

Alley, T. R., et al. (2013). Courtship feeding in humans? The effects of feeding versus providing food on perceived attraction and intimacy. *Human Nature, 24*, 430–443.

Beall, A. T., & Tracy, J. L. (2013). Women are more likely to wear red or pink at peak fertility. *Psychological Science, 24*, 1837–1841.

Cantu, S. M., et al. (2014). Fertile and selectively flirty: Women's behavior toward men changes across the ovulatory cycle. *Psychological Science, 25*, 431–438.

Dunbar, R. I. M. (2010). The social role of touch in humans and primates: Behavioral function and neurobiological mechanisms. *Neuroscience and Biobehavioral Reviews, 34*(2), 260–268.

Durante, K. M., et al. (2008). Changes in women's choice of dress across the ovulatory cycle: Naturalistic and laboratory task-based evidence. *Personality and Social Psychology Bulletin, 34*, 1451–1460.

Elliot, A. J., et al. (2013). Women's use of red clothing as a sexual signal in intersexual interaction. *Journal of Experimental Social Psychology, 49*, 599–602.

Jonason, P. K., et al. (2015). Who engages in serious and casual sex relationships? An individual differences perspective. *Personality and Individual Differences, 75*, 205–209.

Oesch, N., & Miklousic, I. (2012). The dating mind: Evolutionary psychology and the emerging science of human courtship. *Evolutionary Psychology, 10*, 899–909.

Roennedal, D. (2015). The golden rule and the platinum rule. *Journal of Value Inquiry, 49*, 221–236.

Snapp, S., et al. (2015). The upside to hooking up: College students' positive hookup experiences. *International Journal of Sexual Health, 27*, 43–56.

Chapter 20: Having Sex

Popular Books

Bering, J. (2014). *Perv: The sexual deviant in all of us.* New York: Farrar, Straus & Giroux.

Comella, L., & Tarrant, S. (Eds.) (2015). *New views on pornography.* New York: Praeger.

Daedone, N. (2011). *Slow sex: The art and craft of the female orgasm.* New York: Grand Central Publishing.

De Botton, A. (2012). *How to think more about sex.* New York: Picador.

Easton, D., & Hardy, J. W. (2009). *The ethical slut.* Berkeley, CA: Celestial Arts.

Friedman, D. M. (2001). *A mind of its own: A cultural history of the penis.* New York: Penguin.

Hartley, N. (2006). *Nina Hartley's guide to total sex.* New York: Avery Trade.

Joannides, P. (2009). *The guide to getting it on* (6th Ed). Waldport, OR: Goofy Foot Press.

Judson, O. (2003). *Dr. Tatiana's sex advice to all creation.* New York: Vintage.

Kerner, I. (2010). *She comes first: The thinking man's guide to pleasuring a woman.* New York: William Morrow.

Kirschenbaum, S. (2011). *The science of kissing.* New York: Grand Central Publishing.

Klein, M. (2012). *Sexual intelligence.* New York: HarperOne.

Maier, T. (2013). *Masters of sex.* New York: Basic Books.

Makai, M. (2013). *Domination and submission: The BDSM relationship handbook.* CreateSpace.

Martin, R. (2013). *How we do it.* New York: Basic Books.

Meston, C. M., & Buss, D. M. (2009). *Why women have sex.* New York: St. Martin's Griffin.

Murray, C. (2004). *Human accomplishment.* Washington, DC: AEI Press.

Nagoski, E. (2015). *Come as you are.* New York: Simon & Schuster.

Ogas, O., & Gaddam, S. (2012). *A billion wicked thoughts.* New York: Plume.

Roach, M. (2009). *Bonk: The curious coupling of science and sex.* New York: W. W. Norton.

Taormino, T. (Ed.). (2012). *The ultimate guide to kink, BDSM, role play, and the erotic edge.* Berkeley, CA: Cleis Press.

Taormino, T. (Ed.). (2013). *The feminist porn book.* New York: City University of New York Press.

Thomas, K., & Thomas, K. (2005). *The modern Kama Sutra.* Boston: Da Capo Press.

Warren, J., & Warren, L. (2008). *The loving dominant* (3rd Ed.). Emeryville, CA: Greenery Press.

Wolf, N. (2009). *Vagina: A new biography.* New York: HarperCollins.

Selected Academic Papers and Essays (see the ebook or Mating Grounds for full list)

Costa, R. M., & Brody, S. (2007). Women's relationship quality is associated with specifically penile-vaginal intercourse orgasm and frequency. *Journal of Sex & Marital Therapy, 33,* 319–327.

De Jong, P. J., et al. (2013). Giving in to arousal or staying stuck in disgust? Disgust-based mechanisms in sex and sexual dysfunction. *Journal of Sex Research, 50*(3–4), 247–262.

Eberhard, W. G. (2010). Evolution of genitalia: Theories, evidence, and new directions. *Genetica, 138*(1), 5–18.

Ellsworth, R. M., & Bailey, D. H. (2013). Human female orgasm as evolved signal: A test of two hypotheses. *Archives of Sexual Behavior, 42,* 1545–1554.

Hawley, P. H., & Hensley, W. A. (2009). Social dominance and forceful submission fantasies: Feminine pathology or power? *Journal of Sex Research, 46,* 568–585.

King, R., & Belsky, J. (2012). A typological approach to testing the evolutionary functions of human female orgasm. *Archives of Sexual Behavior, 41,* 1145–1160.

Mautz, B. S., et al. (2013). Penis size interacts with body shape and height to influence male attractiveness. *Proceedings of the National Academy of Sciences USA, 110*(17), 6925–6930.

Pham, M. N., & Shackelford, T. K. (2013). Oral sex as infidelity-detection. *Personality and Individual Differences, 54,* 792–795.

Prause, N., & Fong, T. (2015). The science and politics of sex addiction research. In L. Comella & S. Tarrant (Eds.), *New views on pornography* (pp. 431–446). New York: Praeger.

Sela, Y., et al. (2015). Do women perform fellatio as a mate retention behavior? *Personality and Individual Differences, 73,* 61–66.

Geoff's Work

Costa, R. M., et al. (2012). Women who prefer longer penises are more likely to have vaginal orgasms (but not clitoral orgasms): Implications for an evolutionary theory of vaginal orgasm. *Journal of Sexual Medicine, 9,* 3079–3088.

Costa, R. M., et al. (2013). Penis size and vaginal orgasm. *Journal of Sexual Medicine, 10,* 2875–2876

Prause, N., et al. (under revision). "Clitoral" versus "vaginal" orgasms: False dichotomies and differential effects. *Journal of Sexual Medicine.*

Prause, N., et al. (under review). Women's preferences for penis size: A new method using selection among 3D-printed models. *PLOS ONE.*

Zietsch, B. P., et al. (2011). Female orgasm rates are largely independent of other traits: Implications for "female orgasmic disorder" and evolutionary theories of orgasm. *Journal of Sexual Medicine, 8* (8), 2305–2316.

INDEX

beards, 145, 203
Beatles, The, 186
beauty, female
   long-term relationships and, 258–59
   male conception of, 39–40
   self-consciousness about, 38–41
   sexual or romantic success and, 45
   unrealistic expectation of, 32
bedroom, 84–85, 207
benevolent sexism, 156
Berry, Halle, 39
Biel, Jessica, 39–40
birth control, 44
boasting, verbal, 168, 171
bodybuilders, 81, 95
body fat
   female, 34, 39–40, 145
   male, 80–81, 308, 311
body hair, 205
body language, 95, 278
   assertive, 158
   encouragers in, 284
   SOFTEN, 280–81
body odor, 45, 206
body ornamentation, 170–71, 256
body shape/size, 80, 170, 308
body-weight exercises, 93
boyfriend-girlfriend relationships. *See* long-term relationships
brain, 28, 102, 123
breaking up, 251
breath odor, 204–5
broadcasting vs. narrowcasting, 214–15
Burgundy, Ron, 218
buried penis syndrome, 311
Burning Man, 77
Busey, Gary, 99

C
Camus, Albert, 99
cancer, shift work and, 86
capability cues, female, 39–40
car, cleaning up, 207, 212
carbohydrates, 89–91, 103
cardiovascular fitness, 82
cardio workouts, chronic, 91–92
casual dating, 12
   See also dating; medium-term relationships
casual sex, 51
   See also sex; short-term relationships
children, taking care of, 83, 152
   See also fatherhood
Chuck E. Cheese, 110–11
churches, 269
Ciardi, John, 201
circadian rhythm, 86

cities, mating markets in, 238–43
cleanliness, general, 145–46, 207, 212
   See also grooming
Clinton, Bill, 120
clothing, 207–12
   female, 40, 255–56, 302
   scent in, 207
   signaling with, 170
clubs, 184, 254–55, 262–63
clutter, cleaning up, 212
Cocteau, Jean, 196
cognitive behavioral therapy, 106
college(s), 128–30
   activities at, 267–68
   mating markets in, 238, 240, 244
   prestigious, 129
   waiting to start, 127–28
cologne, 206
combat sports, 97
commitment, 57–59
   female competition for, 248
   irrational, 226
   paternal, 75–76
   romantic proof of, 216–17
   saying "no" to, 250
   See also long-term relationships
commonality, establishing, 225, 281–82, 284
communication. *See* conversation; language
compassion, self-, 108, 135, 137–39
competence
   confidence reflecting, 19–22
   domains of, 24–25
competition, 41, 238–39, 248
complaining, 115
compound-movement exercises, 92
computer gaming, 180
condoms, 44
conferences, 268
confidence, 19–20
   building, 22–23
   domain-specific, 24
   faking, 21, 287–88
   mating, 24–25
   momentum effect in, 25–26
   projecting, 178–79, 307
   pushing through low, 27–29
   showing verbal, 157
   takeaways for, 29
conflict, male-female, 149–50
conscientiousness, 136
   See also willpower
conspicuous consumption, 169, 188, 193–94
consumerism, 41, 180, 188
contact calls, 224
continuing-education classes, 268
contraception, 44

ABOUT THE AUTHORS

Tucker Max is the author of *I Hope They Serve Beer in Hell,* which was a #1 *New York Times* bestseller and has over 2 million copies in print worldwide, as well as *Assholes Finish First* and *Hilarity Ensues,* which each have over a million copies in print worldwide.

Geoffrey Miller is a tenured associate professor of psychology at the University of New Mexico, where he teaches courses on evolutionary psychology, human sexuality, intelligence and creativity, and human emotions. He has also worked at NYU Stern Business School, UCLA, University College London, the London School of Economics, QIMR in Brisbane, Australia, and the Max Planck Institute for Psychological Research in Munich, Germany. Geoff has a B.A. from Columbia University and a Ph.D. from Stanford University, and is best known for his books *The Mating Mind* (2001) and *Spent* (2009), which have been published in over a dozen languages. He has over 120 academic publications, and has given over 170 talks in 14 countries. His research has been featured in *Nature, Science, The New York Times, The Washington Post, New Scientist,* and *The Economist,* on NPR and BBC radio, and in documentaries on CNN, PBS, Discovery Channel, National Geographic Channel, and BBC. Geoff has consulted for a variety of Fortune 500 companies, governments, NGOs, advertising agencies, market research companies, and social media companies. He won the 2008 Ig Nobel Prize in Economics for showing that lap-dancers earn higher tips when they're ovulating.